# Handbook on Innovations in Learning

Editors

Marilyn Murphy
Sam Redding
Janet Twyman

INFORMATION AGE PUBLISHING, INC.
Charlotte, NC • www.infoagepub.com

**Library of Congress Cataloging-in-Publication Data**

A CIP record for this book is available from the Library of Congress
http://www.loc.gov

ISBN: 978-1-62396-607-2 (Paperback)
 978-1-62396-608-9 (Hardcover)
 978-1-62396-609-6 (ebook)

Copyright © 2014 Information Age Publishing Inc.

All rights reserved. No part of this publication may be reproduced, stored in a retrieval system, or transmitted, in any form or by any means, electronic, mechanical, photocopying, microfilming, recording or otherwise, without written permission from the publisher.

Printed in the United States of America

## Acknowledgements

The editors wish to acknowledge several colleagues for their contributions to the production of this volume. Our thanks to Stephen Page for his thoughtful and insightful editorial expertise and cover design, and to Robert Sullivan for his skillful copyediting of the volume and development of the glossary. We thank Pam Sheley for designing, coordinating, and overseeing the book's publication and Lori Thomas for reviewing and proofreading multiple drafts. Allison Crean Davis gave us feedback on key chapters, and Karen Mahon provided a complete, external review of the book.

www.centeril.org

The Center on Innovations in Learning (CIL) is a national content center established to work with regional comprehensive centers and state education agencies (SEA) to build SEAs' capacity to stimulate, select, implement, and scale up innovations in learning.

Learning innovations replace currently accepted standards of curricular and instructional practice with new practices demonstrated to be more effective or more efficient in the context in which they are applied.

The Center on Innovations in Learning is administered by the Institute for Schools and Society (ISS) at Temple University, Philadelphia, Pennsylvania, in partnership with the Academic Development Institute (ADI), Lincoln, Illinois.

The Center is funded by the U.S. Department of Education, Office of Elementary and Secondary Education (OESE), under the comprehensive centers program, Award # S283B120052-12A.

The opinions expressed herein do not necessarily reflect the position of the supporting agencies, and no official endorsement should be inferred.

Cover Design: Stephen Page

# Table of Contents

**Foreword and Overview** ........................................................................................ vii
   *Marilyn Murphy*

## Part 1: Innovation in Learning

**What Is an Innovation in Learning?** .......................................................................... 3
   *Sam Redding, Janet S. Twyman, and Marilyn Murphy*

**Stimulating Innovation (or Making Innovation Meaningful Again)** ....................... 15
   *Maureen M. Mirabito and T. V. Joe Layng*

**Innovation, Implementation Science, and Data-Based Decision Making: Components of Successful Reform** ...................................................................................................... 31
   *Ronnie Detrich*

**The Logic of School Improvement, Turnaround, and Innovation** .......................... 49
   *Sam Redding*

## Part 2: The Student in Learning Innovation

**Innovative Practice in Teaching the English Language Arts: Building Bridges Between Literacy In School and Out** ........................................................................................ 61
   *Michael W. Smith*

**Innovations in Language and Literacy Instruction** ................................................ 75
   *Michael L. Kamil*

**Specialized Innovations for Students With Disabilities** ........................................ 93
   *Joseph R. Boyle*

**Getting Personal: The Promise of Personalized Learning** .................................... 113
   *Sam Redding*

## Part 3: Technology in Learning Innovation

**Education + Technology + Innovation = Learning?** ............................................. 133
   *T.V. Joe Layng and Janet S. Twyman*

**Games in Learning, Design, and Motivation** ........................................................ 149
   *Catherine C. Schifter*

**Advances in Online Learning** ................................................................................. 165
   *Herbert J. Walberg and Janet S. Twyman*

**Learning, Schooling, and Data Analytics** .............................................................. 179
   *Ryan S. J. d. Baker*

## Part 4: Reports From the Field: Innovation in Practice

**Idaho Leads: Applying Learning In and Out of the Classroom to Systems Reform** ......... 193
   *Lisa Kinnaman*

**Using Response to Intervention Data to Advance Learning Outcomes** ................ 207
   *Amanda M. VanDerHeyden*

**Innovation in Career and Technical Education Methodology** .............................. 227
   *Mark Williams*

**Glossary** ................................................................................................................ 247
   *Robert Sullivan*

**Authors' Biographies** ............................................................................................ 263

# Foreword and Overview
*Marilyn Murphy*

The *Handbook on Innovations in Learning* focuses on innovations—both methodological and technological—in teaching and learning that promise to surpass standard practice in achieving learning outcomes for students. The experts who have written chapters in this *Handbook* first identify the underlying principles of learning and then describe novel, balanced approaches, based on these principles, to accelerate learning.

The idea for the *Handbook* emerged from a policy context ripe for such a contribution to practice. In November 2010, a national education technology plan (NETP) was released by the U.S. Department of Education, a project led by the department's Office of Educational Technology. The purpose of the report and the corresponding initiative, according to Secretary of Education Arnie Duncan, was to "leverage the innovation and ingenuity this nation is known for to create programs and projects that every school can implement to succeed" (2010). The plan describes a model of learning centered around personalized learning experiences, with a reliance on state-of-the-art technology as a vehicle to help all students reach their learning potential. The notion of harnessing innovation as a lever to improve success in schools is referenced numerous times in the NETP report, as is the call to power learning by technology.

Ultimately, the purpose of the national technology initiative is about the student in the classroom and the learner outside the classroom. One might rightly ask, "What would success look like in these contexts?" A successful initiative would see teachers energized and empowered to be more effective in their craft with better knowledge of the best and most promising practices and the tools to implement them strategically and effectively. Outside the classroom, a generation of students would emerge who are engaged, excited, and—having embraced and cultivated 21st-century skills—ready to continue lifelong learning.

In its 2012 competition for its comprehensive centers, the U.S. Department of Education invited proposals to establish a new content center dedicated to discovering, supporting, and disseminating "innovations in learning." In its successful response to this call for proposals, the team at Temple University in Philadelphia and its partner, the Academic Development Institute (ADI) in Illinois, presented a design of work that linked the practices of instruction and their underlying principles of learning. To define the work of the newly funded center, learning principles and variations in standard practice would be identified with an eye to their potential as an improvement on what is currently accepted standard practice—innovations. The center would focus on the instructional core—teachers, students, and content—while addressing the recently expanded nature of learning environments and, at the same time, enhancing the teaching and learning process with novel solutions—innovations (Redding, 2012).

As pointed out in the NETP report and taken as axiomatic in the foundation of the new center, technology is a vehicle for managing, delivering, and engaging students in a rich curriculum and exciting learning activities. What exactly is innovation? Innovation is a slippery concept, chameleon-like in its ability to change aspects according to varying contexts. Godin (2013) reminds us that the term dates back to the Greeks and Romans, coming into widespread use after the Reformation. Derived from the Latin "innovare," meaning "to renew," "to alter," it first appears in English in the 16$^{th}$ century, when it was used mainly pejoratively in reference to new religious practices and political revolution but, in some contexts, only "something newly introduced." Now, generally meaning "something new; a new idea, method, or device," the word has undergone semantic amelioration and is frequently used with strongly positive connotations, often suggestive of a significant, even momentous advance. Applied in the exaggerations of advertising, "innovation" is often attributed to some product or process a mere degree beyond "imitation," something that seems at first glance different but which, on a more careful examination, reveals only superficial change rather than substantial differences in utility or efficiency. We all know this game. Education is not unlike other professions or disciplines, where designating something as "innovative" is given broad parameters. As Huberman (1973) correctly notes, "The educational system is too often prone to change in appearance as a substitute for change in substance" (p. 6).

The chapters in this *Handbook* consider best practice from the perspective of topics emerging as priorities in education. Each of the authors presents a concise review of the literature on the topic of the chapter, an explanation of what the topic means in relation to education, and, importantly, suggests action principles for states, districts, and schools. The *Handbook* is structured into four parts. Part One deals with Innovation in Learning and opens with the chapter *What Is an Innovation in Learning?* Authors Sam Redding, Janet Twyman, and Marilyn Murphy grapple with defining innovation in the context of learning and teaching. The chapter provides guidance on the necessary conditions for innovation, including recognizing what a culture of innovation looks like, and suggests a framework for identifying innovations in learning.

In *Stimulating Innovation* (or *Making Innovation Meaningful Again*), Maureen Mirabito and Joe Layng probe the contexts and conditions in which innovation can flourish, noting that "innovation is as much about systemic change as it is about leadership and culture." They argue for intentional planning, a realistic approach, and creativity in encouraging a culture willing to embrace innovation.

Ronnie Detrich considers the importance of the "science of implementation" in his chapter *Innovation, Implementation Science, and Data-Based Decision Making: Components of Successful Reform*. The author includes several guiding principles for the effective diffusion of innovations and seven principles of successful implementation. A cautionary tale on the failed California class size reduction initiative provides a graphic lesson of an undisciplined and uncoordinated attempt to implement change. In *The Logic of School Improvement, Turnaround, and Innovation*, Sam Redding takes a bird's-eye view of the world of school improvement in the last 20-plus years and identifies a hopeful pattern of potential success. Redding looks at the processes of school improvement, turnaround, and innovation, and finds commonalities in what we learn from each that bode well for a positive trajectory of student achievement.

Part Two, The Student in Learning Innovation, considers the student in the innovation process. In their respective chapters, authors Michael Smith and Michael Kamil consider literacy instruction and practice. Smith's *Innovative Practice in Teaching the English Language Arts: Building Bridges Between Literacy In School and Out* reflects on his previous studies of the literate lives of adolescent boys and recommends that some of his findings about what boys read outside of school be harnessed to advance their in-school literacy practice. In Kamil's chapter on *Innovations in Language and Literacy Instruction*, we are urged to be deliberate about selecting "mature" innovations that are evidence driven. Foremost among these innovations in language instruction, as noted by the author, are three efforts to improve instruction: use of standards, application of research, and assessment for accountability.

The chapter *Specialized Innovations for Students With Disabilities*, by Joseph Boyle, explores the challenges of not only providing access to the general education curriculum for students with disabilities but also of engaging these students as active participants in mastering the Common Core State Standards. He surveys methodological and technological innovations in instructional strategies for literacy, mathematics, and science in special education. Sam Redding's chapter, *Getting Personal: The Promise of Personalized Learning*, defines personalized learning and includes classroom examples of how his theory of personalized learning would play out in different scenarios. Redding provides an historical overview, framing the concept as an inroad to the acquisition of 21st-century skills.

Part Three, Technology in Learning Innovation, includes chapters on the relationship between learning and the technology that is becoming more and more a part of the education landscape. In the chapter *Education + Technology + Innovation = Learning?* by Joe Layng and Janet Twyman, we learn of the continuing disjunction between technological advances and unchanging instructional methods. The authors describe the landscape of "current, mainstream K–12 hardware and software," showing how we can use technology to improve student learning.

Catherine Schifter looks at the learning potential in gaming as a driver of education in *Games in Learning, Design, and Motivation.* Schifter provides an overview of the nature and variety of games and how the skills and motivation intrinsic to gameplaying can be used to cultivate desirable learning skills. Next, Herbert Walberg and Janet Twyman discuss the history of distance learning in their chapter *Advances in Online Learning.* The chapter overviews a selection of popular distance learning programs and platforms, including the rapidly expanding application of MOOCs, that is, massive, open, online classes.

Ryan Baker's *Learning, Schooling, and Data Analytics* concludes Part Three by examining the emerging fields of learning analytics (LA) and educational data mining (EDM), areas showing promise in establishing a better understanding of the factors contributing to learning, including social motivation. Baker considers the historic context of these emerging fields and provides a wealth of action principles to guide the use of data to improve practice.

In Part Four, Reports From the Field: Innovation in Practice, three authors report on their experiences using various innovative strategies in practice. A chapter on innovation at work is provided by Lisa Kinnaman in her description of Idaho Leads, an effort to build leadership capacity across the state, including regional and local communities, districts, and schools. This capacity-building effort embraced innovative leadership-building activities and technologies. *Idaho Leads: Applying Learning In and Out of the Classroom to Systems Reform* includes vignettes of seven "studio districts" identified as project exemplars.

Amanda VanDerHeyden's chapter on *Using Response to Intervention Data to Advance Learning Outcomes* examines a system of service delivery that includes adjustments for students who have not been successful learners. VanDerHeyden suggests a systematic process to guide the reader in using data to make informed instructional decisions. Mark Williams's chapter *Innovation in Career and Technical Education Methodology* looks at the potential rethinking of the high school curriculum to encompass the best aspects of academic and vocational learning to better prepare today's students for success in college and careers.

The author traces the history of vocational education as a lens for examining potential for today's educational marketplace, with the goal of education being more than a pipeline for employment.

We have included a *Glossary* of terms found throughout these essays. The authors of the chapters in this volume have examined innovation in effective practice with an eye to what it means for state and local educational systems and how innovation can become standard practice. The Center on Innovations in Learning will continue to supplement this work and seek innovations that will help inform the field in their efforts to improve schools and schooling for the students we are charged to serve.

## References

Godin, B. (2013, April). *The unintended consequences of innovation studies.* Paper presented at Policy Implications Due to Unintended Consequences of Innovation, Special Track at European Forum for Studies of Policies for Research and Innovation, Madrid.

Huberman, A. M. (1973). *Understanding change in education: An introduction.* Paris, France: United Nations Educational, Scientific, and Cultural Organization.

Redding, S. (2012). *Innovations in learning.* Unpublished manuscript, Academic Development Institute, Lincoln, IL.

U.S. Department of Education, Office of Educational Technology. (2010). *Transforming American education: Learning powered by technology* (National Educational Technology Plan). Washington, DC: Author.

U.S. Department of Education, Office of Elementary and Secondary Education. (2012). *Application for new grants under the Comprehensive Centers Program* (CFDA 84.283B). Washington, DC: Author.

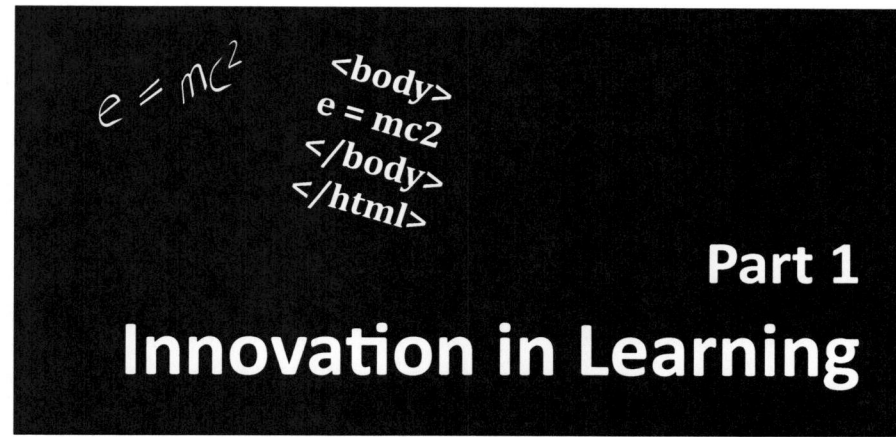

# What Is an Innovation in Learning?
## Sam Redding, Janet S. Twyman, and Marilyn Murphy

> *But Smithies not only taught us particular things. He got us to think—often by questioning us in a way that forced us to follow out the logic of what we were saying to its ultimate conclusion. Often some policy that sounded wonderful, if you looked only at the immediate results, would turn out to be counterproductive if you followed your own logic beyond stage one.*
> Thomas Sowell describing his teacher, Professor Arthur Smithies, in an essay titled *Good Teachers* (para. 9)

What's new? Americans have a penchant for the new. Always expecting a better tomorrow, we are not ones to look back. Thomas Paine wrote, and we have forever believed, "We have it in our power to begin the world over again." We are innovators.

Seeking innovations in learning, we inhabitants of the Information Age reflexively turn our eyes to technology. Rightly so, given the vast improvements technology has brought to our lives. But an innovation is a different way of doing something that is also a *better* way of doing something. In education, an innovation is a deviation from the standard practice that achieves greater learning outcomes for students than the standard practice given equal (or lesser) amounts of time and resources. Innovation does not always involve a mechanical, electronic, or digital device. To condense a few historical narratives, we might say that Benjamin Franklin discovered electricity, Thomas Edison invented the light bulb, and John Travolta danced to innovative disco lights. Or, more to our point, Alan Turing discovered computing, Steve Jobs invented the iPad, and educators made use of the iPad in blended learning. If proved more effective than the standard practice of teacher-directed, face-to-face instruction, blended learning (with an iPad) would be an *innovation in learning*. So, any new device is really just an invention, and only the successful use of it—its application—for a specific purpose, in a specific context, makes it an innovation. The innovation may be methodological, technological, or both.

While we (rightly) argue that innovation is not necessarily technology but rather a better way of doing something, we cannot ignore the technology tsunami. The technology tsunami brings abundant new devices and capabilities, but its wake is littered with the detritus of failed programs, outdated thinking, and obsolete gadgetry. How do we sort through this morass with any confidence we are making a good choice? How do we keep up with what's new? How do we hold on to what is best?

To identify an innovation in learning, we must define the standard practice as well as the new way and determine that the new way is better. That is a high bar to clear. Validating the comparative advantage of a new practice with gold standard research is a desirable goal but one that lays a cold hand on the experimentation that fosters innovation. However, chasing after the next new thing with little evidence of its efficacy wastes valuable time and money and puts students at risk of missed opportunity to learn. A balance must be struck in highlighting the emerging practices that show promise as true innovation. A proposed innovation can be tested via formative, iterative evaluations prior to the needed validation with randomized, controlled trials (Layng, Stikeleather, & Twyman, 2006).

For decades, we have felt our system of public education creaking and groaning as waves of reforms have attempted to dramatically lift the trajectory of student learning. "Innovations" in education seem to occur based on each new societal demand placed on the educational system (Miles, 1964). The mildest reforms aim at improving the implementation of standard practice—simply getting better at what we are already doing. The boldest reforms seek transformation of the entire system through what Frederick Hess (2013) calls "cage-busting leadership"—smashing the debilitating glacier of bureaucracy, over-regulation, collective bargaining, and small thinking. Innovation is a third way—replacing standard practices in teaching and learning with demonstrably better practices.

Innovation is valued as a catalyst to growth. Other sectors have invested in the study of innovation: They have defined it, documented it, and attempted to spread it to obtain results that add value to desirable objectives (see Mobbs, 2010). The process of adopting new innovations has been studied for almost a half a century, with the work of Everett M. Rogers (especially his ground breaking 1962 book *Diffusion of Innovations*) setting the stage for research on innovation. As defined by Rogers (1983), an innovation is "an idea, practice, or object that is perceived as new by an individual or another unit of adoption" (p. 11). An innovation provides an alternative solution to a problem or creates a novel solution to meet needs for an individual, group, or organization:

> The effectiveness of innovation, no matter at what level it is initiated in a school organization, is dependent on the extent to which the people

concerned perceive a problem and hence realize the existence of a need, are knowledgeable about a range of alternative solutions, and feel themselves in a congenial organizational climate. (Karmel et al., 1973, p. 126)

The "newness" of an innovation does not just involve new knowledge, but also new ways to approach the problem (Rogers, 1983, 2003). As stated, and by extension of that idea, innovation may also come from a different way of "connecting the dots," thus providing a solution to a need we might not have even known we had.

In education, innovation has been poorly or inconsistently defined, undermining our ability to harness and scale "it" for better, more efficient learning results. Without a standard for innovation, everything—or nothing—qualifies. A common understanding, with shared definitions, language, and measures, will allow us to describe the characteristics of learning innovations, the trajectories of their adoption, and the ways in which they are spread from one group to another, within and across layers in our education systems. This consistency will ultimately help us encourage and stimulate different ways, better ways, and more effective ways of learning—all tied to specific educational practices and student results.

Innovations in learning solve problems and add value. They:
a. provide fresh solutions or remove traditional barriers to existing, articulated challenges in teaching and learning (and add value by building capacity for implementation);
b. identify a previously undetected need or barrier, then enhance the teaching and learning process with a novel solution (and add value by understanding the limiting factor in a new way and responding accordingly);
c. introduce new possibilities to enhance the teaching and learning process (and add value by providing new, more efficient opportunities for obtaining better results); and
d. allow the education system to adjust to new avenues through which students learn (and add value by capitalizing on and directing student use of technology).

In sum, innovation = improvement, but not improvement by simply getting more proficient with the standard practice. Our premise is that the new practice produces observable, measurable, sustainable improvements through replacement of a standard practice rather than more proficient implementation of it. Innovation solves a problem, sometimes by replacing a standard practice and at other times by articulating a previously unfelt problem or need and proposing a solution. If a new practice is implemented (even those using the latest technologies) and it does not result in observable, measurable, sustainable improvements, it is *not* an innovation. By identifying specific practices from which innovations emerge and the conditions under which the innovations are most successful, we will be able to talk specifically and precisely about what innovations in learning are, whom they help most, what they require, and how they work. We begin with the following definitions.

## Defining the Work

***Innovation.*** Innovation is the application of an idea or invention, adapted or refined for specific uses or in its particular contexts (Gertner, 2012; Manzi, 2012). The implementation of an innovation proceeds over time, often with adjustments in course as the innovation is fitted to the context. An innovation replaces the standard product, program, practice, or process with something better, and as the majority adopts it, the innovation then becomes the new standard.

***Learning.*** Learning is a positive change in the learner's cognitive, psychomotor, social, and/or emotional knowledge and skill as exhibited in the learner's behavior.

***Innovation in Learning.*** An innovation in learning occurs in a specific teaching and learning context, improving upon the implementation of the standard practice or introducing a new practice, thus achieving greater learning outcomes. Innovative practices may be ordered into processes and procedures, bundled into programs, and packaged into products.

> *The whole aim of good teaching is to turn the young learner, by nature a little copycat, into an independent, self-propelling creature, who cannot merely learn but study.... This is to turn pupils into students, and it can be done on any rung of the ladder of learning.*
> — Jacques Barzun, *Teacher in America*

***Practice.*** A practice is the specific way an instructor teaches or a student learns. Effective practices are rooted in principles of learning and adapted to the context, including the learning environment and the student's readiness, prior mastery, and motivation. A standard practice is an effective practice that has been widely adopted. An innovative practice improves upon the standard or creates a standard for a previously unarticulated problem or need.

***Processes and Programs.*** An instructional or metacognitive process is an efficient ordering of practices to produce an expected learning outcome. A program is a coherent assemblage of processes and practices, with procedures, instructions, and tools.

***Principles of Learning.*** Principles of learning are the underlying psychological or behavioral principles upon which effective instructional and metacognitive practices, processes, and programs rest.

## A Culture of Innovation

Innovation frequently requires an investment in human capital and tools. Whatever the degree of change an innovation occasions, success depends upon the clear communication of purpose, the personal engagement of everyone involved, the attention to short-term and long-term progress, and the consolidation and institutionalization of the improvements (Kotter, 2012). To make a meaningful difference, the "doing" part of an innovation must be executed systematically, with performance measures for determining progress and making course corrections. As part of a comprehensive initiative to advance the transformation of American education, the Obama administration and the U.S. Department of Education are encouraging a culture of learning powered by technology. Programs and projects within this national plan encourage "a strategy of innovation, careful implementation, regular evaluation, and continuous improvement" (U.S. Department of Education, 2010).

A culture of innovation, within an educational organization or across a system of organizations, systematically institutionalizes a five-phase innovation process that (1) stimulates innovations to improve learning outcomes; (2) enables potential adopters to select innovations appropriate to their context and need; (3) ensures that the innovation is implemented with fidelity to its essential elements and with adaptations to enhance its effectiveness in the given context; (4) facilitates the scaling of the innovation through implementation in multiple classrooms, schools, and districts; and (5) provides a system for monitoring the effects of the innovation and its scaling, implementing change as necessary.

Research can provide the foundation when building and supporting a culture of innovation (Kasper, 2008), which both philanthropic and government-funded incentives can facilitate (e.g., U.S. Department of Education, 2013; Warren, 2013). McGuinn (2012) found that the federal Race to the Top grant program stimulated innovation and "has had a significant impact on the national political discourse around education" (p. 136) by providing a national framework around innovation and helping states build capacity to implement these innovations effectively. Angehrn and colleagues (2009) were able to stimulate and support knowledge, collaborative learning, and innovation across community members by focusing on increasing different types of value (connection, actionable learning, and gratification). The ability to select appropriate innovations should be greatly influenced by the evidence-based framework and practices that assist teachers in making any curricular or instructional choice (Kazak et al., 2010; Miller, 2009).

We know that to support selection and implementation, training should be provided to teachers about an innovation (Fullan, 1982). The growing science of implementation offers guidelines on effective implementation practices (Fixsen & Blase, 2009; Penuel, Fishman, Yamaguchi, & Gallagher, 2007) and identifies specific measures to be used to support instructional fidelity (Fixsen, Blase, Naoom, & Van Dyke, 2010). We can benefit from education's several brushes with large-scale educational reform by reviewing what has and has not worked in the past. Based on a review of previous attempts at large-scale reform, Elmore (1996) offers recommendations for addressing scalability and improving practice in education. Other research helps us define "scale" and its dimensions (such as depth, sustainability, spread, and shift in ownership) to better support and sustain consequential change (see Coburn, 2003). Finally, the research on formative evaluation and iterative testing of a program or process, as well as summative evaluation procedures, can provide useful guidance on evaluating both the overall effects of an innovation, as well as each phase in the process (Layng, Stikeleather, & Twyman, 2006; see also Markle, 1967).

**Evaluating the Innovation Process**

Each of the first four phases of the innovation process applies its own evaluative criteria to determine and improve that phase's effectiveness. Therefore, innovators develop metrics to analyze the degree to which (a) the organization's efforts to stimulate innovation result in innovations taking hold and increased learning taking place, (b) the selection criteria and process match the innovation to the adopter's context and need, (c) implementation adheres to the innovation's essential elements and makes appropriate adaptations, and (d) the innovation is successfully taken to scale.

> *All learning is either by instruction or by discovery; that is, with or without the aid of teachers....The teacher who actually knows something must put himself in the position of inquiring to aid inquiry on the part of the learner, who must inquire in order to learn.*
>
> Mortimer J. Adler,
> *Teaching and Learning*

The fifth phase takes an overarching view of the effect of the innovation, asking, "How well, in this context, does the innovation result in improved outcomes?"

**Conditions for a Culture of Innovation**

A culture of innovation requires leaders who are aware of their organization's capacity, strengths, weaknesses, and needs and who also understand (a) the innovation process and (b) the human dynamics of change (Redding, 2012). The innovation process must be exercised within a climate of clarity and trust that encourages people to seek better ways to teach and learn, and can correct course or adapt when the evidence shows change is needed. The culture of innovation values, assesses, and understands the potential for both reward (e.g., likely positive impact on learning within the organization's particular conditions) and risk (e.g., the chance for diminished learning, wasted resources, and loss of clarity and trust).

## Framework for Innovations in Learning

The following narrative framework provides a conceptual structure for identifying innovations in learning. The framework is organized around three domains: content, instruction, and personalization. Within each domain, principles of learning establish a psychological foundation for the standard practices.

The standard practices provide a basis for comparison in assessing a new practice's effectiveness and determining its status as an innovation in learning. The text describing the indicators of a standard practice presents in plain language a behavioral illustration of the standard practice's implementation.

## Content

The content is what is to be learned, otherwise known as the curriculum. Educators put in place many practices, processes, and programs to determine and organize the curriculum, including both the core curriculum and each student's opportunity to expand upon the curriculum defined by the school and teacher. Educators organize the content into instructional plans and may choose existing curriculum materials, create their own, or a blend of both. Content (or the curriculum) must be offered on a platform of good instructional design. The design of effective curriculum materials requires a systematic process that includes performing content, task, and learner analyses; clearly defining the learning objectives; determining the criteria and corresponding assessments for understanding or mastery; establishing what entry repertoire would be needed by the student to be successful in the curriculum; and making student motivation more likely by incorporating a program's fundamental principles throughout the instructional sequence (e.g., The goal should not be to make history fun, but to help learners find the fun in history; Tiemann & Markle, 1990; see also Dick & Carey, 1996; Smith & Ragan, 1999; Twyman, Layng, Stikeleather, & Hobbins, 2004).

### *Examples of Principles of Learning for Content*
- **Explicitness:** Learning is most efficient when its intended outcomes are explicit, measurable, and understood by the teacher and student.
- **Cumulative knowledge:** Learning occurs best when new knowledge is built upon prior knowledge.
- **Fluency:** Knowledge and skills that are "fluent" (i.e., automatic) are easier to maintain and apply to other things.
- **Concept formation:** We learn through discrepancies, and we extend what we know through "samenesses."
- **Acquired relevance:** A student's interest in a topic and motivation to pursue learning related to it are amplified by the student's exposure to new topics and engagement with them.

### *Examples of Standard Practices for Content*
a. Establish a team structure with specific duties and time for instructional planning.
b. Engage teachers in aligning instruction with standards and benchmarks.
c. Enable teachers to critically evaluate and select appropriate, relevant curriculum resources.

    d. Engage teachers in assessing and monitoring criterion-based student mastery.
    e. Engage teachers in differentiating and aligning learning activities.
    f. Assess student learning frequently with standards-based assessments.

   ***Examples of Indicators of Standard Practice for Content***
    a. Teachers are organized into grade-level, grade-level cluster, or subject-area instructional teams.
    b. Instructional teams meet for blocks of time (4- to 6-hour blocks, once a month; whole days before and after the school year) sufficient to develop and refine units of instruction and review student learning data.
    c. Instructional teams develop standards-aligned units of instruction for each subject and grade level.
    d. Instructional teams use student learning data to plan instruction.
    e. Instructional teams review the results of unit pre- and post-tests to make decisions about the curriculum and instructional plans and to "red flag" students in need of intervention (both students in need of tutoring or extra help and students needing enhanced learning opportunities because of early mastery of objectives).

**Instruction**

Instruction encompasses the world of ways to get information from one place (a book, a webpage, the teacher's head) to another place (the student's head, shown by a change in the student's behavior). Good instructional delivery requires active learner engagement with frequent opportunities to respond (Rosenshine & Berliner, 1978) and immediate, relevant, and related (i.e., contingent) feedback (Mory, 1992; Shute, 2008). Instruction should support the learner in moving forward at his or her own pace (Wang & Zollers, 1990) so that new material is not presented until the student has demonstrated mastery or application of current material (Bloom, 1968; Keller, 1968; Kulik, Kulik, & Bangert-Drowns, 1990). This progression of instruction and content should be tied to actual measures of student learning and not dictated by curriculum content chunks such as chapters or units or the passage of marking periods or calendar years.

Teachers "deliver" instruction through a variety of modes (including at a distance and via technology) and should provide opportunities for student self-direction and exploration. Student self-assessment is a key component of metacognition, and teacher or program assessment of student learning is critical to effective instruction.

   ***Examples of Principles of Learning for Instruction***
   - ***Exercise:*** Those things most often repeated are best remembered.
   - ***Feedback:*** Students learn best when they receive immediate feedback on their progress toward mastery of specific learning tasks.

- **Pacing:** Students learn best when instruction and the presentation of new material is contingent upon their mastery of current material.
- **Reflection:** Students use background knowledge and real-world prior experience to enhance both comprehension and motivational engagement.

### Examples of Standard Practices for Instruction
a. Expect and monitor sound instruction in a variety of modes (whole-class, teacher-directed groups, student-directed groups, independent work, computer-based, and homework).
b. Expect and monitor sound homework practices and communication with parents.
c. Expect and monitor sound classroom management.

### Examples of Indicators of Standard Practice for Instruction
a. The teacher is guided by a document that aligns standards, curriculum, instruction, and assessment.
b. The teacher develops weekly lesson plans based on aligned units of instruction.
c. The teacher differentiates assignments (individualizes instruction) in response to individual student performance on pretests and other methods of assessment.
d. The teacher maintains a record of each student's mastery of specific learning objectives.
e. The teacher interacts instructionally with students (explaining, checking, giving feedback).
f. The teacher interacts managerially with students (reinforcing rules, procedures).
g. The teacher interacts socially with students (noticing and attending to an ill student, asking about the weekend, inquiring about the family).
h. The teacher uses open-ended questioning and encourages elaboration.
i. The teacher encourages peer interaction.
j. The teacher encourages students to paraphrase, summarize, and relate.
k. The teacher encourages students to check their own comprehension.
l. The teacher uses a variety of instructional modes (whole-class, teacher-directed groups, student-directed groups, independent work, computer-based, and homework).
m. The teacher systematically reports to parents the student's mastery of specific standards-based objectives.
n. The teacher models, teaches, and reinforces social and emotional competencies.

## Personalization

A student's motivation to attempt and persist in learning is centered upon certain psychological principles that are operationalized through teacher–student interaction as well as instructional design, delivery, and personalization. Essential to learning are the student's facility in directing his or her learning, self-assessing mastery, applying learning strategies, using learning tools and technologies, and finding information.

**Examples of Principles of Learning for Personalization**
- ***Readiness:*** Concentration and eagerness stem from the student's prior learning and motivation to learn.
- ***Reciprocity:*** A student learns best in a reciprocal relationship with a teacher whose knowledge of and concern for the student is apparent to the student.
- ***Transferability:*** A student learns best when aware of the current learning task's future applicability, including its usefulness in achieving the student's personal aspirations.
- ***Freedom:*** A student learns best when the student exercises some degree of freedom in selection of the content and application of learning strategies.

**Examples of Standard Practices for Personalization**
a. Use fine-grained data to design for each student a learning path tailored to that student's prior learning, personal interests, and aspirations.
b. Develop each student's metacognitive skills to gauge his or her own mastery, manage his or her learning strategies, use learning tools, and direct his or her learning processes.
c. Allow students freedom to choose learning content and learning activities.

**Examples of Indicators of Standard Practice for Personalization**
a. The teacher encourages self-direction by giving students choice in the selection of topics and the application of learning strategies.
b. The teacher builds students' metacognitive skills by teaching learning strategies and their appropriate application.
c. The teacher builds students' metacognitive skills by providing students with processes for determining their own mastery of learning tasks.
d. The teacher builds students' ability to learn in contexts other than school.
e. The teacher connects students' out-of-school learning with their school learning.
f. The teacher builds students' ability to use a variety of learning tools.
g. The teacher uses appropriate technological tools to enhance instruction.
h. The teacher helps students articulate their personal aspirations and connect their learning to the pursuit of these aspirations.

This conceptual framework provides a starting point for the work of the Center on Innovations in Learning and other groups seeking to identify innovations in learning. We will be considering learning principles, as well as standard practices. Variations in the standard practices and new practices to address previously unarticulated problems will be studied to determine their potential as true innovations.

# References

Angehrn, A. A., Maxwell, K., Luccini, A. M., & Rajola, F. (2009). Designing effective collaboration, learning, and innovation systems for education professionals. *International Journal of Knowledge and Learning, 5*(3), 193–206.

Barzun, J. (1981). *Teacher in America*. Indianapolis, IN: Liberty Fund.

Bloom, B. S. (1968). Learning for mastery. *Evaluation Comment, 1*(2), 1–12.

Coburn, C. E. (2003). Rethinking scale: Moving beyond numbers to deep and lasting change. *Educational Researcher, 32*(6), 3–12.

Dick, W., & Carey, L. (1996). *The systematic design of instruction* (4th ed.). New York, NY: Harper Collins Publishing.

Elmore, R. F. (1996). Getting to scale with good educational practice. *Harvard Educational Review, 66*(1), 1–27.

Fixsen, D. L., & Blase, K. A. (2009, January). *Implementation: The missing link between research and practice* (NIRN Implementation Brief, No. 1). Chapel Hill, NC: University of North Carolina, National Implementation Research Network.

Fixsen, D., Blase, K., Naoom, S., & Van Dyke, M. (2010, October). *Stage-based measures of implementation components*. Chapel Hill, NC: University of North Carolina, National Implementation Research Network.

Fullan, M. (1982). *The meaning of educational change*. New York, NY: Teachers College Press.

Gertner, J. (2012). *The idea factory: Bell Labs and the golden age of American innovation*. New York, NY: The Penguin Press.

Hess, F. (2013). *Cage-busting leadership*. Cambridge, MA: Harvard Education Press.

Karmel, P., Blackburn, J., Hancock, G., Jackson, E. T., Jones, A. W., Martin, F. M., . . . White, W. A. (1973, May). *Schools in Australia*. Report of the Interim Committee for the Australian Schools Commission. Canberra: Australian Government Publishing Service.

Kasper, G. (2008, May). *Intentional innovation: How getting more systematic about innovation could improve philanthropy and increase social impact*. Retrieved from http://www.monitorinstitute.com/downloads/what-we-think/intentional-innovation/Intentional_Innovation.pdf

Kazak, A. E., Hoagwood, K., Weisz, J. R., Hood, K., Kratochwill, T. R., Vargas, L. A., & Banez, G. A. (2010). A meta-systems approach to evidence-based practice for children and adolescents. *American Psychologist, 65*(2), 85.

Keller, F. (1968). "Goodbye teacher...." *Journal of Applied Behavior Analysis, 1*, 79–89.

Kotter, J. (2012, March 1). Leading change: Why transformation efforts fail. In *Reinvention: Turn around your business; transform your career* (pp. 42–49). Harvard Business Review OnPoint.

Kulik, C., Kulik, J., & Bangert-Drowns, R. (1990). Effectiveness of mastery learning programs: A meta-analysis. *Review of Educational Research, 60*, 265–299.

Layng, T. V. J., Stikeleather, G., & Twyman, J. S. (2006). Scientific formative evaluation: The role of individual learners in generating and predicting successful educational outcomes. In R. F. Subotnik & H. J. Walberg (Eds.), *The scientific basis of educational productivity* (pp. 29–44). Charlotte, NC: Information Age Publishing.

Manzi, J. (2012). *Uncontrolled: The surprising payoff of trial-and-error for business, politics, and society*. New York, NY: Basic Books.

Markle, S. M. (1967). Empirical testing of programs. In P. C. Lange (Ed.), *Programmed instruction: Sixty–sixth yearbook of the National Society for the Study of Education* (Part 2, pp. 104–138). Chicago, IL: University of Chicago Press.

Miles, M. B. (1964). Educational innovation: The nature of the problem. In M. B. Miles (Ed.), *Innovation in education* (pp. 1–46). New York, NY: Teachers College Press.

McGuinn, P. (2012). Stimulating reform: Race to the Top, competitive grants, and the Obama education agenda. *Educational Policy, 26*(1), 136–159.

Miller, S. P. (2009). *Validated practices for teaching students with diverse needs and abilities.* Boston, MA: Allyn & Bacon.

Mobbs, C. W. (2010, December). *Why is innovation important?* North Bicester, Oxfordshire, UK: Innovation for Growth. Retrieved from http://www.innovationforgrowth.co.uk/whyisinnovationimportant.pdf

Mory, E. H. (1992). The use of informational feedback in instruction: Implications for future research. *Educational Technology Research and Development, 40*(3), 5–20.

Penuel, W. R., Fishman, B. J., Yamaguchi, R., & Gallagher, L. P. (2007). What makes professional development effective? Strategies that foster curriculum implementation. *American Educational Research Journal, 44*(4), 921–958.

Redding, S. (2012). *Change leadership: Innovation in state education agencies.* Oakland, CA: Wing Institute.

Rogers, E. M. (1962). *Diffusion of innovations.* New York, NY: Free Press.

Rogers, E. M. (1983). *Diffusion of innovations* (3rd ed.). New York, NY: Free Press.

Rogers, E. M. (2003). *Diffusion of innovations* (5th ed.). New York, NY: Free Press.

Rosenshine, B. V., & Berliner, D. C. (1978). Academic engaged time. *British Journal of Teacher Education, 4*(1), 3–16.

Shute, V. (2008). Focus on formative feedback. *Review of Educational Research, 78*(1), 153–189.

Smith, P., & Ragan, T. (1999). *Instructional design* (2nd ed.). New York, NY: John Wiley & Sons, Inc.

Sowell, T. (2002, April 18). *"Good" teachers.* Retrieved from http://townhall.com/columnists/thomassowell/2002/04/18/good_teachers/page/full

Tiemann, P. W., & Markle, S. M. (1990). *Analyzing instructional content: A guide to instruction and evaluation.* Seattle, WA: Morningside Press.

Twyman, J. S., Layng, T. V. J., Stikeleather, G., & Hobbins, K. A. (2004). A non-linear approach to curriculum design: The role of behavior analysis in building an effective reading program. In W. L. Heward et al. (Eds.), *Focus on behavior analysis in education* (Vol. 3, pp. 55–68). Upper Saddle River, NJ: Merrill/Prentice-Hall.

U.S. Department of Education. (2010). *Transforming American education. Learning powered by technology.* Washington, DC: Office of Educational Technology.

U.S. Department of Education. (2013). *Education Department launches 2013 Investing in Innovation competition* [Press release]. Retrieved April 5, 2013, from http://www.ed.gov/news/press-releases/education-department-launches-2013-investing-innovation-competition

Wang, M. C., & Zollers, N. J. (1990). Adaptive instruction: An alternative service delivery approach. *Remedial and Special Education, 11*(1), 7–21.

Warren, J. (2013, April 15). New Kentucky fund will support education innovation across the state. *Lexington Herald-Leader.* Retrieved from http://www.kentucky.com/2013/04/15/2601468/new-kentucky-fund-will-support.html#storylink=cpy

# Stimulating Innovation
# (or Making Innovation Meaningful Again)
*Maureen M. Mirabito and T. V. Joe Layng*

Welcome to the 21st century—a time when every school system in the world is preparing its children to be successful. As educators who face countless changes and requirements with technology and complexities hurtled our way, we can feel as though we are standing helpless in the middle of that Billy Joel song, *We Didn't Start the Fire*—the one with rapid-fire allusions to hundreds of headlines (Joel, 1989). Times are certainly complex, and this *complexity*, according to Michael Fullan, "means change, but specifically it means rapidly occurring, unpredictable, nonlinear change" (2001, p. ix). Innovation is one brand of change. We cannot innovate without doing things differently. Innovation done well, however, is more controlled than simply doing things differently; oftentimes, it can even be predictable. Innovation is planned change. Researchers from the 1970s describe it as "a deliberate, novel, specific change which is thought to be efficacious in accomplishing the goals of a system" (Nisbet & Collins, 1978, p. 6). According to the implications of that definition, stimulating innovation is as much about systemic change as it is about leadership and culture.

As much as we know about change, leadership, and culture now, we still find it difficult to leverage these factors toward the stimulation of focused, connected, and meaningful innovations within *and* across educational system hierarchies. More than 40 years ago, Simpkins and Miller (1972) explained why:

> Disputes arise as to the order of priority of educational objectives which best meets the interests of the individual and society, and agreement is difficult to obtain on appropriate educational ideas and practices. At the point of

implementation, it is not easy to change educational principles and methods, which are well entrenched and sanctified by tradition. (p. 6)

If we compare that statement from 1972 to the current state of education in 2013, we would find little difference in our efforts to innovate except perhaps to acknowledge the impact of federal and state policy on the entire system's ability to fulfill program requirements *and* adequately tend to the personalization of support to districts, schools, and classrooms. States have increasingly more to do and much less to do it with. The good news? Innovation (connected to specific and clear goals) loves that particular challenge.

## Why Is Innovation So Hard?

For a few years now, state education agencies have been building and refining their statewide systems of support. In some cases, states have completely reconfigured their approach to supporting the lowest achieving schools and evaluating their own effectiveness: "Successful state education agencies evaluate themselves—and their systems of recognition, accountability, and support—using the same rigorous performance metrics and evaluation tools that they apply to districts and schools" (Redding, 2013, p. 12). In other cases, these support systems continue to operate as individual, self-contained departments, coordinating one area of functional expertise with another area of functional expertise, often resulting in better coordination of what has always been done.

> *"Successful state education agencies evaluate themselves—and their systems of recognition, accountability, and support—using the same rigorous performance metrics and evaluation tools that they apply to districts and schools."*
> 
> Redding, 2013, p. 12

In all cases, we have yet to see pervasive (or disruptive) transformations in the ways that states, districts, and schools operate and interact, transformations that effect and sustain dramatic and widespread improvements in teaching and learning. This is not to say that structures aren't supportive or improvement isn't occurring. They are. It is. But with so many priorities still to achieve, programs to run, and reports to submit, we too easily forget what we set out to do in the first place—continually provide students with new and effective learning experiences—let alone communicate how we go about it up and down and across system levels.

Michael Fullan observed that our problem is not lack of innovations, but rather "the presence of too many disconnected, piecemeal, superficially adorned projects" (2001, p. 109). States, districts, and schools are so busy trying to just keep up and "keep it together" that the thought of one more thing, even if it is the right thing, seems unbearable. The annual *MetLife Survey of the American Teacher: Challenges for School Leadership* polled a representative sample of 1,000 teachers and 500 principals in K–12 schools across the country and found that "teacher job satisfaction has hit its lowest point in a quarter of a century, and 75 percent of principals believe their jobs have become too complex" (Strauss, 2013). In this world of rapid change and accountability, educators spend more and more time connecting and reporting on moving dots. Change of most sorts is likely to face resistance, particularly when it's unrelated (and/or in addition) to all of the other dots educators are trying to manage and maintain.

In identifying the reasons that people resist change, regardless of the industry under discussion, studies cite the most common resistors to be uncertainty, concern over personal loss, group resistance, dependence, lack of trust in administration, and awareness of weaknesses in the proposed change (Fullan, 2009; Spector, 2011). Whether introducing, implementing, or stimulating new initiatives or innovations, awareness of and attention to these internal forces of resistance are essential, without question.

But there is another force of resistance that has crept onto the scene: fatigue—*innovation fatigue* to be exact. Innovation was once a concept full of meaning and excitement, but its overuse and broad application has created a situation in which many see the word as an empty cliché (everything is innovative and nothing is) or short for "we're going to pressure you for something new, without guidance, resources, or support" (Rehn, 2013, para. 2). Consider these characteristics of innovation fatigue identified by Rehn at each level of the educational system:

- **It's all a joke.** Just mentioning the word innovation or change gets people all riled up, eyes rolling, and guffawing. They've been there and done that with little to no results to speak of and have mentally turned away from the direction you are trying to steer them.
- **New initiatives are met with old solutions**. As Fullan points out, the problem isn't a lack of innovation, it's that there are too many ad hoc, disconnected priorities and programs. It's hard to get staff working in new ways when history tells them there will be another "initiative" or "innovation" right behind this one, so they figure out how to incorporate the new innovative priorities into their existing, comfortable approaches.
- **They beg you to stop**. This type of begging goes beyond the typical resistance factors that were described earlier and speaks more of desperation and hopelessness: "Please stop. There are no people to do it and no resources to support it. We can't do one more thing."
- **They've given up.** Maybe they still fake it, but more than likely, they have completely given up on innovation and real change. At worst, they have given up all together—on innovation, on making a difference in their part of the work; at best, they *only* care about their part of the work and turn all of their energy into doing what they can to improve teaching and learning.

To overcome innovation fatigue, we must get serious about making innovation meaningful again. Broadly, that means stop asking people to just "think outside the box" (another cliché) or "just do this one more thing, and you'll see, it'll be different." We need to make clear what it is that causes us to say things are not right or can be improved. Is there acknowledgement that some things *may* be working? Many may feel that they are asked to change even when they believe what they are doing works. For some, innovation translates into, "How do I fit what I want to do, or have been doing all along, into this call for change?" Stated differently, is there recognition that past innovations have yielded some practices that should be continued? Acknowledging what is working is as important as recognizing what needs to change. It suggests that there can be lasting effects of innovation and that it is not just the latest attempt to look up-to-date. We need to (a) start talking specifically about the role of innovation in the organization and how it connects to very clear goals and priorities; (b) begin eliminating things—programs, practices, processes, and even innovations—that aren't positively impacting teaching and learning; (c) start creating a culture that promotes innovation in both language and action; and (d) begin developing a process to support, manage, and measure innovation.

Education isn't the only field struggling in this endeavor. A 2007 survey conducted by McKinsey & Company, which gauged the practices and perceptions among more than 1,000 senior executives and lower-level management, revealed that 70% of respondents indicated that innovation was a "top priority" for their organization, yet felt that their company approached it in inconsistent and at times counterproductive ways. According to the report, "Although more than a third of top managers [senior VP level and higher] say innovation is part of the leadership team's agenda, an equal number say their companies govern innovation in an ad hoc way" (Barsh, Capozzi, & Mendonce, 2007, pp. 2–3). Episodic innovation is both ineffective and fatiguing. Innovation that works is disciplined and invigorating.

## Remind Me, What Is Innovation Exactly?

Earlier, we described innovation as planned change, a simple enough definition. But there is little else about innovation that is simple: It is hard to do and easy to get wrong. Innovation comes in many shapes, sizes, and classes, but innovation becomes *meaningful* when it is connected to very clear and focused organizational and performance goals, when staff understand and see the value of it, when the evaluation criteria are not only understood but embraced, and when support exists and is evident at all levels of the educational system.

Nisbet defines innovation as "any new policy, syllabus, method, or organizational change, which is intended to improve teaching and learning" (1974, p. 2). Basset (1970, p. 4) classifies innovation into six categories:

a. new educational ideas or practices that were not previously known (inventing something new);
b. adaptations, extensions, or modifications of earlier ideas (adopting something that has been successful elsewhere, improving something that already exists);
c. changed conditions (e. g., class size, better materials, attracting innovative people) under which previously unsuccessful innovations may be successful;
d. changed attitudes on the part of teachers or administrators towards an idea;
e. new situations where the elements combine in new ways, resulting in a better mobilization of influences; and
f. changes that result from the spread of ideas which people had not previously understood or saw as potentially important (seeing something from a different perspective).

Apart from these *categories* of innovation, Clayton Christensen and other innovation experts believe there are (at least) two *kinds* of innovation: sustaining innovations and disruptive innovations. Both are critical to an organization's growth and success but require very different strategies to achieve. Sustaining innovations are intended "to sustain the core"—finding ways to do what is already being done, only better. Disruptive innovations create new markets or completely transform existing ones by focusing less on performance and focusing more on making things simpler, more affordable, more accessible, and/or more customizable. In education, this means new ways of creating and delivering learning environments that are not only different from the standard classroom, but also fundamentally change it. This includes the use of new technologies, such as tablets and interactive whiteboards; new means of research, such as search engines and direct access to outside resources via the Internet; new forms of collaboration made possible by social media; new means of delivering just-in-time learning that provides instruction right when it is needed; and the application of new principles derived from the laboratory, as well as the growing use of "big data" (see Layng & Twyman and also Baker in this *Handbook*).

During the writing of this chapter, the first author had very sick children for what seemed a very long winter. For one child or another, there were pediatrician's office visits every week or more for one reason or another, waiting in rooms on average for one hour or more. At one point, the author learned about a pediatric "minute clinic" that recently opened and promised minimal (almost nonexistent) wait times, a clean and fun environment, high-quality care, and the capacity to fill prescriptions (if needed) on the spot. Almost all insurances were accepted, and no appointment was needed. Employing retired pediatricians or pediatric nurses and physician's assistants looking for flexible work environments, this clinic is definitely disrupting the traditional pediatric care industry.

The two forms of innovation, sustaining or disruptive, "couldn't be more different," says Mark W. Johnson, chairman of Innosight, indicating that they achieve different outcomes and "need different levels of resources and different people who are rewarded in different ways" (Kelly, 2010, p. 2). According to Johnson, one of the biggest mistakes organizations make is treating them as the same. For example, people tasked with fueling the company's future are also expected to sustain the current offerings, splitting their time and resources in ad hoc ways. "Worse," says Johnson, "they subject both kinds of innovations to a single time scale and reward with the same incentives" (Kelly, 2010, p. 2). In his view, organizations need to carefully plan their sustaining innovations in order to maintain their relevance and meet needs in the short term but separately identify and pursue disruptive innovations that will create something new and change the game in productive ways for the future.

> *Innovation is planned change because it requires careful consideration of and alignment to system goals and priorities as well as constant and conscious effort to create a collaborative and supportive culture that promotes, values, and rewards creativity and innovation—sustaining and disruptive—and assigns the right people, the appropriate resources, and different timetables to each.*

Innovation is *planned change* because it requires careful consideration of and alignment to system goals and priorities as well as constant and conscious effort to create a collaborative and supportive culture that promotes, values, and rewards creativity and innovation—sustaining and disruptive—and assigns the right people, the appropriate resources, and different timetables to each. The importance of taking into account the culture, context, and conditions in pursuing innovation cannot be understated. As Nisbet and Collins (1978) also observed, a "too narrow focus on innovation leads to situations where important related factors have been ignored or underestimated" (p. 6). Understanding the interplay between innovation, culture, and context separates successful, strategic innovation from ad hoc, resisted, and usually failed innovation.

## What Does a Culture That Supports Innovation Look Like?

Not all innovative cultures can offer rooftop garden terraces or foosball tables where employees meet to brainstorm and solve problems as does Google, but those things aren't necessarily what make a culture innovative. Despite the theme park-like work setting, Google's description of its culture states that it is really the people that make it the kind of company it is. The statement continues, "We strive to maintain the open culture...in which everyone is a hands-on contributor and feels comfortable sharing ideas and opinions...Our offices...

are designed to *encourage interactions between, within, and across teams* and to spark conversations about work" (italics added; Google, n.d., para. 2).

At Applied Minds, a company that relies exclusively on interdisciplinary approaches to "build things so small you have to look at them under an electron microscope. We design things the size of large buildings" (Jardin, 2005, para. 22), cofounders Bran Ferren and Danny Hillis, former engineers for Walt Disney's Imagineering, rely on artists, scientists, and engineers with wide-ranging skills in architecture, electronics, mechanics, physics, mathematics, software development, system engineering, and storytelling to invent, design, and prototype breakthrough products and services for industry and government (Jardin, 2005). The projects of Applied Minds range from toys and roller coasters to cancer treatments and sound scramble technologies, from buildings to algorithms, and from off-road vehicles to high-resolution displays (Jardin, 2005). Two more detailed examples include an interactive surface map of earth that comes alive with the sweep of a hand, zooming from continent, to country, to state, to city, to parking lot. A swipe of the finger takes you east, west, north, or south. Cupped hands turn the map into a globe that can spin. In 2005, Applied Minds was developing "an online search and collaboration system called Metaweb, a project to identify and match specific cancer treatments based on attributes of a patient's body chemistry" (Jardin, 2005, para. 15).

Hillis and Ferren believe that their cross-disciplinary approach, together with providing internal structures and opportunities that make cross-collaboration easy and expected, is essential to their success. As Hillis puts it, "There are plenty of people out there who could design electronics, psychologists who could tell you that meaning demands attention, and architects who could tell you we need to make open offices work better, but we think about all of these things together" (Jardin, 2005, para. 13).

As educators, we are not likely to benefit from (or require) gadgets that will create sonic privacy in workspaces without walls (another Applied Minds' innovation), but we can benefit from the cross-disciplinary and collaborative culture that Applied Minds has established to develop solutions, create opportunities, and explore possibilities.

Google and Applied Minds are examples of companies which support modern innovative cultures, but innovative cultures can be found in every century. Author Frans Johansson (2004), in his book *The Medici Effect: Breakthrough Insights at the Intersection of Ideas, Concepts, and Cultures*, shares his research (which supports other scholars' findings as well) on what sparked the 14$^{th}$ century Renaissance. Gabriel Kasper and Stephanie Clohesy (2008) use Johansson's research in their report to reveal lessons that hold valuable, 21st century relevance as well:

    a. **Collaborate**. Forget traditional boundaries and divisions and find ways to bring people together from a wide variety of fields and disciplines to work and cocreate. Look both inside and outside your organization for innovative partnerships.

b. **Be systematic**. Develop a culture that supports, nurtures, and develops innovation in a systematic way. Creativity is only one part of the innovation picture. A disciplined yet flexible process is needed to launch new ideas and then scale them to the opportunity or need at hand.

c. **Use change agents**. Senior leadership support for innovation is essential. But an organization also needs people who can foster innovation throughout the organization, both around specific opportunities or needs and structurally to impact daily operations.

d. **Use technology**. German scribes mocked the early printing presses as unreliable "contraptions" that would never replace hand-written books. Innovative cultures should identify, accept, and support new technologies that can increase the flow and dissemination of knowledge and information and simplify operational work.

Silos and working within functional areas are not unique to the educational system; most organizations and companies operate this way. Increasingly, though, the innovative ones have figured out ways to slowly dismantle silos and work cross-functionally to eliminate duplicative or ineffective resources and requirements. Literature on innovation and practice over the last decade reveal that it is possible for an organization to be more systematic about innovation. What was once thought to be an art is actually more of a science, and the general outline of what it takes to successfully manage innovation is beginning to come into focus. Following intentional, repeatable processes can allow an organization to more effectively develop, test, implement, and share new ideas. Innovative organizations continuously engage in this process.

## Cross-Functioning and Collaboration

In 2008, in an effort to redefine work priorities and approaches to identifying and delivering support and services to the lowest performing schools in a state of 24 school systems with proximal access to leading science, education, and technology centers, the Maryland State Department of Education (MSDE) launched the Breakthrough Center. An emphasis on "dismantling the silos" undergirded the development of the Breakthrough Center, with teams expected to work cross-functionally up and down the levels of the educational system to identify needs within the department and across districts and schools in the state (uniquely and commonly). Depending on the needs identified and their context, a cross-functional team would be established to cocreate solutions with districts, schools, and external partners, enlisting both top-down and bottom-up support. Learning from one another would be as valuable to the process as the contribution of expertise and skills.

In addition to its collaborations, the Breakthrough Center also serves as a broker of services between districts, schools, and organizations, as well as the driver of incentives to encourage and identify where exceptional (even innovative) practices are occurring within the state's schools and classrooms. Giving a nod to the idea that disruptive innovation does not happen overnight, the center has adopted a "go slow to go fast" approach to its growth. For all of the excitement that this new way of operating elicited, it generated uncertainty in the early stages as well. Four years into its launch, the center continues to navigate the complexities and nuances of an educational system that adheres to traditional mechanisms for operating, including the allocation and disbursement of funding and services. However, constant efforts to build trusting and collaborative relationships around a crystal clear and shared vision throughout the Maryland State Department of Education and into the districts and schools has resulted in more direct pathways through which teaching and learning have improved.

This type of approach becomes systematic when, as Michael Fullan (2013) observes,

[A] cross-functional team of leaders from multiple departments begin talking about goals and what each department can contribute. They interact continuously in small and big ways and come to have a similar grasp of the core goals as well as the main strategies being employed. This concept is then extended to other levels—district and school. Pretty soon a critical mass of leaders at all levels begin to interact and act in consistent ways, learning from each other and extending learning to the rest of the organization. The system starts to work in a reinforcing way. (p. 62)

## Other Ways of Thinking About Collaboration

Open innovation is another approach that is attracting broad attention in the problem-solving, solution-seeking world. Clayton Christensen, in a September 2012 web log, "Open Innovation and Getting Things Right" (Christensen, 2012), describes it this way, "Open innovation is a method of innovation that has arisen in recent years which allows companies to essentially source some of their innovation efforts to outside parties, often through contests [in which] individuals compete to develop the best solution to the innovation challenge the company has set forth" (para. 2). On a large scale, it involves crowd-sourcing problems to the world's best thinkers who compete to provide solutions to business, technical, policy, and social challenges. Companies like Google, Apple, NASA, and IBM use open innovation to solve some of their greatest challenges. NASA, for example, in trying to solve the problem of health-related issues for long-duration flights, opened this problem

> *Companies like Google, Apple, NASA, and IBM use open innovation to solve some of their greatest challenges.*

up to the crowd—those within their agency that may not have otherwise been brought into the conversation and especially those outside the agency that may have no experience in space travel—in an effort to find the most innovative solution. Referred to as crowd-sourcing, NASA used this approach to solve another problem: how to preserve food for several years in space. The solution came from someone completely outside of the food or space industry ("How Open Innovation Is Solving," 2013).

Though the results of open innovation to overall success are mixed, Christensen, in his September 2012 web log, advises us to be cautious in adopting open innovation too quickly without a precise definition of what it is and how we aim to use it: "For example, open innovation can be an excellent means for innovating around specific technical challenges. In contrast, open innovation may be a less effective means for bigger, larger architectural or business model innovations" (para. 3).

In education, open innovation might just be the approach state education agencies could employ to identify, develop, and scale learning innovations within their state. For example, a district with resources to build and develop a robust curriculum and assessment program that meets the requirements of the Common Core could "sell" its product to the state or to a consortium of smaller districts and schools without the resources or expertise to build such a program on its own. In tough economic times, these external revenue-generating opportunities are attractive to districts with in-house capacity, yet provide an economical solution for states, districts, and schools without such capacity but who might share the cost in purchasing products, programs, or services.

On a smaller but critically important scale, open innovation might prove just the approach for engaging teachers in the innovation process—tapping into their skills and talents for new solutions or different approaches to personalize student learning, for example, and then coming up with creative ways to reward them. Great teachers innovate and personalize learning every day. Finding them is one step of the innovation process; the next and trickier part is identifying the specific practices they have innovated upon and coming up with effective ways to transfer that knowledge and those skills to others. There you have it: your first innovative challenge.

The concept of open innovation is an interesting one for educators. It has the potential to expand the practice of collaboration and interdisciplinary teaming within an organization as well as up and down the levels of its system even further—definitely into classrooms, maybe across state and national lines, possibly into different industries. Of course, as with most types of innovation, it should be approached carefully and be connected to clear and specific goals. It certainly provides new ways of thinking about resources, solving problems, and envisioning possibilities.

## Motivation to Innovate in Education and the Consequences of Not Innovating

Innovation means change, and change has consequences. One consequence is clear: Change implies work. For districts, schools, principals, and teachers, additional work is the last thing they desire. It is important to understand the cost of change for all who are asked to innovate. Even attending a meeting to discuss innovation can be an extra burden. Innovation should be fun; that is, it should produce consequences that are worthwhile for all involved. Innovation policy needs to allow those consequences to have their effect. Israel Goldiamond (1974) noted that consequences often come in packages—a bundle of costs and benefits. Given an array of alternatives, people will distribute their behavior in accord with the costs and benefits contingent on each alternative (Goldiamond, 1984; Herrnstein, 2000). Policymakers may examine the costs and ignore the benefits, emphasize benefits and ignore the costs, or overlook alternative ways of doing things that provide the same benefits at less cost or have the same cost but greater benefits (Goldiamond, 1976).

Every day, educators are faced with these choices. They occur moment to moment—for example, "Do I use precious time to work with one child and forsake having a well prepared lesson for the many?" They also occur in terms of allocating time and effort to innovation. One approach is to make these consequences explicit; that is, describe the costs (including the effort it takes to change and implement change) and benefits of innovating as compared to the costs and benefits of current practices. An example of this can be found in Layng's (1977) analysis of telecommunication vs. transportation trade-offs when delivering instruction to students who must commute long distances to school. Often, the costs and benefits discussed are economic, that is, at least some form of monetary value may be assigned to the consequences under consideration (see, Layard & Glaister, 1994). However, there are other forms of costs and benefits that are consequences of a more personal nature.

There are two major types of personal consequences (Goldiamond, 1974; Layng, 2009). There are those that are extrinsic to the activity, extrinsic meaning that they are arranged by an outside agent, and there are those specific to an activity. Too often policymakers focus on the former and hope for the latter. B. F. Skinner (1953), commenting on why French was easier to learn in France than in the United States, said, "In an American school, if you ask for salt in good French, you get an A. In France, you get the salt" (p. 402). The latter is an example of the kind of built-in consequences Skinner advocated; the former is arranged by others and is extrinsic to the activity, what Skinner (1968) called a "spurious" consequence.

When incentives (benefits) are discussed, they are often only of the activity-extrinsic type, such as merit pay. While pay is important and critical to one's well being, money-based incentives should allow for individual differences in activity-specific consequences. Free choice is defined by the consequences of choice, such as offering equal amounts of money for different activities, thus leaving the selector free to choose which activity is preferred. Consider Goldiamond's (1976) observation that prisoners given time off their sentences for participating in medical trials could not be considered to freely consent to those trials unless time off one's sentence was available for other activities as well. Only then could the costs and benefits for participation be fully considered by the inmate.

We assert that innovations that are embraced and maintained provide activity-specific consequences, while innovations that are transient and feel burdensome are often maintained by spurious, activity-extrinsic consequences. These spurious consequences include the cost of noncompliance, such as failing to appear as a team member or jeopardizing one's evaluation or career advancement, as well as benefits such as merit pay or gold star employee ceremonies. Activity-specific benefits are those for which we may see learner engagement, obvious *aha!* moments in the classroom, improved learner evaluations that demonstrate learner success and inform better practices rather than judge, unanticipated peer acknowledgement, and even paid adoption of teacher, school, or district innovations by others.

Costs can be activity-specific as well. These costs include learning new methods and technologies. For a principal, not only learning but managing these technologies imposes an added burden. There are inventory, storage, wiring, safety, and distribution issues, to name but a few, which when added to an already overwhelming list of responsibilities, make the job increasingly complex. Added complexity at all levels is a cost.

The benefits of innovation should be tangible, activity-specific, and frequent. The costs need to be recognized and minimized where possible. Teacher dissatisfaction may perhaps be traced to a decline in activity-specific benefits, a rise in the activity-extrinsic consequences of compliance or noncompliance (such as meeting new standards), as well as to increases in workload and complexity.

How can innovation be motivated? We offer three proposals.

a. **Conduct a workload audit**. One approach is to conduct what we would call a workload audit and to frame any suggested innovation in this context. For every new program, collaboration meeting, preparation to share best practices, classroom implementation, and so on, specify what is removed to make way for the change. Innovation should not be synonymous with increased workload. Those who are most affected by innovation should not be the ones who bear the brunt of the human cost of innovation. Removing this cost improves the likelihood that innovation benefits will be achieved.

b. **Identify the consequences.** Search for and identify as many activity-specific consequences as possible for those working at implementing innovation at all levels. Ask, "If things were working as we would want them to, what would it look like to us? What would be happening that each of us (administrator, principal, teacher, student, parent) would be thrilled to see?" Those are likely the activity-specific consequences that will maintain innovative behavior.

c. **Plan for maximum benefits, minimum costs**. Devise an innovation plan that maximizes activity-specific benefits and minimizes activity-specific costs, while minimizing spurious consequences of all types.

## Where Do We Go From Here?

Change is messy, even planned change. But to Fullan (2001) and other experts on change and innovation, "The experience of this messiness is necessary in order to discover hidden benefits—creative ideas and novel solutions are generated when the status quo is disrupted" (p. 107).

We have taken note of several of the innovations cited throughout this *Handbook*—some are programs, others practices, some entire systems of innovation. The context and conditions in which these innovations are most successful must not be overlooked. Therefore, before we specify action principles to stimulate innovation and make it meaningful again, we're going to get your creative brain thinking by asking you to consider the context and conditions of an innovation. Pick an innovation or two that you've read about in this *Handbook* and take a reverse approach in your examination of them. On your own, or with your team, ask yourselves:

a. How would this innovation disrupt the status quo in my organization?
b. What need does it address or possibilities does it create for teaching and learning?
c. What conditions (leadership, structures, flexibility, work load) would support the development and implementation of this innovation?
d. What language, actions, and beliefs need to be defined and agreed upon in order to successfully pursue this type of innovation and then make it happen?
e. What types of collaboration and communication occurred at each level of the educational system that enabled building credibility and enthusiasm for the innovation?
f. What motivated these educators to pursue this innovation? What were the possible consequences of not pursuing it?
g. What are the costs and benefits that need to be identified, both activity-specific and activity-extrinsic?
h. How can the benefits of the innovation outweigh its costs, as well as outweigh the benefits and costs of the status quo at every level of participation?

## Action Principles

a. Consider context and culture. When planning for a successful, strategic innovation, think carefully about the context and culture in which it will be implemented and how each may influence the other. Identify ways to leverage the interplay between them.
b. Build an understanding. Communicate the specific role of innovation in your organization (its purpose, what it should achieve, how people will be supported in stimulating it) and connect innovation to very specific goals and priorities.
c. Build a culture of innovation. Simultaneous to building an understanding of what innovation is and what it should achieve, build a culture to support it. Create structures, opportunities, and common practices for people across and within teams or divisions to interact, create, develop new ideas, communicate them to all levels of the system, and scale them. A culture of innovation should be demonstrated at all levels of the system.
d. Make innovation concrete and recognizable. Specify the categories and types of innovation for staff so they begin to see it in tangible form and even start to recognize it in practices they currently employ (and maybe just haven't formalized or shared). Use the definitions and examples provided in this chapter and elsewhere in this *Handbook* to get started.
e. Point out past and ongoing successes. Demonstrate that past innovations have staying power by acknowledging what still works well and continuing it.
f. Differentiate the two types of innovation. Create distinct processes, timelines, and incentives for the two types of innovations—sustaining innovations (more effective and efficient ways of doing what is already being done) and disruptive innovations (creating something new and different, a game-changer for the future).
g. Look, identify, disseminate, and incentivize. Using established criteria for innovation, seek out where it is happening (in classrooms, offices, divisions), identify the specific practices being innovated upon, and establish pathways to transfer that knowledge and those skills to others. Identify the incentives for knowledge transfer.
h. Envision the potential and anticipate the problems. Be up front about the costs and benefits of innovation, identifying as many activity-specific consequences as possible. To start, ask, "If things were working as we would want them to, what would it look like to us? What would be happening that each of us (administrator, principal, teacher, student, parent) would be thrilled to see?"

# References

Barsh, J., Capozzi, M., & Mendonce, L. (2007, October). How companies approach innovation: A McKinsey Global Survey. *The McKinsey Quarterly*. Retrieved from http://www.mckinseyquarterly.com

Bassett, G. W. (1970). *Innovation in primary education*. London, UK: Wiley Interscience.

Christensen, C. (2012, September 19). Open innovation and getting things right [Web log message]. Retrieved from http://www.claytonchristensen.com/open-innovation/

Fullan, M. (2001). *Leading in a culture of change*. San Francisco, CA: Jossey-Bass.

Fullan, M. (2009). *Motion leadership: The skinny on becoming change savvy*. Thousand Oaks, CA: Corwin.

Fullan, M. (2013). *Motion leadership: More skinny on becoming change savvy*. Thousand Oaks, CA: Corwin.

Google. (n.d.). *Our culture*. Mountain View, CA: Author. Retrieved from http://www.google.com/about/company/facts/culture/

Goldiamond, I. (1974). Toward a constructional approach to social problems: Ethical and constitutional issues raised by applied behavior analysis. *Behaviorism, 2*(1), 1–84.

Goldiamond, I. (1976). Protection of human subjects and patients: A social contingency analysis of distinctions between research and practice, and its implications. *Behaviorism, 4*(1), 1–41.

Goldiamond, I. (1984). Training parents and ethicists in nonlinear behavior analysis. In R. F. Dangel & R. A. Polster (Eds.), *Parent training: Foundations of research and practice* (pp. 504–546). New York, NY: Guilford.

Herrnstein, R. J. (2000). *The matching law: Papers in psychology and economics*. Cambridge, MA: Harvard University Press.

How Open Innovation is Solving Some of NASA's Trickiest Problems. Knowledge@Wharton (2013, April 03). Retrieved from http://knowledge.wharton.upenn.edu/article/how-open-innovation-is-solving-some-of-nasas-trickiest-problems/

Jardin, X. (2005, June 21). Applied minds think remarkably. *Wired*. Retrieved from http://www.wired.com/science/discoveries/news/2005/06/67951

Joel, B. (1989). We didn't start the fire. On *Storm front* [Record]. New York, NY: Columbia Records.

Johansson, F. (2004). *The Medici effect: Breakthrough insights at the intersection of ideas, concepts, and cultures*. Cambridge, MA: Harvard Business Press.

Kasper, G., & Clohesy, S. (2008). *Intentional innovation: How getting more systematic about innovation could improve philanthropy and increase social impact*. Prepared for the W. H. Kellogg Institute. Retrieved from http://www.monitorinstitute.com/downloads/what-we-think/intentional-innovation/Intentional_Innovation.pdf

Kelly, B. (2010, June 16). Interview with Mark W. Johnson, "Leading the innovative focused organization." *Strategy & Innovation, 8*(5), 1–8.

Layard, R., & Glaister, S. (Eds.). (1994). *Cost-benefit analysis*. New York, NY: Cambridge University Press.

Layng, T. V. J. (1977). Telecommunications–Transportation trade-offs: A brief social contingency analysis of the relationship of petro-energy scarcity to instructional technology. *NSPI Journal, 16*(10), 7–9.

Layng, T. V. J. (2009). The search for an effective clinical behavior analysis: The nonlinear thinking of Israel Goldiamond. *The Behavior Analyst, 32*(1), 163–184.

Nisbet, J. (1974, July). *Innovation–Bandwagon or hearse?* Frank Tate Memorial Lecture (Photocopy).

Nisbet, R. I., & Collins, J. M. (1978). Barriers and resources to innovation. *Australian Journal of Teacher Education, 3*(1), 2–29.

Redding, S. (2013, May). Building a better statewide system of support. In B. Gross & A. Jochim (Eds.), *Leveraging performance management to support school improvement: The SEA of the future* (pp. 9–18). San Antonio, TX: Building State Capacity & Productivity Center at Edvance Research, Inc.

Rehn, A. (2013, January 2). Are you creating innovation fatigue? [Web log message]. Alexandria, VA: American Society for Training and Development. Retrieved from http://www.astd.org/Publications/Blogs/Workforce-Development-Blog/2013/01/ARE-YOU-CREATING-INNOVATION-FATIGUE

Simpkins, W. S., & Miller, A. H. (Eds.). (1972). *Changing education, Australian viewpoints*. Sydney, Australia: McGraw Hill.

Skinner, B. F. (1953). *Science and human behavior*. New York, NY: Macmillan.

Skinner, B. F. (1968). *The technology of teaching*. New York, NY: Appleton Century Crofts.

Spector, B. (2011). *Implementing organizational change: Theory into practice* (international ed.). Upper Saddle River, NJ: Prentice Hall.

Strauss, V. (2013, February 21). U.S. teachers' job satisfaction craters—report. *Washington Post*, Answers Sheet.

# Innovation, Implementation Science, and Data-Based Decision Making: Components of Successful Reform
*Ronnie Detrich*

> *Plans are only good intentions unless they immediately degenerate into hard work.*
> Peter Drucker

Ever since the 1957 Soviet Union's launch of Sputnik, it seems the United States has been in a constant state of school reform. That event galvanized the United States to enact reforms in science and engineering education (Powell, 2007), to be followed over the years by a dizzying array of "innovations" in instructional practices (teacher-led, child-centered, Response to Intervention, evidence-based), in structural innovations (small schools, small class sizes, classrooms without walls, charter schools), in personnel preparation (extra years of training, alternative routes to credentials), and in accountability (pay for performance, value-added modeling, changing evaluation procedures). Yet the student achievement data have remained remarkably flat since the 1970s (National Center for Education Statistics, 2011). During this time, educators have seen reform initiatives quickly come and go; researchers have estimated that the average life span of an educational innovation is only 18–48 months (Aladjem & Borman, 2006; Latham 1988). Each of these reform efforts represents an attempt to solve an educational problem. Despite strong evidence of effectiveness when evaluated in research settings, many of these so-called innovations often returned disappointing results when taken to scale. The problem may be not in the innovations themselves but rather in the manner in which they have been implemented (Fixsen, Naoom, Blase, Friedman, & Wallace, 2005).

Generally, educators adopt educational reforms because they are seen as advantageous, producing either greater benefit to the student (Martens, Peterson, Witt, & Cirone, 1986), equal benefit as current practice but requiring less effort, or equal benefit but more acceptable by being more positive and constructive.

Recent reform efforts include the use of evidence-based interventions to solve educational problems (Coalition for Evidence-Based Policy, 2003). For the promise of the evidence-based reform movement to be realized, the recommended practices will require high-quality implementation. Regrettably, many reform practices do not meet the standards required to consider them evidence-based or to support their claims of effectiveness. To create true change in the effectiveness of schooling, educators must adopt, implement, and scale up only practices that are evidence-based. Not only do school officials have a fiduciary responsibility to spend taxpayer dollars on practices that have evidence of effectiveness, they are ethically bound to provide students the best chance of success. Otherwise, widespread implementation is nothing more than a large research project.

Evidence-based practices selected for implementation constitute an intervention. In this chapter, intervention refers to *any systematic effort to change behavior at any level of the system*. For example, instructional curricula are interventions, as is training staff to implement a curriculum. Providing feedback to principals about how well their schools are performing is also an intervention. This chapter will review what is known from the growing field of "implementation science" that can contribute to high-quality implementation of innovative, effective practices at scale.

## A Framework to Guide Implementation

It is axiomatic that student outcomes are significantly influenced by the quality of the teacher and the classroom environment. Students do well when the teacher is skilled and has created a constructive learning environment. An extension of this logic can only conclude that the school team, the principal, the district, and the state education agency (SEA) are successful to the extent they create supportive functional environments for those operating at lower levels in the system. The ultimate criterion for success is student achievement. Figure 1 describes the interdependence of the different levels in an educational system.

In Figure 1, the student is the focal point of all activity for the other levels in the system, with the student's performance conceptualized as a motivator for change. Viewing student performance in this way affects implementation in two major ways: (a) student underperformance can initiate change; and (b) change initiatives can be evaluated by how they affect student performance. All activities across all levels of the system can be informed by the answer to one critical question: What is necessary for each student to succeed?

Scaling up an innovation is a significant undertaking, requiring many levels in the system to alter the way they do business. As a result, in many instances, reforms intended for students never reach the classroom intact (Brown, Hess,

**Figure 1. The Interdependence of the Different Levels in an Educational System**

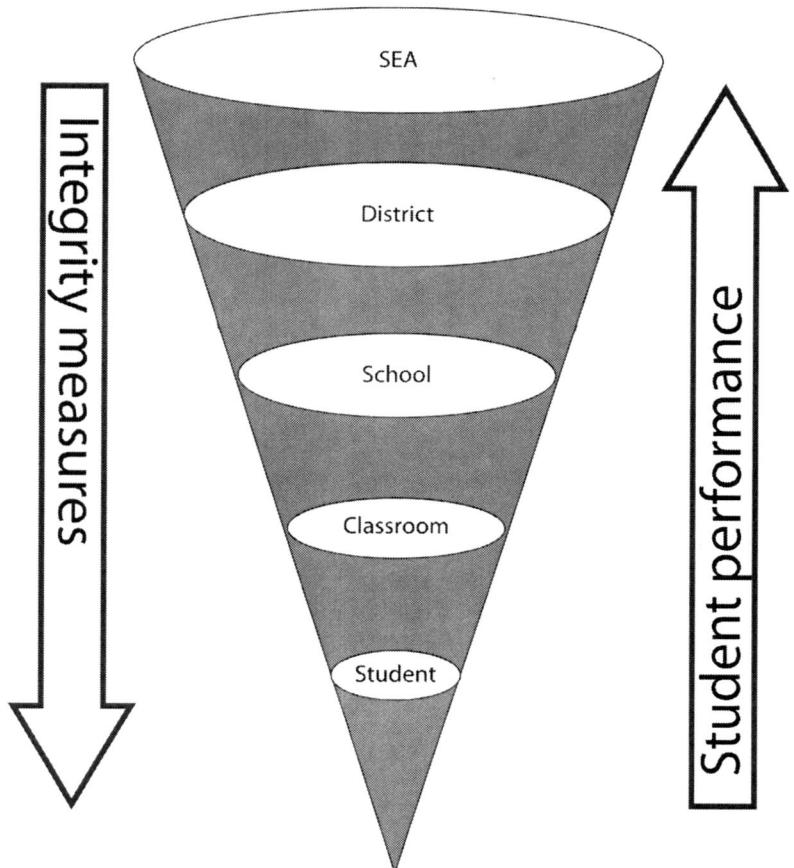

Lautzenheiser, & Owen, 2011), the result of a breakdown in the implementation effort somewhere between the initiating agency and the classroom. Viewing the educational system as an ecosystem highlights the need for all parts of the system to be organized to support the implementation effort. Alignment (i.e., when policies, practices, and goals within a system are organized to facilitate action at other levels of the system, in the service of the same goals) must occur, or the reform effort will not be implemented with fidelity, produce the desired results, or be sustained.

When an innovation is introduced into a system, it is necessary to evaluate its impact. Many of the difficulties associated with implementing innovations in the classroom can be successfully addressed by employing a data-based, decision-making approach in which *all* activities are evaluated for their impact on student outcomes. The data derived from measures of implementation give context and meaning to the data about student performance. That is, understanding student performance data also requires data on how well interventions are implemented in the classroom and how well teachers are supported in their implementation by training, coaching, and constructive feedback. In our multitiered educational system, measures of student performance that can be aggregated into increasingly larger units for higher levels in the system and measures of the quality of implementation at each level are two key features of data-based decision making in implementation.

A broad view of the use of data within systems of education is shown in Figure 1. Data about student achievement are collected at the level of the individual student and classroom and flow up from the student through the various levels of the system to the SEA. Data about the quality of implementation are generally collected at a level above the one responsible for implementation; data flow down the levels in the form of performance feedback to the responsible persons. When this occurs, the system is aligned and working towards the same outcomes. From a top level, SEAs support and evaluate districts' efforts at implementation and understanding performance data, while districts support and evaluate school implementation efforts. When data systems are organized this way, any misalignment between levels can be identified and corrected. For example, if student progress is lacking and data indicate a subpar implementation, a review of the data regarding the training, support, and the sufficiency of the support plan for the teachers can be used to inform system improvement.

> **The research on implementation indicates that even initially high-quality implementations will deteriorate over time without feedback about performance.**

In all cases, the support plan needs to include performance feedback. An extensive literature supports this practice as a means of enhancing the quality of implementation in classrooms and schools (Bartels & Mortenson, 2005; Burns, Peters, & Noell, 2008; Mortenson & Witt, 1998; Myers, Simonsen, & Sugai, 2011; Noell et al., 2000). The research on implementation indicates that even initially high-quality implementations will deteriorate over time without feedback about performance. For example, Newton and colleagues (2009) noted that school-based, problem-solving teams trained to use a specific protocol for decision making will begin basing choices on unalterable and irrelevant variables if they are not provided feedback about how well they are following the protocol.

If data suggest that the teachers are implementing with integrity and that the teacher training and support plan, including performance feedback, are sufficient and being implemented with integrity but student performance does not improve, then it may be reasonable to conclude that the intervention is not effective in a particular context. Some interventions are simply not appropriate for some settings due to the mismatch between the requirements of the intervention and the resources and capacity of the setting. If high-quality implementation cannot be achieved or can be achieved only at great cost, then it may be necessary to abandon the innovation. A careful evaluation of the research base of any given intervention should preclude most discordant applications. Nevertheless, changes in contextual factors—demographics, for example—may impact any intervention, so once a highly successful implementation is achieved, its effects on student performance must continue to be reevaluated.

## The Science of Implementation

"Implementation science" is an emerging field that studies how changes are successfully introduced and implemented within a system. Just as the movement toward evidence-based practices derived from medicine, the systematic study and experimentation of implementation variables also started there (Carroll et al., 2007) and has now moved into education. Currently, the primary methods of analysis for studying the implementation process—both descriptive and experimental methods—are maturing, yet there is much useful information to be gleaned from the data so far (Rubenstein & Pugh, 2006).

Implementation refers to the set of activities that are necessary for an innovative practice to produce desired outcomes (Fixsen et al., 2005). The benefits are most likely to be accomplished by implementing with integrity, that is, with a consistency of values, actions, methods, measures, principles, and, ultimately, outcomes. If a practice—all, not just certain features of it—is not implemented with integrity, it could be argued that it has not actually been implemented. Furthermore, implementation is not complete until the innovation has become routine practice within a school or district and new hires continue to implement it (Coburn, 2003). Since teacher turnover data indicate that almost 50% of teachers leave the profession within 5 years of entry (Heyns, 1988) and Fixsen and colleagues (2005) estimate at least 4–5 years to fully implement an innovation within a system, many teachers will not see the full implementation of an innovation. If an intervention is to be sustained, additional "generations" of teachers will be responsible for implementation. As generations of teachers enter the system, a culture and an infrastructure must be established to support their integration.

So how does an innovation get "fully implemented" within a system? Two approaches have been described to characterize implementation efforts: *letting* it happen and *making* it happen (Greenhalgh, Robert, Macfarlane, Bate, & Kyriakidou, 2004). Given the importance of education, "making" an effective implementation happen is the necessary choice. But how? Rogers (2003) argued that the diffusion of an innovation is a function of social processes more than a matter of its features (counter to the proverbial notion "build a better mousetrap, and the world will beat a path to your door"). Rogers (2003) suggested several guiding principles for the effective diffusion of innovations:

   a. The adoption rate of an innovation is a function of its compatibility with the values, beliefs, and past experiences of the members of a social system.

    b. Innovations have to solve a problem that is important for the person who is expected to adopt it.
    c. The innovation must have a relative advantage over the current practice.
    d. It is necessary to gain the support of opinion leaders within the social system if the adoption of the innovation is to reach critical mass and become self-sustaining.
    e. The innovation is perceived as being simple to understand and implement.
    f. The innovation can be implemented on a small, limited basis before being broadly adopted.
    g. The benefits of innovation are observable to others.

## Seven Principles of Successful Implementation

The next sections consider supporting evidence for Rogers's (2003) principles and describe how these principles can guide "making implementation happen." Throughout this section of the chapter, schoolwide positive behavior support (SWPBS) will be used as an example of thoughtful, systematic implementation and scaling up. SWPBS has been developing and evolving over the past 30 years. Initially, it was implemented in one school in Oregon; now it is used in approximately 16,000 schools nationwide.[1]

A key feature of SWPBS is its emphasis on data-based decision making and development of the internal capacity of the school to solve its own problems. School leadership teams lead the development of interventions and evaluate their impact. The primary measure of effectiveness is changes in office discipline referrals (ODRs). In addition to measuring student behavior, school data are routinely reviewed by administrators or consultants to determine the quality of implementation.

### Principle A: Insure Compatibility With Values, Beliefs, and Experiences

Fixsen and colleagues (2005) have proposed a model of the stages of implementation in which adoption is one of the earliest stages. In many instances, programs are adopted at one level of a system (administration), but if a program is not adopted and accepted by those directly responsible for its implementation, the probability of effectiveness and sustainability are very low. Several authors have argued that educational innovations are more likely to be adopted/accepted if they fit well with the culture of a classroom or a school (Albin, Lucyshyn, Horner, & Flannery, 1996; Detrich, 1999; Kealey, Peterson, Gaul, & Dinh, 2000). Several factors are associated with acceptability (Elliott, 1988), including, for teachers, an intervention's agreement with their view of what constitutes effective instruction or behavior management, the time required to implement it in the classroom, and its perceived ease of implementation. Teachers are more likely to agree to implement interventions if they feel they have the skills and

---

[1] For more detailed information on SWPBS and its methods of behavior management at the school-wide level, see Sugai and Horner (2009).

resources necessary (Elliott, 1988). The data on acceptability illustrate that adoption of an innovation is often less about the scientific evidence of its effectiveness and more about the social acceptability of an innovation, its fit with current practices, the ease of transition and support available, and the consequences of not adopting.

Since the adoption of an innovation and implementation fidelity are influenced by many variables, the introduction of a comprehensive data-based decision-making system into a school or district requires a systematic implementation. When decisions are based on data, the relevant data must be presented in a format that decision makers will use. The function of streaming data up and down the educational system, as depicted in Figure 1, is to provide feedback about the effects of the innovation on students and the effects of the support activities on staff. If the data are to function effectively as feedback, then they must be displayed in a manner that is most likely to get the decision makers to interact with it. One of the considerations of data presentation is the users' preferences about how it will be displayed (Hojnoski et al., 2009). Easton and Erchul (2011) report that educators have preferences about the frequency and the format (graph, written summary of data, face-to-face meetings) of feedback. High-quality implementation of data-based decision making requires interaction with the data. Preferences of the users of the data must be identified and feedback loops developed that match those preferences as much as possible.

> *When decisions are based on data, the relevant data must be presented in a format that decision makers will use.*

## Principle B: Innovation Must Solve a Problem for the Implementer

High-quality implementation is partially a function of the perception of the intervention as solving a problem important to those implementing it (Rogers, 2003). Further, if implementers do not experience a benefit from the intervention, they are unlikely to continue using it (Gingiss, 1992). For example, quick, credible measures of student learning (such as curriculum-based measures, or CBMs) are one way for teachers to perceive the early stage effects of an intervention, just as a scale provides feedback about weight loss before clothes fit differently. CBMs provide timely feedback to teachers, allowing adjustments to the instructional practice and real-time evaluation of its effectiveness. This short cycle of analysis helps implementers to have an indication of effects in time to change practices if necessary. At other levels of the system, data on the quality of implementation provide early feedback about the likelihood of positive student outcomes. By routinely monitoring the quality of implementation across all levels, corrective actions can be taken before student data indicate a problem.

In SWPBS, at least 80% of a school's faculty must identify behavioral problems as one of their three top concerns and commit to working on behavioral issues for at least 3 years; only after these conditions are met will external coaches begin implementation of the SWPBS systems (McIntosh, Horner, & Sugai, 2009). This commitment is established after meetings with school administrators and faculty to describe what SWPBS is and what will be required of the school personnel. Teachers often consider behavior problems to be one of their greatest concerns; however, reaching agreement on how to manage them has proven elusive. Perhaps one of the features of SWPBS that makes it attractive to school personnel is its positive reinforcement of socially desirable behavior, a method rated more highly than negative, consequence-based interventions (Elliott, 1988; Miltenberger, 1990). SWPBS addresses the problem in a way consistent with the values of the teachers responsible for implementation.

### Principle C: The Innovation Must Have an Advantage Relative to Current Practice

Any time teachers are asked to adopt and implement an innovation, they are being asked to replace an existing practice. Harris (1979) has argued that cultural practices are adopted and maintained to the extent that they have favorable outcomes at a lower cost than the alternatives. If teachers perceive no advantage to a new program or practice when compared to the current practice, they are unlikely to adopt it. This principle is related to but distinct from Principle B above. It may be that a proposed innovation solves a teacher-defined problem, as exemplified in Principle B. But if that innovation requires (costs) so much effort that its benefit is negated, it has no advantage over the existing "solution." Such inadequate advantages are likely to occur when the intervention does not directly affect the teacher. For example, teachers do not directly experience the consequences of students failing to make adequate progress in reading in the same way that they experience the effects of poor behavior management practices.

One of the ways that an innovation has an advantage over an existing practice is the reduction in effort required to implement it. Several studies demonstrate the effect of effort as a variable in adopting an intervention (Martens et al., 1986; Martens & Elliott, 1984; Witt, Witt, & Martens, 1983). Demands on time can be conceptualized as a dimension of effort. Teachers frequently cite lack of time as a primary reason for failing to implement an intervention with integrity (Dusenbury, Brannigan, Falco, & Hansen, 2003; Klingner, Vaughn, Hughes, & Arguelles, 1999). The demands of time also impact the acceptability of interventions more broadly (Elliott, 1988), as new interventions almost always require training of those implementing the changes and, often, personnel in other parts of the system. In SWPBS, staff are trained to enter the ODR data and distribute reports to the decision-making teams in a timely manner; yet, over the long run,

SWPBS may reduce time spent addressing issues related to behavior management. When successful, there are fewer ODRs, giving teachers more time for instruction. Principals and administrative staff spend less time dealing with disruptive students. Those are the long-term benefits of SWPBS; yet the short-term costs are real. Informing the school faculty of what is expected of them in an SWPBS implementation and gaining a commitment from 80% of the faculty before initiating often minimizes the negative reaction to time costs when they are directly experienced.

### Principle D: Opinion Leaders Must Support the Innovation

Adopting a practice is a social process (Rogers, 2003), and variables other than the features of the intervention and data about its effectiveness influence decision making. If an opinion leader, a credible individual within the social system, endorses an innovation and becomes a "local champion," others are more likely to adopt it. If there is no local champion, high-quality implementation and sustainability are less likely (Elliot & Mihalic, 2004). In SWPBS, opinion leaders are school leadership teams, comprised of faculty from different disciplines and staff (Sugai & Horner, 2009). The leadership teams can be selected in a variety of ways, but to maximize their influence, it is best when the school faculty has chosen the members. Opinion leaders have established relationships with their colleagues, earned their trust and respect, and gained influence with their peers. The school leadership team, working with the school faculty, establishes the priorities and determines the interventions for the school. Because the school leadership team is made up of credible, influential opinion leaders, proposed solutions stand a better chance of being adopted by the majority of the school faculty.

Strong administrative support is also important to successful implementation. When the principal and other district leaders act as advocates for a particular initiative, it is more likely to be successfully implemented (Fixsen et al., 2005; Han & Weiss, 2005; McIntosh, Filter, Bennett, Ryan, & Sugai, 2010; Simmons et al., 2002; Sugai & Horner, 2009). To build support and garner the positive influence, principals in SWPBS implementations are required to participate in all trainings (Sugai & Horner, 2009). When principals and other school administrators champion an innovation, they can work to resolve institutional barriers to implementation and facilitate alignment across levels.

### Principle E: The Innovation Is Perceived as Simple to Understand and Use

Teachers consistently rate interventions they perceive as being simple to use as more acceptable than those perceived as having greater complexity (Elliott, 1988; Miltenberger, 1990). Innovations are more likely to be perceived as easy to implement if they can be modified to fit local circumstances (Klingner et al., 1999). It has been well demonstrated that teachers adapt programs to better accommodate their own teaching styles, the needs of their students, and the time and material resources available (Dusenbury et al., 2003; Han & Weiss, 2005). Of course, a flexible program design must ensure that any modifications leave its core features intact so as to avoid rendering the program ineffective (McLaughlin & Mitra, 2001). Understanding the permissible latitude in implementation requires training in the details of the intervention and in the principles that inform it. Klingner et al. (1999) demonstrated that yearlong training and support for the implementation of different reading programs resulted in teachers continuing to implement at least one of the programs at moderate levels of integrity three years later. Teachers' familiarity with the principles of an innovation tended to increase the acceptability and likelihood of adoption (Elliott, 1988; Reimers, Wacker, & Koeppl, 1987).

**Principle F: The Innovation Can Be Implemented on a Limited Basis**

Rogers (2003) suggests that innovations are more likely to be adopted if they can be implemented on a small scale, such as a pilot study, before being disseminated more broadly. Implementation sites can be selected that are most able to implement with sufficient quality, providing useful initial data on what might be larger barriers that all schools might encounter, as well as initial conditions for success (Elliott & Mihalic, 2004). Successful outcomes can also increase the interest of other educators in replicating the innovation, while those individuals who participated in the successful pilot implementation can become champions for the intervention and facilitate the dissemination to other sites.

Implementing at a small scale allows those responsible for implementation to identify unanticipated barriers to implementation; as additional schools and districts adopt the innovation, possible solutions to institutional barriers have already been developed. This strategy functions to reduce the effort of later adopters and increases the probability they will maintain the initial implementation until benefits are realized. Implementation on a limited scale is one of the core features of SWPBS (Sugai & Horner, 2009).

Starting small and phasing in an innovation reduces its impact on the resources within a district. If all of its schools were to adopt a new program at once, a district would likely be pressed to assure high-quality implementation. Applying the lessons learned from a small, high-quality implementation can provide better estimates of resources needed as the intervention is expanded in a second phase. As implementation of the intervention expands to other schools, it is more likely that conditions are created to organize internal capacity to support it. Those who were part of the initial implementation may function as coaches for later phases. This is part of the logic of implementing SWPBS (Sugai & Horner, 2009).

**Principle G: The Results of Innovation Are Observable to Others**

This principle is related to Principle F, advocating a limited initial implementation. If a school site successfully implements an innovation that solves a common problem within a district, then these results can motivate other schools to adopt the innovation. For SWPBS, the common measure of success of the program is a reduction in ODRs, and dissemination of early successes is a cornerstone of scaling-up practices within districts and states (Herman et al., 2008, esp. pp. 22–26; Sugai & Horner, 2009). Several mechanisms within the model publicize these successes, such as data sharing at district-wide meetings (informing district leaders of success) or SWPBS school personnel working in leadership teams with other schools (sharing successful practices). By making the outcomes visible, the activities increase the motivation of others to participate. In turn, they help sustain implementation in at least two ways: the reporting of positive effects often results in positive feedback from peers, and an individual's public identification with SWPBS helps maintain commitment to the program.

## An Example of Implementation Failure

The evidence from implementation science demonstrates that for implementation to be successful, careful planning and involvement of multiple levels of the educational system are necessary. High-quality implementation can be time consuming and expensive. It requires vigilance on the part of those responsible, or the initiative will end prematurely or simply fail to effect the desired improvements. California's experience with class size reduction (CSR) should serve as a cautionary tale about failing to follow the principles of implementation science.

The California CSR initiative began in 1996 as the result of a $1 billion windfall in the California budget for education. The governor, Pete Wilson, launched the CSR effort out of his office rather than through the California Department of Education. The initiative was passed in July 1996, taking state and district educational officials by surprise. Districts were directed to reduce class size in grades K–3 to 20 or fewer students by October. This legislation created an overnight need for 18,000 additional classrooms (a 28% increase), 12,000 new teachers for the 1996–1997 school year, and an additional 15,000 over the next 2 years. In the first year, $1 billion was spent on implementation. The second year, $1.5 billion was spent to train teachers and fund facilities (Wexler et al., 1998).

Why did the state of California scale up CSR so rapidly? There were several sources of influence: The budgetary windfall created the fiscal opportunity; the results of a Tennessee experiment with a class size reduction program had garnered significant national attention (Word et al., 1990); and California students' literacy rates ranked next to last among the states in 1994 (Wexler et al., 1998). The effort to improve educational outcomes for California students was a laudable goal for the CSR initiative, but several variables were overlooked in the rush to implement.

One of the findings from the Tennessee CSR effort (Word et al., 1990) was that benefits were obtained when class sizes were between 13–17 students. By setting the maximum class size of 20, California ignored the available evidence about requirements to achieve benefit. Further, by rushing to implement, there was no time to develop a thoughtful, systematic plan to phase in the reduction, and by failing to plan, no contingency was made for the lack of available space or teachers. The Tennessee benefits were obtained when fully credentialed teachers led instruction. No benefits were obtained when instructional assistants taught classes.

In California, the rush to implement resulted in many classrooms being led by teachers with emergency credentials, personnel who may have had less experience in classrooms than Tennessee's instructional assistants. The opening of so many teaching positions also resulted in fully credentialed teachers moving to higher socioeconomic status schools, leaving instruction in the high-poverty, high-minority schools to teachers with emergency credentials. Further, because there was insufficient space for the new classrooms and portable classrooms could not be built and delivered fast enough to keep up with the demand, schools were forced to convert other instructional areas, such as gyms, into classrooms. After billion of dollars spent and a massive disruption of its educational system, California's CSR program improved student test scores only minimally at best (Bohrnstedt & Stecher, 1999).

Could these negative consequences have been avoided? Guidance from implementation science may have minimized some of these missteps. The stated goal of CSR in California was to improve literacy scores; however, the details from Tennessee on its improved outcomes were ignored. CSR—consistent with most educators' values and beliefs about how to best provide instruction—automatically gained widespread support, as evidenced by the participation of 873 of 895 eligible school districts in the 1997–1998 school year. By involving individuals from the California Department of Education and district officials, the governor's office and the legislature could have developed a more systematic implementation plan. Districts that had the capacity (credentialed teachers and space) to immediately implement could have piloted California's CSR and identified difficulties and developed solutions. In the meantime, other districts could have begun to increase their capacity to implement CSR by increasing teacher recruitment activities and purchasing portable classrooms. Those districts with successful early implementations could become champions for class size reduction and supply coaches for other schools beginning implementation. The costs of implementation could have also been phased in over a number of years rather than profligately spent in the first few years of the effort. It is not possible to know if literacy scores would have improved if implementation had been more systematic, but there would have been a better chance for midcourse corrections and adjustments, and the overall costs of CSR would have been smaller.

## Conclusion

No matter how small or how large the size of the change, principles of implementation science must be followed to maximize the benefits of the innovation. We can only wonder how many previous innovations would have succeeded if they had been guided by the principles from implementation science. Certainly, implementation science can provide guidance and improved outcomes for future innovations. There appears to be very little to lose by adhering to these principles and, potentially, a great deal to gain. At minimum, reducing the rapid churn of introducing and discarding effective innovations would be a significant contribution.

This chapter's opening epigraph emphasized that hard work is required to bring about change, an observation certainly true of educational reform. Because innovations are always implemented in a specific human context with its own preferences, values, and beliefs about how to best educate children, those interested in implementing an educational innovation must act as cultural anthropologists. For successful implementation, they must understand that different districts and schools develop different cultures and that the same innovation may have to be introduced and implemented differently across schools. Given the uncertainty of implementation, any systematic effort at change will require ongoing measurement of both the important outcomes and the processes required to produce the outcomes. Implementation is an iterative process; without data to inform what is working and what requires change, decisions will be based on unknown and unreliable variables. If the improvement promised by the innovation is important, then the implementers must care enough to do the hard work.

## Action Principles

### States or Districts

a. Engage all agents. Involve all who will be responsible for an innovation in the planning for implementation. Build partnerships across all levels of the educational system to facilitate implementation of an innovation.
b. Systematize decision making. Systematically introduce or support a comprehensive, data-based, decision-making system, including measurement of the quality of implementation, into a school or district.
c. Start small. Initially introduce new interventions or innovations on a small scale (such as a pilot study) before more broadly disseminating (as early successes are a cornerstone of scaling-up practices within districts and states).
d. Assess the fit. Before introducing an innovation, assess the culture of the setting to assure the "goodness of fit" between the innovation and the setting.

e. Plan support. Establish comprehensive support plans across all levels for those who are responsible for implementation prior to initiating an innovation.
  f. Instill a mindset. Foster a culture of innovation and the implementation practices that support it.

**Schools and Classrooms**
  a. Assess the fit. Select innovations that fit into the culture of the school or classroom and shape the culture to support the innovation.
  b. Set school-specific priorities. Leverage the school leadership team, working with the school faculty, to establish priorities and adopt innovations for the school.
  c. Verify capacity. Ensure that there are adequate time and resources to implement the innovation.
  d. Institute new structures and operating procedures. Build in teacher- and administrator-level data-based decision making and foster development of the internal capacity of the school to use data to solve problems.

**States, Districts, Schools, and Classrooms**
  a. Align problems with appropriate solutions. Ensure that any innovation introduced into the system solves a problem or has a perceived advantage over current practice.
  b. Make data easily useable. Present data on implementation and the effects of an innovation in a format that decision makers will understand and use.
  c. Monitor implementation. Regularly and routinely monitor the quality of implementation of an innovation across all levels, so that corrective actions can be taken early in the process.
  d. Look again. Establish recursive feedback systems across all levels.
  e. Model decision making. Routinely model data-based decision making as the way of doing business.
  f. Provide proactive support. Learning a new skill is difficult and takes time. Support for those learning to implement an innovation should be proactive rather than being reactive and waiting for the learners to identify that there is some difficulty.
  g. Be principled. Follow the principles of implementation to maximize the benefits of the innovation. Use implementation principles to provide guidance and improve outcomes for future innovations.

# References

Aladjem, D. K., & Borman, K. M. (2006). *Summary of findings from the national longitudinal evaluation of comprehensive school reform.* Paper presented at the annual meeting of the American Educational Research Association, San Francisco, CA.

Albin, R. W., Lucyshyn, J. M., Horner, R. H., & Flannery, K. B. (1996). Contextual fit for behavioral support plans: A model for "goodness of fit." In L. K. Koegel, R. L. Koegel, & G. Dunlap (Eds.), *Positive behavioral support: Including people with difficult behavior in the community* (pp. 81–98). Baltimore, MD: P.H. Brookes.

Bartels, S. M., & Mortenson, B. P. (2005). Enhancing adherence to a problem-solving model for middle-school pre-referral teams: A performance feedback and checklist approach. *Journal of Applied School Psychology, 22*(1), 109–123.

Bohrnstedt, G. W., & Stecher, B. M. (1999). *Class size reduction in California: Early evaluation findings, 1996–1998*. Palo Alto, CA: American Institutes for Research.

Brown, C. G., Hess, F. M., Lautzenheiser, D. K., & Owen, I. (2011). *State education agencies as agents of change: What it will take for the states to step up on education reform*. Washington, DC: Center for American Progress. Retrieved from http://www.americanprogress.org/issues/education/report/2011/07/27/9901/state-education-agencies-as-agents-of-change/

Burns, M. K., Peters, R., & Noell, G. H. (2008). Using performance feedback to enhance implementation fidelity of the problem-solving team process. *Journal of School Psychology, 46*(5), 537–550.

Carroll, C., Patterson, M., Wood, S., Booth, A., Rick, J., & Balain, S. (2007). A conceptual framework for implementation fidelity. *Implementation Science, 2*(40), 1–9.

Coalition for Evidence-Based Policy. (2003). *Identifying and implementing educational practices supported by rigorous evidence: A user-friendly guide*. Washington, DC: U.S. Department of Education, Institute of Education Sciences, National Center for Education Evaluation and Regional Assistance.

Coburn, C. E. (2003). Rethinking scale: Moving beyond numbers to deep and lasting change. *Educational Researcher, 32*(6), 3–12.

Detrich, R. (1999). Increasing treatment fidelity by matching interventions to contextual variables within the educational setting. *School Psychology Review, 28*(4), 608–620.

Dusenbury, L., Brannigan, R., Falco, M., & Hansen, W. B. (2003). A review of research on fidelity of implementation: Implications for drug abuse prevention in school settings. *Health Education Research, 18*(2), 237–256.

Easton, J. E., & Erchul, W. P. (2011). An exploration of teacher acceptability of treatment plan implementation: Monitoring and feedback methods. *Journal of Educational and Psychological Consultation, 21*(1), 56–77.

Elliott, S. N. (1988). Acceptability of behavioral interventions in educational psychology. In J. C. Witt, S. N. Elliott, & F. M. Gresham (Eds.), *Handbook of behavior therapy in education* (pp. 121–150). New York, NY: Plenum.

Elliott, D. S., & Mihalic, S. (2004). Issues in disseminating and replicating effective prevention programs. *Prevention Science, 5*(1), 47–53.

Fixsen, D. L., Naoom, S. F., Blase, K. A., Friedman, R. M., & Wallace, F. (2005). *Implementation research: A synthesis of the literature* (FMHI Publication #231). Tampa, FL: University of South Florida, Louis de la Parte Florida Mental Health Institute, The National Implementation Research Network.

Gingiss, P. L. (1992). Enhancing program implementation and maintenance through a multiphase approach to peer-based staff development. *Journal of School Health, 62*(5), 161–166.

Greenhalgh, T., Robert, G., Macfarlane, F., Bate, P., & Kyriakidou, O. (2004). Diffusion of innovations in service organizations: Systematic review and recommendations. *Milbank Quarterly, 82*(4), 581–629.

Han, S. S., & Weiss, B. (2005). Sustainability of teacher implementation of school-based mental health programs. *Journal of Abnormal Child Psychology, 33*(6), 665–679.

Harris, M. (1979). *Cultural materialism: The struggle for a science of culture.* New York, NY : Random House.

Herman, R., Dawson, P., Dee, T., Greene, J., Maynard, R., Redding, S., & Darwin, M. (2008). *Turning around chronically low-performing schools: A practice guide* (NCEE #2008-4020). Washington, DC: National Center for Education Evaluation and Regional Assistance, Institute of Education Sciences, U.S. Department of Education. Retrieved from http://ies.ed.gov/ncee/wwc/PracticeGuide.aspx?sid=7

Heyns, B. (1988). Educational defectors: A first look at teacher attrition in the NLS-72. *Educational Researcher, 17*(3), 24–32.

Hojnoski, R. L., Caskie, G. I., Gischlar, K. L., Key, J. M., Barry, A., & Hughes, C. L. (2009). Data display preference, acceptability, and accuracy among urban Head Start teachers. *Journal of Early Intervention, 32*(1), 38–53.

Kealey, K. A., Peterson, A. V., Gaul, M. A., & Dinh, K. T. (2000). Teacher training as a behavior change process: Principles and results from a longitudinal study. *Health Education & Behavior, 27*(1), 64–81.

Klingner, J. K., Vaughn, S., Hughes, M. T., & Arguelles, M. E. (1999). Sustaining research-based practices in reading: A 3-year follow-up. *Remedial and Special Education, 20*(5), 263–287.

Latham, G. (1988). The birth and death cycles of educational innovations. *Principal, 68*(1), 41–43.

Martens, B. K., Peterson, R. L., Witt, J. C., & Cirone, S. (1986). Teacher perceptions of school-based interventions. *Exceptional Children, 53*(3), 213–223.

McIntosh, K., Filter, K. J., Bennett, J. L., Ryan, C., & Sugai, G. (2010). Principles of sustainable prevention: Designing scale-up of school-wide positive behavior support to promote durable systems. *Psychology in the Schools, 47*(1), 5–21.

McIntosh, K., Horner, R. H., & Sugai, G. (2009). Sustainability of systems-level evidence-based practices in schools: Current knowledge and future directions. In W. Sailor, G. Dunlap, R. Horner, & G. Sugai (Eds.), *Handbook of positive behavior support* (pp. 327–352). New York, NY: Springer.

McLaughlin, M. W., & Mitra, D. (2001). Theory-based change and change-based theory: Going deeper, going broader. *Journal of Educational Change, 2*(4), 301–323.

Miltenberger, R. G. (1990). Assessment of treatment acceptability: A review of the literature. *Topics in Early Childhood Special Education, 10*(3), 24–38.

Mortenson, B. P., & Witt, J. C. (1998). The use of weekly performance feedback to increase teacher implementation of a prereferral academic intervention. *School Psychology Review, 27*(4), 613–627.

Myers, D. M., Simonsen, B., & Sugai, G. (2011). Increasing teachers' use of praise with a response-to-intervention approach. *Education and Treatment of Children, 34*(1), 35–59.

National Center for Education Statistics. (2011). *The nation's report card: Reading 2011* (NCES 2012-457). Washington, DC: Institute of Education Sciences, U.S.Department of Education.

Newton, S. J., Horner, R. H., Algozzine, R. F., Todd, A. W., & Algozzine, K. M. (2009). Using a problem-solving model to enhance data-based decision making in schools. In W. Sailor, G. Dunlap, R. Horner, & G. Sugai (Eds.), *Handbook of positive behavior support* (pp. 551–580). New York, NY: Springer.

Noell, G. H., Witt, J. C., LaFleur, L. H., Mortenson, B. P., Ranier, D. D., & LeVelle, J. (2000). Increasing intervention implementation in general education following consultation: A comparison of two follow-up strategies. *Journal of Applied Behavior Analysis, 33*(3), 271–284.

Powell, A. (2007, October 11). How Sputnik changed U.S.education. *Harvard Gazette*. Retrieved from http://news.harvard.edu/gazette/story/2007/10/how-sputnik-changed-u-s-education/

Reimers, T. M., Wacker, D. P., & Koeppl, G. (1987). Acceptability of behavioral interventions: A review of the literature. *School Psychology Review, 16*(2), 212–227.

Rogers, E. M. (2003). *Diffusion of innovations* (5th ed.). New York, NY: Free Press.

Rubenstein, L. V., & Pugh, J. (2006). Strategies for promoting organizational and practice change by advancing implementation research. *Journal of General Internal Medicine, 21*(S2), S58–S64.

Simmons, D., Kame'enui, E. J., Good, R. H., Harn, B. A., Cole, C., & Braun, D. (2002). Building, implementing, and sustaining a beginning reading improvement model: Lessons learned school by school. In M. R. Shinn, H. M. Walker, & G. Stoner (Eds.), *Interventions for academic and behavior problems II: Preventive and remedial approaches* (pp. 537–570). Washington, DC: National Association of School Psychologists.

Sugai, G., & Horner, R. H. (2009). Defining and describing schoolwide positive behavior support. In W. Sailor, G. Dunlap, R. Horner, & G. Sugai (Eds.), *Handbook of positive behavior support* (pp. 307–326). New York, NY: Springer.

Wexler, E., Izu, J., Carlos, L., Fuller, B., Hayward, G., & Kirst, M. (1998). *California's class size reduction: Implications for equity, practice, and implementation*. San Francisco and Stanford, CA: WestEd and Policy Analysis for California Education, Stanford University.

Witt, J. C., & Martens, B. K. (1983). Assessing the acceptability of behavioral interventions used in classrooms. *Psychology in the Schools, 20*, 510–517.

Witt, J. C., Martens, B. K., & Elliott, S. N. (1984). Factors affecting teachers' judgments of the acceptability of behavioral interventions: Time involvement, behavior problem severity, and type of intervention. *Behavior Therapy, 15*(2), 204–209.

Word, E., Johnston, J., Bain, H. F., Fulton, B. D., Zaharias, J. B., Lintz, M. N., et al. (1990). *Student/Teacher Achievement Ratio (STAR) Project. Final summary report, 1985–1990*. Nashville, TN: Tennessee State Department of Education.

# The Logic of School Improvement, Turnaround, and Innovation
*Sam Redding*

The process of improving school performance has maintained a consistent logic at least since the advent of curriculum standards and state assessments in the 1990s. Over the past half-decade, Secretary of Education Arne Duncan's (2009) charge for the nation to turn around its 5,000 lowest-achieving schools has introduced an impetus for innovation that may leaven the stolid logic. We are only now on the cusp of evaluative research, especially that related to the U.S. Department of Education's School Improvement Grant (SIG) and Investing in Innovation (I3) programs, research that will let us distill from the myriad of approaches those that may alter our understanding of how schools improve. This distillation of successful strategies will then legitimately carry the stamp of "innovation," as the new strategies alter the logic we have previously applied.

The logic of school improvement begins with a statement of the ultimate goal of K–12 (or preK–12) schooling. The conventional goal, echoed across the landscape of public education, is that all students will leave the 12$^{th}$ grade ready for college and careers. The true measure of this goal's attainment by a school system would be the degree of success in college and careers (over the course of a lifetime) attained by its graduates. Longitudinal studies of postsecondary success are enlightening, but not particularly useful in a school improvement process that requires more easily retrievable feedback on a school's effectiveness. For school improvement purposes, we turn to measurements of students' knowledge and skills within and upon exiting the school system.

Curriculum standards, including the Common Core State Standards, and graduation requirements articulate a body of knowledge and skill thought to prepare a student for college and career. State assessments and end-of-course tests provide measures of a student's acquisition of the necessary knowledge and skills defined by the standards and graduation requirements. Preparation for college and career is a solid, practical, and utilitarian goal, and we have miles to go before achieving it for all students. In time, however, we may find the goal unduly narrow and incapable of encompassing all that we desire for our children's lives both during their school years and beyond senior year. We already know that social and emotional competencies, not commonly included in our catalog of necessary knowledge and skills, are essential to success in college and career as well as every other aspect of life.

A school system's performance is measured by what it adds to its students' knowledge and skills as evidenced in the state assessments, end-of-course tests, and fulfillment of graduation requirements. In other words, its students demonstrate their readiness for college and career by meeting standards, and the degree to which its students do so provides a summative metric for determining the school system's performance. Grade-level and subject benchmarks ladder the $12^{th}$ grade standards down through the grades to kindergarten or prekindergarten so that each student's progress toward the ultimate standards and the system's goal can be tracked. The performance of each school in the system, and each grade level in the school, is thereby measured according to the benchmarked progress of students.

School improvement is the process by which the school adds to its students' knowledge and skills through intentional efforts to enhance school effectiveness. A productivity calculation determines how efficiently the school achieves its results—the ratio of school resource inputs to student outcomes. Intentional efforts to enhance school effectiveness and productivity include:

a. **Variety and Choice**: allowing parents to choose the school their children attend in order to provide market incentives for the school to improve.
b. **Governance**: changing the school's decision makers and/or decision-making processes.
c. **Structure**: changing the way the school, its personnel, and its students are organized.
d. **Program**: changing the school's curricular and co-curricular offerings.
e. **Practice**: changing or improving the fidelity of implementation of professional practice by school personnel.

Parental choice and change in governance, structure, and program are all designed to ultimately improve the professional practice of school personnel, so change in practice is the core driver of school improvement. Professional practice is improved by increasing implementation fidelity to standard practice (the assumed most effective practice) or replacing the standard practice with a more effective practice, which is innovation.

## Changing Adult Practice to Improve Student Learning

The bedrock of school improvement is change in adult professional practice, the chief contributor to student performance and gains in student learning. In its simplest form, this is accomplished through a process in which school personnel, in a culture of candor and trust, examine their practice and strive to improve it, typically facilitated by professional development and coaching. In this model, as illustrated in Figure 1, adult performance represents the degree to which professional personnel implement effective practice. Student performance stands for the work of the students in the learning process. Student learning is measured by summative assessments aligned with standards. Coaching and feedback are in response to data about all three components of the cycle and are directed primarily at adult performance in order to improve practice.

**Figure 1: Interplay of Adult Performance, Student Performance, and Student Learning**

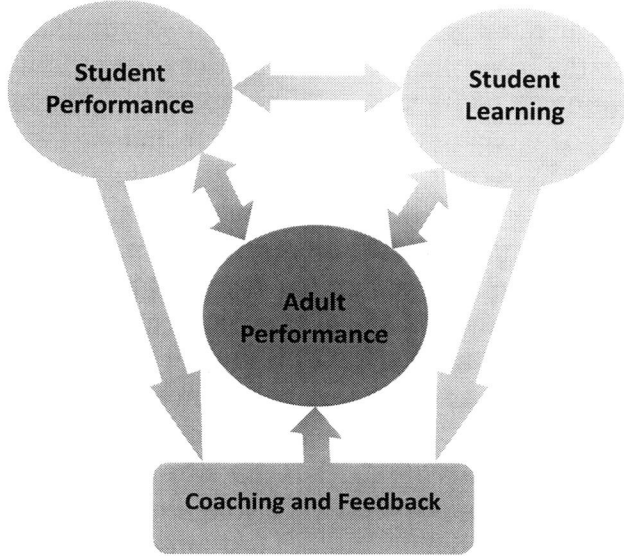

## Improvement Planning

The conventional school improvement process centers around a plan responding to student learning data, such as that derived from the assessment of students' progress relative to benchmarked standards, end-of-course tests, and graduation rates. The plan is revised annually as new student learning data become available. Typically, the school's administrators develop the annual plan for submission to the district and state, and the plan features a few major goals aligned with areas of deficiency revealed in the student data. Ideally, the administrators engage a representative team of teachers and stakeholders in reviewing the data and developing the plan. The annual school improvement plan (SIP) commonly introduces programmatic interventions (for example, new curriculum, professional development, technology) to address its goals, with objectives defined for the interventions and outcome targets for the goals. Rarely does the plan address specific professional practices or provide targets and metrics for them. The programmatic interventions are assumed to change professional practice.

The conventional annual SIP has succeeded in focusing school personnel on student learning data, but has been less successful in linking the data back to the professional practices that led to the outcomes in the first place. Annual plans provide a strategic roadmap, but they are prone to becoming static and not facilitating the routine adjustments in course informed by frequent feedback loops. Further, the SIP process assumes that the school personnel are adept at constructing the right goals from analysis of the student data and aligning those goals with the programmatic interventions with the greatest impact. Layering on programmatic solutions often results in initiatives working at cross purposes and creates inextricable managerial webs that distract administrators and teachers from attention to the basic professional practices they intend to impact.

The annual SIP appears on its surface to comport with the tenets of performance management. "The basic structure of a performance management system is simple," according to Betheny Gross and Ashley Jochim (2013, p. 3) of the Center on Reinventing Public Education and the national Building State Capacity and Productivity Center. Gross and Jochim proffer a simple three-part process for the structure of a performance management system: (1) set high performance standards and goals; (2) systematically assess performance and evaluate progress; and (3) improve or adapt. Where the annual SIP falls short is in its tendency to define "performance" only as student performance and not adult performance, thus giving too little attention to the change in discreet professional practices that, cumulatively, drive improvement. Also, the annual SIP rarely includes the metrics, feedback loops, and opportunities for ongoing adjustment in professional practice that move the dial on student learning. School improvement processes have recently adopted an indicator-based approach to improvement that bridges the ultimate goals to the more immediate, operational objectives that allow for nimble response.

## Indicators as Performance Feedback

Students' performance on standards-based assessments and their fulfillment of rigorous graduation requirements are *indications* of their readiness for college and career. In an improvement process, these student outcome measures are considered *lagging indicators* because they tend to follow changes in professional practice. In fact, changes in professional practice may themselves follow changes in school enrollment options, school governance, school structure, and programs designed to improve practice. So the lag in time can be considerable and not immediately useful as feedback in a nimble performance management system. More immediate indications of change in professional practice, called *leading indicators*, include such quantifiable markers as student attendance, teacher attendance, discipline referrals, and formative assessments. Finally, the most direct indication of change in professional practice is the observable demonstration of these practices. These direct determinations of professional practice are *effective practice indicators*, also called *implementation indicators*.

The use of specific indicators of effective practice to guide and assess school improvement processes is derived from performance management methodology. This methodology emphasizes evidence-based procedures that achieve results as exemplified by Wiseman et al. (2007). Indicators are employed in many fields as intermediate and specific measures of more general concepts, and they are highly promising in education. See, for example, the performance management literature from the field of business, such as Frear and Paustian-Underdahl (2011).

Effective practice indicators state in plain language how the practice looks when observed. Observation includes direct witnessing of the practice as well as examination of documents that confirm the practice. For classroom instruction, an effective practice might be that *the school expects and monitors sound classroom management* (Redding, 2007a; Redding, 2007b), a practice based on research on the relationship between classroom management methods and student learning outcomes. Effective practice indicators could then describe classroom behaviors associated with this sound classroom management, such as:

a. When waiting for assistance from the teacher, students are occupied with curriculum-related activities provided by the teacher.
b. Transitions between instructional modes are brief and orderly.
c. The teacher maintains well-organized student learning materials in the classroom.
d. The teacher displays classroom rules and procedures in the classroom.
e. The teacher corrects students who do not follow classroom rules and procedures.
f. The teacher reinforces classroom rules and procedures by positively teaching them.

These indicators can be observed in a classroom, and by observing them in all classrooms, the patterns of professional practice for the school are calculated.

Another effective practice is that *the school has established a team structure with specific duties and time for instructional planning* (Redding, 2007a; Redding, 2007b), a practice based on research confirming the importance to student learning outcomes of instructional planning by teacher teams. Effective practice indicators for instructional planning by teacher teams might include:

a. Teachers are organized into grade-level, grade-level cluster, or subject instructional teams.

b. Instructional teams meet for blocks of time (4- to 6-hour blocks, once a month; whole days before and after the school year) sufficient to develop and refine units of instruction and review student learning data.
c. Instructional teams develop standards-aligned units of instruction for each subject and grade level.
d. Instructional teams use student learning data to plan instruction.
e. Instructional teams review the results of formative assessments to make decisions about the curriculum and instructional plans and to "red flag" students in need of intervention (both students in need of tutoring or extra help and students needing enhanced learning opportunities because of early mastery of objectives).

For these specific indicators of effective instructional team practices, a document review of the schedules, agendas, and work products of the teams would serve as confirmation of their implementation.

The indicator of effective practice is the finest grained metric for determining the level of effective practice in a school. To put this in perspective, school improvement might be organized by domain, practice, and indicators. For example, the domains might be leadership and decision making, professional development, curriculum, assessment, instructional planning, classroom instruction, classroom management, and family engagement. Within each domain, several effective practices would be cited, and for each effective practice, a number of specific, behavioral indicators given.

The school's leadership team is the ideal vehicle for managing the improvement process (Louis et al., 2010). The leadership team assesses each indicator and determines if it is *fully* implemented, yielding a binary measure for each—yes or no. The percent of indicators fully implemented for an effective practice would quantify that practice's degree of implementation. Likewise, the percent of indicators fully implemented for a domain would quantify that domain's degree of implementation. Finally, a tally of the percent of indicators fully implemented across all domains would quantify the current status of the school. As indicators are reassessed, following efforts to reach their full implementation, the new tallies compared with the earlier assessments would provide a measure of change or improvement.

The leadership team cycles through this process of securing data to assess current practice, developing plans to reach full implementation, monitoring progress, and reassessing to confirm implementation. This cyclical process is similar in approach to that described by Wiseman et al. (2007), making sense within the context of the school and including actionable tasks, persons responsible, and timelines. Figure 2 illustrates this process for continuous school improvement.

**Figure 2. Process of Continuous School Improvement**

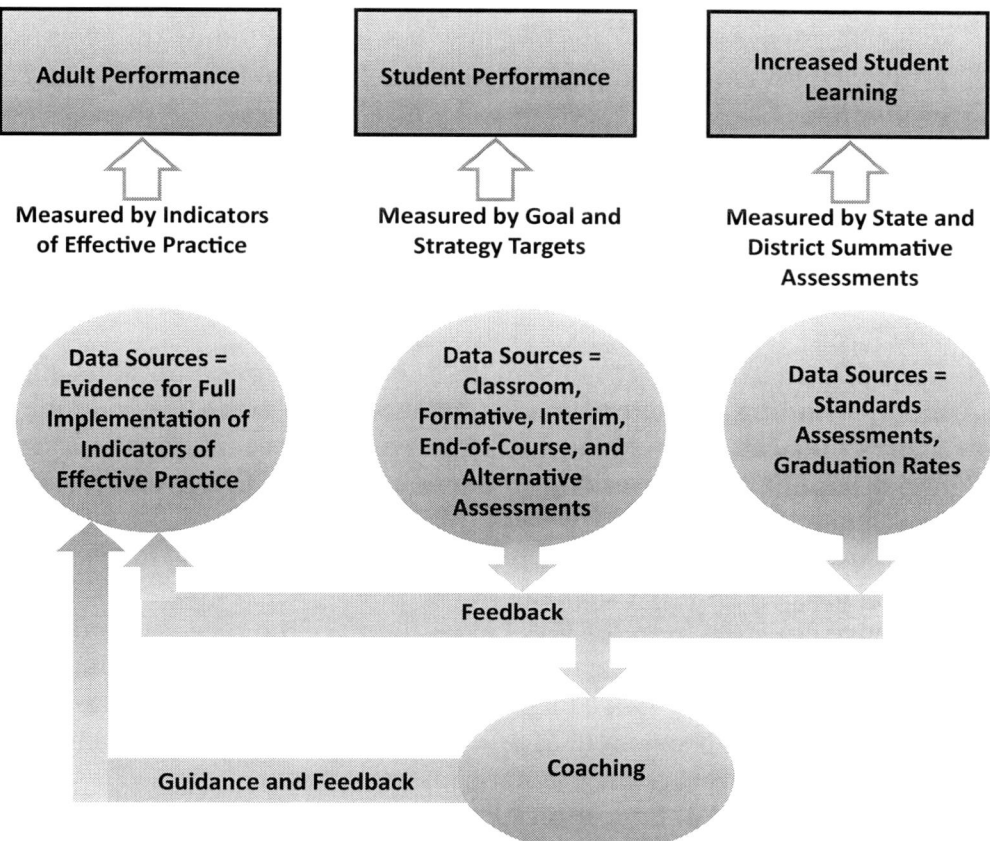

## Improvement, Turnaround, and Innovation

Ratcheting up the degree of implementation of effective practice, as evidenced in achieving specific indicators, is a recursive process. It is premised upon the acceptance of standard (effective) practices and the school's candid efforts to assess current practice and improve upon it. Improvement implies an incremental process, while turnaround calls for more dramatic change. On a scale of intensity, a turnaround strategy, as opposed to an improvement strategy, would include a shorter timeline for change and the inclusion of practices and indicators based on evidence of successful turnaround. For example, the practices might be aligned with the seven turnaround principles identified by Redding (2012) and the U.S. Department of Education (2011), with the topics of the turnaround principles serving as domains of effective practice:

a. **Leadership**: providing strong leadership by reviewing the performance of the current principal, replacing the current principal or ensuring the principal is a change leader, and providing the principal, with operational flexibility.

b. **Effective Teachers**: ensuring that teachers are effective and able to improve instruction by reviewing all staff and retaining those determined to be effective; carefully selecting new teachers, including transfers; and providing job-embedded professional development informed by teacher evaluation.
c. **Extended Learning Time**: redesigning the school day, week, or year to include additional time for student learning and teacher collaboration.
d. **Strong Instruction**: strengthening the school's instructional program based on student needs and ensuring that the instructional program is research-based, rigorous, and aligned with state academic content standards.
e. **Use of Data**: using data to inform instruction and for continuous improvement, including providing time for collaboration on the use of data
f. **School Culture**: establishing a school environment that improves safety and discipline and addressing students' social, emotional, and physical health needs.
g. **Family and Community Engagement**: providing ongoing mechanisms for family and community engagement.

As evidence emerges from the great experiment of the recent School Improvement Grants, we will learn more about turnaround. In particular, we will know if school choice and change in governance, structure, and program are necessary precursors to improvement of practice. We will also know which practices provide the greatest leverage for dramatic improvement.

The U.S. Department of Education's Investing in Innovation (I3) grants will also begin yielding an evidence base for innovation, as will evaluation of the many innovations sponsored by private companies, states, and districts. We will look for innovation in practice, and we will redefine effective practices and their indicators accordingly.

The Center on Innovations in Learning, one of seven federally funded national content centers, is poised to interpret emerging research on innovative practice and assist the field in making prudent decisions about it. Simply arriving at a sound and widely accepted definition of innovation is not an easy task. In the field of education this is especially true, as educators look back at a history of seemingly good ideas gone fallow. But the advent of powerful new technologies, coupled with the evidence emerging from large-scale efforts to improve and transform schools, gives us reason for optimism.

Figure 3 shows schooling's path toward the ultimate goal of college and career readiness. It also illustrates the points at which innovation will disrupt convention and pave a new and better pathway.

## Figure 3: Schooling's Path and Points of Innovation

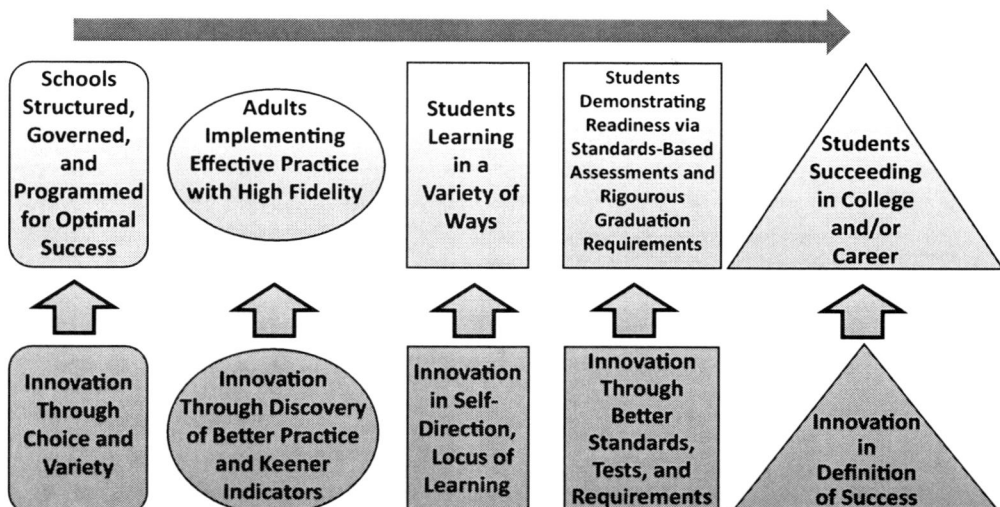

## Conclusion

The processes of school improvement, turnaround, and innovation are different but interrelated and reinforce each other. In continuous school improvement, we focus on fidelity to the implementation of evidence-based practice—doing well what we think we should do. In a turnaround situation, the pace of change is more rapid and the precursors for changed practice more dramatic. Innovation steps in from aside the process, looks at the currently recognized best (standard) practices, and discovers more effective practices that then replace the standards. What we learn from turnaround informs our understanding of school improvement, and the infusion of successful innovation raises the trajectory of improvement and turnaround. We are able to accomplish more than we realized.

## Action Principles

a. Establish an inventory of research-based practices with specific, behavioral indicators that describe their implementation.
b. Charge the school leadership team with the responsibility for managing an improvement process based on the continuous assessment, implementation, and monitoring of effective practices and their indicators.
c. Include three data sources in determining the school's progress: adult performance data, student performance data, and student learning data.
d. Provide feedback for the continuous improvement process, including coaching by school improvement specialists and district personnel.
e. Report progress periodically by generating reports of the ongoing work of the leadership team and the student learning outcomes.

f. Gear the effective practices and indicators for schools in need of rapid improvement to turnaround strategies.
g. Innovate by determining the power of particular professional practices and their indicators, and amend or replace the practices and indicators with ones deemed to have greater power.

## References

Duncan, A. (2009, June 14). *States will lead the way toward reform*. Keynote address presented at the 2009 Governors Education Symposium, Cary, NC. Retrieved from: http://www.ed.gov/news/speeches/states-will-lead-way-toward-reform

Frear, K. A., & Paustian-Underdahl, S. C. (2011). From elusive to obvious: Improving performance management through specificity. *Industrial and Organizational Psychology, 4*, 198–200.

Gross, B., & Jochim, A. (2103). *Leveraging performance management to support school improvement*. San Antonio, TX: Edvance Research.

Louis, K. S., Leithwood, K., Wahlstrom, K. L., Anderson, S. E., Michlin, M., Mascall, B.,...Moore, S. (2010). *Investigating the links to improved student learning* (Final report of research findings). Minneapolis, MN: Learning from Leadership Project, University of Minnesota. Retrieved from http://www.wallacefoundation.org/knowledge-center/school-leadership/key-research/Pages/Investigating-the-Links-to-Improved-Student-Learning.aspx

Redding, S. (2007a). Indicators of successful restructuring. In H. Walberg (Ed.), *Handbook on restructuring and substantial school improvement* (pp. 113–132). Lincoln, IL: Center on Innovation and Improvement. Retrieved from http://www.adi.org/about/publications.html

Redding, S. (2007b). Systems for improved teaching and learning. In H. Walberg (Ed.), *Handbook on restructuring and substantial school improvement* (pp. 99–112). Lincoln, IL: Center on Innovation and Improvement. Retrieved from http://www.adi.org/about/publications.html

Redding, S. (2012). *Change leadership: Innovation in state education agencies*. Oakland, CA: Wing Institute. Retrieved from http://www.adi.org/about/publications.html

U.S. Department of Education. (2011, September). *ESEA flexibility*. Washington, DC: Author. Retrieved from http://www.ed.gov/esea/flexibility/documents/esea-flexibility.doc

Wiseman, S. M., Chinman, P., Ebener, P. A., Hunter, S. B., Imm, P., & Wandersman, A. (2007). *Getting to outcomes: 10 steps for achieving results-based accountability*. Santa Monica, CA: RAND Corporation. Retrieved from http://www.rand.org/pubs/technical_reports/TR101z2

# Part 2
# The Student in Learning Innovation

# Innovative Practice in Teaching the English Language Arts: Building Bridges Between Literacy In School and Out
*Michael W. Smith*

The research that Jeff Wilhelm and I did on the literate lives of adolescent boys both in and out of school (Smith & Wilhelm, 2002) was motivated by the fact that all available data demonstrates that boys underperform girls on measures of reading and writing. This underperformance is sometimes attributed to boys' rejection of reading because they see it as a feminized, or at least as an inappropriate masculine activity (e.g., Martino, 1994, 1998). As a consequence, we began our research with the expectation that the young men in our study would reject literacy. But, strikingly, they didn't. Instead, we found that all of the boys in our study were actively engaged in literacy outside school. Their rejection of school literacy, therefore, has to be seen not as a function of their attitude toward literacy in general but rather as a comment on the particular kinds of literate activity they typically encounter in school. In this chapter, I'll argue that a powerful educational innovation would involve capitalizing on adolescents' engagement in literacy outside school by building bridges between what they do out of school and what we want them to do in school.

## Some Good News and Some Bad

First, some background. Our study focused on a very diverse group of 49 boys from four different schools in three different states (Smith & Wilhelm, 2002). The boys varied in terms of their ethnicities, social classes, and levels of academic achievement. We collected and analyzed four different kinds of data: an interview on our participants' favorite activities; an interview on their responses to a series of short profiles that highlight different ways of being literate; three monthly interviews on the literacy logs that the boys kept in which they tracked all of the reading, writing, listening, and viewing they did in and out of school; and think-aloud protocols on four stories that differed in terms of the sex of the main character and the relative emphasis on action versus character.

As I noted above, one of our chief findings stands in stark contrast to conventional wisdom about boys and literacy. Far from rejecting literacy, ALL of the boys in the study embraced reading in one form or another, though only seven of them were book readers. Surprisingly, this embrace was especially clear in remarks from the boys who struggled most with school literacy. For example, Mick, a 10th grader and functional illiterate, regularly bought four magazines (one each on cars, model cars, professional wrestling, and hip hop) despite living in very dire economic circumstances. He'd look at the pictures and then find someone to read to him when the picture told him that the magazine included something he needed to know.

> **So, the good news is that young men value literacy. The bad news is that they tend not to value the kind of literacy that matters in school.**

So, the good news is that young men value literacy. The bad news is that they tend not to value the kind of literacy that matters in school. Mick, for example, yearned to read and identified his own problems as "I don't read that good." But what he yearned to read was not what was assigned in school. He wasn't alone on that score. Brandon, a highly competent reader, warned us "not to confuse this [my school reading] with my real reading [what he was pursuing at home]." His "real reading" was about "stuff that interests me," stuff that would help him pursue his real world interests in the here and now.

Our findings resonate with those of other researchers who have examined adolescents' out-of-school literacies. For example, Weinstein (2009) studied the out-of-school writing of nine urban adolescents from Chicago, primarily their raps and spoken-word poetry. She argues that her research helps educators understand the "funds of knowledge" (Moll & Greenberg, 1990) upon which students could draw if they were given the opportunity to do so, though the writers themselves saw little connection between what they must do in school and the writing they freely chose to do outside school. Studies in this tradition have a hortatory function (cf. Smith & Moore, 2012), encouraging literacy educators to recognize "the power that literacy has for young people of all classes and ethnoracial descriptions" (Weinstein, 2009, p. 159).

Why do students who are deeply committed to literacy reject school literacy? Dewey (1916) provides one possible explanation: "Children live proverbially in the present; that is not a fact to be evaded, but it is an excellence!" (p. 55). However, according to Dewey, educators too often see education solely as preparation for the future, which works against the power of the present moment, resulting in "a loss of impetus" and promoting an attitude of "shilly-shallying and procrastination." Dewey further argues that this future orientation keeps teachers from focusing on the specific human beings who are their students. Instead of seeking a thorough understanding of who their students are in the present and directing instruction to their students' current selves, educators base their instruction on "a vague and wavering opinion" (p. 55) of what their students may be expected to become. Dewey then discusses a final problem with future-based teaching:

> Finally, the principle of preparation makes necessary recourse on a large scale to the use of adventitious motives of pleasure and pain. The future having no stimulating and directing power when severed from the possibilities of the present, something must be hitched on to make it work. Promises of reward and threats of pain are employed. Healthy work, done for present reasons and as a factor in living, is largely unconscious. The stimulus resides in the situation with which one is actually confronted. But when this situation is ignored, pupils have to be told that if they do not follow the prescribed course, penalties will accrue; while if they do, they may expect, some time in the future, rewards for their present sacrifices. Everybody knows how largely systems of punishment have had to be resorted to by educational systems which neglect present possibilities in behalf of preparation for the future. (pp. 55–56)

## An Innovative Possibility

A way to engage kids in the healthy work of the present is to use their out-of-school literacies as bridges to developing their canonical literacies. Lee, for example, has long championed the transformative power of drawing on students' cultural resources, the everyday literate practices in which students' engage, what she calls "cultural modeling." Her line of inquiry began nearly 20 years ago with the publication of a research report (1993) that demonstrates the effectiveness of using African American students' understanding of signifying, a form of ritual insult, that includes "playin' the dozens" (e.g., "Yo mama so dumb she thought a quarterback was a refund."); "sounding" (i.e., when conversational partners try to outdo each other by building one insult upon another using the same theme); and "marking" (i.e., sarcastically emulating the words of another). Students were given three dialogues of extended signifying taken from Mitchell-Kernan's (1981) research and were asked to interpret what each speaker in the dialogue meant by each conversational turn, as well as the criteria they employed to determine the meaning. Students generated a set of criteria comparable to those that expert readers use to understand irony in literature, according to Booth (1974) and Smith (1991). Students in the cultural modeling group improved in their

> *A way to engage kids in the healthy work of the present is to use their out-of-school literacies as bridges to developing canonical literacies.*

comprehension of literature from pretest to posttest over twice as much as did students in a control group.

In a recent review, Ball, Skerrett, and Martinez (2011) discuss the potential power of such an approach, though they note the need for additional research and more funding to do that research. Another testimony to the power of cultural modeling is the extent to which Lee's ground-breaking work has been generative for other scholars seeking ways to leverage the power of cultural practices employed out of school to develop academic understandings. Orellana and Reynolds (2008), for example, studied how Mexican immigrant children's experience translating for their families might be employed in teaching them how to paraphrase texts, an important academic skill.

Related work is grounded in a new literacies perspective that holds, according to Morrell (2002), that marginalized students are indeed highly literate but that "their literacies have little connection with the dominant literacies promoted in public schools" (p. 72). He details a unit of instruction in which he and his students used hip-hop music as a lens to understand canonical poetry and reports that his students

> generated quality interpretations and made interesting connections between the canonical poems and the rap songs....Their critical investigations of popular texts brought about oral and written critiques similar to those required by college preparatory English classrooms. (p. 72)

In a similar vein, Hill's (2009) study of students' engagement in an after-school, hip-hop curriculum demonstrates that students who were alienated from school could nonetheless act as "cultural critics who deploy critical literacies in order to identify and respond to structures of power and meaning within hip-hop texts" (p. 122). Also operating in this theoretical tradition, Vasudevan (2010) argues that "definitions of literacy and learning that operate in schools today are often far removed from the actual practices in which children and youth engage" (para. 5). She makes the compelling point that urban youth "live digital lives" but are "confined to analog rights in school" (para. 5) because of the policies prohibiting the use of mobile technologies in which they are expert. Her case study of one adolescent demonstrates how his smartphone "provided a chance to participate in new discursive communities; to take on and be recognized for new identities; and to gain new audiences for his writing" (para. 46).

A closely related perspective, that of multiliteracies, was introduced by the New London Group (1996) who called for a pedagogy centered on the notion of design and the recognition that

> increasingly important are modes of meaning other than linguistic, including visual meanings (images, page layouts, screen formats); audio meanings (music, sound effects); gestural meanings (body language, sensuality); spatial meanings (the meanings of environmental spaces, architectural spaces); and multimodal meanings. Of the modes of meaning, the multimodal is the most

significant, as it relates all the other modes in quite remarkably dynamic relationships. (p. 80)

In this same tradition, Alvermann (Alvermann & Moore, 2011) notes that "interactive communication technologies and a definitional broadening of *text* to include moving images, words, sounds, gestures, and performances support the folding of literacy practices, regardless of their place of origin" (p. 157). When such folding occurs, according to Alvermann, "research suggests that youth-produced digital media texts generated in classrooms provide opportunities for students to examine their identities in relation to a curriculum's master narratives and to push back with their own counterstories" (p. 157), with the result that kids who were on the margins of classroom life may no longer be so. Alvermann closes her argument by suggesting a sieve metaphor for "noticing relationships between in-school and out-of-school literacy learning that have been obscured previously" (p. 158). In like manner, Dyson (1999) has called for schools to develop curricula that are "permeable"—that is, that allow free movement between what students do inside and outside of school.

> *Hip hop, spoken word, digitalk, gaming, and fan fiction are popular forms of out-of-school literate activity, ones that are sure to resonate with many adolescents.*

Consider what could follow if these metaphors prevail. Turner (2010) notes that teachers and the popular press present texting and other forms of what she calls "digitalk" as enemies of literacy teachers. She argues that "rather than seeing it as a deficiency, a lazy representation of Standard English, we should recognize its power in the digital, adolescent community" (p. 46) and that we should use students' understanding of texting as a way to help them become conscious of the language choices they make.

In a similar fashion, Abrams (2009) has documented the potential benefits of gaming, another practice long thought to be an enemy to literacy teachers. More specifically, her research documents how gaming helped three struggling 11th grade students develop understandings that enabled them to learn classroom material.

Roozen (2009) makes a similar argument in his study of how writing fan fiction—that is, fiction that fans of a movie, television show, book, or story write employing the characters or storyline of the source text—supported one student's trajectory into graduate school English studies. That student explained the support she experienced:

> I don't think that I ever thought of them as separate. I've always been combining them. When we read the *Masque of the Red Death* in 10th grade, I wrote a funny play version of it using the people in the class as characters, and when I showed it to the teacher she let us [perform] it for class. And so even back then, like I rewrote *Everyman*, the medieval play, with my own characters in

it and that kind of thing, so I've always been combining school work and fan fiction. (p. 148)

Hip hop, spoken word, digitalk, gaming, and fan fiction are popular forms of out-of-school literate activity that are sure to resonate with many adolescents. A permeable curriculum could also allow students to make use of their unique out-of-school literacies in service of developing traditional academic literacies and, in doing so, personalizing their instruction in some fashion. In one example of permeable curriculum, Wilson and Boatright (2011) provide a case study analysis of an American Indian student for whom grass dancing was central to his identity. He danced in full regalia at his school's talent show. But he also was allowed to bring his expertise into the classroom. His teacher shared a compact disc the student had compiled on intertribal music. The student also explained videos of American Indian dancing to several language arts classes. Wilson and Boatright attribute the case participant's success as a communicator to be a function of his being allowed to "combine and use modes whose affordances offset and complemented other modes' affordances and constraints" (p. 274).

The list could go on and on. Smagorinsky (2011), for example, discusses his investigations of a wide variety of literacies, from drawing to choreography to model building to mask making. Taken together, Smagorinsky's studies provide compelling evidence of the power of these alternative forms of literate engagement.

Interestingly, the arguments made by the sociocultural thinkers cited above resonate with perspectives of cognitive scholars. One of the most important educational insights from cognitive science over the last 50 years is schema theory, a theory that establishes that all learning proceeds by connecting the known to the new. If new knowledge is consistent with previous knowledge, it is added to existing schema—an organized set of knowledge pertaining to foundational ideas or processes—in an act called assimilation. If what was previously known is inconsistent, it must be accommodated to the new learning. Otherwise, people will not only fail to understand the new data, but they will also quickly revert to prior misconceptions (Science Media Group, 1989). Cognitive science, like sociocultural theory, teaches us that the only resource a learner can employ to learn something new is what she already knows and can do.

In summary, what is important here is not providing a comprehensive list of all the ways teachers of the English language arts have drawn on out-of-school literacies or all of the research and theory that supports doing so. Rather, what is important is to understand how generative the related perspectives of cultural modeling, new literacies, multiliteracies, and schema theory can be in fostering innovative teaching practices by encouraging teachers to recognize that what students do outside school can be a critically important resource in helping them do what they need to do inside school.

## Barriers to Innovation

If the theory and research grounding the use of out-of-school literacies in the development of academic literacies has been in place for 20 years, what makes the practices innovative? They have not been adopted by schools to any significant extent. As Redding (2012) has argued, an innovations in learning occurs when a currently accepted standard of curricular or instructional practice is replaced by a more effective practice. Put simply, innovation in learning is changing what teachers do and how they do it to achieve better results for students.

That's a challenge because the innovative practices described above are at odds with some foundational assumptions of literacy teachers. In the first place, literacy teachers regard many of the new literacies as their enemies, something to be overcome rather than employed. Buck (2012) puts it this way:

> Our continued disciplinary emphasis on static text, and our reliance on theories derived from print texts...not only puts us out of step with students and the larger culture, but also blinds us to many of the rhetorical affordances of new media. (p. 11)

Moreover, including the new literacies may challenge the assumptions about the very nature of literacy classrooms and how they work. A number of scholars have employed Bakhtin's (1981) concept of the chronotope to explain this nature. A classroom chronotope is a repeated pattern in the use of time and space, a way of being, if you will, that frames the way that students, teachers, literacy practices, and so on are understood. Matusov (2009), for example, argues that the chronotope of the conventional classroom positions the teacher as sole authority. The theoretical traditions that call for embracing out-of-school literacies position students as experts. Prior (1998) explains that the chronotope of traditional classrooms "sever[s] relations of the classroom to other times and places" and that it presents "persons only in their institutional capacities, obscuring other activity footings or social identities within the classroom itself" (p. 251). The theoretical traditions that call for embracing out-of-school literacies seek to employ rather than obscure other activity footings and social identities.

Second, a recent educational initiative, the Common Core State Standards (CCSS), seems likely to make things worse and inhibit real innovation. By their very nature, the CCSS reify the future directedness that Dewey critiques. The mission statement of the CCSS makes their future directedness clear:

> The Common Core State Standards provide a consistent, clear understanding of what students are expected to learn, so teachers and parents know what they need to do to help them. The standards are designed to be robust and relevant to the real world, reflecting the knowledge and skills that our young people need for success in college and careers. With American students fully prepared for the future, our communities will be best positioned to compete

successfully in the global economy. (Council of Chief State School Officers & the National Governors Association Center, n.d.)

One might stipulate to the importance of the CCSS's goal of "ensur[ing] that all students are college and career ready in literacy no later than the end of high school" by "shift[ing] content...toward higher levels of cognitive demand" (Porter, McMaken, Hwang, & Yang, 2011, p. 106). However, the demands of the standards may militate against schools' making use of the funds of knowledge students have developed in their literate activity outside of school.

Although the standards' document explicitly says that the CCSS do not "define how teachers should teach" or describe "all that can or should be taught," (Council of Chief State School Officers & the National Governors Association Center, 2010), the English Language Arts Standards' emphasis on text complexity would seem to work against the likelihood that teachers would make increasing use of the prior knowledge students have gained in their extramural literate activities. Cunningham (in press) argues that "the most widely discussed reading instructional change called for by the CCSS is a significant increase in text complexity." He argues further that "those who have not read the standards and only listened to the chatter about them may well have concluded that this is the only major change in reading instruction the CCSS entails." That change would seem to work against attempts to make more use of the texts with which adolescents engage out of school as resources to draw on in their encounters with those readings. Indeed, the table in the CCSS document illustrating the complexity, quality, and range of student reading, Grades 6–12, is dominated by canonical literary (e.g., *Macbeth*) and informational texts (e.g., *Narrative of the Life of Frederick Douglass, an American Slave*).

In addition, David Coleman (2011), one of the chief authors of the CCSS and perhaps their most influential proponent, has promoted an approach to instruction that seems to be at odds with approaches that seek to bridge students' in-school and out-of-school literacies. Rather than encourage teachers to build textual bridges, he instead has encouraged teachers "to think of dispensing for a moment with all the apparatus we have built up before reading and plunge into reading the text. And let it be our guide into its own challenges. That maybe those challenges emerge best understood from the reading of it" (p. 17). Given the influence of standards and their assessments, such calls will almost certainly result in curricular and instructional retrenchment rather than the innovative expansion of curricular and instructional understandings signaled by research and theory exploring students' out-of-school literacies.

Finally, literacy teachers by and large have not been prepared to make use of students' out-of-school literacies. Gritter (2012) calls for teachers to employ permeable textual discussion that "values what students already know and can do and informs students they bring important schema to literature, allowing them to interpret or recast texts in new and exciting ways" (p. 257). She recognizes, however, that the teachers she studied did not have the preparation to do so.

## So What to Do?

Complex problems defy simple solutions; however, understanding the barriers to innovation points the way to developing action principles to overcome those barriers. The following five action principles could be enacted at the state, district, or school level.

**Make sure that teachers and administrators understand the standards.** Misunderstandings of the CCSS abound, some, as I argued previously, promulgated by the authors of the standards themselves. The concerns that instruction employing students' out-of-school literacies is not in line with the CCSS's emphasis on text complexity can be reduced by understanding that the CCSS explicitly state that "the Standards define what all students are expected to know and be able to do, not how teachers should teach" and that they "do not define the intervention methods or materials necessary to support" students who may encounter difficulties in meeting the CCSS. It is also important to know what is in the standards themselves and what is in the ancillary materials designed to support their enactment. States voted to adopt the standards. They did not vote to accept the instructional ideas in those ancillary materials.

**Reevaluate policies that create barriers to linking in-school and out-of-school literacies.** Many schools ban the use of cell phones. It is hard to imagine sending a clearer signal that school and home are radically at odds. If, instead, schools allowed the responsible use of cell phones, teachers could begin to use them as powerful instructional tools. Texting is a fertile ground to develop important rhetorical understanding, but that's just the tip of the iceberg. A search on the internet with the words "cell phones as instructional tools" yielded over 5,000,000 hits! A thoughtful cost-benefit analysis of this kind of policy may result in giving teachers and students access to powerful resources they currently do not employ.

**Reevaluate curricular structures that create barriers to linking in-school and out-of-school literacies.** Some traditional curricular structures make it difficult to enact the kind of innovative instruction called for here. A quick example: British and American literature classes are typically organized chronologically. Applebee, Burroughs, and Stevens (2000) found that teachers employing this organizational structure seldom engaged students in developing historical understandings that would support students' interpretive work, so the benefits of such an organization are unclear. But the cost of not being able to put contemporary popular cultural and canonical literary texts into meaningful conversation is manifest.

**Give ongoing support to both inservice and preservice teachers as they develop new practices.** I've argued in this chapter that teachers may resist employing students' out-of-school literacies because making use of them runs counter to the chronotope of the literacy classroom. That means that teachers who are working to change their practice will need plenty of support. The question is how to provide that support, given limited professional development resources. One innovative possibility is employing Indistar®, a sophisticated, web-based, change management system developed by the Academic Development Institute. Indistar's platform allows a school-based leadership team to assess the current implementation of effective practices with guidance from rubrics, research briefs, and coaches, and implement plans to improve the practices. The team determines the evidence necessary to confirm that the practices are fully implemented, and gathers and documents the evidence.

What's true for inservice teachers is true for preservice teachers as well. A wealth of research documents the disconnect faced by preservice teachers when they go into the field, a disconnect that echoes the research–practice divide discussed above. They often do not see the innovative practices espoused in their preparation programs being practiced in their schools. As Smagorinsky, Rhym, and Moore (2013) point out, these "competing centers of gravity" make it difficult to develop a coherent approach to teaching.

Juzwik and her colleagues (2012) offer one innovative approach to teacher education that may help preservice teachers overcome the problem of conflicting settings. They worked to foster dialogically organized classroom interactions through a pedagogy informed by multiliteracies using a Web 2.0-mediated process of video-based response and revision. Four times over the course of their internships, teacher candidates recorded videos of their teaching and posted them to an online social network, ultimately creating a culminating digital reflection on their materials. The interns also commented on each other's practices and reflected on the feedback they received from their colleagues and teachers. Instead of having their field of vision limited to one site, these preservice teachers and their university professors were able to see how the instruction advocated in their teacher preparation programs played out in multiple settings. Although the additional demands of the video-based response and revision created challenges both to the preservice teachers and their supervisors, Juzwik and her colleagues conclude that emerging digital technologies offer an "unprecedented opportunity" (p. 33) to reduce the university–schools divide and, in so doing, to create opportunities for preservice teachers to collaborate in developing effective practices over time.

**Cast teachers as researchers.** The gap between educational research and practice has been long lamented. Overcoming teachers' suspicion of educational research, powerful and long-held beliefs about the nature of their discipline, and their worries about preparing students to meet state and national standards makes clear that it will take far more than an occasional inservice program acquainting teachers with new practices and the research that supports them to make them willing and able to make use of students' out-of-school literacies as instructional resources. McIntyre (2005) argues that one way to bridge the divide is to engage teachers in the evaluation of research-based practice in the context of their own practice. As I have argued elsewhere (Smith, Wilhelm, & Fredrickson, 2012), the CCSS can act as a lever to do just that. That is, if a curricular or instructional innovation can be shown to achieve the standards, then its implementation becomes far more likely. School teams of literacy educators could select particular approaches to drawing on students' out-of-school literacies, develop measures for testing the extent to which they achieve the CCSS, and share their findings.

## Conclusion

Gritter (2012) offers an apt summary for the lines of research that support innovative ideas for making more use of students' out-of-school literacies: "A basic but profound truism of teaching and learning is that no one learns anything without knowing something first. Learning in classrooms is about connections made with prior knowledge and also with human beings" (pp. 257–258).

Particular suggestions for making connections between what students know and do outside of school with what they need to learn and do inside school abound. But those suggestions are far too seldom taken up by teachers. That's understandable given the barriers that exist for doing do. However, given the stakes of the game, accepting those barriers is unsustainable. Instead, schools must create structures to overcome them so that promising innovative practices can flourish.

## Action Principles

**For State Education Agencies**
 a. Work with institutes of higher learning to encourage use of digital technologies to reflect on real-world teaching experiences.
 b. Re-evaluate policies that might create barriers to making best use of current technologies.

**For Local Education Agencies**
 a. Provide opportunities for professional development on ways to teach common core standards in individual contexts and cultures.
 b. Provide research materials to your teaching staff on new literacies and different ways of approaching literacy.
 c. Provide opportunities for teachers to focus on alternative ideas of how to teach literacy using less traditional materials.

**For Teachers**
 a. Be aware of the value of the non-standard literacy practices of your students and what is currently being used by them.
 b. Start where the student currently is in their reading practice and proceed from there.

c. Expand the scope of required readings to include less traditional literacy of value.

## References

Abrams, S. S. (2009). A gaming frame of mind: Digital contexts and academic implications. *Educational Media International, 46*(4), 335–347.

Alvermann, D., & Moore, D. W. (2011). Questioning the separation of in-school and out-of-school contexts for literacy learning: An interview with Donna Alvermann. *Journal of Adolescent & Adult Literacy, 55*(2), 156–158.

Applebee, A. N., Burroughs, R., & Stevens, A. (2000). Creating continuity and coherence in high school literature curricula. *Research in the Teaching of English, 34*, 396–428.

Bakhtin, M. (1981). *The dialogic imagination: Four essays by M. M. Bakhtin.* (C. Emerson & M. Holquist, Trans.; M. Holquist, Ed.). Austin, TX: University of Texas Press.

Ball, A. F., Skerrett, A., & Martinez, R. A. (2011). Research on diverse students in culturally and linguistically complex language arts classrooms. In D. Lapp & D. Fisher (Eds.), *Handbook of research on teaching the English language arts* (3rd ed., pp. 22–29). New York, NY: Routledge.

Booth, W. (1974). *A rhetoric of irony.* Chicago, IL: The University of Chicago Press.

Buck, A. (2012). Examining digital literacy practices on social network sites. *Research in the Teaching of English, 46*, 9–38

Coleman, D. (2011, April 28). *Bringing the Common Core to life* [Transcript of a Webinar]. Albany, NY: New York State Department of Education. Retrieved from http://usny.nysed.gov/rttt/docs/bringingthecommoncoretolife/fulltranscript.pdf

Council of Chief State School Officers, & the National Governors Association Center for Best Practices. (2010). *Common Core State Standards for English language arts and literacy in history/social studies, science, and technical subjects.* Retrieved from http://www.corestandards.org/ELA-Literacy

Council of Chief State School Officers, & the National Governors Association Center for Best Practices. (n.d.). *Mission statement.* Retrieved from http://www.corestandards.org/

Cunningham, J. W. (in press). Research on text complexity: The Common Core State Standards as catalyst. In S. B. Neuman & L. B. Gambrell (Eds.), *Reading instruction in the age of Common Core State Standards.* Newark, DE: International Reading Association.

Dewey, J. (1916). *Democracy in education.* New York, NY: The Free Press.

Dyson, A. H. (1999). Coach Bombay's kids learn to write: Children's appropriation of media material for school literacy. *Research in the Teaching of English, 33*, 367–402.

Gritter, K. (2012). Permeable textual discussion in tracked language arts classrooms. *Research in the Teaching of English, 46*, 232–259.

Hill, M. L. (2009). *Beats, rhymes, and classroom life: Hip-hop pedagogy and the politics of identity.* New York, NY: Teachers College Press.

Juzwik, M., Sherry, M. B., Caughlan, S., Heintz, A., & Borsheim-Black, C. (2012). Supporting dialogically organized instruction in an English teacher preparation program: A video-based, web 2.0-mediated response and revision pedagogy. *Teachers College Record, 114*(3), 1–42.

Lee, C. (1993). *Signifying as a scaffold for literary interpretation: The pedagogical implications of an African American discourse genre* (NCTE Research Report No. 26). Urbana, IL: National Council of Teachers of English.

Martino, W. (1994). Masculinity and learning: Exploring boys' underachievement and underrepresentation in subject English. *Interpretations, 27*(2), 22–57.

Martino, W. (1998). "Dickheads," "poofs," "try hards," and "losers": Critical literacy for boys in the English classroom. *English in Aotearoa (New Zealand Association for the Teaching of English), 25*, 31–57.

Matusov, E. (2009). Pedagogical chronotopes of monologic conventional classrooms: Ontology and didactics. In F. Matusov (Ed.), *Journey into dialogic pedagogy* (pp. 147–206). Hauppauge, NY: Nova Publishers.

McIntyre, D. (2005). Bridging the gap between research and practice. *Cambridge Journal of Education, 35*, 357–382.

Mitchell-Kernan, C. (1981). Mother wit from the laughing barrel. In A. Dundes (Ed.), *Signifying, loud-talking, and marking* (pp. 310–328). Englewood Cliffs, NJ: Prentice Hall.

Moll, L. C., & Greenberg, J. B. (1990). Creating zones of possibilities: Combining social contexts for instruction. In L. C. Moll (Ed.), *Vygotsky and education: Instructional implications and applications of sociohistorical psychology* (pp. 319–348). New York, NY: Cambridge University Press.

Morrell, E. (2002). Toward a critical pedagogy of popular culture: Literacy development among urban youth. *Journal of Adolescent and Adult Literacy, 46*, 72–77.

New London Group. (1996). A pedagogy of multiliteracies: Designing social futures. *Harvard Educational Review, 66*(1), 60–92.

Orellana, M. F., & Reynolds, J. (2008). Cultural modeling: Leveraging bilingual skills for school paraphrasing tasks. *Reading Research Quarterly, 43*, 48–65.

Prior, P. (1998). *Writing/Disciplinarity: A sociohistoric account of literate activity in the academy*. New York, NY: Routledge.

Porter, A., McMaken, J., Hwang, J., & Yang, R. (2011). Common Core Standards: The new U.S. intended curriculum. *Educational Researcher, 40*, 103–116.

Redding, S. (2012). *Change leadership: Innovation in state education agencies.* Oakland, CA: Wing Institute.

Roozen, K. (2009). "Fan fic-ing" English studies: A case study exploring the interplay of vernacular literacies and disciplinary engagement. *Research in the Teaching of English, 44*, 136–169.

Science Media Group. (1989). *A private universe*. Cambridge, MA: Harvard University, Smithsonian Institution.

Smagorinsky, P. (2011). *Vygotsky and literacy research: A methodological framework*. Rotterdam, Netherlands: Sense.

Smagorinsky, P., Rhym, D., & Moore, C. (2013). Competing centers of gravity: A beginning English teacher's socialization process within conflictual settings. *English Education, 45*, 147–183.

Smith, M. W. (1991). *Understanding unreliable narrators: Reading between the lines in the literature classroom*. Urbana, IL: National Council of Teachers of English.

Smith, M. W., & Moore, D. W. (2012). What we know about adolescents' out-of-school literacies, what we need to learn, and why studying them is important: An interview with Michael W. Smith. *Journal of Adolescent and Adult Literacy, 55*, 745–747.

Smith, M. W., & Wilhelm, J. (2002). *"Reading don't fix no Chevys": Literacy in the lives of young men.* Portsmouth, NH: Heinemann.

Smith, M. W., Wilhelm, J., & Fredrickson, J. (2012). *O, yeah?!: Putting argument to work both in school and out.* Portsmouth, NH: Heinemann.

Turner, K. H. (2010). Digitalk: A new literacy for a digital generation. *Phi Delta Kappan, 92*(1), 41–46.

Vasudevan, L. (2010). Education remix: New media, literacies, and the emerging digital geographies. *Digital Culture and Education, 2*(1), 62–82. Retrieved from http://www.digitalculturean-deducation.com/uncategorized/vasudevan_2010_html/

Weinstein, S. (2009). *Feel these words: Writing in the lives of urban youth.* Albany, NY: SUNY.

Wilson, A. A., & Boatright, M. D. (2011). One adolescent's construction of native identity in school: Speaking with dance and not in words and writing. *Research in the Teaching of English, 45,* 252–277.

# Innovations in Language and Literacy Instruction
*Michael L. Kamil*

The title of this chapter intentionally uses the word "instruction" rather than learning. An explanation of this usage is in order. Learning is an intervening variable between instruction and some outcome measure. That simply means that what we label learning is not directly observable—it must be inferred by showing that some measure improves (or not) as a result of some instruction. Outcome measures are many and varied. They can be simple measures—answering questions about text or responding to oral language in a variety of appropriate ways. If learning has occurred, the performance after instruction will be better than it was prior to instruction. Learning is not under the direct control of either a learner or a teacher. What is under the teacher's control is instruction. Instruction can take many different forms. A traditional form is for a teacher to deliver a curriculum. Other forms include instruction without a traditional teacher delivered either by textbooks, computers, or even trial and error. A learner can, for example, choose to spend more time repeating or practicing material in order to improve outcomes. Learning to speak a language, for example, involves just such a format. What can be manipulated (or innovated) are the external conditions, not the internal learning. This chapter will deal with the innovations in these external conditions.

Over the last two decades or so, the greatest innovations in language instruction have been the results of three efforts to improve general instruction: the use of standards to guide instruction, the application of research to determine effective instruction, and the consistent use of assessment for accountability in achievement. All three of these innovations can be classed as mature, which means they have been used, vetted, and improved, but are still not universal. These innovations shape the form of the material in this chapter.

While there are many nascent innovations, most of them have little or no research to demonstrate the effectiveness of their applications. Standards are a relatively recent development but have a relatively high adoption rate because of federal and state educational policy. The refinement in the use of standards has been the adoption of the Common Core State Standards (CCSS) by most of the states. The major innovation involved in CCSS is that it provides a common framework for instruction so that students receive consistent instruction across schools, districts, and even states, with few exceptions. The other innovation is that CCSS calls for increased rigor and complexity compared to other standards.

Accompanying the development of CCSS has been the development of assessments that are consistent with those standards—a necessity given that the CCSS incorporate a large increase in the rigor as well as an extended range of analysis of language. The development of the CCSS was based on the best available research and drew on the best of the available standards at the time, reflecting the second innovation already noted. The new assessments are currently under development.

> **Research has always been promoted as a path to higher student achievement by the education research community, but it took an act of Congress to move this emphasis into widely adoped educational practice.**

However, the use of assessments has been adopted by a portion of the educational practice community. The innovation is that teaching is guided by a series of assessments to measure progress and determine what is needed either to prevent or correct difficulties in learning.

Research has always been promoted as a path to higher student achievement by the education research community, but it took an act of Congress to move this emphasis into widely adopted educational practice. The federal initiative that established the National Reading Panel (NRP; National Institute of Child Health and Human Development [NICHHD], 2000) was an instantiation of the attempt to improve practice by applying relevant research. The research syntheses conducted by the NRP became policy, particularly for the Reading First Program under the No Child Left Behind Act of 2001, and have been implicated in the improvement in reading achievement since their implementation. The use of research findings is an innovation because educational materials were (and often still are) adopted without consideration for their effectiveness.

There are many nascent innovations that have been and are being offered as improvements in instruction. They are not the focus here because many of them have little or no evidence for their effectiveness. As these newer innovations are implemented and tested, they may well take their place among the more reliable and mature innovations that are the focus of this chapter.

In what follows, I will address the language areas in so far as there is research to support recommendations. The areas to be considered are reading, writing, speaking, and listening. This chapter will also consider some recommendations for early childhood education and some recommendations for second-language learners. For each of these areas, I will review some of the relevant research and recommendations for policy and implementation. Because the body of research is so extensive, reliance is placed on meta-analyses and other reviews of the research.

## Reading and Language Instruction in Early Childhood Education

A major component of early childhood education is language instruction because literacy instruction is based in oral language. In what follows, I focus on the elements of early education that are related to later literacy learning. The National Early Literacy Panel (2008) conducted extensive meta-analyses of research on the variables in early language that produced improved outcomes in literacy in later grades, including the following:
   a. alphabet knowledge
   b. phonemic awareness
   c. concepts about print (knowledge of print conventions, e.g., left–right, front–back, and concepts like title page, author, etc.)
   d. oral language
   e. print awareness (combines elements of alphabet knowledge, concepts about print, and protodecoding, i.e., beginning or early decoding)
   f. writing or writing one's name
   g. rapid automatic naming (RAN) of letters and digits
   h. RAN of objects and colors
   i. phonological short-term memory
   j. visual perception

Research on some of these variables has produced evidence supporting the efficacy of incorporating them into instruction to improve later literacy. For example, there is ample evidence that teaching students phonemic awareness skills leads to improved reading. On the other hand, it is not clear that phonological memory can be taught in an effective way to produce better literacy outcomes. Alphabet knowledge, concepts about print, oral language, print awareness, and writing would seem to be clear and appropriate targets of instruction. While the other variables are indicators of later achievement and might suggest the need for some instruction, the exact form of the appropriate instruction is not clear.

Shared book reading and dialogic book reading (Lonigan & Whitehurst, 1998) in early childhood have also been shown to have a positive effect on oral language and later reading achievement. In these methods, which are related but somewhat different, an adult reads a book with children, asking questions, modeling responses, and asking for predictions as the story continues. A summary of these results is available from the What Works Clearinghouse (2007).

Hart & Risley (1999) have shown deficits in the vocabulary of students of lower socioeconomic status. Because vocabulary is such a critical facet of literacy development, any sort of intervention to address this deficit must begin before children enter formal schooling. Any intervention seeking to augment a child's lexical abilities should be part of a comprehensive effort, such as that developed by Dickinson and his colleagues (Dickinson, McCabe, Anastasopoulos, Peisner-Feinberg, & Poe, 2003), in which vocabulary, phonological sensitivity, and print knowledge are combined.

Given the large variability in early childhood programs, there is a great deal of difficulty in guaranteeing that students receive the appropriate sorts of instruction. This problem is further exacerbated by the patchwork of credentialing for early childhood educators. Nevertheless, in their edited volume, Neuman and Kamil (2010) present evidence demonstrating that effective practices in professional development can endow early childhood educators with the skills to provide solid foundations for their students.

**Recommendations**

The research findings described in the preceding paragraphs should be used to guide instruction. In addition, ways to help ensure that instructional practices are implemented effectively are needed. The following are offered as a partial list of ways to assist state education agencies (SEAs) and local education agencies (LEAs) in implementation:
  a. SEAs: Require that credential or certificate programs include current research-based practices to prepare early childhood educators to deliver high-quality instruction that will prepare students for later success in school.
  b. LEAs and their schools: Ensure that a comprehensive program of instruction connects early childhood instruction to instruction in elementary grades and ultimately through high school.
  c. LEAs: Provide continual professional development for inservice teachers.

## Reading in the Elementary Grades

The National Reading Panel (NICHHD, 2000) was established to determine what instructional regimens should be implemented with a high probability of succeeding in raising reading achievement. While the technical charge was to examine research from elementary grades through high school, the most intensive uses of the National Reading Panel (NRP) were by teachers in elementary grades. The greater uses are likely a function of the greater prevalence of reading instruction in elementary grades. The NRP recommended practices in five areas:

***Phonemic awareness:*** the ability of students to focus on or manipulate the sounds (phonemes) of the language. The NRP found that phonemic awareness (PA) instruction was effective for students in kindergarten and first grade but was far less effective for students in higher grades. Moreover, if PA was taught for too many hours, its effect was mitigated. One interesting finding was that PA instruction was more effective for small groups than for individuals or for whole classes.

*Phonics:* the ability to translate print into oral language. The NRP reported that phonics instruction was effective for students up to second grade but had diminishing returns (in terms of improvement in reading achievement) from second to sixth grade.

*Fluency:* the ability to read with speed, accuracy, and appropriate expression. The NRP found that fluency was the indicator of appropriate progress in reading in the early grades. A lack of fluency is the indication that students need some intervention in order to make progress in learning to read.

*Vocabulary:* the ability to understand the meanings of individual words. The NRP found that explicit vocabulary instruction increased vocabulary and comprehension.

*Comprehension strategies:* procedures that guide students as they read and write. The NRP identified eight types of comprehension strategy instruction that were effective:

   a. comprehension monitoring
   b. cooperative learning
   c. curriculum integration
   d. graphic organizers
   e. question answering
   f. question generation
   g. story structure (maps)
   h. summarization

Of these, the most effective were question generation and summarization, even though all had substantial support in the research literature.

In addition to the five areas of instruction, the NRP detailed the effectiveness of professional development in improving student reading achievement. The report also summarized the research on applications of technology in reading instruction. Although there was less of a body of research to analyze for technology applications compared to studies of the efficacy of professional development, the NRP did show that technology could be used effectively in instruction to raise student achievement.

The Institute of Education Sciences has produced a number of documents describing instructional practices for a range of topics from reading to mathematics to school reform. For each of these "practice guides," five instructional recommendations are presented, along with the research evidence and an assessment of the amount of support for the recommendation. For elementary grades, a practice guide was developed for improving reading comprehension in kindergarten through Grade 3 (Shanahan et al., 2010). The five recommendations were rated according to the amount of evidence substantiating them:

a. Teach students how to use reading comprehension strategies. (strong)
   b. Teach students to identify and use the text's organizational structure to comprehend, learn, and remember content. (moderate)
   c. Establish an engaging and motivating context in which to teach reading comprehension. (moderate)
   d. Guide students through focused, high-quality discussion on the meaning of text. (minimal)
   e. Select texts purposefully to support comprehension development. (minimal)

Some of these recommendations clearly reiterate items in the NRP list, but recommendations "c" and "d" are new. Given the overall agreement of both lists, it is clear that the research findings provide some obvious guidance for instruction. (Note: The rating of "minimal" suggests that there are few studies, but the data from those studies do support the recommendation.)

## Recommendations

The preceding summaries of recommendations for instruction in the elementary grades provide a great many detailed suggestions for instructional practice. As with early childhood education, there is a need to consider some factors in implementing those practices.

   a. Although not specified in the brief review of research described above, it is important for SEAs to have both a diagnostic (progress monitoring) program and the resources to address student difficulties as they arise. After identification of reading difficulties (or potential difficulties), it is important to follow up on the diagnosis of difficulties with sufficient instruction to correct them. The resources for such remedial or supplemental instruction are often insufficient.
   b. LEAs: Shift the focus of instruction as students progress through the grades; that is, ensure that students receive a strong but not exclusive foundation in decoding skills in early grades, shifting to higher level comprehension skills.
   c. LEAs: Provide a coherent program of professional development (and coaching). If done correctly, such a program will enable teachers to continually update their skill sets and so deliver the most effective instruction possible.

## Reading Instruction in Middle and High School

As early as 1944, Artley expressed a concern about the adequacy of reading instruction in the content areas with his oft-quoted phrase, "Every teacher a teacher of reading." While that may be going too far, the recent development of standards (Common Core State Standards, 2012) suggests a current and critical need for reading instruction in the content areas, particularly in science, social studies, and history. The findings of the NRP, as well as other research, suggest that the focus of reading instruction for improving adolescent literacy is different from that required for earlier grades. In particular, the structures and discourse of individual content areas require specialized instruction for each area. For example, through about Grade 3, vocabulary expansion is mostly from oral language, whereas the new words learned beyond Grade 3 derive mainly from text (Sticht & James, 1984). CCSS addresses these concerns by including standards for science, history, social studies, and technical material beginning at the elementary levels.

Obviously, reading instruction should build on the work done by teachers in earlier grades, but with an eye to the work that will have to be done in subsequent grades. Another IES practice guide concerned with improving adolescent literacy (Kamil et al., 2008) addresses some of the needs of students in Grades 4–12 by making the following recommendations:

a. Provide explicit vocabulary instruction. (strong)
b. Provide direct and explicit comprehension strategy instruction. (strong)
c. Make available intensive and individualized interventions for struggling readers, interventions that can be provided by trained specialists. (strong)
d. Provide opportunities for extended discussion of text meaning and interpretation. (moderate)
e. Increase student motivation and engagement in literacy learning. (moderate)

This practice guide acknowledges that students in Grade 4 have different needs from students in Grade 12. However, an examination of all of the recommendations across the range of middle and high school settings does show some general commonalities: an emphasis on vocabulary and comprehension and on improving students' motivation and engagement. In addition, it seems clear that provisions should be made for struggling readers by providing targeted tutoring that will address the reasons for their difficulties.

## Recommendations

a. SEAs and LEAs: Provide extra instructional time, targeted to need, for struggling readers. This additional time will involve assessments and appropriate instructional regimens based on those assessments.
b. LEAs: Provide professional development for teachers in middle and high school to assist them in delivering high-quality instruction. Extend professional support to all content area teachers and not limited to English language arts teachers.
c. LEAs and schools: Provide content area teachers with the tools to detect and to address difficulties in learning that are related to their specific disciplines.

## Writing Across the Grades

A practice guide that addresses the issues of writing in elementary schools provides four recommendations (Graham et al., 2012):
  a. Teach students to use the writing process for a variety of purposes. (strong)
  b. Teach students to become fluent with handwriting, spelling, sentence construction, typing, and word processing. (moderate)
  c. Provide daily time for students to write. (minimal)
  d. Create an engaged community of writers. (minimal)

In a meta-analysis of writing research about improving writing for students in Grades 4–12, Graham and Perin (2007) offered another set of recommendations. Their research and the resulting 11 recommendations focused strictly on improving writing, without consideration for other literacy skills. Notable in their report are effect sizes differentiating highly effective practices from less effective ones:
  a. writing strategies (effect size = .82)
  b. summarization (effect size = .82)
  c. collaborative writing (effect size = .75)
  d. specific product goals (effect size = .75)
  e. word processing (effect size = .55)
  f. sentence combining (effect size = .50)
  g. prewriting (effect size = .32)
  h. inquiry activities (effect size = .32)
  i. process writing approach (effect size = .32)
  j. study of models (effect size = .25)
  k. writing for content learning (effect size = .23)

Of these, writing strategies, summarization, collaborative writing, and having specific product goals have such substantial effects that they should be unquestioned parts of the curriculum. Studying models and writing for content learning provide relatively less improvement and should be implemented only with lower priority. While some of these effect sizes are relatively small, they may be worth the effort given the general difficulty of improving writing ability for adolescents.

Another set of recommendations about writing focuses on the improvements in reading that occur when writing is added to the curriculum (Graham & Hebert, 2010). As with both the other sets of recommendations above, some of these are highly effective and others less so. This set of recommendations focuses on students in Grades 1–12 and are grouped in three categories:
  A. Have students write about the text they read. (effect size = 0.40)
      1. Have students respond to a text. (effect size = 0.77)
      2. Have students write summaries of a text. (effect size = 0.52)
      3. Have students write notes about a text. (effect size = 0.47)

4. Have students answer or create and answer questions about a text in writing. (effect size = 0.27)
B. Teach the process of writing, text structures, and paragraph or sentence construction skills. (effect size = 0.18 )
C. Increase how much students write. (effect size = 0.30)

There is substantial overlap in the recommendations on writing instruction from the three sources. It is also the case that the expected improvement varies by the context and the purposes for including writing in the curriculum. Perhaps the most interesting recommendation is that simply increasing the amount that students write will improve their reading by close to one third of a standard deviation. This is a more than reasonable return for a simple intervention.

**Recommendations**
a. SEAs: Stipulate in teacher credentialing requirements that preparation for writing instruction is a fundamental part of teacher preparation.
b. LEAs: Ensure that writing is integrated into the literacy curriculum and taught in combination with reading and other literacy skills.
c. LEAs: Direct teachers to conduct writing instruction in contexts that are as authentic as possible so that students will not view writing as divorced from real life.

## Listening and Speaking

In spite of the recent developments in technology—audio books and podcasts—and their place in learning and literacy, mainstream literacy research has not focused on listening and speaking as targets of literacy instruction. This knowledge deficit is rendered more puzzling by the evidence of an emphasis in early grades instruction on both listening and speaking and the transition to reading as documented by Sticht and his colleagues (Sticht et al., 1974; Sticht & James, 1984). Although there is little guidance specifically about improving instruction in listening and speaking, the Common Core State Standards have set specific standards for what students should learn in these areas.

**Recommendations**
a. LEAs: Add both listening and speaking to the curriculum across all grades, not just the elementary grades.
b. LEAs: Promote the teaching of listening and speaking in the context of reading and writing and also as independent skills.

## Second-Language Learning

No one is a stranger to the fraught relationship of Americans to languages other than English. Our Founders relied on the English language as a unifier and as a way of insuring that ties with the lands of immigrants would be severed. Even our great early linguists, such as Noah Webster, supported the belief that suppressing languages other than English would serve the betterment of English specifically and the American educational system in general. In fact, until World War II, the only obvious role given to languages other than English was for the "reading purpose," for the study of foreign literatures.

This status changed dramatically during World War II, as the military in particular confronted the grave dilemma of having Americans totally unprepared to participate with others (friends or foes) on the world stage in a language other than English. The response was the rapid development of an audio-lingual pedagogy in which students were immersed in foreign language study for 10–12 hours per day. Although adult students in a pressure-filled environment demonstrated success, the pedagogy was not sustainable in a school setting. The 1950s and 1960s saw language learning as a stimulus–response endeavor, where individual words and phrases in one language are paired with those in another. This produces, at best, an impoverished learning. Many adults to this day claim to be able to ask some questions in the second language but then have no understanding of an answer when it deviates from the learned pairing. This resulted in the general societal belief that Americans are somehow genetically incapable of learning a language other than English and perpetuated a philosophy that others must be compelled to learn and use English at the expense of all other languages. A full discussion of this history is found in Bernhardt (1999).

> *Many adults to this day claim to be able to ask some questions in the second language but then have no understanding of an answer when it deviates from the learned pairing.*

The 1970s witnessed massive immigration of individuals fleeing repression rather than only seeking opportunity. Schooling at all levels had to respond to massive numbers of individuals needing useful and usable English quickly, not merely for the "reading purpose." Linguistics probed the nature of the useful and usable and focused on the nature of *functional* language—in other words, on the nature of what individuals could *accomplish* with language, rather than just what they *knew* about language. The concept of *doing*, known technically as *proficiency*, is probably the most influential concept to have been infused into the language landscape in the past 30 years. This concept of language proficiency attaches to significant and renewed insights into the language learning brought forth by the research process, specifically in two areas: oral proficiency development in a second language (Doughty & Long, 2004), and second-language reading (Bernhardt, 2011).

## Oral Proficiency

Research in oral proficiency development has led to the recommendation that, at the school level, children should be encouraged to speak English and also to the admonition that instructors must understand that oral language is merely a surface manifestation of student learning. Research in oral proficiency development also implies that, at the district level, mechanisms should be in place to permit learners to use and access their strongest language (which may be their home language) in their classrooms and in tutorials as well as in high-stakes content assessments.

Research in second-language oral proficiency indicates that linguistic forms develop over time as a response to the efficacy and frequency of particular forms within a language environment. As an example, the present progressive in English, formed with the *–ing* (*I am going to school*) is a form learned early in English regardless of native language background. Present progressive is the most frequently occurring form of the present tense in English. The verbal inflection *–(e)s* for the third-person singular is learned late in English language acquisition and oftentimes never: *My mother goes to the market every day* is often rendered as *\*My mother go to the market every day* even among highly fluent and competent speakers. While incorrect in standard English, this latter utterance is fully comprehensible, never interfering with communication. Yet learners are often penalized early and frequently for not developing a command of all the standard forms of English. Such corrections reinforce teachers' beliefs that students cannot learn a second language until they have a complete command of all forms and learners' beliefs that they will never succeed in that task. Research indicates that English language learners need minimally 6 years in an English-speaking environment to have an oral command somewhat equivalent to native-speaking peers. Said differently, instruction relying exclusively on oral language performance tends to put learners into a very threatening position. Signals are sent that the oral performance should be grammatically flawless and that the performance should be spontaneous when neither is possible with second-language learners. Second-language learners and users often need more time than native speakers to articulate an utterance, often reporting that by the time they have formulated a response an instructor has moved on. To reduce the pressure on speech performance, teachers should employ several alternate strategies in the classroom, such as telling students in advance what questions will be posed, permitting them to work in groups to formulate answers, and having language learners "try out" their answers with peers before speaking publically. At the district level, mechanisms should be in place to allow students additional tutorial time for practicing speech. Tutorial time is often at the level of grammatical form. What learners actually need is time to practice and articulate oral speech: Retelling events, explaining processes, and describing are language functions that learners need to practice and to be given feedback on. Teachers should also be given professional development opportunities to learn new languages. Taking a language course at a local college or university will bring enlightenment regarding the learning processes and frustrations of language learners in classrooms more concretely than any additional summer workshop ever could (Teemant, Bernhardt, Rodrîguez-Muñoz, & Aiello, 2000).

**Recommendations**
a. SEAs and LEAs: Ensure that policies encourage the use of native language in the acquisition of second languages.
b. SEAs and LEAs: Include all communicative forms in second-language instruction—reading, writing, and listening, in addition to speaking.
c. LEAs: Provide professional development in current research-based practices for teaching second languages.

## Second-Language Literacy

In addition to recommendations from studies of oral proficiency, SEAs and LEAs can improve instruction for English language learners by attending to research in second-language literacy.

At the classroom level, students should be encouraged to use their native language literacy as a critical tool in their English language learning. At the district level, libraries should be equipped with materials such as encyclopedias, handbooks, and digital material that articulate in a language familiar to students the expository content material they are learning in English.

Reading in a second language entails, according to research across a number of age groups and languages, three variables: first-language literacy, second-language knowledge, and background knowledge and affect.

Generally, the more able readers are in their first-language reading, the greater the contribution (upwards of 20%) to second-language reading (Bernhardt & Kamil, 1995). This understanding of the importance of first-language literacy is recent. When Rossell and Baker (1996) reviewed the research on bilingual education, they concluded that it was not beneficial for students. However, Greene (1997) did a meta-analysis of the studies in the Rossell and Baker research review and found that methodologically sound studies yielded a different conclusion. Greene concluded that at least the use of some native language in learning English produced moderate effects. These data are supportive of the conclusion of Bernhardt and Kamil. The understanding of the contribution of first-language reading is one of the main reasons that learners in school should be encouraged to use some of what they know in their native language when using their second language. It will improve learning outcomes, and they will be more able to focus on the content of reading material. In fact, much of the technical vocabulary related to content material is Latinate, and, consequently, many learners who come to school speaking Spanish already have a sense of this particular technical vocabulary. Of course, when reading material is exclusively narrative fiction, any vocabulary advantage for non-native learners is mitigated; the vocabulary is not necessarily Latinate, and the content often has little or no factual basis.

The second variable entailed in second-language reading is grammatical knowledge of the second language. Ironically, this knowledge accounts for no more than 30% of the process of second-language reading (Greene, 1997). If teachers force students to focus on language form while ignoring content, they do little to actually help learners to read and understand.

The third element is the importance of background knowledge and affect. Research has revealed the importance of background knowledge and affect—around 50% of the second-language reading process (Greene, 1997). All readers have some content knowledge that engages them and interests them. For some, that content knowledge might be about animals or trains; for others, fashion and games. That content knowledge is generally housed for the particular reader in a language other than English. It is not that knowledge does not exist; it is that it might not be visible to a teacher in English.

The important conclusion of this research is not that the three elements listed above are distinct from each other. Rather, it is that they are interdependent, and they compensate for each other. In other words, if a learner has knowledge of a process in his or her first language, the learner can use that knowledge to compensate for a lack of knowledge in grammar and syntax in the new, second language. In like manner, an acute understanding of language forms can help a reader through the signaling system of a text, helping to point out redundancies and references that assist a reader in comprehending new vocabulary. And, of course, motivation and the desire to learn can help a struggling learner of English strive to understand more about animals or how to play a game more effectively.

> *Students should learn to talk about and write about what they read.*

The recommendations listed here are interdependent. Students should learn to talk about and write about what they read. They should be encouraged to elaborate and to extend their utterances so that they practice upper registers of speech. What learners read, whether in their first or second language, provides the content and the motivation to write and speak. If schools or districts have staffs that fail to see or to utilize this interdependence, their students will continue to have difficulty in middle and high school and will fail to learn to use all the resources they possess and therefore fail to take on the challenges of college-level material.

Gersten et al. (2007) produced a U.S. Department of Education practice guide with recommendations for teaching English language learners in elementary school. Those recommendations, with the assessments of the strength of the evidence of their effectiveness, are:

a. Conduct formative assessments with English learners using English language measures of phonological processing, letter knowledge, and word and text reading. (strong)
   b. Provide focused, intensive small-group interventions for English learners determined to be at risk for reading problems. (strong)
   c. Provide high-quality vocabulary instruction throughout the day. Teach essential content words in depth. In addition, use instructional time to address the meanings of common words, phrases, and expressions not yet learned. (strong)
   d. Ensure that English learners participate for 90 minutes per week in instructional activities that pair students at different levels of proficiency in English. (strong)
   e. Ensure that the development of formal or academic English is a key instructional goal for English learners, beginning in the primary grades. (low)

In addition to these explicit recommendations, the authors also strongly urge an appropriate use of native languages in instruction for English language learners. Generally, the explicit recommendations (a) through (e) overlap substantially with those for teaching language skills to native speakers of English, but that should not obscure the real differences in learning English as a second language from native English learners.

In a synthesis of research on adolescents learning English, Short and Fitzsimmons (2007) formulated both general policy recommendations (e.g., refining definitions of English language learners) and instructional recommendations. For the purposes of this discussion, I focus on the instructional recommendations:
   a. Integrate all four language skills into instruction.
   b. Teach components and processes of reading and writing.
   c. Teach reading comprehension strategies.
   d. Focus on vocabulary development.
   e. Build and activate background knowledge.
   f. Teach language through content and themes.
   g. Use native language strategically.
   h. Pair technology with existing interventions.
   i. Motivate English language learners through choice.

This list clearly overlaps both the set of native English learner recommendations and the other English language learner recommendations presented above. A substantial amount of transfer between languages (Dressler & Kamil, 2006; Genesee, Geva, Dressler, & Kamil, 2008) accounts for the similarities of the recommendations. In spite of the similarities, a caution in assessing the recommendations is in order. While the body of research in first-language literacy is extensive, the volume of research in second-language literacy is far smaller.

Consequently, there may be many issues for which there is little or no guidance for instruction of English language learners.

Many of the recommendations cited above also, obviously, are reflected in the Common Core State Standards (CCSS)—particularly those recommendations that emphasize all four literacy domains. However, CCSS are not explicitly about second-language learners, and some types of accommodations need to be made to instruction for them. To address the differences between standards for native speakers and standards for English language learners, the WIDA (World-Class Instructional Design and Assessment) Consortium developed its own set of expectations for learners (WIDA, 2012). These standards were designed to highlight the ways in which second-language learners can be taught to the same standards as the CCSS.

### Recommendations

a. SEA policies: Allow the use of native language in the instruction of English language learners to make such instruction more effective.
b. SEAs and LEAs: Ensure that teachers receive appropriate preparation in teaching English language learners both in preservice and inservice settings.
c. SEAs and LEAs: Use assessments that take into account the native language abilities of students for both formative and summative purposes.

## Summary

Many recommendations included in this discussion of language and literacy overlap. Care must be taken to understand how each of the recommendations may be instantiated differently across different grade levels. Thus, for example, vocabulary instruction in early grades should be focused primarily on oral language, whereas instruction for older students should focus on print vocabulary. Similar examples could be generated for almost all of the recommendations. Clearly, the needs and experiences of elementary students are different from those of middle and high school students.

Very little has been included about the assessments that attend these instructional recommendations because assessments are now being developed for CCSS. Although there are assessments for the WIDA standards, they might have to be revised when the CCSS assessments are finalized. Until "the dust settles," teachers, administrators, and policymakers need to be tuned in to new developments. The guidance given in the various recommendations above should be followed insofar as possible until "official" guidance is available.

This chapter has provided a broad range of recommendations. Any such review will eventually become outdated. Thus, there is no substitute for keeping up with the research literature. New findings may alter old recommendations, and new findings may uncover areas not in the scope of current recommendations. A good source for research-based information on instructional programs is the What Works Clearinghouse (http://ies.ed.gov/ncee/wwc/) which publishes reports on research that evaluates such materials.

Professional learning groups should focus not only on current practices, but also on ways to read, digest, and implement new research-based practices. The improvement in achievement of the last decades in reading and mathematics can largely be attributed to the use of such practices, assessments to monitor student progress, and data-based decision making to focus instruction on student needs. Keeping up with research will allow for continual improvement in educational practice.

As noted in the opening paragraphs of this chapter, there are many innovations that have been developed that are not the focus of the chapter. Some of these are certainly worth watching—those involving technology are among the most promising, but those are also among the developments that have not been extensively tested. For example, whether widespread use of smartphones, tablets, Ultrabooks, or other computers will improve learning is still to be determined. There is a need to teach students about the uses of technology regardless of its ultimate effects on achievement simply because the world that students will enter is increasingly filled with technology. Similar concerns about multimedia texts, electronic textbooks, and other digital media have to be raised. Educational policymakers and practitioners will have to be more vigilant about developers and will have to keep current on a wider range of issues.

Finally, there will never be a substitute for principled evaluations of any innovations (or conventional materials) that are adopted. This is a corollary to the application of research to practices but is a special case. If adopted materials do not provide appropriate improvements in learning for students they *must* be changed or discarded. The only way to do this is to have local evaluations of programs to determine whether innovations promoted by popularity are truly effective in local contexts. Such a procedure is entirely consistent with the innovation of using research-based practices. If consistently implemented, it will improve practice and force producers of materials to raise the currency and quality of their products.

## References

Artley, S. (1944.) A study of certain relationships existing between general reading comprehension and reading comprehension in a specific subject matter area. *Journal of Educational Research, 37,* 464–473.

Bernhardt, E. B. (1999). Socio-historical perspectives on language teaching in modern America. In H. Byrnes (Ed.), *Perspectives on research and scholarship in second language learning* (pp. 39–57). New York, NY: Modern Language Association.

Bernhardt, E. B. (2011). *Understanding advanced second-language reading.* New York, NY: Routledge.

Bernhardt, E., & Kamil, M. L. (1995). Interpreting relationships between L1 and L2 reading: Consolidating the linguistic threshold and the linguistic interdependence hypotheses. *Applied Linguistics, 16,* 15–34.

Common Core State Standards Initiative. (2012). *Common Core State Standards*. Retrieved from http://www.corestandards.org/about-the-standards

Dickinson, D. K., McCabe, A., Anastasopoulos, L., Peisner-Feinberg, E. S., & Poe, M. D. (2003). The comprehensive language approach to early literacy: The interrelationships among vocabulary, phonological sensitivity, and print knowledge among preschool-aged children. *Journal of Educational Psychology, 95*(3), 465–481.

Doughty, C., & Long, M. (Eds.). (2004). *The handbook of second language acquisition*. Malden, MA: Blackwell.

Dressler, C., & Kamil, M. L. (2006). First- and second-language literacy. In D. August & T. Shanahan (Eds.), *Developing literacy in second-language learners: Report of the National Literacy Panel on language-minority children and youth* (pp. 197–238). Mahwah, NJ: Erlbaum.

Genesee, F., Geva, E., Dressler, C., & Kamil, M. L. (2008). Cross-linguistic relationships in second-language learners. In D. August & T. Shanahan (Eds.), *Developing reading and writing in second-language learners: Lessons from the Report of the National Literacy Panel on Language-Minority Children and Youth* (pp. 153–183). New York, NY: Routledge.

Gersten, R., Baker, S. K., Shanahan, T., Linan-Thompson, S., Collins, P., & Scarcella, R. (2007). *Effective literacy and English language instruction for English learners in the elementary grades: A practice guide* (NCEE 2007-4011). Washington, DC: National Center for Education Evaluation and Regional Assistance, Institute of Education Sciences, U.S. Department of Education. Retrieved from http://ies.ed.gov/ncee/wwc/publications/practiceguides

Graham, S., & Hebert, M. A. (2010). *Writing to read: Evidence for how writing can improve reading. A Carnegie Corporation Time to Act Report*. Washington, DC: Alliance for Excellent Education.

Graham, S., Bollinger, A., Booth Olson, C., D'Aoust, C., MacArthur, C., McCutchen, D., & Olinghouse, N. (2012). *Teaching elementary school students to be effective writers: A practice guide* (NCEE 2012-4058). Washington, DC: National Center for Education Evaluation and Regional Assistance, Institute of Education Sciences, U.S. Department of Education. Retrieved from http://ies.ed.gov/ncee/wwc/pdf/practice_guides/writing_pg_062612.pdf

Graham, S., & Perin, D. (2007). *Writing next: Effective strategies to improve writing of adolescents in middle and high schools* (A report to the Carnegie Corporation of New York). Washington, DC: Alliance for Excellent Education.

Greene, J. (1997). A meta-analysis of the Rossell and Baker review of bilingual education research. *Bilingual Research Journal, 21*(2), 103–122.

Hart, B., & Risley, T. R. (1999). *The social world of children learning to talk*. Baltimore, MD: P. H. Brookes.

Kamil, M. L., Borman, G. D., Dole, J., Kral, C. C., Salinger, T., & Torgesen, J. (2008). *Improving adolescent literacy: Effective classroom and intervention practices: A practice guide* (NCEE #2008-4027). Washington, DC: National Center for Education Evaluation and Regional Assistance, Institute of Education Sciences.

Lonigan, C. J., & Whitehurst, G. J. (1998). Relative efficacy of parent and teacher involvement in a shared-reading intervention for preschool children from low-income backgrounds. *Early Childhood Research Quarterly, 13*(2), 263–290.

National Early Literacy Panel. (2008). *Developing early literacy: Report of the National Early Literacy Panel: A scientific synthesis of early literacy development and implications for intervention*. Washington, DC: National Institute for Literacy. Retrieved from http://lincs.ed.gov/publications/pdf/NELPReport09.pdf

National Institute of Child Health and Human Development. (2000). *Report of the National Reading Panel: Teaching children to read: An evidence-based assessment of the scientific research literature on reading and its implications for reading instruction: Reports of the subgroups.* Washington, DC: Author.

Neuman, S. B., & Kamil, M. L. (Eds.). (2010). *Preparing teachers for the early childhood classroom: Proven models and key principles.* Baltimore, MD: P. H. Brookes.

Rossell, C. H., & Baker, K. (1996). The educational effectiveness of bilingual education. *Research in the Teaching of English, 30*(1), 7–74.

Shanahan, T., Callison, K., Carriere, C., Duke, N. K., Pearson, P. D., Schatschneider, C., & Torgesen, J. (2010). *Improving reading comprehension in kindergarten through 3rd grade: A practice guide* (NCEE 2010-4038). Washington, DC: National Center for Education Evaluation and Regional Assistance, Institute of Education Sciences, U.S. Department of Education. Retrieved from whatworks.ed.gov/publications/practiceguides

Short, D., & Fitzsimmons, S. (2007). *Double the work: Challenges and solutions to acquiring language and academic literacy for adolescent English language learners* (A report to Carnegie Corporation of New York). Washington, DC: Alliance for Excellent Education. Retrieved from http://www.all4ed.org/files/DoubleWork.pdf

Sticht, T., Beck, L., Hauke, R., Kleiman, G., & James, J. (1974). *Auding and reading: A developmental model.* Alexandria, VA: Human Resources Research Organization.

Sticht, T. G., & James, J. H. (1984). Listening and reading. In P. D. Pearson, R. Barr, M. L. Kamil, & P. Mosenthal (Eds.), *Handbook of reading research* (Vol. I, pp. 293–317). White Plains, NY: Longman.

Teemant, A., Bernhardt, E., Rodrîguez-Muñoz, M., & Aiello, M. (2000). The insights of dialogue: Teacher collaboration benefits second language learners. *The Middle School Journal, 32*(2), 30–38.

What Works Clearinghouse. (2007). *Dialogic reading.* Retrieved from http://ies.ed.gov/ncee/wwc/pdf/intervention_reports/WWC_Dialogic_Reading_020807.pdf

Weir, R. H. (1962). *Language in the crib.* The Hague: Mouton.

WIDA. (2012). *The English language development standards, kindergarten–Grade 12.* Madison, WI: Board of Regents of the University of Wisconsin System. Retrieved from http://www.wida.us/standards/eld.aspx

# Specialized Innovations for Students With Disabilities
*Joseph R. Boyle*

In the United States, a number of educational reforms have occurred over the past several years. Among these is the standards-based reform. The standards-based reform is comprised of three main components: higher content standards, assessments to determine whether students have met the standards, and accountability criteria for both students and schools (Nolet & McLaughlin, 2005). For students with disabilities—particularly high-incidence disabilities (e.g., learning disabilities, emotional/behavioral disorders, high-functioning autism, ADHD, and mild intellectual disabilities)—these reforms have changed the way that they are taught and assessed in the general education curriculum.

First, higher standards are now the norm and are often tied to teachers' daily lesson plans in most states. In fact, 45 states have adopted the Common Core State Standards (CCSS), and efforts are underway to develop a national standards-based test to assess whether students have met common core components (Haager & Vaughn, 2013). Second, states have developed assessments to determine if students have met their own state's standards. In many cases, these are aligned with or are the same as the CCSS. Under certain circumstances, some students with disabilities may opt out of such tests (e.g., students who are unable to participate in an assessment with reasonable accommodations); however, for most students with high-incidence disabilities, participation in such testing is required (McLaughlin & Thurlow, 2003). Third, schools are now accountable for their students' meeting the set standards on state tests. Currently, 26 states have exit exams that students must pass to move on to the next course, grade level, or to graduate from high school (Center on Education Policy, 2012; Deshler, Schumaker, Bui, & Vernon, 2006). Finally, changes in the Individuals with Disabilities Education Act (IDEA) in 1997, and subsequently in 2004, now require schools to provide students with disabilities greater access to the general education curriculum. It is believed that *meaningful access* to the general education curriculum will allow these students to learn core content and, in the process, prepare them to pass state tests (Deshler, Schumaker, Bui, & Vernon, 2006).

## Research Synthesis

As more states and schools implement standards with assessments that are required for students to advance, teachers are being presented with the new challenge of teaching students with more diverse disabilities in their classes. For many teachers this means changing how content is presented, how students are engaged with the content, and how students are assessed on the content (Nolet & McLaughlin, 2005). Consequently, classroom innovations, either technological or methodological, are now becoming more prominent in assisting students with disabilities to learn and teachers to teach in inclusive or general education classes. While many of the technological innovations (e.g., word prediction and text-to-speech software) were originally designed to assist persons with disabilities (Kurzweil, 1999; Swiffin, Arnott, Pickering, & Newell, 1987), today, these innovations have been adopted for use by the general population and are incorporated into the tools (e.g., cell phones, computers) that we use every day.

> *Special education innovations should improve on current instructional practice. An ideal special education innovation would allow a student with a disability to compete on the same level as peers without disabilities.*

Special education innovations should improve on current instructional practice. An ideal special education innovation would allow a student with a disability to compete on the same level as peers without disabilities. In other words, innovations should not only increase achievement or improve behavior for students with disabilities, but effect a positive change large enough so that students with disabilities who use the innovation can achieve at the same level as peers (without disabilities) who are using established best practices. *Technological innovations* mentioned in this chapter are typically one of three types: (a) those that represent advances in technology, such as smartpens and tablet applications (i.e., "apps"); (b) those that apply traditional technology in new and innovative ways, such as content acquisition podcasts (CAPs); and (c) those traditional teaching methodologies that now incorporate components of technology, such as repeated readings that use text-to-speech technology. On the other hand, *methodological innovations* typically are of two types: (a) those strategies or procedures that try to mediate the learning process so that students can now efficiently learn the content (e.g., strategic note-taking, concrete-representational-abstract teaching sequence), and (b) those that try to teach skills and problem-solving procedures in new and innovative ways (e.g., STAR, LAP strategies, see below). Today, many methodological and technological innovations in education can be applied to different content areas and to students of different ages. For the purpose of this chapter, two broad areas—literacy, and mathematics and science—will be presented, as well as examples of special education innovations in these areas.

## Literacy Innovations in Special Education

In reading, students with disabilities have well-documented difficulties, including reading at appropriate rates when compared to peers without disabilities (Jenkins, Fuchs, van den Broek, Espin, & Deno, 2003), learning sight words and vocabulary (Jenkins et al., 2003; Wolf & Bowers, 1999), making inferences (Cain & Oakhill, 1999), and comprehending information read from text (Jenkins et al., 2003; Wagner et al., 1997). In writing, students with disabilities have problems that range from lower order mechanical problems to higher order strategic problems (Wong, 1997). Specifically, these problems include low levels of productivity; weak mechanical skills; and difficulty in planning, generating, organizing, revising, and editing (Graham, Harris, MacArthur, & Schwartz, 1991; Lewis, Graves, Ashton, & Kieley, 1998; Mayes, Calhoun, & Lane, 2005). To address these problems among students with disabilities, researchers have developed a number of literacy innovations.

One innovation in literacy instruction is methodological but also incorporates technology: a repeated readings intervention developed to improve reading fluency and comprehension.[1] Although the repeated reading intervention has been used in schools for some time, this recent twist on it integrates Kurzweil 3000 software into the repeated reading process. In one study, Coleman and Heller (2010) used repeated reading with computer modeling among students with disabilities. In this intervention, the student read the passage aloud for the first, third, and fifth time. In the second and fourth readings, the computer, via the Kurzweil software, read the passage as the student read along silently with the passage on the computer screen. In those instances when the student read the passage aloud, he or she was provided with a correction on any errors made while reading. In the first and fifth reading, the student was also asked comprehension questions. The advantage of incorporating software into the intervention was that each word was highlighted as it was read aloud by the computer (i.e., computer modeling). According to the researchers, all students who used the repeated readings procedure with computer modeling were able to increase reading fluency, accuracy, and comprehension from first to fifth readings. In addition, most of the students demonstrated slight increases in reading fluency on novel passages.

---

[1] See Chard, Vaughn, & Tyler, 2002 and Therrien, 2004 for in-depth discussions of the effectiveness of repeated readings.

Another literacy innovation, strictly methodological, teaches an inference strategy, INFER, to students with disabilities to improve their reading comprehension (Fritschmann, Deshler, & Schumaker, 2007). This innovation goes beyond seeking a mere literal comprehension and helps students mediate text so that they can achieve the more difficult inferential comprehension. This inference strategy employs a first-letter mnemonic device, an acronym, which prompts students to respond to a variety of inference questions. Using the acronym "INFER" as the mnemonic device keyed to a five-step process, students perform five actions while reading a passage. In the first step, *I—Interact*, students *interact with a text* and the questions by previewing the passage and reading the comprehension questions at the end of the passage. Next, they categorize the questions into factual and inferential questions and further categorize the inferential questions into four types: purpose, main idea/summarization, prediction, and clarification questions. In the second step, *N—Note*, students *note what they know* to activate any background knowledge relating to the information, underline key words in the questions, as well as place code letters next to each question based upon the four types. Next, in the third step, *F—Find*, students *find the clues* by reading the passage and underlining clues that are related to key words in the questions and remembering the answers. Next, for *E—Explore,* students *explore more details* by looking for additional information to support their answers. Finally, in step five, *R—Return*, students *return to the question* to make sure that they have answered it. When the INFER strategy was taught to ninth-grade students with disabilities, students improved their comprehension from 32% during the baseline phase to 77% during the instructional phase.

A third innovation in literacy instruction is the use of "quick writes" to improve writing skills of students with disabilities (Mason, Kubina, & Hoover, 2011; Mason, Kubina, & Taft, 2009). Quick writes are 10-minute writing responses to an open-ended question (e.g., Should students your age be given a laptop computer for school? Explain why or why not. Should students your age have cell phones? Explain why or why not.). These writing activities can be used to support content learning by assigning a brief writing activity to students in a nonthreatening and informal manner (e.g., Should a species like the mountain lion, that was originally found in Pennsylvania, be reintroduced back into Pennsylvania?). Quick writes are meant to encourage free expression; therefore, writing mechanics are not taken into account. They teach effective writing skills with different genres such as narrative, persuasive, and informative writing. Quick writes incorporate two learning strategies: POW and TREE. These strategies help students with both prewriting tasks and the actual writing. Using the acronym POW (i.e., pick my ideas, organize my notes, write and say more) facilitates students' planning out their ideas by getting them down on paper and elaborating on them prior to writing. Using the acronym TREE (i.e., topic sentence; reasons, three or more; examine; ending) provides students the ability to transform their ideas into an essay. Results from studies that taught students with disabilities to use quick writes have demonstrated that students can improve in the number of parts to their writing, the number of words written, and the quality of their written essays (Mason et al., 2011; Mason et al., 2009).

Another innovation for improving the writing skills of students with disabilities is the use of word prediction software (see Peterson-Karlan, 2011, for a full review of technology to support writing for students with disabilities). Word prediction software works by offering the user a list of word choices, appearing after the first letter of the word is typed. Most programs also contain a read-back function (via text-to-speech software) for students to check spelling and grammar (Grant, 2009). Recent studies (Evmenova, Graff, Jerome, & Behrmann, 2010; Handley-More, Deitz, Billingsley, & Coggins, 2003; Mirenda, Turoldo, & McAvoy, 2006) that examined the effectiveness of word prediction software for improving the writing skills of students with writing disabilities and of students with physical disabilities have found positive effects on performance. Handley-More et al. (2003) found that when the program *Co-Writer* was used by students with learning disabilities, students showed improvements in legibility and spelling. Likewise, when Mirenda et al. (2006) had 24 students with physical disabilities use word processing with *Co-Writer*, students exhibited significant differences using word processing with word prediction software than when using handwriting skills. These differences were found among legible words, correctly spelled words, percentage of correct word sequences, and average total length of correct word sequences in essays. Finally, Evmenova et al. (2010) compared the effects of three word prediction software programs (*WordQ*, *Co-Writer*, and *WriteAssist*) against word processing alone (i.e., baseline condition). In this study, the researchers found that, regardless of the word prediction software, students with mild disabilities improved written spelling accuracy. When using any one of the three programs, students also increased the total number of words produced and the rate at which they composed, though increases varied according to the program.

## Math and Science Innovations in Special Education

In mathematics education, students with disabilities have difficulties in a number of areas that include memory problems, such as retrieving math facts (Garnett & Fleischner, 1983), remembering and using multiple steps to solve problems (Bley & Thornton, 1995; Bryant, Bryant, & Hammill, 1990), comprehending math vocabulary, understanding and solving math word problems, using procedural strategies and rules, and understanding math concepts (Maccini, Strickland, Gagnon, & Malmgren, 2008). In science education, students with disabilities have difficulty recording notes during lectures and discussions (Boyle, 2010a), understanding and using reasoning skills on categorical reasoning tasks (Scott & Greenfield, 1991, 1992), and effectively using problem-solving skills on science tasks, particularly inquiry-based science activities (Dalton, Morocco, Tivnan, & Mead, 1997).[2] To address these issues and help students learn more efficiently in these areas, researchers have developed several innovations in mathematics and science instruction.

To teach abstract mathematics concepts to students with disabilities, researchers have advocated the use of the concrete-representational-abstract (CRA) teaching sequence. Even though CRA was first used in 1988 (Peterson, Mercer, & O'Shea, 1988), it is only now becoming the preferred method to teach mathematical problem solving to this population. The CRA sequence helps students gain a conceptual understanding of many different subdomains in math such as addition, subtraction, multiplication, division (Flores, 2010; Miller & Kaffar, 2011; Miller, Stringfellow, Kaffar, Ferreira, & Mancl, 2011; Morin & Miller, 1998), integers (Maccini & Hughes, 2000; Maccini & Ruhl, 2000), and solving equations (Witzel, Mercer, & Miller, 2003). Instruction using CRA begins with the use of manipulatives (i.e., concrete), advances to the use of pictures or tallies (i.e., representational), and eventually moves to solving problems using only numbers (i.e., abstract).[3] Typically, students receive a few lessons at each stage. For example, Miller and Kaffar (2011) taught students with and without disabilities to regroup in addition over five concrete lessons, three representational lessons, and eight abstract-level lessons. These lessons used explicit instruction, teacher modeling and demonstrations, guided practice with supports, and independent practice. Results from several studies indicate that CRA instruction was more effective than traditional instruction. For example, Miller and Kaffar (2011) found that students who were instructed using the CRA sequence performed better than students in a comparison group in terms of accuracy of computational regrouping and fluency of computational regrouping (i.e., number of problems correctly solved per minute; Miller & Kaffar, 2011). Likewise, Flores (2010) used CRA among students with math difficulties and found increases in students' scores on subtraction with regrouping from baseline to instructional phases.

Another methodological innovation is strategy instruction in math. The use of first letter mnemonic strategies (e.g., LAP, STAR) is changing the way teachers teach math to students with disabilities, particularly with more complex mathematical content, such as fractions and word problems. For example, one study taught students with learning disabilities to solve problems involving the addition and subtraction of fractions (Test & Ellis, 2005). The LAP fraction strategy incorporates three mnemonically keyed steps: *L—Look* at the sign and denominator, *A—Ask* yourself the question, and *P—Pick* your fraction type. During the L step, students *look* at the addition or subtraction sign in their problem and *ask*

---

[2] For more detailed information about the mathematical and science problems among students with disabilities, see the following reviews: Dalton, Morocco, Tivnan, & Mead, 1997; Jordan & Hanich, 2003; Swanson & Jerman, 2006.
[3] See Flores, 2010, for a detailed explanation of CRA that includes solved examples.

themselves, "Will the smallest denominator divide into the largest denominator an even number of times?" Students then *pick* one of three fraction types and follow the procedures for solving that particular fraction. Once students were able to recite the strategy steps at 100% mastery, they moved to a practice session in which they practiced identifying and dividing the smallest denominator into the largest denominator. Next, students practiced the LAP steps to solve different fraction types. Finally, every 10 days over a 6-week period, students were given the LAP fractions strategy test and the LAP fractions test. During instruction, the researcher modeled problems while thinking aloud, provided guided practice, and had students solve problems independently. Results from this study found that students could apply the LAP strategy to successfully solve addition and subtraction problems involving fractions.

A second strategy instruction, the STAR strategy, was incorporated into CRA instruction to teach students with disabilities to correctly solve algebraic word problems (Maccini & Hughes, 2000; Maccini & Ruhl, 2000). The steps for the strategy are as follows: *S—Search* the word problem; *T—Translate* the problem; *A—Answer* the problem; and *R—Review* the solution. In their first study, Maccini and Ruhl (2000) taught eighth-grade students with disabilities to use the STAR strategy combined with CRA. Using the STAR strategy, students were taught to solve problems over three phases: concrete, semiconcrete, and abstract. Across all three phases, students made substantial average gains in their accuracy of solving the problems: The average baseline accuracy rate was 35%, and the rate increased to 85% in the concrete phase, dipped to 78% in the semiconcrete phase, and increased to 89% in the abstract phase. For the most part, scores were maintained during near transfer, far transfer, and maintenance phases as well. Another study (Maccini & Hughes, 2000) that used the same training and similar procedures again resulted in increases in the correct solution and answer.

Finally, in a third study that combined CRA and the math instruction strategy FAST DRAW, Morin and Miller (1998) taught students with disabilities to solve multiplication problems. In this effort, three lessons were taught at the concrete level, three at the representational (i.e., semiconcrete) level, one lesson on the use of the DRAW strategy, and three lessons at the abstract level. The DRAW strategy (mnemonically, *D—Discover* the sign; *R—Read* the problem; *A—Answer*, or draw and check; and *W—Write* the answer) was first taught to students, then the FAST strategy, again through lessons at the concrete, representational, and abstract levels. The steps identified by the FAST acronym are *F—Find* what you are solving for; *A—Ask* yourself, "What are the parts of the problem?"; *S—Set* up the numbers; and, *T—Tie* down the sign. The FAST DRAW steps were taught to students who were solving traditional paragraph word problems, both with and without extraneous information in the problem. The results from this study found that of the 63 lessons taught, only four times did students' problem solving of multiplication problems drop below 80%. Even when used with word problems involving multiplication, students with disabilities were able to correctly solve these types of problems.

A methodological innovation for helping students learn science content is the strategic note-taking (SN) intervention (Boyle, 2010b, 2013; Boyle & Weishaar, 2001; Lee, Lan, Hamman, & Hendricks, 2008). This intervention is comprised of both the mnemonic CUES strategy and SN paper. This strategy was developed to assist students in retaining information during science lectures by incorporating steps that help them focus attention on teacher cues and science vocabulary in the lecture, as well as providing steps—such as clustering similar lecture ideas and categorizing summarized lecture points—to help them organize lecture content. In the strategy, each step prompts the student to perform an action using lecture information and the SN paper. In the first step, the *C—Cluster* step, students aggregate lecture information into manageable units of three to six related ideas and record the chunked ideas on the SN paper. The *U—Use* step prompts students to pay attention and listen for teacher cues (i.e., number cues and importance cues) during the lecture and, when they hear these cues, to record the lecture points that are associated with them. In the next step, *E—Enter*, students listen for vocabulary words in the lecture and record them in the appropriate area on the SN paper. In the *S—Summarize* step, students write a word or words that would categorize the three to six lecture points they have already listed (i.e., clustered together) on the SN paper.

The SN paper was developed based on Mayer's select-organize-integrate (SOI) model of learning (Mayer, 1996), as well as other research on generative note-taking (Peper & Mayer, 1986), and designed specifically for science lectures. At the top of the SN paper, students would quickly identify the lecture topic and relate the topic to their own background knowledge of it. In the next portion of the SN paper, students clustered together three to six main lecture points with details, as they were being discussed in the lecture. Next, students summarized (or categorized) clustered ideas. If there were any new science vocabulary words, students would also list these in the appropriate section of the SN paper, under "New Vocabulary or Terms." The steps of naming three to six main points, summarizing immediately after naming lecture points, and listing new vocabulary were repeated on additional pages until the lecture ended. The last page directed students to write five main points from the lecture with descriptions of each.[4]

In the studies of the SN strategy, students participated in two training sessions. During the first 50-minute session, the investigator followed a scripted lesson and trained students how to use the SN strategy with the SN paper. Throughout the training, the investigator provided a brief description of SN,

---

[4] For copies of the actual SN paper see the following website: https://sites.temple.edu/snotetaking

modeled the technique, and guided students through practice portions of a videotaped lecture. During the second session, students used the same videotape, but new SN paper. Unlike the first session, during which the lecturer periodically paused for student feedback, the second session played the videotaped lecture in its entirety without interruption so that students could become acclimated to a typically paced lecture. Results from the Boyle (2013) investigation best exemplify the effectiveness of SN for middle school students with and without disabilities. Boyle reported that both students with and without disabilities who used the intervention scored better on measures of the cued lecture points recorded (e.g., emphasis and organization cued lecture points), total lecture points recorded, number of science vocabulary recorded by students, and total words in notes. In addition, students with learning disabilities in the SN group scored as well as or better than students without disabilities in the control group. Results from other studies (Boyle, 2010b; Boyle & Weishaar, 2001) also demonstrate that students with disabilities who were taught SN outperformed peers with disabilities who used traditional note-taking to record notes during lectures.

## Promising Technologies

One innovative technology, called content acquisition podcasts (CAPs), provides vocabulary instruction to high school students with and without disabilities (Kennedy, 2011; Kennedy & Wexler, 2013). CAPs use digitized or multimedia content to teach science and social studies vocabulary while incorporating research-based methodologies such as morphemic analysis, context analysis (Baumann et al., 2002; Ebbers & Denton, 2008; Nagy, 2007), and keyword mnemonic instruction (Mastropieri, Scruggs, & Levin, 1987).[5] CAPs are produced by creating slides that display the vocabulary word; its pronunciation, definition, and morphemes; keyword; and its synonyms and antonyms. These slides are then synchronized with narration explaining the different components of the slide. Once created, the file is saved as a movie and imported into a moviemaking or video program on a computer. Each CAP is typically 3 to 5 minutes in length. Students then play the CAP and learn the vocabulary word. Kennedy (2011) reported that for students with disabilities, CAPs that integrated morphemic and contextual analysis, along with the keyword mnemonic method, were more effective than CAPs that contained only the word, definition, and pictures. Students who used CAPs improved their performance from pretests to posttests on both an open-ended measure (i.e., students write the definition, a synonym, an antonym, and any additional information they might know about vocabulary) and a multiple-choice measure (i.e., given the stem for each word, students choose the appropriate definition of the word, given the answer and distractors).

---

[5] Please see Brigham, Scruggs, & Mastropieri, 2011, for a detailed explanation of how the keyword method is used to support the learning of science vocabulary.

Another promising technological innovation that helps students compensate for poor note-taking skills is the *smartpen* (Hannon, 2008; Stachowiak, 2010). A smartpen is an electric pen that contains a micro-camera that records information when students write lecture information on special dot paper. At the same time, the pen simultaneously records the audio portion of the lecture. The dot paper contains microdots that tell the location of the pen on the paper through the pen's micro-camera. The pen's camera takes 72 snapshots per second, sufficient to capture anything written on the paper. Each picture is decoded by software in the smartpen to provide an (x, y) coordinate pair, telling the smartpen exactly where the pen tip is on any given page and synchronizing these coordinate pairs with the audio recording. For example, if a student is only able to record a partial lecture point (e.g., *plasma*) on the dot paper, after the lecture ends, the student taps the written word *plasma* and that particular audio portion of the lecture will be played (e.g., *Plasma is the fourth state of matter. It is an ionized gas.*), enabling the student to amend his or her lecture notes by adding to or correcting information. Of course, any training should involve the teacher modeling how to use the smartpen, followed by guided practice to ensure students' fluent use prior to independent practice.

> *As students with disabilities enroll in larger numbers in challenging and advanced courses and are required to pass state tests in order to graduate from high school, merely gaining access to the general education curriculum is no longer sufficient.*

Even though only a few studies of this innovation have been conducted to date, mostly exploratory in nature, the smartpen has been recommended for use with students with disabilities (Van Schaack, 2009).

One final technological innovation that should be mentioned is the use of handheld tablets (e.g., iPads, iPods) in special education. Over the past several years, iPad and iPod applications (apps) have become increasingly popular for use in special education classrooms to assist students in monitoring their behaviors/social skills (Blood, Johnson, Ridenour, Simmons, & Crouch, 2011) and their academic performance (Haydon, Hawkins, Denune, Kimener, McCoy, & Basham, 2012; Kagohara, 2011; Nordness, Haverkost, & Volberding, 2011). For example, when three second-grade students with disabilities used a math application called Math Magic on iPads 3 days per week (10 minutes per session) over 4 to 15 weeks, students improved over baseline scores on two-digit subtraction problems and improved scores by an average 17% on a standardized district test (Nordness et al., 2011). In another study (Haydon et al., 2012), high school students with emotional disturbance were taught to use iPad apps on targeted math skills (e.g., coin math, fractions, patterns, and operations); they were able to improve on the number of correctly solved math problems versus traditional worksheet sessions, and students exhibited higher rates of engagement.

## Summary

Recent articles in the field of special education reflect the challenges in trying to help students access the general education curriculum to address Common Core State Standards. As students with disabilities enroll in larger numbers in challenging and advanced courses and are required to pass state tests in order to graduate from high school (Deshler, Schumaker, Bui, & Vernon, 2006), merely gaining access to the general education curriculum is no longer sufficient (Lynch & Taymans, 2004). In fact, students with disabilities need to be *active participants* in the general education curriculum in order to ensure that they progress and are prepared to pass state tests (DeSimone & Parmar, 2006). Many have argued that *genuine access* to the general education curriculum can only come about through new innovations in teaching and proper class supports that focus on what is taught and how the curriculum is delivered (Soukup, Wehmeyer, Bashinski, & Bovaird, 2007).

## Action Principles for SEAs, LEAs, and Schools

The action principles are meant to serve as suggestions and recommendations for agencies seeking to encourage the use of innovations in public schools, to show how districts can support teachers who want to learn about or who use innovation in their classrooms, and to suggest what teachers can do to increase the likelihood that innovation will be successful in the classroom.

### State Education Agency (SEA)

a. Develop a state website solely dedicated to innovations in special education. The first step might be for SEAs to develop a website on innovations in special education. This website should be separate from the state education website. Because state websites are so large, they are tedious to maneuver through and find the information that a person is seeking. A dedicated innovations website could contain examples of how innovations are used in schools throughout the state and the country. Examples might include video clips of teachers using technological or methodological innovations in the classroom with students. Teachers in the videos could point out the advantages of the innovation, identify potential problems in using it in the classroom, and offer tips for teachers about it. The website could also contain links to journal articles or websites on each innovation, as well as to upcoming training sessions on the innovations.

b. Develop a state conference on innovations in special education. SEAs could sponsor a state conference on innovations in special education. These conferences could provide stipends to teachers to help defray the cost for their attendance. The conference should include a mix of informational sessions about different innovations and "hands on" workshops in which teachers can learn in depth about an innovation and create materials related to the session, materials which they could then use, in turnkey fashion, in their classrooms. The conference could feature national speakers who developed an innovation, as well as federal grant awardees who could discuss findings from projects that used, developed, and evaluated innovations. These awardees could discuss the findings from their research and offer suggestions for using their innovation in different environments (e.g., urban, rural, and suburban) and with different populations of students (i.e., How did general education students respond to the innovation? How did students with autism spectrum disorders respond to the innovation? Students with learning disabilities?).

c. Reward schools for using innovations to teach students with disabilities. Each SEA should try to identify and recognize effective schools within its borders that use innovations. These schools could serve as models, and their personnel could serve as resources for teachers throughout the state. Too often, school personnel within a state, and in some cases within each of its districts, are unaware of colleagues using effective teaching innovations. Often teachers must go it alone to try to teach students with disabilities when, in fact, other teachers in the state have already developed successful innovations for their classrooms. Schools' efforts should be recognized and highlighted on SEA websites for others to learn about and copy. Schools could also offer small monetary awards for teachers who use or develop innovations.

d. Encourage state laboratory schools or university–school partnerships. SEAs could help bring together researchers from universities and school personnel who are looking for innovations. Often, faculty are looking to assess and research a new innovation and, at the same time, schools are in need of an innovation. These schools could serve as laboratory/experimental schools and may well be sites that are using some of the latest innovations in special education. In 2012, the Institute of Education Sciences, an arm of the U.S. Department of Education, offered a grant competition titled Researcher–Practitioner Partnerships in Education Research. This competition solicited proposals from university researchers who would evaluate a school's data and help identify potential problem areas that, in subsequent years, could be addressed through innovations or current best practices. The hope is that these 2-year funded partnerships will be the beginning of long-term collaborations. Initially, funds would be used to help schools identify weak areas and, in subsequent funding cycles, develop interventions and assess the effectiveness of those interventions on student learning and behavior. In many ways, SEAs could take this federal program and use it as a template. State competitions could offer funding that would encourage such partnerships, perhaps in the form of seed money or small grants.

e. Develop materials that show how to integrate innovations into the curriculum. Provided the innovations have been shown to be effective for both students with and without disabilities, the latest innovations should be embedded in the curriculum for teachers to use in their classes. Once an innovation is embedded within the curriculum, the better the chance that teachers will use it on a consistent basis. Lenz and Deshler (2004) have observed from their many years of strategy research that elementary schools are able to seamlessly weave new strategies or innovations into their curriculum; in spite of their general applicability, however, these practices are not often adopted in secondary schools. Further, Lenz and Deshler show that, with proper supports, teachers can use these innovations to help all students learn content.

## Local Education Agencies

a. Allocate resources for technology and professional development. If school districts want teachers to learn new skills/innovations, they can either send teachers out for training or bring the training into schools. Schools should offer travel funds for teachers who will target a new innovation that they want to learn. Teachers can then attend the training or workshop to learn it and report back to the school district how the innovation is being used in their classroom. If schools have inclusive classes, co-teachers can attend workshops and then demonstrate to other teachers how the innovations are used in co-taught classes. Another option for school districts is to provide professional development in schools. In either case, the old model of one-shot professional development has been shown to be ineffective. More efficient training involves locating teachers who have a need to learn an innovation and a desire to use it in their classroom. Districts should target these teachers for professional development and then follow up using turnkey methods, such as having the expert model the innovation in the teacher's class and then letting the teacher use it, receiving feedback from the expert. Experts may have to return a few times to help the novice teacher refine how the innovation is used in that particular classroom.

b. Provide a support network after training. For teachers trained to use innovations, districts should provide them a support network in order to share ideas and solicit advice when they encounter problems. An electronic discussion board or chat board can serve as a virtual meeting place for discussions about better ways to teach students with disabilities. The site might also contain other resources like video clips that demonstrate effective teaching using innovations or web articles about innovations.

c. Develop district-wide innovation coaches. Mentors could teach part-time and mentor teachers part-time. They should also be tasked with staying abreast of and being trained in the latest educational innovations for teaching students with disabilities. With such duties, they could serve as professional developers in the district, introducing innovations to teachers. When serving as coaches, they could assess the fidelity of teachers' implementation of innovations and assist in assessing the effectiveness of innovations on student learning.
d. Districts should assess their teachers' and students' attitudes about new innovations. If teachers don't enjoy using an innovation or don't see its value, they are unlikely to use it consistently in the classroom. Therefore, districts need to assess attitudes through customer surveys that ask teachers about an innovation's usefulness, what they like and dislike about it, and what changes could improve its use in the classroom. Students are also consumers of teachers' methods, strategies, and technologies, so they too should provide input about classroom innovations. Further, students should be asked about or interviewed on how they feel the innovation has changed the way they think about content or the learning process while using the innovation. Student input can help the district decide whether changes should be made in the way the innovation is taught to teachers or the way teachers implement the innovation.

**Schools**
a. Make innovations work for students with disabilities. As noted earlier in this chapter, teachers need to use explicit instruction, especially when introducing a new instructional method or technology. In explicit instruction, a teacher first models or demonstrates an innovation, followed by guided practice with feedback, and ending with the student using the innovation independently. Teachers should strive to teach students innovations that allow them to become autonomous and independent learners. So instead of relying on a note-taker, a student with disabilities should learn the skills (e.g., strategic note-taking) necessary for recording his or her own notes. Teachers should express their high expectations of students; mediocrity never advanced civilization.
b. Tie strategy instruction to the teaching of new technology. For technological innovations, it may be more effective to teach students a strategy that helps them use the new technology in authentic classroom settings. For example, the InSPECT strategy (McNaughton, Hughes, & Ofiesh, 1997) was taught to students with learning disabilities to help them successfully use the spell checker in word processing programs. With new technology, such as smartpens and iPads, it may be necessary to teach students a strategy so that they can use the technology properly and effectively. Regardless of

the technique or strategy, explicit instruction is still needed to insure that students learn to use technology effectively.

c. Teachers need to insure that new innovations transfer to the classroom. Once students learn to use the innovations, teachers should make sure that students with disabilities can generalize the innovation to different contexts with different content. This stage of instruction teaches students how to use the innovation in a flexible manner—modifying steps of the strategy when necessary or modifying how technology is used in new situations. This adaptation of an innovation may also necessitate teaching students its use in those classes with more advanced content.

d. Train with fidelity using all training steps. The idea of fidelity in interventions refers not only to teachers following the prescribed implementation procedures for an innovation, but also to how much time (e.g., days, sessions) teachers spend—sometimes referred to as intensity—on specific training steps when training students how to use student strategies (Swanson, Wanzek, Haring, Ciullo, & McCulley, 2012). Intervention fidelity is important because it determines whether an innovation fails or succeeds, especially in special education classrooms where students require explicit step-by-step instruction and scaffolding to master a skill or innovation. Therefore, the more complex an innovation, the more critical it becomes for teachers to follow the prescribed training procedures.

e. Monitor the progress of learning by identifying specific skills to be assessed and use benchmark tests that parallel components of state tests. As with any innovation or intervention, it is important to assess student progress. Progress is typically assessed daily for a newly implemented innovation and then periodically once it is determined that the innovation is working as intended. When measuring an innovation's effectiveness, teachers should focus on its usability (i.e., Can students use it successfully?), students' fluency in using it (i.e., Can students use it quickly without making too many mistakes?), and its effectiveness as measured by outcomes (i.e., For a math innovation, have students increased the number of correct problems solved compared to previous measures?). Finally, since the goal of the kind of academic innovations discussed here should be to increase students' skills to a level comparable to that of nondisabled peers, teachers should consider using a districtwide benchmark measure (i.e., smaller tests whose questions are similar to state tests) to insure that students are on track to do well with district and state measures.

## References

Baumann, J. F., Edwards, E. C., Tereshinki, C. A., Kame'enui, E. J., & Olejnik, S. (2002). Teaching morphemic and contextual analysis to fifth-grade students. *Reading Research Quarterly, 37*(2), 150–176.

Bley, N. S., & Thornton, C. A. (1995). *Teaching mathematics to students with learning disabilities* (3rd ed.). Austin, TX: Pro-Ed.

Blood, E., Johnson, J. W., Ridenour, L., Simmons, K., & Crouch, S. (2011). Using an iPod Touch to teach social and self-management skills to an elementary student with emotional/behavioral disorders. *Education and Treatment of Children, 34*, 299–321.

Boyle, J. R. (2010a). Note-taking skills of middle school students with and without learning disabilities. *Journal of Learning Disabilities, 43*(6), 530–540.

Boyle, J. R. (2010b). Strategic note-taking for middle school students with learning disabilities in science classrooms. *Learning Disability Quarterly, 33*(2), 93–109.

Boyle, J. R. (2013). *Strategic note-taking for inclusive middle school science classrooms. Remedial and Special Education* (RASE). Advance online publication. doi: 10.1177/0741932511410862

Boyle, J. R., & Weishaar, M. (2001). The effects of a strategic note-taking technique on the comprehension and long term recall of lecture information for high school students with LD. *LD Research and Practice, 16*(3), 125–133.

Brigham, F. J., Scruggs, T. E., & Mastropieri, M. A. (2011). Science education and students with learning disabilities. *Learning Disabilities Research & Practice, 26*, 223–232.

Bryant, D. P., Bryant, B. R., & Hammill, D. D. (1990). Characteristic behaviors of students with LD who have teacher-identified math weaknesses. *Journal of Learning Disabilities, 33*, 168–177.

Cain, K., & Oakhill, J. V. (1999). Inference making and its relation to comprehension failure. *Reading and Writing, 11*, 489–503.

Center on Education Policy. (2012). *State high school exit exams: A policy in transition.* Washington, DC: Author.

Chard, D. J., Vaughn, S., & Tyler, B. (2002). A synthesis of research on effective interventions for building reading fluency with elementary students with learning disabilities. *Journal of Learning Disabilities, 35*, 386–406.

Coleman, M. B., & Heller, K. W. (2010). The use of repeated readings with computer modeling to promote reading fluency with students who have physical disabilities. *Journal of Special Education Technology, 25*, 29–41.

Dalton, B., Morocco, C., Tivnan, T., & Mead, P. (1997). Supported inquiry science: Teaching for conceptual change in urban and suburban classrooms. *Journal of Learning Disabilities, 30*, 670–684.

Deshler, D., Schumaker, J., Bui, Y., & Vernon, S. (2006). High schools and adolescents with disabilities: Challenges at every turn. In D. D. Deshler & J. B. Schumaker (Eds.), *Teaching adolescents with disabilities: Accessing the general education curriculum* (pp. 1–34). Thousand Oaks, CA: Corwin Press.

DeSimone, J. R., & Parmar, R. S. (2006). Issues and challenges for middle school mathematics teachers in inclusion classrooms. *School Science and Mathematics, 106*, 338–348.

Ebbers, S. M., & Denton, C. A. (2008). A root awakening: Vocabulary instruction for older students with reading difficulties. *Learning Disabilities Research & Practice, 23*, 90–102.

Evmenova, A., Graff, H., Jerome, M., & Behrmann, M. (2010). Word prediction programs with phonetic spelling support: Performance comparisons and impact on journal writing for students with writing difficulties. *Learning Disabilities Research & Practice, 25*, 170–182. doi: 10.1111/j.1540-5826.2010.00315.x

Flores, M. M. (2010). The effects of strategic instruction and the concrete-representational-abstract sequence on students' subtraction with regrouping. *Remedial and Special Education, 31*, 195–207.

Fritschmann, N. S., Deshler, D. D., & Schumaker, J. B. (2007). The effects of instruction in an inference strategy on the reading comprehension skills of adolescents with disabilities. *Learning Disabilities Quarterly, 30*, 244–264.

Garnett, K., & Fleischner, J. E. (1983). Automatization and basic fact performance of normal and learning disabled children. *Learning Disability Quarterly, 6*, 223–230.

Graham, S., Harris, K., MacArthur, C., & Schwartz, S. (1991). Writing and writing instruction for students with learning disabilities: Review of a research program. *Learning Disability Quarterly, 14*, 89–114.

Grant, K. (2009). System planning for inclusive technology: Applying the "Then What" factor or what to do BEFORE the technology is purchased. *Special Education Technology Practice, 11*, 15–18.

Haager, D., & Vaughn, S. (2013). The Common Core State Standards and students with learning disabilities: Introduction to the special issue. *Learning Disabilities Research & Practice, 28*, 1–4.

Handley-More, D., Deitz, J., Billingsley, F., & Coggins, T. (2003). Facilitating written work using computer word processing and word prediction. *American Journal of Occupational Therapy, 57*(2), 139–151.

Hannon, C. (2008). Paper-based computing. *Educause Quarterly, 4*, 15–16.

Haydon, T., Hawkins, R., Denune, H., Kimener, L., McCoy, D., & Basham, J. (2012). A comparison of iPads and worksheets on math skills of high school students with emotional disturbance. *Behavioral Disorders, 37*, 232–243.

Jenkins, J. R., Fuchs, L. S., van den Brock, P., Espin, C., & Deno, S. L. (2003). Accuracy and fluency in list and context reading of skilled and RD groups: Absolute and relative performance levels. *Learning Disabilities Research and Practice, 18*, 237–245.

Jordan, N. C., & Hanich, L. B. (2003). Characteristics of children with moderate mathematics deficiencies: A longitudinal perspective. *Learning Disabilities Research and Practice, 18*, 213–221.

Kagohara, D. (2011). Three students with developmental disabilities learn to operate an iPod to access age-appropriate entertainment videos. *Journal of Behavioral Education, 20*, 33–43.

Kennedy, M. (2011). *Effects of content acquisition podcasts on vocabulary performance of secondary students with and without learning disabilities* (Doctoral dissertation). Retrieved from UMI Proquest Dissertations and Theses.

Kennedy, M., & Wexler, J. (2013). Helping students succeed within secondary-level STEM content. *Teaching Exceptional Children, 45*, 26–33.

Kurzweil, R. (1999). *The age of spiritual machines*. New York, NY: Penguin Books.

Lee, P., Lan, W., Hamman, D., & Hendricks, B. (2008). The effects of teaching note taking strategies on elementary students' science learning. *Instructional Science, 36*, 191–201. doi:10.1007/s11251-007-9027-4

Lenz, B. K., & Deshler, D. D., (with Kissam, B. R.). (2004). *Teaching content to all: Evidence-based inclusive practices in middle and secondary schools*. Boston, MA: Pearson Education.

Lewis, R., Graves, A., Ashton, T., & Kieley, C. (1998). Word processing tools for students with learning disabilities: A comparison of strategies to increase text entry speed. *Learning Disabilities Research and Practice, 13*, 95–108.

Lynch, S., & Taymans, J. (2004). The challenge of academic diversity and systemic reform. In B. K. Lenz & D. D. Deshler (Eds.), *Teaching content to all* (pp .19-46). Boston, MA: Pearson Education.

Maccini, P., & Hughes, C. A. (2000). Effects of a problem-solving strategy on the introductory algebra performance of secondary students with learning disabilities. *Learning Disabilities Research & Practice, 15*, 10–21.

Maccini, P., & Ruhl, K. L. (2000). Effects of a graduated instructional sequence on the algebraic subtraction of integers by secondary students with learning disabilities. *Education and Treatment of Children, 23*, 465–489.

Maccini, P., Strickland, T., Gagnon, J. C., & Malmgren, K. (2008). Accessing the general education math curriculum for secondary students with high-incidence disabilities. *Focus on Exceptional Children, 40*, 1–32.

Mason, L. H., Kubina, R., & Hoover, T. (2011). Effects of quick writing instruction for high school students with emotional and behavioral disabilities. *Journal of Emotional and Behavioral Disorders*. Advance online publication. doi: 10.1177/1063426611410429.

Mason, L. H., Kubina, R., & Taft, R. (2009). Developing quick writing skills of middle school students with disabilities. *Journal of Special Education, 44*, 205–220.

Mastropieri, M. A., Scruggs, T. E., & Levin, J. R. (1987). Learning-disabled students' memory for expository prose: Mnemonic versus nonmnemonic pictures. *American Educational Research Journal, 24*, 505–519.

Mayer, R. E. (1996). Learning strategies for making sense out of expository text: The SOI model for guiding three cognitive processes in knowledge construction. *Educational Psychology Review, 8*, 357–371.

Mayes S. D., Calhoun, S. L., & Lane, S. E. (2005). Diagnosing children's writing disabilities: Different tests give different results. *Perceptual Motor Skills, 101*, 72–78.

McLaughlin, M. J., & Thurlow, M. (2003). Educational accountability and students with disabilities: Issues and challenges. *Journal of Educational Policy, 17*(4), 431–451.

McNaughton, D., Hughes, C., & Ofiesh, N. (1997). Proofreading for students with learning disabilities: Integrating computer and strategy use. *Learning Disabilities Research & Practice, 12*(1), 16–28.

Miller, S. P., & Kaffar, B. J. (2011). Developing addition with regrouping competence among second-grade students with mathematics difficulties. *Investigations in Mathematics Learning, 4*(1), 25–50.

Miller, S. P., Stringfellow, J. L., Kaffar, B. J., Ferreira, D., & Mancl, D. (2011). Developing computation competence among students who struggle with mathematics. *Teaching Exceptional Children, 44*(2), 38–46.

Mirenda, P., Turoldo, K., & McAvoy, C. (2006). The impact of word prediction software on the written output of students with physical disabilities. *Journal of Special Education Technology, 21*(3), 5–12.

Miller, S. P., & Kaffar, B. J. (2011). Developing addition with regrouping competence among second-grade students with mathematics difficulties. *Investigations in Mathematics Learning, 4*(1), 25–50.

Morin, V. A., & Miller, S. P. (1998). Teaching multiplication to middle school students with mental retardation. *Education and Treatment of Children, 21*, 22–36.

Nagy, W. E. (2007). Metalinguistic awareness and the vocabulary–comprehension connection. In R. K. Wagner, A. E. Muse, & K. R. Tannenbaum (Eds.), *Vocabulary acquisition: Implications for reading comprehension* (pp. 52–77). New York, NY: Guilford.

Nolet, V., & McLaughlin, M. J. (2005). *Accessing the general curriculum, including students with disabilities in standards-based reform* (2nd ed.). Thousands Oaks, CA: Crowin Press.

Nordness, P., Haverkost, A., & Volberding, A. (2011). An examination of hand-held computer-assisted instruction on subtraction skills for second grade students with learning and behavioral disabilities. *Journal of Special Education Technology, 26*, 15–24.

Peper, R. J., & Mayer, R. E. (1986). Generative effects of note-taking during science lectures. *Journal of Educational Psychology, 78,* 34–38.

Peterson, S. K., Mercer, C. D., & O'Shea, L. (1988). Teaching learning disabled students place value using the concrete to abstract sequence. *Learning Disabilities Research, 4,* 52–56.

Peterson-Karlan, G. (2011). Technology to support writing by students with learning and academic disabilities: Recent research trends and findings. *Assistive Technology Outcomes and Benefits, 7,* 39–62.

Scott, M. S., & Greenfield, D. B. (1991). The screening potential of a taxonomic information task for the detection of learning disabled and mildly retarded children. *Journal of Applied Developmental Psychology, 12,* 429–446.

Scott, M. S., & Greenfield, D. B. (1992). A comparison of normally achieving, learning disabled, and mildly retarded students on a taxonomic information task. *Learning Disabilities Research & Practice, 7,* 59–67.

Stachowiak, J. (2010). Universal design for learning in postsecondary institutions. *The Johns Hopkins University New Horizons for Learning, 8.* Retrieved from http://jhepp.library.jhu.edu/ojs/index.php/newhorizons/article/view/68

Soukup, J., Wehmeyer, M., Bashinski, S., & Bovaird, J. (2007). Classroom variables and access to the general curriculum for students with disabilities. *Exceptional Children, 74*(1), 101–120.

Swanson, E., Wanzek. J., Haring, A., Ciullo, S., & McCulley, L. (2012). Intervention fidelity in special and general education research journals. *Journal of Special Education.* Advance Online Publication. doi: 10.1177/0022466911419516

Swanson, H. L., & Jerman, O. (2006). Math disabilities: A selective meta-analysis of the literature. *Review of Educational Research, 76,* 249–274.

Swiffin, A. L., Arnott, J. L., Pickering, J. A., & Newell, A. F. (1987). Adaptive and predictive techniques in a communication prosthesis. *Augmentative and Alternative Communication, 3,* 181–191.

Test, D., & Ellis, M. F. (2005). The effects of LAP fractions on addition and subtraction of fractions with students with mild disabilities. *Education and Treatment of Children, 28,* 11–24.

Therrien, W. J. (2004). Fluency and comprehension gains as a result of repeated reading. *Remedial and Special Education, 25,* 252–261.

Van Schaack, A. (2009). New smartpen and paper to help teach blind college students. *Science Daily.* Retrieved from http://www.sciencedaily.com/releases/2007/12/071203121438.htm

Wagner, R. K., Torgesen, J. K., Rashotte, C. A., Hecht, S. A., Barker, T. A., Burgess, S. R.,…Garon, T. (1997). Changing relations between phonological processing abilities and word-level reading as children develop from beginning to skilled readers: A 5-year longitudinal study. *Developmental Psychology, 33,* 468–479.

Witzel, B. S., Mercer, C. D., & Miller, M. D. (2003). Teaching algebra to students with learning difficulties: An investigation of an explicit instruction model. *Learning Disabilities Research & Practice, 18*(2), 121–131.

Wolf, M., & Bowers, P. G. (1999). The double-deficit hypothesis for the developmental dyslexias. *Journal of Educational Psychology, 91*(3), 415–438.

Wong, B. Y. L. (1997). Research on genre-specific strategies for enhancing writing in adolescents with learning disabilities. *Learning Disability Quarterly, 20,* 140–159.

# Getting Personal: The Promise of Personalized Learning
*Sam Redding*

Personalized learning's basic premise—that instruction should be tailored for each student and that the student should be the prime actor in directing learning—is not new. Four tensions in education, however, are reigniting interest in personalized learning:
   a. The curriculum is under pressure to expand in scope and depth, though the amount of time in school remains stubbornly constant (Kaplan & Chan, 2011).
   b. Teachers struggle, given limited time for training and planning, to use data and individualize instruction to meet the expectation that all students perform proficiently on methodically structured, standards-based assessments (Hassel & Hassel, 2012).
   c. Low achievement and unacceptable dropout rates point to waning student motivation as an underlying cause (Christensen, Horn, & Johnson, 2008).
   d. Familial and societal fragmentation and disconnection jeopardize young people's social and emotional well-being (Jackson, 2008).

Accompanying the impetus to address these problems and the resulting revival of interest in personalized learning is the sense that new technologies may actually make such learning feasible. By reforming schooling's time–pace–place traditions and utilizing new technologies, personalized learning proponents assert that the bulging curriculum could be accommodated, data and instruction efficiently managed, students motivated, and people connected. Figure 1 illustrates the problematic tensions in education, the possible technological solutions, and the application of the technologies in the practice of personalization.

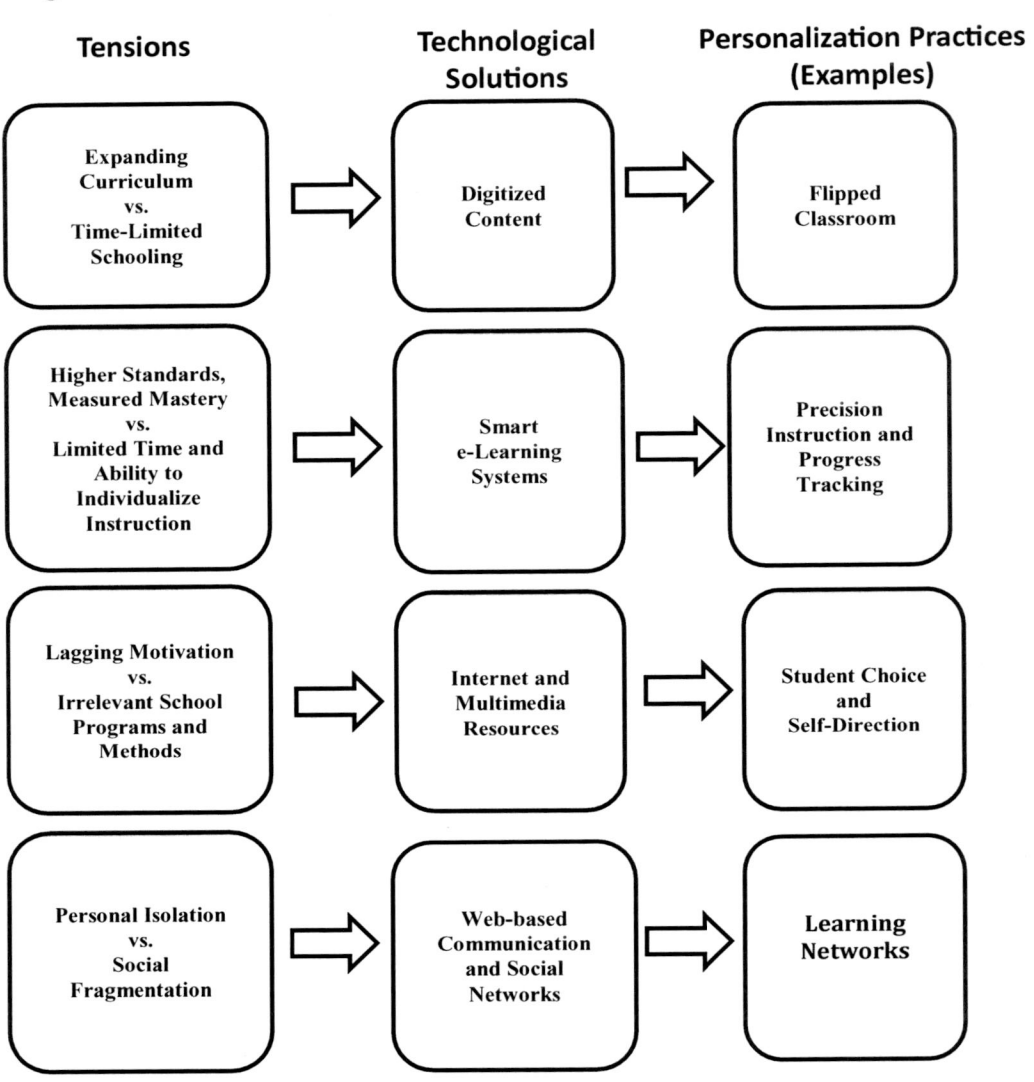

Figure 1. Tensions, Technological Solutions, and Personalization Practices

New technology makes possible ways to teach and learn that were unfathomable only a short time ago. Approaching technology's multitude of possibilities, we are at once hopeful and cautious. Maggie Jackson (2008) is cautious, asking:

> Do we yearn for such voracious virtual connectivity that others become optional and conversation fades into a lost art? For efficiency's sake, do we split focus so finely that we thrust ourselves in a culture of lost threads? Untethered, have we detached from not only the soil but the sensual richness of our physical selves? Smitten with the virtual, split-split, and nomadic, we are corroding the three pillars of our attention: focus (orienting), judgment (executive function), and awareness (alerting). The costs are steep: we begin to lose trust, depth, and connection in our relations and our thought. (p. 215)

Clearly, technology is not and should not be the whole of personalized learning lest it fail as an antidote to the tensions in education. The expanding curriculum may fracture into incomprehensible, digital disarray. Reliance on radical individualization may rob students of common experience and overlook the proven facility of explicit and direct instruction. Excessive student choice may result in no appreciable unity of understanding and wasted time. Social connection mediated by electronic devices may further isolate young people and hamper social and emotional maturation.

To succeed, personalized learning will have to choose its technology judiciously and adhere to sound principles for how students learn. Frederick Hess advises, "Given our scant experience with digital provision, it seems prudent to avoid sweeping national policies or requirements, at least at this stage" (Hess, 2012, pp. 49, 51). The same caution is appropriate for states, districts, and schools for any introduction of technology.

## What, Exactly, Is Personalized Learning?

David Brooks, in his 2011 best seller *The Social Animal*, describes the fictional Ms. Taylor, a high school English teacher whose "goal was to turn her students into autodidacts. She hoped to give her students a taste of the emotional and sensual pleasure discovery brings—the jolt of pleasure you get when you work hard, suffer a bit, and then something clicks" (p. 82). Ms. Taylor sought to press beyond her students' blasé exteriors, discover each one's inner being, and understand what would open his or her mind. She would then think of just the right book for that student at that time.

Ms. Taylor waited to find Harold, a student, alone in the hallway. "She pressed a slim volume into Harold's hand. 'This will lift you to greatness!' she emoted. And in a second she was gone. Harold looked down. It was a used copy of a book called *The Greek Way* by a woman named Edith Hamilton. Harold would remember that moment forever" (p. 83). Ms. Taylor did not stop there. Over the coming weeks, as Harold responded to the book and raised questions that went beyond its scope, Ms. Taylor pointed him to other books and suggested topics for his papers. From Ms. Taylor, Harold learned the discipline of research and the joy of learning. Ms. Taylor took this approach with all of her students, personalizing her instruction.

We can appreciate the principles of personalized learning that Ms. Taylor employed—matching the right content to each student's interests and readiness at just the right moment and extending learning beyond the classroom. You might even say she flipped her classroom, with students reading late into the night and coming to school charged with ideas to discuss. What we might ponder is the extent to which Ms. Taylor's own passion for learning and personal interest in her students contributed to her success as a teacher, apart from the mechanics of paced learning tailored to learning preferences and the interests of the learner.

In other words, can a computer do it better? Or even as well? Perhaps Ms. Taylor, with the aid of technology, strikes the right balance.

Personalized learning is a hot topic these days, raising both hopes and concerns: Is it a fad that will pass or an idea whose time has come? Does personalized learning disregard interpersonal learning? Will personalized learning give us the big jump in student achievement we desperately seek? Does personalized learning mean kids spending more time staring into electronic devices? What, exactly, is personalized learning? Here is how the U.S. Department of Education (USDOE) defines it:

> Personalization refers to instruction that is paced to learning needs [i.e., individualized], tailored to learning preferences [i.e., differentiated], and tailored to the specific interests of different learners. In an environment that is fully personalized, the learning objectives and content as well as the method and pace may all vary. (2010, p. 12)

It is telling that this USDOE definition of personalized learning was put forward in the department's launch of a major technology initiative, a concurrence that illustrates the present-day merger of personalized learning philosophy with technological application. A 2010 symposium on personalized learning sponsored by the Software and Information Industry Association, in collaboration with ASCD (formerly the Association for Supervision and Curriculum Development) and the Council of Chief State School Officers, made the connection between personalization and technology. The symposium's report (Wolf, 2010) states:

> Personalized learning requires not only a shift in the design of schooling, but also a leveraging of modern technologies. Personalization cannot take place at scale without technology. Personalized learning is enabled by smart e-learning systems, which help dynamically track and manage the learning needs of all students, and provide a platform to access myriad engaging learning content, resources, and learning opportunities needed to meet each student's needs everywhere at any time, but which are not all available within the four walls of the traditional classroom. (p. 10)

The symposium advocated as much for the use of technology as for the efficacy of personalized learning, marrying the two to demonstrate technology's power to make personalized learning practical.

The symposium participants identified the top five essential elements of personalized learning as follows:

   a. flexible, anytime/everywhere learning;
   b. a redefined role for teachers and an expanded sense for "teacher";
   c. project-based, authentic learning;
   d. a student-driven learning path; and
   e. mastery/competency-based progression/pace (Wolf, 2010).

This list of essential elements of personalized learning adds specificity to the USDOE's definition as previously cited. The symposium singled out the redefinition of the use of time and the Carnegie Unit as the "single most significant policy enabler for personalized learning....Personalized learning models reverse the traditional model that views time and place (that is, seat-time) as the constant and achievement as the variable. Instead, personalized learning ensures all students gain proficiency independent of time, place, and pace of learning" (Wolf, 2010, p. 7).

## The Ways We Learn

In warping the traditional model for time, pace, and place as suggested by the symposium's identified priorities, personalized learning cannot loosen itself from psychological and behavioral principles of how people learn. In fact, the promise of personalized learning rests heavily on its ability to open our eyes to learning's many paths and choose them wisely. Technology may make this feasible. The following fictional vignettes describe the many ways we learn.

**We learn informally and incidentally.** Long before Sally steps foot into a classroom, she will learn to speak, walk, identify and categorize hundreds of objects, respond to social cues, and act on her environment. She jumps on her daddy's lap, tilts her little head, smiles, and says, "Petey good doggie. Petey come inside and play with me?" Somehow Sally mastered an immeasurable array of psychomotor, cognitive, and affective skills in order to gain her father's assent. This is informal or incidental learning, and Sally will go on learning in this manner the rest of her life.

**We learn through self-directed, intentional study, monitoring our progress and adjusting our strategies.** James is bound and determined to get his driver's license. He pours over the *Rules for the Road*, underlining key passages, dog-earing a couple pages, closing the book, and quizzing himself. No one assigned this learning task to James. His learning is self-directed toward a goal he has set for himself, with strategies he has chosen to employ.

**We learn when our objectives are explicit and we get plenty of practice.** Edna Filbert thinks of herself as an old-school educator. Come hell or high water, no child will leave her second-grade class without solid reading and math skills. "Sure we have fun. Learning is fun. But, by golly, it is the most fun when we know we got it right. My kids know their phonics, and they know their math facts. I drill them in class, and they practice. No such thing as 'drill and kill' in my book. Drilling itself is fun. When I present a flash card and the kids respond in unison with the right answer, I see the smiles on their faces. I like to create verses that include a few new words. We sing the verses together, and the kids get familiar with the words. Then, they spell the words out on their papers, and I quiz them on the meaning. They understand what I want them to learn, and they are happy when they do it." In Mrs. Filbert's class, personal satisfaction is derived from collective pursuit, a sense of accomplishment, and seeing Mrs. Filbert applaud.

**We learn through discovery and acquired relevance.** When surfing the Internet to find pictures of her favorite U.S. presidents, Marie inadvertently lands on a site about the Lincoln automobile. Something catches her eye. It is a picture of a woman holding a sketch of a new car design, and in the background is a silver-colored convertible trailing an electric cord plugged into the wall. Marie clicks on the picture to learn more. A video clip explains the elements of the new car design narrated by a young engineer. Marie downloads a brochure on careers in automotive design and engineering. Marie has discovered a new interest and gained new knowledge unrelated to her original search.

**We are motivated to learn when our teacher connects personally with us.** To most of his teachers, Phillip is an indifferent learner. His math teacher, Miss Alvarez, is not satisfied with that appraisal. "What's planned for your weekend?" Miss Alvarez asks. "Nothing much," Phillip responds. "So what does your Saturday look like?" Miss Alvarez presses. "Helping dad in the store," Phillip replies. "What's the job?" Miss Alvarez inquires. "Pricing and stocking crates of oranges," Phillip offers. "How do you know what price to put on the oranges?" "It depends on how many are spoiled, how many are ripe, and what we think the customers will pay." "Very interesting. So you must have some formulas for making these decisions. Do you sample a few crates to determine the percentage of oranges that are spoiled or ripe?" "Yes, something like that." "And do you calculate what the oranges cost you, including the shipping?" "Of course, we have to make money." "Sounds like you work with a lot of math." "I never thought of it that way." "Well, I think I have an idea for a homework assignment, just for you." Miss Alvarez found a way to make learning personal for Phillip, and Phillip now thinks of Miss Alvarez as different from other teachers—in a good way.

**We learn by example as well as through intentional instruction.** "I don't know where to draw the line between what I teach by example and what I teach more directly," says Dennis McWhorter. "I like to think that I model the social behaviors that I want my students to emulate, but I also teach them specific social skills. I teach learning strategies, and I also 'think out loud' with the class as we ponder a problem and determine together how best to approach it. We can't take for granted that kids will absorb social and emotional learning by osmosis, and we can't assume they develop metacognitive abilities purely through trial and error." Dennis McWhorter models and teaches social and metacognitive skills.

**We learn efficiently when the learning tasks build from our current mastery, stretching us just the right amount.** Bill Bostek's fellow teachers call him "Mr. Fanatic." "They think I am obsessed with data and that I work day and night," Bill explains. "I keep telling them that the data are only part of the story. In fact, data are a small part. The big job is in constantly adapting each student's assignments in response to the data. That is the time-consuming part, but also the part that makes the difference. I have a system for it. Everything I teach is aligned to standards, of course. All the teachers do that. But I am very specific in developing my objectives for what I want the kids to learn. Then I develop several ways for a student to master each objective—multiple learning activities. I embed my assessments in the work, so I can keep making adjustments in what I want each student to do. At least twice a week I make adjustments for each student in each subject. I group and regroup students based on their progress. I pull together a few students for reteaching when I sense they have a common need. Some kids learn quickly, and I feed them more work at a higher level. I don't want them to get bored. Other kids take more time, and I want to be sure they have mastered each objective before moving on. That works for most of them, but for some it seems the school day isn't long enough. I stay after school for what the kids call 'Bostek Hour,' and I tutor them. Sometimes we meet at the school on Saturdays, and I try to make it fun for them. Yes, it is a heck of a lot of work, but it pays off. My students learn. All of my students." Bill Bostek differentiates his instruction and applies mastery learning techniques the old-fashioned way, and that requires an extraordinary amount of planning time and attention to each student's progress, each day. He is a fanatic.

**We learn enthusiastically when we are actively engaged in the process.** Cynthia Greenberg is a technology native and knows every new device and software application that comes on the market. Her science classroom is wired to the hilt. "What the old-timers call programmed learning has really evolved," she says. "It is no longer an isolated student plunking through computer screens to make the red light flash. The software I use includes sophisticated algorithms and precisely scaffolds each student's learning path and gives me real-time data on each student's progress. It probes the students to learn their special interests and takes that into account in their assignments. It saves me hours of preparation time. But it also helps me group students for project work, links to videos that the kids love, and encourages discovery. Each student has a folder on our server, and they use word processing programs, spreadsheets, and databases in their work. They snap pictures from the electronic microscopes and include them in their reports. Students use presentation software and embed videos in the presentations they make to the class. Yes, there is a lot of activity in my classroom, but it is all for a purpose. And the progress data for each student lets me know exactly where they are so that I know they are learning science. Cool stuff." Cynthia Greenberg's facility with technology enables her to efficiently incorporate the principles of personalization.

In summary, much learning is incidental; it just comes naturally. Some learning is self-directed, requiring facility in setting goals, self-assessing mastery, applying learning strategies, using learning tools and technologies, and finding information. Formal learning takes practice, work, repetition, and persistence.

We sometimes acquire new interests by serendipity, discovering realms of knowledge previously unexplored, when we are given choice in directing our learning. When our teacher shows that she really knows us and cares about us, we eagerly accept her instruction and are inspired by her example. We learn vicariously as well as from instruction and study. We pursue learning tenaciously when the task is sufficiently challenging but also within our reach. We invest ourselves fully in learning when given choices in the process. We thrive on variety, and we like to show off what we know. Tapping into these various ways in which we learn, personalized learning, at its best, expands our conception of where, when, and how learning occurs.

The term "personalized learning" begs the question: Who does the personalizing? The examples of the ways we learn (cited above) include student-driven learning processes in which the student chooses the topic, time, strategy, and outcome. Other examples place the teacher in the dominant role, designing instruction and adapting it to each student. School-based personalized learning models typically include both personalization by the teacher and by the student. These models include individual student work as well as group work. Technology may be an aid to both the teacher and the student. Technology enables teachers to efficiently manage curriculum, precisely assess each student's mastery, organize multiple paths to mastery, assign learning tasks aligned with each student's interests and readiness, communicate with each student, and present instruction through a variety of modes. Technology enables students to manage their work; learn outside the school; self-assess their mastery; conveniently access resources; communicate with the teacher, other students, and other teachers and experts; and present and share their work in a variety of modes.

> **The term "personalized learning" begs the question: Who does the personalizing?**

## Research Synthesis

Personalized learning, as the term is used today, rests upon strands of education philosophy and methodology with a considerable lineage. Research on personalized learning, then, derives from studies relevant to its individual strands or on specific applications of elements of its approach.

### Personalized Learning's Pedigree

Despite the current emphasis on technology as the chief enabler of personalized learning, the concept has a lengthy pedigree that predates the digital age. Its predecessors chipped away the lock-step approach to education, likened to factory production lines, that arose in the nineteenth century when bureaucratic public school systems emerged and emulated industrial age business practices (Jeynes, 2007). Ironically, the standardized, assembly line model replaced, in many regions, one-room schoolhouses that operated in accordance with some of the principles we now ascribe to personalized learning—minus, of course, the technology.

Personalized learning theories today are infused with educational philosophy from the Progressive Era, especially John Dewey's (1915, 1998) emphasis on experiential, child-centered learning; social learning; expansion of the curriculum; and preparation for a changing world. The expansionist, progressive philosophy is counterbalanced in contemporary personalized learning approaches by the science of education introduced by Lee Cronbach (1949), Benjamin Bloom (Bloom & Krathwohl, 1956), and others in the mid-twentieth century, who advocated the careful measurement of student mastery of predetermined objectives. This scientific approach took full flight in the standards movement of the late-twentieth century. Technology is viewed by personalized learning advocates as the necessary linchpin to efficiently wed an expanded curriculum and varied instructional modes with the exacting requirements of learning standards and assessed student mastery (Wolf, 2010).

Personalized learning, as recently defined by the U.S. Department of Education, is a concept advanced from those of individualization and differentiation. Individualized instruction is paced according to the learning needs of different learners, as in mastery learning (Bloom, 1971). Differentiated instruction is tailored to the learning preferences of different learners and guided by what research shows is best for students like them (Tomlinson, Brimijoin, & Narvaez, 2008). Personalized instruction encompasses both individualization and differentiation, adapting for both pace and preference. Personalized instruction also adapts learning objectives and content as well as method and pace, remaining cognizant of the objectives' relationship to content standards (USDOE, 2012).

Margaret C. Wang combined aspects of differentiation and mastery learning in a teacher-planned approach that included student self-direction in managing learning tasks. Wang's Adaptive Learning Environments Model (ALEM; Wang, 1992) was designed to meet the challenges of diverse student backgrounds, interests, and prior learning that increasingly characterized classrooms in public schools. Especially, ALEM addressed the diversity propelled by inclusion of students with disabilities in regular classrooms. Wang proposed meticulously planned, differentiated learning activities assigned to each student through fluid "prescriptions" (student learning plans) that the teacher modified on-the-fly as students demonstrated mastery of leveled objectives. The ALEM classroom was organized into learning centers, and students self-scheduled their rotations through the centers as they worked on their individual plans. The student learning plans included both independent work and group work. The teacher introduced new material in whole-class, direct instruction and reinforced it in teacher-directed small groups. ALEM included most of the elements of personalized instruction but required an immense amount of teacher preparation, which

Wang suggested was best done by teacher instructional teams.

Mastery learning (Bloom, 1971) shattered the time barriers teachers placed on the acquisition of teacher-determined objectives—more time for some students, less for others, until the objectives were met. Differentiated instruction (Tomlinson, Brimijoin, & Narvaez, 2008) paved multiple pathways to the same objective, and adaptive learning (Wang, 1992) insisted that the teacher adapt her objectives, activities, classroom configurations, and modes of instruction in accordance with the assessed readiness of each student. Together, these concepts set the stage for technology's ability to provide wide-ranging and audience-specific content and to gather and manage data. Technology has the potential to make practical the management of curriculum, instructional differentiation, and assessment of mastery required to personalize learning: "Digital learning makes it easier to personalize instruction, which many average teachers find difficult or impossible to achieve with whole classrooms of students with a wide array of needs" (Hassel & Hassel, 2012, p. 13).

## Technology in Personalized Learning

The concept of personalized learning predates the introduction of technology to facilitate its practice, but technology may provide the means for doing it well. "Personalization has and can take place without technology, but not at scale. Technology dramatically increases a teacher's ability to identify and manage the needs of many students, and for students to access a large variety of interventions, content, resources, and learning opportunities everywhere at any time" (Wolf, 2010, p. 10). Technology provides more efficient ways to personalize (Crosbie & Kelly, 1993). Technology can assist in all areas of teaching and learning, including (a) initial student assessment to determine current strengths, weaknesses, and needs; (b) selecting, aligning, and managing curriculum; (c) managing student profile data to document individual needs, preferences, and interests; (d) assessing student mastery to inform instruction; (e) creating multiple, teacher-prepared lessons for targeting individual student needs, preferences, and interests; (f) delivering media-rich instruction; (g) giving students access to resources and an interactive network of teachers and students; (h) aiding students in project development and presentation; (i) providing computer-based, computer-assisted, and online learning; and (j) providing teachers, administrators, parents, and students with a wealth of data-based metrics and analytics reporting individual student learning as well as classroom, school, district, and state progress and performance.

Personalized learning requires a shift not only in the design of schooling (i.e., time, curriculum, and instructional delivery methods), but also in how educators view and use technologies. When judiciously selected and appropriately implemented, technologies can enhance efforts to personalize instruction through (a) smart e-learning management systems that can dynamically track and manage the learning needs of individual students and whole classrooms; (b) intelligent, automated tutoring systems that provide immediate and customized coaching, feedback, and ongoing performance assessments to students; (c) platforms that allow students to connect with engaging learning content; (d) access to real-time, up-to-date resources and learning opportunities that engage learners and meet individual learning needs anywhere and anytime; (e) expanded assessment opportunities; and (f) learning communities extending beyond the classroom (Dede & Richards, 2012; Wolf, 2010).

For some students, personalized learning may include online classes. In a blended learning approach, technology is not seen as a replacement for the traditional classroom, but rather as a powerful tool to enhance what is already proven to be effective pedagogy. "In this hybrid conception of personalization, educators can carry out a series of practices to make sure that technology and data enhance relationships, but do not pretend to substitute for them" (Sandler, 2012, p. 1). For other students, technology may simply make classroom learning activities more viable. For example, a project at Temple University Institute for Schools and Society (ISS) is developing an iPad application that may enable students with learning disabilities to take better class notes. This technological innovation can improve students' abilities to learn through better knowledge transfer.

> *In a blended learning approach, technology is not seen as a replacement for the traditional classroom, but rather as a powerful tool to enhance what is already proven to be effective pedagogy.*

## 21st-Century Skills

The 21st-century skills model, advocated by Bernie Trilling and Charles Fadel (2009), has been adopted by school districts across the country over the past few years. This model contains many of the elements associated with personalized learning, especially the use of technology to manage an expanded curriculum, options and choices for students, and attention to the complex of personal, social, and academic competencies necessary for success in life. A framework for learning, based on the model and advocated by the Partnership for 21st Century Skills (www.p21.org), combines core subjects with current, interdisciplinary themes: global awareness; financial, economic, business, and entrepreneurial literacy; civic literacy; health literacy; and environmental literacy.

In the framework, the thematic approach aims at developing students' 21st-century skills, itemized as:

1. Learning and innovation skills
   a. creativity and innovation
   b. critical thinking and problem solving
   c. communication and collaboration

2. Information, media, and technology skills
   a. information literacy
   b. media literacy
   c. ICT (information, communication, and technology) literacy
3. Life and career skills
   a. flexibility and adaptability
   b. initiative and self-direction
   c. social and cross-cultural skills
   d. productivity and accountability
   e. leadership and responsibility (Partnership for 21st Century Skills, n.d.)

According to its developers, the framework's support systems "help students master the multidimensional abilities that will be required of them" (para. 1). The 21st-century skills model seeks to expand and integrate the curriculum, build personal skills, and utilize technology as an instructional tool and to equip students to succeed in an increasingly technological world.

## Direct, Explicit Instruction and Personalized Learning

Personalized learning proponents do not so much disparage direct and explicit instruction as ignore it. When direct instruction is mentioned, it is contrasted with personalized learning. On their blog, "Personalize Learning," McClaskey and Bray (2012) say this: "Traditional teaching practice usually involves explicit direct instruction. In this case, everything depends on the teacher, the hardest working person in the classroom. To really learn something, the learner needs to be challenged and motivated enough to want to learn" (para. 5). In other words, direct instruction is teacher-centered (a bad thing in personalized learning) and does not engage or motivate students.

In fact, direct instruction's central tenet is that the teacher is responsible for what the student learns. Rather than warping the time–pace–place structure of schooling, direct instruction makes maximum use of every available instructional minute through the teacher's meticulous planning and efficient delivery of instruction to the whole class or group of students. The direct instruction model (Adams & Engleman, 1996) centers on seven major steps:

1. The teacher clearly determines learning intentions—what is to be learned.
2. The teacher establishes the success criteria for student performance.
3. The teacher "hooks" the students' interest to build commitment and engagement.
4. The teacher presents the lesson with modeling, input, and checking for understanding before proceeding, reteaching when necessary.
5. The teacher gives students guided practice activities and moves about the room to determine mastery and provide feedback.
6. The teacher provides closure for the lesson, summarizing and drawing together loose ends.

7. The teacher assigns independent practice to reinforce what the students have mastered.

Despite its indifference for most of the tenets of personalized learning, direct, explicit instruction has demonstrated significant results in student learning outcomes. John Hattie (2009), in his much-cited *Visible Learning*, synthesized 800 meta-analyses relating to achievement, showing the effective size of dozens of education practices and influences. In commenting on the massive, federally funded Project Follow Through, a controlled study completed in the 1970s that evaluated the effects on student learning of several programs, Hattie observed, "All but one program had close to zero effects (some had negative effects). Only Direct Instruction had positive effects on basic skills, on deeper comprehension measures, on social measures, and on affective measures" (p. 258). The programs that achieved little or no effect included ones with strong similarities to personalized learning, characterizing themselves as "holistic," "student-centered learning," "learning-to-learn," "active learning," "cooperative education," and "whole language." In introducing direct instruction, Hattie adds a personal note:

> Every year I present lectures to teacher education students and find that they are already indoctrinated with the mantra 'constructivism good, direct instruction bad.' When I show them the results of these meta-analyses, they are stunned, and they often become angry at having been given an agreed [upon] set of truths and commandments against direct instruction. (p. 204)

Further support for direct instruction comes from an analysis of comprehensive school reform models by the Comprehensive School Reform Quality Center (CSRQC; 2006a, 2006b) at the American Institutes for Research. That study found only two elementary school models, both instructionally focused, prescriptive, and based on direct instruction methodology, to show moderate strength of effect. CSRQC found no middle school or high school models with evaluations that showed moderate strength of effect. No models at any grade level demonstrated a strong effect.

One wonders if direct instruction could be woven into a personalized learning model, and certainly digital learning could be utilized in several of direct learning's steps. In addition to direct instruction's structured methodology, the process places the person of the teacher in a primary relationship with students. In understanding what motivates students to learn, separating the personal contributions of the teacher from the methods the teacher employs requires careful dicing of variables. As teachers step aside for a facilitative role and rely more heavily on technology in instruction, we must consider what may be lost.

## Personalization at Home

If there is one venue where personalized learning should be natural it is in homeschooling, and we have evidence that many homeschooled youngsters develop an enviable sense of self-direction and academic attainment (Ray, 2010).

When provided by savvy parents, homeschooling also enables flexible adaptation of instruction that incorporates the student's interests and nurtures incipient talent. Homeschooling parents have used digital learning and internet-based programs to provide the meat of instructional content and to determine their children's progress. Homeschooling is the ultimate transformation of schooling's time–pace–place structures and provides a fertile laboratory for understanding what is most promising about personalized learning.

## Conclusions

Personalized learning traces its philosophical roots to strands of American education that have attempted to break the lock-step of graded classrooms and rigid curricula, integrate school learning and life experience, and equip the student with the skills necessary for self-directed learning and choice in learning pathways. Yet many of the previous efforts to achieve these aims have fallen fallow because of the time required for teachers to plan and deliver individualized and varied instruction within the confines of class periods and curricular requirements. New technology provides efficiencies for the teacher and greater opportunity for both the teacher and the student. Technology and technology-assisted programs, especially those that utilize the internet, engage students with learning in ways that enhance student motivation to learn and provide valuable and frequent feedback on their mastery.

> *Personalization ensues from the relationships among teachers and learners and the teacher's orchestration of multiple means for enhancing every aspect of each student's learning and development.*

Personalization ensues from the relationships among teachers and learners and the teacher's orchestration of multiple means for enhancing every aspect of each student's learning and development. Even with the application of technology to achieve the goals of personalization, the teacher remains a source of motivation for students through her relational suasion with them. The teacher builds the student's metacognitive competencies to effectively direct his own learning and make choices about it. The teacher models and instructs social and emotional learning and behavior. The teacher fosters a classroom culture in which learning and learners are respected, and the thrill of mastery is reinforced. Most of all, the teacher organizes and orchestrates instruction in the ways most effective for each of her students. Personalized learning places the teacher in a multidimensional role that requires a basket of skills and mindsets that honor the supremacy of her position in students' learning.

## Action Principles

### For the State Education Agency
a. Remove statutory and regulatory barriers that constrict a district's or school's ability to modify the time–pace–place structure of learning.
b. Provide information for districts and schools on emerging personalization practices that show promise.
c. Showcase districts that systematically and effectively utilize personalized learning methods.
d. Include preparation in personalized learning concepts and methods in leader and teacher licensure requirements.
e. Provide districts and schools with evaluative criteria to determine the effectiveness of personalized learning methods in their contexts.

### For the Local Education Agency
a. Be cautious of programs described as "personalized"; the term is being used in various ways, so be sure the program fits your purposes.
b. Give parents a choice in selecting schools and programs, especially when introducing dramatically new methods that some parents may not desire for their children.
c. Provide technology for administrators and teachers to manage curriculum, instruction, student data, and communication.
d. Provide ample professional development for school leaders and teachers to successfully integrate technology and personalization methods into their instruction.
e. Consider the time–pace–place structures in the schools and how they can be changed to promote learning any time and everywhere.

### For the School and Classroom
a. Provide teachers with bridges between conventional teaching methods and personalized methods (especially with technology) to allow them to assimilate the different ways of teaching.
b. Begin, as they say, with the end in mind—what you want students to acquire—and then consider if the new method or new technology is a better way to achieve the result.
c. When asking students to use technology outside of school, ensure that all students have access to the technology and know how to use it.
d. Balance the use of technology to facilitate communication among students and teachers with the need for face-to-face interaction.
e. Consider both technological and non-technological ways to tailor instruction for each student and to give students choice in directing their learning.

f. Intentionally build students' skills with metacognition, self-direction, and use of multiple sources of information.

## References

Adams, G. L., & Engelmann, S. (1996). *Research on direct instruction: 25 years beyond DISTAR.* Seattle, WA: Educational Achievement Systems.

Bloom, B. S. (1971). Mastery learning. In J. H. Block (Ed.), *Mastery learning: Theory and practice* (pp. 47–63). New York, NY: Holt, Rinehart, & Winston.

Bloom, B., & Krathwohl, D. (1956). *Taxonomy of educational objectives.* New York, NY: McKay.

Brooks, D. (2011). *The social animal.* New York, NY: Random House.

Christensen, C., Horn, M., & Johnson, C. (2008). *Disrupting class: How disruptive innovation will change the way the world learns.* New York, NY: McGraw Hill.

Comprehensive School Reform Quality Center. (2006a). *Report on elementary school comprehensive school reform models.* Washington, DC: Author.

Comprehensive School Reform Quality Center. (2006b). *Report on middle and high school comprehensive school reform models.* Washington, DC: Author.

Cronbach, L. (1949). *Essentials of psychological testing.* New York, NY: Harper & Row.

Crosbie, J., & Kelly, G. (1993). A computer-based personalized system of instruction course in applied behavior analysis. *Behavior Research Methods, 25*(3), 366–370.

Dede, C., & Richards, J. (Eds.). (2012). *Digital teaching platforms: Customizing classroom learning for each student.* New York, NY: Teachers College Press.

Dewey, J. (1915). *The school and society.* Chicago, IL: Chicago Press.

Dewey, J. (1998). *Experience and education* (60th anniversary ed.). West Lafayette, NY: Kappa Delta.

Hassel, B. C., & Hassel, E. A. (2012). Teachers in the age of digital instruction. In C. E. Finn, Jr., & D. R. Fairchild (Eds.), *Education reform for the digital age* (pp. 11–34). Washington, DC: Thomas B. Fordham Institute.

Hattie, J. (2009). *Visible learning: A synthesis of over 800 meta-analyses relating to achievement.* New York, NY: Routledge.

Hess, F. M. (2012). Quality control in K–12 digital learning: Three (imperfect) approaches. In C. E. Finn, Jr., & D. R. Fairchild (Eds.), *Education reform for the digital age* (pp. 35–54). Washington, DC: Thomas B. Fordham Institute.

Jackson, M. (2008). *Distracted: The erosion of attention and the coming dark age.* Amherst, NY: Prometheus Books.

Jeynes, W. (2007). *American educational history: School, society, and the common good.* Thousand Oaks, CA: Sage Publications.

Kaplan, C., & Chan, R. (2011, September). *Time well spent: Eight powerful practices of successful, time-expanded schools.* Boston, MA: National Center on Time and Learning.

McClaskey, K., & Bray, B. (2012, October 19). The expert learner with voice and choice [Web blog]. Retrieved from http://www.personalizelearning.com/2012/10/the-expert-learner-with-voice-and-choice.html

Partnership for 21st Century Skills. (n.d.). Framework for 21st century learning. Retrieved from http://www.p21.org/overview

Ray, B. D. (2010). Academic achievement and demographic traits of homeschool students: A nationwide study. *Academic Leadership: The Online Journal, 8.* Retrieved from http://content-cat.fhsu.edu/cdm/compoundobject/collection/p15732coll4/id/456

Sandler, S. (2012). People v. 'Personalization': Retaining the human element in the high-tech era of education. *Education Week, 31*(22), 20–22.

Tomlinson, C. A., Brimijoin, K., & Narvaez, L. (2008). *The differentiated school: Making revolutionary changes in teaching and learning.* Alexandria, VA: Association for Supervision and Curriculum Development.

Trilling, B., & Fadel, C. (2009). *21st century skills: Learning for life in our times.* San Francisco, CA: John Wiley & Sons.

U.S. Department of Education. (2010). *Transforming American education: Learning powered by technology.* Retrieved from http://www.ed.gov/technology/netp-2010

U.S. Department of Education. (2012). *Learning: Engage and empower.* Retrieved from http://www.ed.gov/technology/netp-2010/learning-engage-and-empower

Wang, M. C. (1992). *Adaptive education strategies: Building on diversity.* Baltimore, MD: Paul H. Brookes.

Wolf, M. (2010). *Innovate to educate: System [re]design for personalized learning.* A report from the 2010 symposium. Washington, DC: Software & Information Industry Association. Retrieved from http://siia.net/pli/presentations/PerLearnPaper.pdf

# Part 3
# Technology in Learning Innovation

# Education + Technology + Innovation = Learning?
## T.V. Joe Layng and Janet S. Twyman

Close your eyes, and think of the word "technology." What thoughts and images come to mind? Your smart phone? Computers? Hardware or digital things, or information in bits and bytes floating around in the "cloud" above your head? Now, pause to pay attention to the feelings that you associate with "technology"? Do you feel comfortable, or sense stirrings of concern? Is there eagerness, or do you have a sense that things could very easily be out of control?

Technology is the use and knowledge of tools, techniques, systems, or methods in order to solve a problem or serve some purpose. What we view as new technology evolves and advances persistently. A technological innovation—stone tools—is said to be a driver behind early human migration (Jacobs et al., 2008). Agriculture and pottery were innovative "technologies" to our Neolithic ancestors (Cole, 1970), as was the light bulb to Edison and his contemporaries (Hargadon & Douglas, 2001). Technology arose through our need to solve problems, whatever problems we as individuals or as societies were faced with at any given time. We learned to use materials from the environment (e.g., tools), or our own ingenuity (e.g., processes), to create new things and solve our problems. Across every endeavor known to mankind, we continue to advance knowledge and technology with each new discovery made or problem solved (Douglas, 2012). Innovative technology is rarely the result of a "eureka moment," but of much more. Due to human endeavor, the march of innovation and new technology continues through time.

In 1968, at the dawn of the "modern" technology revolution, B. F. Skinner called for the development and growth of a "technology of teaching." This technology would extend the progression of scientific discoveries made in the psychology laboratory into the school classroom. Although Skinner did create one of the first "teaching machines" (Skinner, 1968), he did not mean that teaching required machines. Instead, he advocated a "technology" of teacher/learner interactions that could greatly improve the likelihood of learner success (Skinner, 1954, 1984). As noted by Twyman (in press), Skinner outlined "a technology of instruction based on the behavioral principles of small, incremental steps, simple to complex sequencing, high rates of learner interaction, reinforcement of correct responses, and individual pacing" (n.p.) and thus commenced an instructional technology revolution featuring carefully designed instruction, thorough scientific validation, and automated (mechanical) delivery systems (Rumph et al., 2007).

Yet, almost 50 years later, Skinner's vision still has not come to pass. Few of the discoveries made in the psychological, behavioral, and cognitive laboratories have made their way into educational practice (Lagemann, 2002; Slavin, 2002). Instead, when we hear the words educational technology these days, we do not think of teaching processes or ways of learning; we think of laptops, tablets, apps, and other forms of hardware and software.

> *Modern technologies allow data collection on student responses, learning patterns, content access, and a myriad of information on learning effects.*

There is a storied history of "hardware" technology invented for or used in the classroom. A timeline of classroom technology often includes advances from papyrus (at about 3000 B.C.), to the quill pen, the hornbook, the magic lantern, chalkboards, pencils, the overhead projector, the slide projector, the teaching machine, handheld calculators, the desktop computer, interactive whiteboards, student response systems, and now powerful, Internet-connected, mobile, personal digital devices, such as tablets and smartphones (Wilson, Orellana, & Meek, 2010). These more modern listings represent a tremendous evolution in the technology of "tools" used daily in schools. But has the technology in processes, in how we teach and learn, equally evolved? The answer, if we use student learning outcomes as our measure, is unfortunately "no."

Even as our tools advance, there seems too little change in the way we teach (Allington, 1994). Just as the era when filmstrips and then the TV were introduced into classrooms, short videos accessed over the Internet are hailed as major breakthroughs, touted as revolutionizing education (Vetter & Severance, 1997). However, anything beyond a cursory look reveals that this "revolution" still relies on the age-old model of information presentation, individual or group study, some sort of test (perhaps), and then the hoped-for learning. And we have seen that these methods produce some students who do learn; however, most do not. Instructors may add questions and suggest discussion topics (as is often done by companies offering video selections from current television networks), but these are minor additions to what is otherwise a very noninstructional technological approach.

Other examples missing a true teaching technology abound. Search engines have dramatically increased our access to information. We live in an information-rich culture where there are few facts we can't locate in but a few minutes (Leu, Kinzer, Coiro, & Cammack, 2004; Smith, 2011). Yet these articles and webpages, just seconds away from our fingertips, are still mostly passive information for us to "absorb" and "retain" and even evaluate for reliability (Ybarra & Suman, 2006) the best we can. Most online courses tend to be replicas of traditional classrooms modified for asynchronous delivery. And much like the traditional classroom, some of these online courses are poorly organized and delivered, while others may be well organized and engaging; yet, pedagogically, there is little real difference between the two. Tablets put computing power (figuratively) in the hands of our children, providing 24/7 access if wanted (Shih, 2007). Touch interfaces invite interaction, and mastery of the interface often requires little training, but with what are our K–12 learners spending an average of 7.5 hours a day interacting (Means, Toyama, Murphy, & Jones, 2010; Rideout, Foehr, & Roberts, 2010)? This chapter, while providing an overview of current, mainstream K–12 hardware/software educational technology, will focus on more critical aspects of education technology: teaching and learning and how we can use a technology of teaching to improve outcomes for all learners.

The history of failure in education reform (Kazdin, 2000; Kliebard, 1988; Sarason, 1990) has caused many to ask, "What do we need to do, as a system and a society, to improve schooling?" We further the question by asking, "Can we do what has eluded us to this point, that is, create a real technology of teaching and learning? Is there any hope that our practices can be informed by the sciences of behavior, learning, and cognition? What role can current (and future) digital technology and new devices play in making this happen?"

## The Technology of Tools

Technology tools, both hardware and software, have been lauded as the panacea for what ails the American classroom (e.g., Katten Muchin Rosenman, 2013). Whether or not they can or will fulfill that promise is still subject to great debate (Brady, 2012). While various tool technologies have improved some facets of education—such as greater information access, increased variety of content creation tools, broader access to instruction, automated data collection, and behavior management tools—the seamless blending of instructional design, pedagogy, and technology tools has been much harder to achieve. An example of that seamless blending is described in a recent white paper by Layng (2012):

> Imagine a reading comprehension program that was designed to take advantage of a wide range of technology available in a classroom, including computers, interactive whiteboards, and perhaps iPads. A teacher might begin

by assigning the first three lessons of the program to be completed online as homework (e.g., Leon et al., 2011). Learners could access the lessons using a notebook or iPad they have at home, or perhaps use a computer that may be located in a library or computer lab at school. The teacher could access reports that not only let her know if the work was done, but also describe the precise performance of each learner. The online application featuring continuous adaptation would catch and correct many of the errors made by the learner. The program would provide individualized correction based on the type of error that occurs. The teacher would know how many questions were answered correctly the first time, versus after a correction. Learners with many corrections would eventually answer correctly, but could be flagged as perhaps needing more attention. The teacher could then provide whole-classroom interactive whiteboard lessons that review and extend the material learned online. Learners would be able to participate and verbalize the strategies they learn. No interactive whiteboard? Teacher guides and learner response materials could be provided to help transfer and extend skills learned in the program.

The teacher may find that some of the learners do not have the basic decoding skills necessary for the lessons. A brief two-minute assessment administered to each learner might find that some need to begin in the second half of an online phonics program, while others need to begin earlier.

As the program proceeds, skills learned online become the basis of collaborative in-class activities. The activities extend beyond the multiple-choice, inquiry-based lessons provided online, and give learners the opportunity to construct open-ended answers to literal, inferential, derived vocabulary, and main idea questions. Material from a range of subjects might be included in the collaborations as the programs progress and the learners master increasingly complex reading tasks. We should see learners eagerly extend their new comprehension abilities to new areas.

Other teachers may focus on the whole-classroom lessons, and reserve online or iPad work for those learners who seem to be having trouble in class. Yet others may rely on the online program and use the interactive classroom lessons for small-group instruction for targeted learners. And yet others may begin with the interactive whiteboard lessons and subsequently rely more on the online lessons as a result of acquiring iPads for their classrooms. The options are many and the flexibility great. What all of these teachers want, however, is content that will help them achieve their classroom goals—no matter what technology is theirs to use, or how they choose to use it.

In summary, schools need to be able to take advantage of any or all instructional technology found in any combination that meets their needs. They might introduce iPads in one classroom, but have learners in other classrooms access the same lessons on a computer. If a classroom has no computers, but does have an interactive whiteboard, students should still be able to learn the same material. What's more, teachers should be able to take advantage of each technology's special features, such as whole-group or small-group instruction using interactive whiteboards, individualized instruction using computers, or mobile learning using iPads. (pp. 3–4)

This scenario may seem idealistic and futuristic, but, in fact, it exists today (see Layng, 2013a). We can learn a great deal about the use of education technology by examining what is involved in the scenario. First, there are the tools. The author talks about four: computers, interactive whiteboards, iPads, and (good old) print material. However, what makes their use compelling is not the individual devices, but how they all work together to achieve a valued educational outcome: reading comprehension. Further, all work together, not rigidly nor in a scripted lock-step curriculum, but afford a range of options that meet the learning goals. What ties the tools together is a unified curriculum instantiated within a software framework.

> *Tools and their software must be considered as a unit and perhaps evaluated as such.*

The hardware/software technologies are tools that assist and enhance the learning process, but should not drive learning goals (National Education Association, 2013; see also McHaney, 2011). It is the software infrastructure across devices that combines each separate device into a unified whole. A teacher may choose a computer, an iPad, or an interactive whiteboard and also supplement with print if desired. While differential costs might influence use, it is the flexibility in how each is used that allows the teacher to meet the specific needs and technology requirements of the school, the classroom, and the learners. Thus, tools and their software must be considered as a unit and perhaps evaluated as such.

## Tools and Data

We hear a great deal about data these days as well. The data generated by individual software programs and the instructional delivery platform that manages our learning tools are indeed important. Yet data alone may not be very helpful. In a recent demonstration of the use of "adaptive" data, a vendor proudly showed how the evening's homework assignment provided individualized, one-page reports for each subject in which each student was engaged. The data were displayed attractively; student strengths and weaknesses were highlighted. By examining the page, a teacher could spot certain learner weaknesses and subsequently design an intervention to address the problem. It all sounded quite compelling, that is, until one does the math. If a fifth-grade teacher teaches five subjects per day to 30 students, that means 150 pages of reports would be produced daily. How does one overworked teacher even begin to make use of that much data? Even in cases in which teachers may have time to contemplate a detailed report, what is to be done with the information? How is an instructional intervention or change designed and delivered, and how is it tracked and evaluated?

Data, instead of being a path to great outcomes, may instead lead to even greater stress on our teachers and principals (Cambell & Gross, 2012). Our data need to be tied to the practices of teaching and learning. Data should be smart (giving us insight), targeted (focused on the variables of concern), and informative (leading to immediate, evaluated interventions). What is needed are "smart reports" that provide critical information for 30 learners on one page, not 30 pages of reports. Our tools need to be linked in ways that provide continuous, formative evaluation, not of students, but of the effectiveness of the instruction or learning environment, and provide a basis to improve that effectiveness.

In summary, the successful integration of a technology tool for learning generally goes hand-in-hand with changes in teacher training, curricula, and assessment practices (Ertmer, 1999; Kopcha, 2012). Integration must occur not only with current devices, but with evolving devices as well. A school should not constantly face the threat that devices purchased this year will be totally useless in two years. This will require the development of software in the form of an instructional delivery platform that evolves to integrate old devices with new, across device manufacturers, for both the individual and whole classroom. These tools, while being developed and tested, are not yet ubiquitous (Edutopia, 2007). These devices are not cheap, and investments must be protected. Systems that rely on a single device or operating system are too limiting and restricting. Devices need to be integrated such the data produced are useful, easy to use, and easy to apply. And, if we have all this, will we be in reach of providing the very best education for our learners? The answer is, sadly, not quite.

## The Technology of Process

Duke Ellington has been quoted (Markle, 1990) as saying, "Beauty without utility is an ornamental lump." Regrettably, our tools of technology may end up being just that. One approach to solving this dilemma is to focus on improving what is actually done with the tools, that is, to focus on the practices used in teaching and learning. We often hear that "teaching" remains largely an art. But recent advances in the technology of the teaching and learning process suggest we may be beginning to combine the science of learning with the art of teaching. There are three nonexclusive ways in which we may do this. One uses a technology of data analysis to make explicit currently implicit practices that may succeed, or at least provide information about what will happen to our learners given certain curricula (see Anderson, Gulwani, & Popovic, 2013; and the series of articles by Layng, Sota, & Leon, 2011; Leon, Layng, & Sota, 2011; and Sota, Leon, & Layng, 2011). A second approach systematically applies a scientific research and development process in the production of the software applications sold to schools (Layng, Stikeleather, & Twyman, 2006). The third explicitly applies practices that the learning sciences have determined to be effective, thereby making use of work in the experimental and applied learning sciences in our teaching (see Twyman, Layng, Stikeleather, & Hobbins, 2004).

## Big Data: Making the Implicit Explicit

One approach employs "big data" to mine the art of teaching in order to provide effective practices. Proponents of big data maintain that solutions for teaching and learning can emerge from collecting and analyzing as much data as we can from as many learners as we can (Greller & Drachsler, 2012; West, 2012). But what is meant by "big data," and what does it mean for education?

Using data to drive decision making is not new to school districts. In fact, most districts are flooded with data. Everything from attendance, to bus ridership, to number of cafeteria meals served, to program usage rates, to teacher sick days, to student test scores and more are collected and used to make decisions. Many schools have adopted classroom reporting systems that describe what students are doing, their grades, homework, and so forth. These data are often available to students and parents as well. Schools strive to find data that help them make sense of what they are trying to do, and perhaps indicate what works, and even predict outcomes given certain practices. Often the word most frequently used is "accountability" (Ehren & Swanborn, 2012). Data are frequently used to compare outcomes between schools. Sometimes data are used to help identify successful practices that might be shared in some way, yet at other times they are used to reward or punish administrators or teachers (Burnett, Cushing, & Bivona, 2012).

Big data is none of that. Big data often makes few or no assumptions about what the data show. Data are not chosen to show this or that. Instead, every bit of data collected, from just about every source, is used. For schools, this would mean all the data listed above and more—including data publicly available but not collected by the school, such as census data. This inclusiveness is why it is called "big data." But it is not simply the amount of data, but how the data are used that is important (Greller & Drachsler, 2012; Siemens & Gasevic, 2012). In most instances, "genetic algorithms" are used to find patterns and highlight relationships in the data (Beasley, Martin, & Bull, 1993; see also Ryan Baker's chapter on data analytics in this *Handbook*). Used correctly, these algorithms can potentially diagnose learner problems, suggest solutions, make predictions, and even design instruction.

The algorithms are referred to as "genetic" because the principles of selection, much like those found in nature, are applied to the outcomes of looking for relations in the data (Johnson, 1999). By looking at learner characteristics, academic history, economic and social demographics, assignments made, assignments completed, quiz scores, grades on projects, and so forth, one algorithm may predict at a 50% correct rate that learners who have certain characteristics and experience may be successful in a given curriculum, and another algorithm might predict at a 60% correct rate that learners who have slightly different characteristics and experience may be successful in the curriculum. Thus, an initial population of hypotheses is generated. The "fitness" of each hypothesis is computed based on how closely each hypothesis predicts actual outcomes. Two hypotheses from the old generation are selected for mating; that is, genetic operators are used on this pair to create at least two offspring. The fitness of the two offspring is computed, and the ones selected that make the better prediction, these offspring are added to the new generation. This process continues until the best possible algorithm evolves that results in the most accurate predictions. Since this is done with very powerful computers, calculations occur very rapidly. With these data, a school knows which learners with identifiable characteristics will likely succeed with a given curriculum. The school can now more effectively match learners to curricula. Sometimes, hundreds of algorithms can be tested against one another in just a few minutes. Such procedures can make very clear, more quickly and reliably than ever before, that certain methods have not worked with a particular group of learners while another has. Or, based upon data not previously considered, schools might be better able to identify and assist those at risk. For example, it may be found that attendance for the first 20 days of high school predicts the graduation rate for a particular set of high schools. With those data, a school could immediately target students likely not to graduate. There would be no need to wait for test scores or other results. It may well be possible to then predict which intervention may be more likely to succeed.

This process continually learns from itself with new incoming data. Ultimately, the data generated from a great variety of sources gets combined with the day-to-day activities of teachers to produce and test more algorithms. Everything a teacher does, the lesson plans, the worksheets, the projects, the homework, and all the student data from all of those elements would be fed into the database. Data from thousands and perhaps someday millions of learners would be entered daily into the programs. In time, the most effective practices would emerge. As these practices are used and teachers vary the recommendations, these data would find their way back and new practices would be selected. In theory, the very best educational practices should emerge that most closely meet the requirements of each learner. Further, if instruction is being designed, the paths in the instruction can quickly be evaluated and altered until the best instructional sequence emerges.

There are critics of this use of big data (see Simon, 2013). One clear challenge is privacy (see Strauss, 2013). By its very nature, big data searches and keeps searching for every bit of data collected about a person, generating an unfathomable 2.5 quintillion bytes of data about our existence every single day (IBM,

2013). In education, this includes everyone—administrators, teachers, and students. While big data advocates argue that the individual data is not important apart from the whole, it is still collected and stored. Further, are there questions of the data that should not be asked? What may prevent data from being used to single out a small group and sort the remaining into tracks with fewer resources? Careful consideration must be given to the types of data stored, how it is stored, and who has access to it. The U.S. Department of Education has recently released two publications (including policy drafts) to assist educators and administrators with understanding and using digital big data (see U.S. Department of Education, 2012a, 2012b).

## The Scientific Research and Development Process

Another approach that can contribute to a technology of learning is to be found in the learning sciences laboratories and in scientifically designed learning environments. In the latter, learning scientists use scientific methods to actually design or "engineer" the learning environment. This approach is highly dependent on a very precise, integrated research and development process, a type of scientific formative evaluation. Layng, Stikeleather, and Twyman (2006) described it in detail; we have paraphrased it below:

> Scientists and engineers whose responsibility it is to design complex systems, such as an airplane, rely on thorough formative evaluation to produce a vehicle that will fly the first time. For example, careful wind tunnel and other experiments test how the materials perform, how much lift is provided by the wings, and how the overall aerodynamics are implemented. Each revision is retested until the component meets a predetermined standard. Only after thorough testing of the components, both separately and together, is the final question asked, "Does it fly?"
>
> Each flight is considered a replication; the more conditions encountered, the more systematic the replication. Design modifications determined from test flights improve stability and reliability even more. Rigorous formative evaluations can have the same effect on instructional program development. By ensuring that each component meets a specified quality standard, which in the case of instruction would be a high mastery standard achieved by the learners tested, we can design and build instructional programs that have the same high likelihood of success as when building a modern aircraft. Rigorous "single-subject" iterative cycles (test–revise–test) provide great confidence that all aircraft built in accord with the design and development process will fly—without the need for tests comparing groups of aircraft. A similar approach to educational program development can provide comparable confidence.

By employing a scientific formative evaluation process that saw its beginnings in the 1950s (Markle, 1967) and has continued today (Layng et al., 2006;

Twyman et al., 2004), learning environments may be created that are the products of rigorous developmental testing and that will produce the outcomes required for learner success. Efforts are underway to help automate this process, thereby making it accessible to a larger curriculum development community (see Anderson, Gulwani, & Popovic, 2013). This process is increasingly used by educational publishers and others looking to build replicable and scalable learning environments. Those purchasing applications for their tablets, computers, or whiteboards should determine if those applications have gone through such a process (see Leon et al., 2011, for an example of this process applied to teaching reading comprehension.)

> *One major question raised by this technology is, "Who pays for it?"*

One major question raised by this technology is, "Who pays for it?" The scientific development process is not cheap. Few start-ups can afford it, and few established publishers feel the need to do it since districts may often purchase "good enough" products, particularly if "good enough" is less expensive (see Janzen & Saiedian, 2005).

## Direct Application of Learning Science to Teaching

Educational practices can also be informed by the work of learning scientists as they increasingly attempt to bring the laboratory to school. The results of years of important learning sciences research has yet to find its way into the classroom. This is troublesome. Scientists have investigated all types of learning and have often developed optimal strategies for producing each type. Different types of learning have been identified, and researchers have found that teaching methods appropriate for one type of learning is not appropriate for another. Various categorizations of content analysis and matched teaching applications have been proposed, categorizations which are intended to provide a useful guide for the analysis of content and the application of effective teaching/learning methods.

One categorization (Tiemann & Markle, 1991) separates learning into three main categories: psychomotor, simple cognitive, and complex cognitive. Though the categories offer broad classification, learner behavior may not necessarily fall cleanly into one or the other. Each category can be further subdivided into basic relations, linked relations, and combined relations. Within the psychomotor category, the focus is on learning how to physically do something. Holding a pencil properly (basic relation), swinging a golf club (linked relation, a component is dependent on preceding one), and performing a complex ice-skating routine (combined relation, components are combined and recombined to form new routines) all fall in this psychomotor learning category. What separates psychomotor learning from other types are the physical training required and the events (kinesthetic stimuli) that guide behavior often arise from within one's own body. Simply showing a learner how something is done is seldom adequate. Learners must learn to sense changes in muscle movement and certain temporal–spatial relations (see Mechner, 1994 for a comprehensive discussion).

Within the simple cognitive category, basic relations include (a) paired associate learning (e.g., given a country, name its capital), multiple discrimination learning (e.g., shown numbers 0 through 9, pick out each when asked), and simple serial learning (e.g., counting). Linked relations include sequence learning (e.g., recite *Macbeth*), conditional sequence (algorithms) learning (e.g., complete a long division problem), and combined relations learning (such as verbal relations in which performances are described but not necessarily demonstrated, e.g., describe how a play at third base is made). The primary goal for simple cognitive learning involves learning to perform a task one can already do in the presence of new events. Testing for simple cognitive learning typically involves determining if the learner can do precisely what has been taught. Here, providing enough practice and proper presentation of events to be learned is important.

The complex cognitive category involves concepts such as solid, liquid, and gas (basic relations), which are defined by a set of "must have" features that every instance of the concept shares, but each instance also has certain "can have" features that are not shared and do not enter into the definition of the concept. The goal is to have learners classify instances versus non-instances based on the "must have" features and be able to identify instances not provided during instruction as an example of the concept. Further, learners must be able to correctly reject noninstances that lack one or more of the "must have" features. Next come principles and other higher order linking of categorical learning (linked relations). A principle, for example, describes the relation between concepts, and can often be stated as an if–then relation. It may be a statement of a law such as, "for every action, there is an equal and opposite reaction." The four key concepts being linked are equal, opposite, action, and reaction. The application of the principle, even if one can state it, will be determined, in part, by how well one understands the four concepts. Not being able to distinguish action from reaction and not being able to recognize each instance across a wide range of "can have" features make understanding the principle nearly impossible. Strategies (combined relations) make up the last category of complex cognitive relations. These are self-discovery strategies that learners use to analyze and create new insights and rules. Considerable work has been done on how to teach learners these strategies (see Robbins, 2011; Whimbey &Lochhead, 1999). Rarely do we see them used in the classroom.

Though materials are available for training teachers in these methods, one will not likely find them in colleges of education. Yet more are being developed all the time. It is now possible using new learning technologies to rapidly teach vocabulary (four new words fully taught in 5 minutes), by combining research in what is called "stimulus equivalence" with research in what is called "fast mapping" (Sota, Leon, & Layng, 2011). We can even teach for generativity and recombinatorial insights (Robbins, 2011). A technology of learning is possible.

Interestingly, some of these methods have been available for decades. For example, there is consensus on how best to teach concepts, whether using direct teaching, peer-teaching, inquiry, games, or projects (e.g., Layng, 2013b). As early as 1971, D. Cecil Clark reviewed about 235 concept-learning studies from a range of laboratories and applied classroom experiments. He found a remarkable consensus on what is effective when teaching concepts (Clark, 1971). Inexplicably, even though subsequent work over the years has supported Clark's conclusions, the methods have yet to be incorporated into classroom teaching, the design of textbooks, or apps.

To make these methods available to schools would, of course, require a massive investment in professional development. Where does that money come from? Who determines where to start? How are teachers supported as they try to introduce these methods into their classroom?

We have briefly addressed two types of learning technologies: tools and processes. Now, what would happen if these three technologies of process were combined with the rapidly growing technology of tools? We may be able to overcome the shortcomings and challenges of each. Educators can encourage vendors, device manufactures, and developers to provide tools that include technologies for the collection and use of big data and content products that are based on a strong scientific formative evaluation—the results of which inform and are continually informed by big data—and to ensure that these tools and products use the most up-to-date learning sciences methods as possible. Further, these products should come with professional development that itself is informed by and informs all of these. By allocating scarce resources to those who provide these tools, districts can help ensure they are investing in more than ornamental lumps.

## Action Principles

### State and Local Education Agencies
   a. Ensure equity of access to broadband Internet, for all students.
   b. Ensure that technology and digital tools work together, in concert, to produce educational outcomes.
   c. Provide administrators with training and guidelines on how to make informed decisions about purchasing equipment, technology use, educational applications, and data systems.
   d. Provide assessment and accountability systems (or guidelines for careful development) that ensure academic integrity and accurately measure the impact on students in terms of psychomotor, simple cognitive, and complex cognitive learning.

e. Foster in-house "big data" expertise, including developing a training plan for analytical skills and the understanding of interrelationships between data sets.
f. Collaboration with a national agency and work towards competency certification for teachers of online learning.
g. Encourage preservice and inservice programs to provide instruction and professional development related to the application of learning science principles, including making use of work from the experimental and applied learning sciences in teaching.
h. Encourage preservice and inservice programs to provide instruction and professional development related to the successful engineering of learning environments.

**Schools and Classrooms**
a. Provide ongoing professional development for all personnel on how to use technology effectively. This includes access to relevant, high-quality, interactive professional development on how to integrate the technology of tools and the technology of process into their instruction and practice.
b. Provide all educators with training and assistance in determining what procedures and products use the most up-to-date findings from the learning sciences for effective teaching and learning.

# References

Allington, R. L. (1994). The schools we have. The schools we need. *Reading Teacher, 48*, 14–14.

Anderson, E., Gulwani, S., & Popovic, Z. (2013, April–May) *A trace-based framework for analyzing and synthesizing educational progressions.* Paper presented at ACM SIGCHI Conference on Human Factors in Computing Systems, Paris, France.

Beasley, D., Martin, R. R., & Bull, D. R. (1993). An overview of genetic algorithms: Part 1. Fundamentals. *University Computing, 15*(2), 58–69.

Brady, T. (2012, August). What will the ed tech revolution look like? *Co.Exist.* New York, NY: Mansueto Ventures, LLC. Retrieved from http://www.fastcoexist.com/1680231/what-will-the-ed-tech-revolution-look-like

Burnett, A., Cushing, E., & Bivona, L. (2012). *Uses of multiple measures for performance-based compensation.* Washington, DC: Center for Educator Compensation Reform. Retrieved from http://0-cecr.ed.gov.opac.acc.msmc.edu/pdfs/CECR_MultipleMeasures.pdf

Campbell, C., & Gross, B. (2012, Sept.). *Principal concerns: Leadership data and strategies for states.* Seattle, WA: Center for Reinventing Public Education. Retrieved from http://www.crpe.org/publications/brief-principal-concerns-leadership-data-and-strategies-states

Cole, S. M. (1970). *The Neolithic revolution.* London, UK: British Museum.

Clark, D. C. (1971). Teaching concepts in the classroom: A set of teaching prescriptions derived from experimental research. *Journal of Educational Psychology, 62*(3), 253–278.

Douglas, D. G. (2012). Forward. In W. E. Bijker, T. P. Hughes, & T. Pinch (Eds.), *The social construction of technological systems: New directions in the sociology and history of technology* (pp. vii–ix). Cambridge, MA: MIT Press.

Edutopia. (2007, November 5). *What is successful technology integration?* San Rafael, CA: The George Lucas Educational Foundation. Retrieved from http://www.edutopia.org/technology-integration-guide-description

Ehren, M. C., & Swanborn, M. S. (2012). Strategic data use of schools in accountability systems. *School Effectiveness and School Improvement, 23*(2), 257–280.

Ertmer, P. A. (1999). Addressing first- and second-order barriers to change: Strategies for technology integration. *Educational Technology Research and Development, 47*(4), 47–61.

Greller, W., & Drachsler, H. (2012). Translating learning into numbers: A generic framework for learning analytics. *Educational Technology & Society, 15*(3), 42–57.

Hargadon, A. B., & Douglas, Y. (2001). When innovations meet institutions: Edison and the design of the electric light. *Administrative Science Quarterly, 46*(3), 476–501.

IBM. (2013). *Big data at the speed of business: What is big data?* Armonk, NY: IBM Corporation. Retrieved from http://www-01.ibm.com/software/data/bigdata

Jacobs, Z., Wintleb, A. G., Dullerb, G. A. T., Robertsa, R. G., & Wadleyc, L. (2008). New ages for the post-Howiesons Poort, late and final Middle Stone Age at Sibudu, South Africa. *Science, 372*, 733–735.

Janzen, D., & Saiedian, H. (2005). Test-driven development concepts, taxonomy, and future direction. *Computer, 38*(9), 43–50.

Johnson, V. S. (1999). *Why we feel: The science of human emotions*. Reading, MA: Perseus Press.

Katten Muchin Rosenman. (2013, February 28). *The intersection of education and technology: Do we finally have the tools to save education?* [Video file]. Chicago, IL: Katten Muchin Rosenman, LLP, and the Illinois Technology Association. Retrieved from http://www.kattenlaw.com/files/upload/video/education_technology_seminar.wmv

Kazdin, A. E. (2000). *Psychotherapy for children and adolescents: Directions for research and practice*. New York, NY: Oxford University Press.

Kliebard, H. M. (1988). Success and failure in educational reform: Are there historical "lessons"? *Peabody Journal of Education, 65*(2), 143–157.

Kopcha, T. J. (2012). Teachers' perceptions of the barriers to technology integration and practices with technology under situated professional development. *Computers & Education, 59*, 1109–1121.

Lagemann, E. C. (2002). *An elusive science: The troubling history of education research*. Chicago, IL: University of Chicago Press.

Layng, T. V. J. (2012). *Technology changes in the classroom: In search of effective, flexible solutions* [White paper]. Retrieved from http://www.mimio.com/~/media/Files/Downloads/Partner-Resources/Whitepapers/Mimio_WhitePaper_TechnologyChanges.ashx

Layng, T. V. J. (2013a). *MimioReading Comprehension Suite: An effective, flexible solution to the changing technology in the classroom* [White paper]. Retrieved from http://www.mimio.com/~/media/Files/Downloads/Partner-Resources/Whitepapers/Whitepaper_MimioReadingComp.ashx

Layng, T. V. J. (2013b). *Understanding concepts: Implications for science teaching* [White paper]. Retrieved from http://www.mimio.com/~/media/Files/Downloads/Partner-Resources/Whitepapers/whitepaper_science_teaching.ashx

Layng, T. V. J., Sota, M., & Leon, M. (2011). Thinking through text comprehension I: Foundation and guiding relations. *The Behavior Analyst Today, 12*, 3–11.

Layng, T. V. J., & Stikeleather, G., & Twyman, J. S. (2006). Scientific formative evaluation: The role of individual learners in generating and predicting successful educational outcomes. In R. F. Subotnik & H. Walberg (Eds.), *The scientific basis of educational productivity* (pp. 29–44). Greenwich, CT: Information Age Publishing.

Layng, T. V. J., Twyman, J. S., & Stikeleather, G. (2004). Selected for success: How Headsprout Reading Basics™ teaches children to read. In D. J. Moran & R. W. Malott (Eds.), *Evidence-based education methods* (pp. 171–197). St. Louis, MO: Elsevier/Academic Press.

Leon, M., Layng, T. V. J., & Sota, M. (2011). Thinking through text comprehension III: The programing of verbal and investigative repertoires. *The Behavior Analyst Today, 12*, 21–32.

Leu, D. J., Kinzer, C. K., Coiro, J. L., & Cammack, D. W. (2004). Toward a theory of new literacies emerging from the Internet and other information and communication technologies. *Theoretical Models and Processes of Reading, 5*, 1570–1613.

Markle, S. M. (1967). Empirical testing of programs. In P. C. Lange (Ed.), *Programmed instruction: Sixty-sixth yearbook of the National Society for the Study of Education* (Vol. 2, pp. 104–138). Chicago, IL: University of Chicago Press.

Markle, S. M. (1990). *Designs for instructional designers*. Seattle, WA: Morningside Press.

Markle, S. M., & Tiemann, P. W. (1967). *Programming is a process* [film]. Chicago, IL: University of Illinois at Chicago.

McHaney, R. (2011). *The new digital shoreline: How Web 2.0 and millennials are revolutionizing higher education*. Sterling, VA: Stylus Publishing, LLC. Retrieved from http://books.google.com/books?hl=en&lr=&id=nuBywhoNRGkC&oi=fnd&pg=PR3&dq=The+new+digital+shoreline:+How+Web+2.0+and+millennials+are+revolutionizing+higher+education&ots=A1e1DrRrSS&sig=IsAWrz9bBETrds9uH-XNzHjMuXo

Means, B., Toyama, Y., Murphy, R., & Jones, K. (2010). *Evaluation of evidence-based practices in online learning: A meta-analysis and review of online learning studies* [Revised September 2010]. Washington, DC: U.S. Department of Education, Office of Planning, Evaluation, and Policy Development, Policy and Program Studies Service.

Mechner, F. (1994). *Learning and practicing skilled performance*. New York, NY: The Mechner Foundation. Retrieve from http://mechnerfoundation.org/pdf_downloads/skilled_performance.pdf

National Education Association. (2013). *Policy statement on digital learning*. Washington, DC: Author. Retrieved from http://www.nea.org/home/55434.htm

Rideout, V. J., Foehr, U. G., & Roberts, D. F. (2010). *Generation M2: Media in the lives of 8- to 18-year-olds*. Menlo Park, CA: Henry J. Kaiser Family Foundation.

Robbins, J. K. (2011). Problem solving, reasoning, and analytical thinking in a classroom environment. *The Behavior Analyst Today, 12*, 40–47.

Rumph, R., Ninness, C., McCuller, G., Holland, J., Ward, T., & Wilbourn, T. (2007). Stimulus change: Reinforcer or punisher? Reply to Hursh. *Behavior and Social Issues, 16*(1), 47–49.

Sarason, S. B. (1990). *The predictable failure of educational reform: Can we change course before it's too late?* The Jossey-Bass Education Series and the Jossey-Bass Social and Behavioral Science Series. San Francisco, CA: Jossey-Bass, Inc.

Shih, Y. E. (2007). Setting the new standard with mobile computing in online learning. *The International Review of Research in Open and Distance Learning, 8*(2). Retrieved from http://www.irrodl.org/index.php/irrodl/article/view/361/872.

Siemens, G., & Gasevic, D. (2012). Learning and knowledge analytics. *Educational Technology & Society, 15*(3), 1–2.

Simon, S. (2013). *K–12 student database jazzes tech startups, spooks parents.* New York, NY: Thomson Reuters. Retrieved from http://www.reuters.com/article/2013/03/03/us-education-database-idUSBRE92204W20130303

Skinner, B. F. (1954). The science of learning and the art of teaching. *Harvard Educational Review, 24*(2), 86–97.

Skinner, B. F. (1968). *The technology of teaching.* New York, NY: Appleton-Century-Crofts.

Skinner, B. F. (1984). The shame of American education. *American Psychologist, 39*(9), 947–954.

Slavin, R. E. (2002). Evidence-based education policies: Transforming educational practice and research. *Educational Researcher, 31*(7), 15–21.

Smith, A. G. (2011). Testing the surf: Criteria for evaluating Internet information resources. *Public Access-Computer Systems Review, 8*(3). Retrieved from http://journals.tdl.org/pacsr/index.php/pacsr/article/viewFile/6016/5645

Sota, M., Leon, M., & Layng, T. V. J. (2011). Thinking through text comprehension II: Analysis of verbal and investigative repertoires. *The Behavior Analyst Today, 12*, 12–20.

Strauss, V. (2013). Lawsuit charges Ed Department with violating student privacy rights [Web log message]. Washington, DC: Washington Post. Retrieved from http://www.washingtonpost.com/blogs/answer-sheet/wp/2013/03/13/lawsuit-charges-ed-department-with-violating-student-privacy-rights/

Tiemann, P. W., & Markle, S. M. (1991). *Analyzing instructional content.* Seattle, WA: Morningside Press.

Twyman, J. S. (in press). Behavior analysis in education. In F. K. McSweeney & E. S. Murphy (Eds.), *The Wiley-Blackwell handbook of operant and classical conditioning.* Hoboken, NJ: Wiley-Blackwell.

Twyman, J. S., Layng, T. V. J., Stikeleather, G., & Hobbins, K. A. (2004). A non-linear approach to curriculum design: The role of behavior analysis in building an effective reading program. In W. L. Heward et al. (Eds.), *Focus on behavior analysis in education* (Vol. 3, pp. 55–68). Upper Saddle River, NJ: Merrill/Prentice-Hall.

U.S. Department of Education, Office of Educational Technology. (2012a). *Enhancing teaching and learning through educational data mining and learning analytics* [Issue brief]. Washington, DC: Author.

U.S. Department of Education, Office of Educational Technology. (2012b). *Expanding evidence approaches for learning in a digital world.* Washington, DC: Author.

Vetter, R. J., & Severance, C. (1997). Web-based education experiences. *Computer, 30*(11), 139–143.

West, D. M. (2012). *Big data for education: Data mining, data analytics, and web dashboards.* Governance Studies. Washington, DC: Brookings Institute. Retrieved from http://www.brookings.edu/~/media/Research/Files/Papers/2012/9/04%20education%20technology%20west/04%20education%20technology%20west.pdf

Whimbey, A., & Lochhead, J. (1999). *Problem solving and comprehension.* New York, NY: Routledge.

Wilson, C., Orellana, M., & Meek, M. (2010, September 15). The learning machines. *The New York Times.* Retrieved from http://www.nytimes.com/interactive/2010/09/19/magazine/classroom-technology.html

Ybarra, M. L., & Suman, M. (2006). Help seeking behavior and the Internet: A national survey. *International Journal of Medical Informatics, 75*(1), 29–41.

# Games in Learning, Design, and Motivation
*Catherine C. Schifter*

Games in education have been studied for the last 40 years (Abt, 1970; Egenfeldt-Nielson, 2007; Loftus & Loftus, 1983). These works and others discussed in this paper espouse the potential for game-based education to support students' learning content as well as leadership and collaboration skills through imaginative, intriguing, and challenging play. Egenfeldt-Nielson (2011) noted that, while these claims are consistent over time, game-based learning has yet to be integrated into formal education. The research on games and education is vast but not conclusive, even though a number of journals and conferences are dedicated to the subject. In this research, games are termed serious games (Abt, 1970), video games (Gee, 2003), computer or digital games (Huang, 2012), and simulations (Bredemeier & Greenblat, 1981). One problem with games over the decades is the disconnect between game design and curricular goals. Likewise, the term "games" is all-encompassing and relates to situations in which an individual can play alone or with others, on a field (e.g., soccer or baseball), with a game board (e.g., *Monopoly* by Magie & Darrow in 1936), on a computer or not (e.g., *Dungeons & Dragons* by Gygax & Arneson in 1974, or *Vampire, the Masquerade* by Rein-Hagen in 1991), or with a game console (e.g., Wii, Xbox 360).

The Pew Internet & American Life Project (2008) is a report summarizing how popular video games are in the lives of young people. The authors state, "Video gaming is so widespread among American teenagers that to paint a portrait of a typical teen gamer is to hold a mirror to the population of teens as a whole. Nearly every teen plays games in some way, regardless of gender, age, or socioeconomic status" (Lenhart et al., 2008, p. 7). The Pew study surveyed approximately 1,100 participants, of which one third (31%) reported playing a game every day; of those daily gamers, 50% reported playing in "clans" or "guilds" (p. 10), which means they play with others online, sometimes in massively multiplayer online role-playing games. Additionally, the Entertainment Software Association (2011) reported that 72% of American households play computer or video games, with the average age of a player being 37 years. Thus, electronic games and gameplay are reported to be ubiquitous in the United States.

Games in the 21st century may be dependent on computers or not. For instance, *Minecraft* (Persson & Bergensten, 2009) and *SimCity* (Wright, 1989) are computer-based, sand-box type games, comparable to *Legos* (the building-block game) in that they present no prescribed story line or narrative progression but rather allow the player to imaginatively create a story. In these games, players roam a virtual world and change it at will. The point of the classic version of *Minecraft* is to explore the world presented in the game (which is random; each time a new world is created), mine building materials (e.g., wood or bricks to build, coal and a stick for a torch), and, if play is conducted in "survivor mode," to build a secure shelter against the "evil spiders" and "creepy-crawlers" that come out at night. The game can be played by a single individual on a desktop computer, laptop, or tablet, or by multiple players on a dedicated, secure server requiring permission to access.

Although *Minecraft* is a product of technology, its virtual activities may be made corporeal. A group of boys on a playground were asked what they were doing. They replied, "Playing *Minecraft* without the computer." They were pretending to mine supplies to build a structure to keep them safe from the creepy-crawlers. They were still playing the game *Minecraft*; it did not matter to the boys that there was no computer involved. They were "playing" a game that they knew how to play with or without technology to facilitate the play. They were taking what they learned by playing *Minecraft* on a computer and adapting that play to a different location, that is, transferring knowledge from one situation to another. This is one example of how children can take skills they learn in playing a game and apply those skills to another setting or problem (Shaffer, 2007), which is one of the skills set forth by the Partnership for 21st Century Skills (2011).

For schools and teachers to determine whether games of any form meet their curricular goals, they must first know what they mean by a "game." As noted above, research on games of all kinds has been published for over 40 years with mixed results for impact on education. For games to meet the goals of the Partnership for 21st Century Skills, a clear understanding of the broad scope of games in education is important. This chapter will first explore definitions and classifications of games or playing a game, looking at digital and nondigital games, and will then explore how games have been used in education to date. The chapter also includes proposed principles for how games can be used by state education agencies (SEAs), local education agencies (LEAs), and schools to address student learning and motivation to learn.

## What Makes a Game?

Most of us know a game when we see one. But trying to define a game is not straightforward, because there are classifications that have to do with (a) the number of players, such as solo-played games (e.g., solitaire, in all its variations), paired games (e.g., chess or handball), and team-based games (e.g., football or doubles tennis); and (b) type of activity, such as role-playing games (e.g., *Vampire, the Masquerade* not on a computer [Rein-Hagen, 1991] or *World of Warcraft* on a computer [Pardo, Kaplan, & Chilton, 2004]). A number of authors have attempted to provide guidelines for defining games (Avedon & Sutton-Smith, 1971; Caillois, 1961; Costikyan, 2005; Crawford, 1984; Huizinga, 2000; Parlett, 1999; Salen & Zimmerman, 2004; and Suits, 1978). This chapter focuses on Huizinga's seminal work and how a few others have modified it.

Huizinga, a Dutch cultural historian, wrote *Homo Ludens* ("Man the Player") in 1938.[1] He noted differences between the "game" as it is defined or described and "playing" the game, or the act of playing the game. Clearly, one is static and the other dynamic. Huizinga studied the act of playing games as elements of culture and suggested that to understand games or gaming one must understand how to play the game. Constance Steinkuehler (2005) also emphasized that one must play a game in order to understand the game and gameplay (e.g., mechanics), much as Huizinga proposed. According to Huizinga (2000, pp. 9–13), the central elements of playing a game include:

a. **Freedom**: Play is not work and is done during leisure time.
b. **Distinction**: Play is not what we do every day and, thus, is not ordinary. To play, we leave everyday life behind; play is totally separate from everyday life, in another location—real or imaginary.
c. **Order**: Play is orderly compared with everyday life.
d. **Beauty**: Play can be beautiful by enchanting and captivating our attention.
e. **Tension**: Play can be tense with competition and goals.
f. **Rules**: All play has rules that are binding and provide no doubt about the boundaries of play.
g. **Community**: Play creates community or a feeling of bonds between participants, clubs, teams, and so on.
h. **Secrecy**: Play includes pretense and disguise, masks, and fantasy—thus, secrecy (i.e., *Vampire, the Masquerade* [Rein-Hagen, 1991]).

Huizinga (2000) states his theory this way:
Summing up the formal characteristics of play we might call it a free activity standing quite consciously outside "ordinary" life as being "not serious," but at the same time absorbing the player intensely and utterly. It is an activity

---
[1] The work was first translated into English in 1949, with several reprints, including in 2000.

connected with no material interest, and no profit can be gained by it. It proceeds within its own proper boundaries of time and space according to fixed rules and in an orderly manner. It promotes the formation of social groupings which tend to surround themselves with secrecy and to stress their difference from the common world by disguise or other means. (p. 13)

In terms similar to Huizinga's, Bernard Suits, a philosopher, described "play as active, voluntary, goal oriented, bound by rules, inefficient, and based on the acceptance of the limitations of rules set for the game" (Suits, 1978, as quoted in Mortensen, 2009, p. 12). Roger Caillois (1961), a sociologist, added two additional features: "uncertainty" and the "absence of productivity." The outcomes are uncertain from the beginning; thus, each time play is enacted, the outcome or the circumstances of the outcome is different. For instance, you may play chess with the same opponent several times and win the game each time; however, the play of the pieces and how you won the game may be different each time, producing uncertainty. Lastly, other than professional players who play for money, lack of productivity relates to a lack of financial income as a result of play. The point of playing *World of Warcraft* (Pardo, Kaplan, & Chilton, 2004) is not to gain financial income, but to build a community or a "guild" made up of multiple players from around the world who work together to achieve a task or a challenge offered through the game. Trying to combine the 20th century gameplay definitions by Huizinga, Suits, and Caillois, Mortensen (2009) proffered these elements for "what makes playing a game different from regular, mundane activities: voluntary, bounded by rules, outside of the everyday, limited in time and space, tense, risky, inefficient, and unproductive" (p. 15). Most recently, Huang suggested that playing a game is associated with "goal-driven behaviors, complex tasks, active problem-solving, teamwork/autonomy, motivation to initiate and sustain behaviors, engagement to sustain behaviors, and enriched interactions between players and other players and the gaming system" (2012, slide 13). These traits or characteristics of game play are consistent with the skills set forth by the Partnership for 21st Century Skills (2011).

> *The point of playing World of Warcraft (Pardo, Kaplan, & Chilton, 2004) is not to gain financial income, but to build a community or a "guild" made up of multiple players from around the world who work together to achieve a task or a challenge offered through the game.*

Thus, from 1938 to 2012, how a game or gameplay is defined or identified as such has not changed significantly. What has changed is the media through which games are encountered. In the world known by Caillois and Suits, games were played on a field, game board, or through the imagination. Games since the advent of the microcomputer have added computer-based and video-based gameplay to the mix. However, we argue that any distinction to be made between games that are computer based and those that are not is irrelevant to the definition of a game; the inclusion of computer-based games within the broad range of games merely adds a medium or location for gameplay to occur. While there are games that were initially designed to be computer-mediated (e.g., *Minecraft*), they can be played without the computer, if imagination allows. This also applies to games initially designed to be played without a computer (e.g., *Solitaire*); however, playing on a computer obviates opportunities for cheating.

## Games in Education

While games of various types have been used in education since schooling began—including individual and team sports, board games (e.g., chess), and games created by children—educational games used in the 21st century arose in the 1950s through 1980s as alternatives to drill and practice, for enrichment activities, or as computer-assisted/programmed instruction systems (such as the PLATO system from the University of Illinois). The PLATO system consisted of a central computer connected to terminals by telephone lines or satellite. It was used for individual or small-group instruction and began being used in 1958 (Office of Technology Assessment, 1981). The first wave of educational software to emerge included *Number Munchers* and *Oregon Trail* developed by the Minnesota Education Computing Consortium, *Reader Rabbit* developed by The Learning Company, and *Where in the World is Carmen Sandiego* developed by Brøderbund Software, to name a few, when the mini-computer was introduced into classrooms in the 1980s. Where used, these software programs replaced educational playthings, like blocks and puzzles. In a review of educational games versus "edutainment" from the 1970s and 1980s, Mizuko Ito reported that "educational games put gaming at the center of the enterprise" (2008, p. 92). She stressed how what she called "children's software" (p. 92) was attempting to bridge the divide between education and the new concept of edutainment. Ito defined edutainment as an attempt by software developers to blend education and entertainment, thinking that entertainment would catch children's imagination and learning would be better than traditional education methods. She noted further that, as the educational software industry grew, three genres of edutainment developed initially: the academic, which embeds traditional academic content into games and is associated with behaviorist approaches and external rewards; the entertainment genre, which presents family-friendly, prosocial content appropriate for young children (e.g., nonviolent); and the construction genre, which focuses on constructing and authoring activities, not age specific, with Seymour Papert's *LOGO* as the prime example, along with *Kid Pix* (Brøderbund Software, 1991) and HyperStudio (Wagner, 1989). The construction genre software was not obviously educational or entertainment oriented. Ito suggested that as the educational software matured, these three genres devolved into two: software with mostly academic goals and software with mostly entertainment goals. In her review of educational software (2008), including educational games and edutainment, Ito concluded that many video games created in the 1980s for educational purposes, which she labeled academic, "focused on curricular content, rather than innovative gameplay," emphasized external rewards (i.e., badges or points), and reinforced school-like tasks (2008, pp. 93–94). She further suggested that, in putting educational content into video games with the intent on teaching children through gameplay or fun, developers and educators ran the risk of children recognizing the difference between fun, or entertainment, and school, or education.

> *A major difference between 21st century "serious games" and those from the 1980s is the ability to immerse the player into a virtual world where they perceive themselves as being part of the world rather than merely playing in the world.*

Dennis Charsky (2010), writing on the development of serious games from edutainment and supporting the work of Ito, reported that "edutainment and instructional computer games were once touted as the savior of education because of their ability to simultaneously entertain and educate" (p. 177). However, he goes on to remind us that after many years of implementing these games in schools, they had developed the reputation for being drill and practice masquerading as engaging play. Thus, while the educational software industry was partly established to move away from drill and practice, as illustrated by the PLATO system, teachers saw the products of this new industry as doing exactly what it was trying to replace.

## Digital or Serious Games in Education

As educational games have continued to progress since their initial development in the 1980s, they are termed "serious games" in the early 21st century. Serious games combine characteristics of video and computer-based games for immersive learning experiences intended to deliver specific goals, outcomes, and experiences (de Freitas, 2006). A major difference between 21st century "serious games" and those from the 1980s is the ability to immerse the player into a virtual world where they perceive themselves as being *part of* the world rather than merely *playing in* the world. In observing general trends in game research, de Freitas & Oliver (2006) note "an increasing popularity amongst learners for using serious games and simulations to support curricula objectives" (p. 250). Thus, it is not surprising that newer computer games are generating much interest across many educational arenas (e.g., classroom education, government, business, healthcare, hospitality). Garris, Ahlers, and Driskell (2002) posit the rise of serious games in educational settings is due to three factors. First, there is the emergence of a new paradigm in education, moving away from the teacher-centered model toward a more student-centered, experiential mode of teaching and learning and applied learning versus remembering information. Second, new interactive technologies have been developed over the last two decades allowing for computers to support interactivity between individuals who are separated spatially, even if only in the next classroom, along with tools that will record these activities into a database for analysis purposes. Third, serious games have the capacity, if designed appropriately, to capture students' attention and hold it through various activities. Mayo (2007) suggests the advantages to using serious games in education include, but are not limited to, experiential learning, inquiry-based learning, goal setting, cooperation or competition, continuous feedback, and time on task. Expanding on the work of Garris et al. (2002) and Mayo (2007), Wrzesien and Alcañiz Raya (2010) advocate for the use of serious games in education for three main reasons which take into account the skills proposed in the Framework for 21st Century Learning first published in 2002 (Partnership for 21st Century Skills, 2011): (a) They use actions rather than explanations and create personal motivation and satisfaction; (b) they accommodate multiple learning styles and abilities; and (c) they foster decision making and problem solving in virtual settings, thus allowing students to affect the virtual world and see potential impacts of decisions, or return and try another solution for comparison.

James Gee (2004), a linguist by training, notes that as games have become more complex (i.e., serious games), they have incorporated scaffolding, intelligent tutors, and affinity groups for learning. He further suggests serious games represent experiential learning spaces where learners encounter rich, collaborative, and cooperative activities and interactions. In these spaces, they offer learners complex tools and resources for complex problem solving (Gee, 2003). Using personal experiences with *World of Warcraft* (Pardo et al., 2004) and observational data of children engaged with gaming environments, Gee argues that children learn more and better through these environments, if the games are designed appropriately to stimulate higher-order thinking and collaborative activities. Thus, his argument agrees with that of Garris et al. (2002), as noted above, that serious games may be more likely to address 21st-century skill development through scaffolding of learning, active rather than passive interactions, support of multiple learning styles by using intelligent tutors and affinity group support, cooperative and collaborative experiences/activities/interactions, and complex problem solving.

## Paradigm of Game-Based Learning

Shaffer (2007) noted that researchers have shown that well-designed computer/video games can teach players innovative and creative ways of thinking, deep understanding of complex academic content, and valuable forms of real-world skills, given their ability to provide rich, complex, and compelling virtual worlds (see Adams, 1998; Barab, Hay, Barnett, & Squire, 2001; Gee, 2003; Shaffer,

2005, 2007; Starr, 1994). A new paradigm of game-based learning has emerged, one centered on theories of situated cognition, arguing that people learn best when engaged in activities that are goal-directed so they are meaningfully engaged and invited to be "experts" in some area of the game (Gee, 2003; Shaffer, 2007; Shaffer, Squire, Halverson, & Gee, 2005). According to Squire (2007), "These games give us access to the ways of thinking (including knowledge, skills, values, and dispositions) of experts, and invite us to experience the world in new ways" (p. 53).

Integration of games into teaching and learning activities has been a challenge from the beginning for many reasons. As noted, game development has not been in sync with curriculum needs. Although the digital or immersive delivery format in modern games is new, the experience for many teachers in schools using these games is strangely similar to what happened with bringing electronic technology (e.g., films, video, television) into schools over approximately 75 years: There was a disjunction between the new technology and what needed to be taught (the curriculum). While games may provide interesting formats and add motivation to various activities, a missing critical piece is helping teachers learn how to think about games within teaching content. Regardless of delivery, as educators we must remember that content is what is important. If content (and outcomes) are separate from the activity, teachers tend to think of games as trivial, unimportant, or time fillers. For a truly beneficial integration of games into education, the issues around what teachers are asked to teach (e.g., the curriculum) and the tools provided must be connected.

In her review of educational games cited above, Ito (2008) stated that original educational software intended for use on mini-computers was not designed with curricula in mind, nor vice versa. This is also true with the new, serious games; thus, if a teacher finds a serious game that his or her students find engaging and motivating, that same game may or may not coincide with the goals of the curriculum in use. Barriers to game use in schools include a lack of access to equipment, especially up-to-date equipment (e.g., graphics/video cards), preventing the use of newer, sophisticated game programs in classrooms (de Freitas, 2006). Multiplayer, serious game platforms popular with teens and adults and rich in imagery provide opportunities to "visit" the U.S. Capitol Building without needing to travel to Washington, DC or go through the security barriers. These platforms are powerful for introducing historical events or conditions, but they can be unmanageable for teachers uncomfortable with the game genre. Also, some instructional technology policies prevent accessing Internet sites identified with games, thus blocking access for meaningful interaction between players at a distance. Because these serious game environments are highly immersive and collaborative, teachers' supervision of the classroom and students can be challenging. As stated at the beginning of this chapter, key findings from the literature suggest that—in spite of a preponderance of articles, journals, and conference papers devoted to how games, in their various forms, can support teaching and learning—the empirical evidence is inconclusive to support claims that games in any format transform teaching and learning for all.

Richard Van Eck notes that young children today, those part of the net generation, "require multiple streams of information, prefer inductive reasoning, want frequent and quick interactions with content, and have exceptional visual literacy skills" (2006, p. 16). Understanding these children and their approaches to learning is a challenge to teachers schooled during the era of text-based teaching and teacher-centered instruction. Thus, if these 21st-century games are to be included by teachers to support their teaching and students' learning through differentiated instruction, connections between the games and instructional strategies must be explicit. Using the new types of serious games or even new versions of well-traveled games (e.g., *Where in the World is Carmen Sandiego* [Brøderbund Software, 1985]) without considering the new types of students and how they learn may miss the mark.

## Proposed Principles for SEAs, LEAs, and Schools on Games in Education

As discussed above, the possible combinations of game features—such as number of players, venue, nature of rewards—is large. The biggest challenge for any game is to fit into a curriculum or, at minimum, fit a particular teacher's instructional style. A new report from the Joan Gantz Cooney Center at Sesame Workshop puts it this way:

> Making games work in the classroom requires an understanding not only of issues specific to learning games, but also of the systematic barriers to entry and constraints of the K–12 environment for any supplemental product in the K–12 space. The dominance of a few entrenched players, the long buying cycle, the multi-layered decision making process, the fragmented marketplace, the demand for curriculum alignment, the requirement of a research base, and the need for professional development all will [have an] impact. (Richards, Stebbins, & Moellering, 2013, p. 53)

Larry Cuban (1985) documented how each new technology invented to make education easier for teaching and learning—moving from still images to film to "talkies" to television to computers—has not delivered on its promise. In fact, he noted that problems with technology (e.g., filmstrips breaking, projector bulbs burning out, and more) made it more likely that teachers used technology merely as a supplement, as opposed to infusing it into the teaching and learning process. Even in the more recent era of digital technologies, the case continues to be made that without the integration of educational programs, technology, and theory, significant progress in learning and instruction will not occur (Spector, 2001).

Given Cuban's and others' rather bleak picture of technology's limited ability to support teaching and learning over time, how are SEA, LEA, and school administrators to move forward with current educational software, and games in particular? The first principle is to connect the curriculum and the games to be used, or identify what goals/objectives/competencies are addressed through the educational software or game that cannot be achieved through other means. As noted by Charsky (2010), there are different types of games, but educational games tend to be seen by students as representing old ways of teaching (e.g., drill and practice) rather than engaging and motivating to learn. So here the point is not to make a list of games that may be relevant but to work with game developers and game researchers to identify games that specifically meet the goals of education at different levels (e.g., pre-K, elementary and middle grades, and high school). Ito suggests the construction genre of games has the best chance for transforming the conditions of childhood learning since they are participatory and may include opportunities for self-authoring, digital authoring, online journaling, and social networking—all aspects of 21st-century skills (Partnership for 21st Century Skills, 2011). Supporting local educational administrators and teachers by helping them work through how educational games can be harnessed for learning is essential.

The difficulties are the same for SEAs, LEAs, and even individual teachers: How can connections between computer software and games and curricula be made? How do we sift through the myriad of offerings to find quality instruction? One source of guidance is a paper by Klopfer, Osterweil, and Salen (2009) entitled *Moving Games Forward: Obstacles, Opportunities, and Openness*. The authors stress that the first goal is to identify the obstacles to incorporating games, serious or otherwise, into the learning process. Recent work by product developers toward aligning computer software (including games) to the Common Core may also be of assistance, as noted in the recent article, *Games and the Common Core: Two Movements That Need Each Other* (Chen, 2013).

Principles for schools in implementing or infusing games into lessons are more specific. Alexander, Eaton, and Egan (2010) proposed three main approaches for teachers, principles, parents, and others who oversee public education to understanding the connection between games and education: (a) seeing games as teaching desirable learning skills through play; (b) focusing on integration of curriculum content into games (but cf. Ito's perspective, above); and (c) extracting learning principles embedded in e-games and applying those to the educational context. Here, the foremost point is that teachers and school administrators must see that desirable learning skills can be attained through playing games. If this proposition is not accepted, then games will never be included at any level. Making the connection between curriculum and game content helps teachers, principals, and other administrators to make connections for students. However, Ito's warning—that students will perceive the scam of games masquerading as education—underscores the need to think through how the games really support the curriculum. Here, school administrators might consider the construction genre of games in which mathematics, social studies, and writing could be incorporated. However, this approach requires knowledge of the games and the curriculum to help teachers and parents see the connections.

Another approach to understanding the connection between computer software and games to 21st-century classrooms, teaching, and learning is to consider the skills and abilities to be acquired through the games—analysis, deduction, discrimination, and rule following, among other skills. In this approach, learning is active because players must interact with the game in order to learn the skills. This approach resonates with the work of Gee (2003), Ko (2002), and Moreno and Mayer (2007), who all suggest that in order for children to glean the most from educational games, they must be actively engaged.

One more approach to understanding the connection between computer software and games to 21st-century classrooms, teaching, and learning is to consider how serious games can be used to teach content. For this application, games are used as an external motivator, whether for drill and practice or for other types of learning. As noted by Lenhart et al. (2008) in a report for the Pew Research Center, most American teenagers are playing games, so this transfer could be important. Games can be used to practice information (e.g., the use of *Jeopardy* [Griffin, 1964] in any subject). Although these games may not have been designed for educational purposes, adapting them can support learning by reinforcing students' knowledge. The problem is that they are perhaps not as interactive as e-games, as supported by Gee (2003). As more games are being designed specifically with the classroom in mind, such as *Quest Atlantis* (Barab, Thomas, Dodge, Carteaux, & Tuzun, 2005), it is essential to ensure that the learning outcomes match the educational aims of using the games. As noted by Alexander, Eaton, and Egan (2010), "It is not at all clear that game requirements do not inadvertently compete with and displace intended curricular objectives" (p. 1838).

> *One more approach to understanding the connection between computer software and games to 21st-century classrooms, teaching, and learning is to consider how serious games can be used to teach content.*

The last approach to improving the effective use of games in the classroom entails teachers analyzing what is engaging about an online game, and then applying it to curriculum. The aspects of online games that players enjoy include the narrative structure (beginnings, middles, and ends), "heroic" human qualities ("secrecy" from Huizinga), vivid images and emotional engagement ("beautiful" from Huizinga), distant locations or events ("extraordinary" from Huizinga), and role playing, which invokes rules. Capitalizing on how these aspects can be used in any area of teaching and learning will be essential.

For administrators of SEAs, LEAs, and schools, the key to getting teachers to infuse games into teaching and learning will be helping them see the relationship between the content within the game and curricular goals/competencies to be attained. Most teachers are not going to establish effective gaming classrooms by themselves, and they are not going to learn how to establish them in a teacher education program or an afternoon or summer professional development program. An ongoing support network for teachers interested in infusing game features into their practice needs to be created, a network comprised of the principal and colleagues equally engaged in the effort, and further supported with time for the teachers to see how gaming works for others and in their own classrooms (Schifter, 2008). Without a model to support teachers' exploration of games in their practice, teachers will resort to those teaching methods they understand best. Games, like educational software, have been shown in studies to have positive impacts on learning in laboratory settings (Barab et al., 2001; Shaffer, 2007), but when implemented in classrooms, they have been less than stellar (Ito, 2008; Charsky, 2010). The problem is not necessarily with the games themselves as with the lack of support and understanding of how change in teaching cultures happens over time.

## Action Principles

a. Align games with curriculum content objectives, including the Common Core Standards.
b. Decide what learning skills need improvement or development and choose games which address those skills, rather than the other way around.
c. Provide opportunities for teachers to be part of manufacturers' demonstrations to ensure a thorough understanding of how the game is intended to work and how to maximize student outcomes.
d. Encourage partnerships between educators and game manufacturers, particularly in a game's development stage.
e. Contact manufacturers and volunteer to be part of teacher focus groups as games are developed.
f. Choose games that consider engagement factors, such as action, imagery, role playing, and so forth.
g. Be knowledgeable about hardware–software compatibility, upgrades, licensing fees, shelf-life, and so on when choosing games. Keep in mind the total cost of purchases.

## References

Abt, C. (1970). *Serious games*. New York, NY: Viking Press.

Adams, P. C. (1998). Teaching and learning with SimCity 2000. *Journal of Geography, 97*(2), 47–55.

Alexander, G., Eaton, I., & Egan, K. (2010). Cracking the code of electronic games: Some lessons for educators. *Teachers College Record, 112*(7), 1830–1850.

Avedon, E. M., & Sutton-Smith, B. (1971). *The study of games*. New York, NY: John Wiley & Sons.

Barab, S. A., Hay, K. E., Barnett, M. G., & Squire, K. (2001). Constructing virtual worlds: Tracing the historical development of learner practices/understandings. *Cognition and Instruction, 19*(1), 47–94.

Barab, S. A., Thomas, M., Dodge, T., Carteaux, R., & Tuzun, H. (2005). Making learning fun: Quest Atlantis, a game without guns. *Educational Technology Research and Development, 53*(1), 86–107.

Bredemeier, M. E., & Greenblat, C. S. (1981). The educational effectiveness of simulation games: A synthesis of findings. *Simulation & Gaming, 12*(3), 307–331.

Brøderbund Software. (1985). *Where in the World is Carmen Sandiego*. Eugene, OR: Author.

Brøderbund Software. (1991). *Kid Pix*. Eugene, OR: Author.

Caillois, R. (1961). *Man, play, and games*. New York, NY: Free Press of Glencoe.

Charsky, D. (2010). From edutainment to serious games: A change in the use of game characteristics. *Games & Culture, 5*(2), 177–198.

Chen, M. (2013, April). *Games and the Common Core: Two movements that need each other*. Palo Alto, CA: The George Lucas Educational Foundation. Retrieved from http://www.edutopia.org/blog/games-common-core-need-each-other-milton-chen

Costikyan, G. (2005, June). *Game styles, innovation, and new audiences: An historical view*. Paper presented at the meeting of the Digital Games Research Association (DiGRA), Vancouver. Retrieved from http://www.digra.org/digital-library/publications/game-styles-innovation-and-new-audiences-an-historical-view/

Crawford, C. (1984). *The art of game design*. Berkeley, CA: Osborne/McGraw-Hill.

Cuban, L. (1985). *Teachers and machines: The classroom use of technology since 1920*. New York, NY: Teachers College Press.

de Freitas, S. (2006). *Learning in immersive worlds: A review of game-based learning*. Prepared for the JISC e-learning programme. Retrieved from http://www.jisc.ac.uk/media/documents/programmes/elearninginnovation/gamingreport_v3.pdf

de Freitas, S., & Oliver, M. (2006). How can exploratory learning with games and simulations within the curriculum be most effectively evaluated? *Computers & Education, 46*, 249–264.

Egenfeldt-Nielson, S. (2007). *The educational potential of computer games*. New York, NY: Continuum Press.

Egenfeldt-Nielson, S. (2011). The challenges of diffusion of educational computer games. In T. Connelly (Ed.), *Leading issues in games-based learning research* (Vol. 1, pp. 141–158). Reading, UK: Ridgeway Press.

Entertainment Software Association. (2011). *Essential facts about the computer and video game industry*. Washington, DC: Author. Retrieved from http://www.theesa.com/facts/pdfs/ESA_EF_2011.pdf

Garris, R., Ahlers, R., & Driskell, J. E. (2002). Games, motivation, and learning: A research and practice model. *Simulation & Gaming, 33*(4), 441–467.

Gee, J. P. (2003). *What video games have to teach us about learning and literacy*. New York, NY: Palgrave Macmillan.

Gee, J. P. (2004). *Situated language and learning: A critique of traditional schooling*. New York, NY: Routledge.

Griffin, M. (1964). *Jeopardy*. New York, NY: NBC Studios.

Gygax, G., & Arneson, D. (1974). *Dungeons & Dragons*. Geneva Lake, WI: TSR, Inc.

Huang, W. D. (2012, April). *Fully immersive digital game-based learning (FIDGBL) in e-learning*. Paper presented at the meeting of the American Society for Training and Development (ASTD), Denver, CO.

Huizinga, J. (2000). *Homo Ludens: A study of play-element in culture*. London, UK: Routledge.

Ito, M. (2008). Education vs. entertainment: A cultural history of children's software. In K. Salen (Ed.), *The ecology of games* (pp. 89–116). Cambridge, MA: The MIT Press.

Klopfer, E., Osterweil, S., & Salen, K. (2009). *Moving games forward: Obstacles, opportunities and openness*. Cambridge, MA: The Education Arcade, Massachusetts Institute of Technology. Retrieved from http://education.mit.edu/papers/MovingLearningGamesForward_EdArcade.pdf

Ko, S. (2002). An empirical analysis of children's thinking and learning in a computer game context. *Educational Psychology, 22*, 219–233.

Lenhart, A., Kahne, J., Middaugh, E., Macgill, A. R., Evans, C., & Vitak, J. (2008, September). *Teens, video games, and civics: Teens' gaming experiences are diverse and include significant social interaction and civic engagement*. Washington, DC: Pew Internet & American Life Project. Retrieved from http://www.pewinternet.org/~/media//Files/Reports/2008/PIP_Teens_Games_and_Civics_Report_FINAL.pdf.pdf

Loftus, G. R., & Loftus, E. (1983). *Mind at play*. New York, NY: Basic Books.

Magie, E., & Darrow, C. (1936). *Monopoly*. Salem, MA: Parker Brothers.

Mayo, M. J. (2007). Games for science and engineering education. *Communications of the ACM, 50*(7), 31–35.

Moreno, R., & Mayer, R. (2007). Interactive multimodal learning environments. *Educational Psychology Review, 19*, 309–326.

Mortensen, T. E. (2009). *Perceiving play: The art and study of computer games*. New York, NY: Lang.

Office of Technology Assessment. (1981). *Information technology and its impact on American education*. Washington, DC: U.S. Government Printing Office. Retrieved from http://books.google.com/books?id=mi1hy_DYW_kC&printsec=frontcover#v=onepage&q&f=false

Pardo, R., Kaplan, J., & Chilton, T. (2004). *World of Warcraft* [Massively multiplayer online role-playing game]. Irvine, CA: Blizzard Entertainment.

Parlett, D. S. (1999). *The Oxford history of board games*. Oxford, UK: Oxford University Press.

Partnership for 21st Century Skills. (2011). *Framework for 21st century learning*. Washington, DC: Author. Retrieved from http://www.p21.org/overview

Persson, M., & Bergensten, J. (2009). *Minecraft*. Stockholm, Sweden: Mojang, AB.

Rein-Hagen, M. (1991). *Vampire, The Masquerade*. Stone Mountain, GA: White Wolf Publishing.

Richards, J., Stebbins, L., & Moellering, K. (2013). *Games for a digital age: K–12 market map and investment analysis*. New York, NY: Joan Gantz Cooney Center at Sesame Workshop. Retrieved from http://www.joanganzcooneycenter.org/wp-content/uploads/2013/01/glpc_gamesforadigitalage1.pdf

Salen, K., & Zimmerman, E. (2004). *Rules of play: Game design fundamentals*. Cambridge, MA: MIT Press.

Schifter, C. (2008). *Infusing technology into the classroom: Continuous practice improvement*. Hershey, PA: IGI Global.

Shaffer, D. W. (2005). Epistemic games. *Innovate, 1*(6). Retrieved from http://edgaps.org/gaps/wp-content/uploads/ShafferEpistemic_games_2005.pdf

Shaffer, D. W. (2007). *How computer games help children learn*. New York, NY: Palgrave Macmillan.

Shaffer, D. W., Squire, K., Halverson, R., & Gee, J. P. (2005). Video games and the future of learning. *Phi Delta Kappan, 87*(2), 104–111.

Spector, J. M. (2001). An overview of progress and problems in educational technology. *Digital Education Review, 3*, 27–37.

Squire, K. (2007). Games, learning, and society: Building a field. *Educational Technology, 4*(5), 51–54.

Starr, P. (1994). Seductions of Sim: Policy as a simulation game. *The American Prospect, 5*(17), 19–29.

Steinkuehler, C. A. (2005). *Cognition and learning in massively multiplayer online games: A critical approach* (Doctoral dissertation). University of Wisconsin–Madison.

Suits, B. (1978). *The grasshopper: Games, life, and utopia*. Toronto, Canada: Toronto University Press.

Van Eck, R. (2006). Digital game-based learning: It's not just the digital natives who are restless. *EDUCAUSE Review, 41*(2), 16–30.

Wagner, R. (1989). *Hyperstudio*. Boston, MA: Software MacKiev.

Wright, W. (1989). *SimCity*. Redwood, CA: Electronic Arts.

Wrzesien, J., & Alcañiz Raya, M. (2010). Learning in serious virtual worlds: Evaluation of learning effectiveness and appeal to students in the E-Junior project. *Computers & Education, 55*, 178–187.

# Advances in Online Learning
## Herbert J. Walberg and Janet S. Twyman

The fundamental idea of distance education can be traced to the emergence of cuneiform and pictographic records that transmitted ideas across distance and time from one person to another, often instructing them on how to proceed with a task. Perhaps the origin of modern distance education is best traced to the University of Chicago, which offered mail correspondence courses for college credit beginning in 1892. The University of Iowa pioneered television broadcast courses in 1933, and at the same time, various efforts were begun in Australia to reach remote outback schools and in England to reach those that were unable to attend college classes.[1]

In 1971, the Advanced Research Projects Agency Network made possible the speedy electronic transmission of data—the origin of the global Internet, which was further opened to increasingly more users by IBM's personal computer for use in homes, schools, and offices. Not long after, universities began offering courses online. Heralded as one of the most significant trends in higher education in decades, online course offerings experienced meteoric growth in the 1990s and 2000s. While the rate of new online courses offered has leveled off to around 10% a year over the past decade, online education has made significant inroads in institutions of all types (Allen & Seaman, 2011). For example, the University of Phoenix, probably the best-known online university, enrolled 380,000 students in 2010 and had the highest student enrollment of any postsecondary institution in the U.S. (National Center for Education Statistics, 2011). In the last few years, Harvard, MIT, Stanford, and other universities have begun offering free, nondegree online courses taught by top professors to interested students

---

[1] For the history and older findings and principles described in this chapter, see Ely and Plomp's comprehensive *International Encyclopedia of Educational Technology* (1996).

anywhere in the world with Internet access, and many colleges today offer some courses online.

## Advances in Online Education

This capsule history suggests the potential of online education to make high-quality education readily and cheaply available to vast numbers of students anywhere in the world—"24/7/365." Online courses (those delivered digitally) may be delivered with the teacher in the room or thousands of miles away. The advent, quick adoption, and now widespread prevalence of Internet-connected mobile devices, the ubiquity of high-speed Wi-Fi connections, the availability of video- and screen-capturing, and the explosion of digital content have fueled the growth of online courses. If a course is to be used by tens or hundreds of thousands or even millions of students, it is worthwhile to prepare it thoroughly in terms of the currency and accuracy of the content, the best means of instruction, the optimal use of media—auditory and visual—and the selective use of interaction among students and course leaders. Teams of specialists in these areas can far exceed the knowledge and skills of even the greatest teachers working alone.[2] The course materials and procedures can be tried out and critically evaluated by the team and, preferably, by others who have not participated in its development, thereby lending objectivity and additional perspectives. Modern technologies allow data collection on student responses, learning patterns, content access, and a myriad of information on learning effects. On the basis of what is gleaned, the course may be revised and improved, then used repeatedly, perhaps even for a decade, for skills and subjects that do not change rapidly such as algebra, ancient history, second language learning, and grammar and spelling.

> *Modern technologies allow data collection on student responses, learning patterns, content access, and a myriad of information on learning effects.*

Courses may be assembled from preexisting modules or discrete lessons, and courses may be planned as a series of modules. These may be used in a fixed sequence, which is more necessary in some subjects, for example, in algebra. Alternatively, curriculum consultants, teachers, and students can assemble a variety of multiyear programs of study from modules, courses, and experiences, depending on state and local curriculum requirements. Along with the subject matter and skills acquired in online learning, students gain exposure to modern technology skills such as advanced Internet searching, information curating, and social networking that are becoming essential in modern life, including occupations and professions. Of course, many students below the age of 18 have had

---

[2] For empirical evidence on the accomplishments, further potential, and criticism of online learning, see Casey & Lorenzen, 2010; Dickey, 2005; and Oblinger, 2000.

considerable experience with online technology and have far greater speed and skill than many older adults, including most traditional educators, making young students more comfortable with online learning.

Remote high schools in sparsely settled areas can offer courses to a few advanced students who would otherwise be denied such courses as calculus, differential equations, and animal husbandry. Since online education can be delivered day and night in many nonconventional school settings, it offers the possibility of great savings in the cost of erecting and maintaining traditional school buildings and the waste of student travel time.

## Accommodating the Individual Student

Students need not take online courses only in school, and such courses can serve equally well a variety of students in highly varied circumstances, regardless of sociometric status, residence area, gender, ethnicity, race, and age. Children with disabilities or those who are ill can take courses at home or in hospitals and other institutions. Few traditional elementary school students have access to the study of Latin or Swahili, but these might be offered online, as can a multitude of other subjects and topics.

A careful selection of lessons, modules or units, and courses to suit individual learners in online programs can far better accommodate such student diversity than can traditional schools. In addition, online education programs are increasingly incorporating what is analogous to tutoring in traditional education but which has been seldom used for most students because of its cost. Advanced online programs can continuously track each individual's responses to elements of the lessons. In the event of an error, the programs can provide repetition of the lesson's element or a new way of presenting it such that the student avoids practicing errors and the probability of his or her mastery is greatly increased, particularly for lessons, topics, and courses that are inherently sequential. When instruction is delivered online, it can be customized and its user's achievement instantly measured, all resulting in a greater personalized learning experience.

## Unwarranted Criticism of Online Programs

Though usually lacking scientific evidence and often concerned about competition and job security, traditional educators have leveled much criticism of online learning. They usually cite the lack of stimulation elicited by stirring lectures, insights prompted by the give-and-take of class discussion, and the opportunity to respond to students' questions. Traditional lectures (of the "sage on the stage") are a one-way means of transmitting knowledge and understanding. For one-way transmission, however, reading is hard to beat. By the middle grades, students can typically read 3 times faster than adults, including teachers, ordinarily can speak. Moreover, fluent readers can suit the pace of the reading to what they need; they may skip over parts they already know, and they may spend far more time than others on the parts that are difficult for them to master. In addition, if lectures are preferred, perhaps on the grounds that they are especially motivating, they may easily be (and often are) incorporated into online education, as in the short, stimulating TED lectures by outstanding, well-prepared performers. In addition, professionally prepared illustrative graphics and short films teachers may find difficult to prepare can be incorporated into online programs.

The other frequent claim against online education is that it lacks the superior socialization of traditional schools and the stimulation of classroom discussion, much less the excitement of out-of-school life. More than a half century ago, James Coleman (1961) pointed out the intensity of the adolescent society often in opposition to responsible adults and how preoccupations with cars, clothes, and dating undermine education. Perhaps today's intense involvement with sports, unconstructive Internet surfing, and walking the shopping malls have added to the adolescent distractions from learning. Similar to the problem of lecturing, instruction geared to, say, the middle of the class may be too difficult for the slower learners and already known and comprehended well by advanced learners, thus wasting the time and adding to the boredom of both. Student questions and comments typically have the same problem of suiting the level of the lesson to learners with varying interests, abilities, prior knowledge, and speeds of learning.

Perhaps a warranted criticism of online instruction, however, may be that many of today's instructors are unfamiliar or untrained in the use of online instructional tools and online pedagogy. A particular skill set and understanding of how online learning opportunities can be created and enhanced are required to make an effective education course. Designers and instructors of online education courses not only need to be well versed in the traditional skills—such as knowledge of the subject matter, proficiency in designing instruction, and active student learning with clear expectations and timely feedback—they also must be proficient in the tools of technology and expectations that come with online learning. Learning management systems, chat or discussion boards, and other social networking tools, shared online (increasingly "cloud"-based) repositories, planning synchronous (simultaneous) as well as asynchronous learning experiences, and the awareness of accessibility standards are just a few of the skills needed to successfully teach an online course. This need is beginning to be addressed through the use of online communities, informal and formal professional development, training (free or paid) offered by content or system providers, and even certificate programs in e-learning.

## Barriers to Online Education

There is a widespread but perhaps diminishing attitude among administrators and educators, especially at the K–12 level, that online or distance education courses are not as rigorous as traditional bricks and mortar programs. A 2011

Sloan Consortium report indicated that less than one third of chief academic officers say their faculty see the value and legitimacy of online education (Allen & Seaman, 2011). This may be a result of concern over a teacher's assumed ability to "directly" monitor the student during the learning process (i.e., while in the classroom) and instead having to resort to online testing, or products produced by the student, or other methods typically considered "indirect" measures of student learning. Proponents argue that online experiences provide much richer opportunities for learning and accessing a breadth of course material, and the evolving tools for monitoring and assuring student participation remove many of the causes of concern regarding independence of student work. The causal reasoning on both sides of this argument is speculative, but evidence cited below supports online methods with respect to achievement outcomes.

Another barrier at the K–12 level is the practice of reimbursing school districts for student "seat time," the amount of time students spend in the classroom, typically 180 days per year minimum. Schools are grappling with how to account for online or distance education within the seat time formula, with 36 states creating policies that take into account credit-for-performance in addition to or in lieu of physical time spent in class (Cavanagh, 2012). More

> *"Transitioning away from seat time, in favor of a structure that creates flexibility, allows students to progress as they demonstrate mastery of academic content, regardless of time, place, or pace of learning."*
> U.S. Department of Education, 2013

guidance for states on how to accomplish this may be forth-coming, as the U.S. Department of Education also is deemphasizing seat time, stating: "Transitioning away from seat time, in favor of a structure that creates flexibility, allows students to progress as they demonstrate mastery of academic content, regardless of time, place, or pace of learning" (2013, para. 1). Increased standardization of digital content, program interface, and reporting systems may also need to occur before the effectiveness of online education becomes fully realized at scale. Currently, educators often need to learn several different tools with unique interfaces and differing operations. In addition, these independent (unconnected) learning systems may not provide the interoperability essential to build useful extensive data systems and networks of information to be used or shared by multiple teachers, schools, districts, or systems. As part of the digital education movement, both governmental programs (e.g., the State Educational Technology Directors Association) as well as private organizations (e.g., IMS Group; the Association of Educational Publishers) are promoting the use of common standards for digital materials, allowing digital products from any source to be readily integrated into a school's or college's learning management system.

## Online Education Principles Exemplified

Though hundreds of online programs could be cited and described, two seem particularly valuable to illustrate the benefits of digital education: the Khan Academy and the MimioSprout and MimioReading suite of products. Each of these programs offers the following features, which are representative of the best in online learning:

- personalization of learning and instruction;
- the potential to increase motivation;
- increased access across locations and times of the day;
- improved abilities to collect and evaluate data;
- increased resources for teacher training;
- the potential to streamline systems and processes; and
- the ability to generate learning analytics (see Twyman, 2013).

### Khan Academy

As an outgrowth of his response to a young relative's need for school tutoring and instruction, Bangladeshi-American Salman Khan, a graduate of the Massachusetts Institute of Technology and the Harvard Business School, created his eponymous nonprofit academy in 2006. By 2012, it provided free, short online video tutorials in mathematics, physics, general and organic chemistry, biology, healthcare and medicine, macro- and microeconomics, finance, astronomy and cosmology, history, American civics, art history, and computer science.

Each tutorial is a complete, custom, self-paced learning tool. The system provides custom-tailored help for students with problems, and awards points and badges to measure and incentivize student progress. Coaches, parents, and teachers can view a student's progress in detail and analyze multiple students' progress for targeted interventions.

The aim of the Khan Academy is to provide tens of thousands of lessons to serve anyone, anywhere, anytime—a world-class education for the worlds of children, adolescents, and adults. By 2012, Khan Academy had served more than 200 million students and many uncounted more with philanthropically sponsored, offline versions for economically underdeveloped areas of Africa, Asia, and Latin America (see Khan Academy, 2013; Noer, 2012; Rasicot, 2011; Young, 2010).

### MimioSprout and MimioReading

Two pioneer programs, Headsprout Early Reading and Reading Comprehension, provided online individualized instruction that employed engaging animation and colorful graphics and was highly refined with psychological principles as well as formative and summative evidence on effects. Now known as MimioSprout and MimioReading (see Mimio, 2013), these products were built and released in the early 2000s, just as parents and educators were beginning to realize the power of the Internet in providing quality instruction as a supplement to or replacement for teacher-delivered, classroom-based instruction. A review of the features of these programs clearly illustrates the utility and power of online education.

Both Internet-based reading programs developed their content and teaching interactions from current evidence and known best practice. Headsprout Early Reading/MimioSprout teaches the research-based fundamental skills identified by the National Reading Panel (National Institute of Child Health and Human Development, 2000) as critical to reading success. The content of Headsprout Reading Comprehension/MimioReading is based not only on a scientific analysis of what it means to comprehend text (e.g., Goldiamond & Dyrud, 1966), but also on a systematic review of how comprehension is taught and what works in schools. The development method included formative evaluation (see Layng, Stikeleather, & Twyman, 2006) and a nonlinear, behavior-analytic design process. This development process involved initial testing with hundreds of children, producing over 250 million data points, to refine the program and its instruction (see Twyman, Layng, Stikeleather, & Hobbins, 2004).

The resulting products individualize teaching for each student; the programs automatically and continuously track each learner's performance and immediately adjust instruction and branching based on the analysis of individual responses, patterns of errors, and correct responses. Hallmarks of good instruction, including frequent opportunities to respond (Gettinger & Seibert, 2002), relevant feedback (Cossairt, Hall, & Hopkins, 1973), reduced error learning (Touchette & Howard, 1984), visual displays of progress (Fuchs, 1986), mastery before moving on (Kulik, Kulik, & Bangert-Drowns, 1990), direct practice (Hall, Delquadri, Greenwood, & Thurston, 1982), and meaningful application are embedded into the programs. Tens of thousands of learners from all over the world have used the programs, including students in public schools, private and charter schools, virtual schools, homeschools, and even those in hospitals and orphanages. Independent summative evaluations (see Clarfield & Stoner, 2005; Huffstetter, King, Onwuegbuzie, Schneider, & Powell-Smith, 2010) validate not only the instructional outcome of learning to read but also the power of online learning.

## Other Online Programs

This new learning paradigm is further exemplified by the for-profit company, K12 (http://www.k12.com/), which provides à la carte online courses and full-time online schooling programs to parents and schools in 28 states and 36 countries. K12 students engage in independent online study, with supporting teachers available by email and by phone. Monitoring and assessment occurs either online, in person in blended settings, or using other technologies (e.g., phone and video).

Many districts and schools have adopted a blended model, one in which students learn partially through the online delivery of content and instruction and partially via a supervised brick-and-mortar location other than the home. The blend may be for a single course of study or for a combination of courses. In a private or public–private partnership, programs such as Achievement First (see Achievement First, 2013) or the Knowledge is Power Program (http://www.kipp.org/results) charter school network have shown an increase in student attendance and participation and improvement in both standardized and competency-based test scores.

Education technology entrepreneurs are rapidly expanding the kind of adaptive software and "cloud ware" available. They concentrate not only on content alone but also on classroom and behavior management tools. Launched in 2011, for example, ClassDojo (http://www.classdojo.com/) is an online program that allows teachers to continually track and manage student behavior in class, awarding points for specific good behavior like attentiveness and politeness and subtracting them for poor behavior such as being disruptive or not turning in homework. Teachers can choose to make students' points visible to the class throughout the day. While the principles of behavior at work are similar to those in the Good Behavior Game (see Embry, 2002), the automatic public visibility of Class Dojo may provide even greater motivation to students to behave well.

Goalbook (https://goalbookapp.com/) is another program for students with special needs. It allows all of a child's teachers and assistants to update his or her individualized education plan simultaneously, if they like, thus keeping everyone on track with the child's education without requiring constant conversations and paperwork. This program allows teachers to set personal learning goals for each child—say, reading a third-grade-level book or mastering the 9-times multiplication tables—and track learner progress. The system also allows for instant reports and data gathering of the child's progress on each measure. Another resource, Edmodo (https://www.edmodo.com/), offers free Internet-based software aimed at schools, students, and teachers. It functions somewhat like Facebook, only tailored to education. Once teachers and their students sign up to use Edmodo, they can exchange assignments, view the class calendar, and start and respond to online discussions. Teachers can post polls and quizzes and immediately track student progress through such assignments on any device that accesses the Internet. Goalbook looks like and acts similarly to Edmodo but provides goals and assessments for special needs students, such as those with various psychological handicaps.

Adaptive technology can be successful even without expert teachers. In one program, for example, high school students were recruited to teach Head Start preschoolers to read using a computer program called Funnix (http://www.funnix.com/) in a low-income, half-minority Georgia community. The students were much more successful in teaching reading than the regular teaching staff, who used conventional methods. Funnix uses a step-by-step, sequential approach to teaching phonics that is highly scripted but also personalized through the computer program. The Funnix group was better at skills like naming letters, identifying the initial sounds of words, and reading nonsense words halfway through the year and reached reading levels of about a year ahead of the control group (Stockard, 2009).

## MOOCs

Perhaps one of the most innovative recent trends in education is the arrival of massive, open, online classes (MOOCs), currently offered at the university level but with the potential to be adapted to secondary school instruction. MOOCs offer (mostly) free online college-level classes taught by noted lecturers to anyone who wants to enroll, anywhere in the world. They are revolutionary in both the openness of access and in the typically high quality of instruction offered. The original MOOC was a University of Manitoba course titled "Connectivism and Connective Knowledge," co-taught by George Siemens and Stephen Downes to 25 tuition-paying students and over 2,000 nonpaying students from around the world (Siemens, 2012). Perhaps the most notable MOOC has been an artificial intelligence course offered in 2011 by Stanford professor Sebastian Thrun and Google colleague Peter Norvig; it enrolled 160,000 students across 190 nations (DeSantis, 2012). Seeing the potential of MOOCs, Thrun went on to found Udacity, which—along with other new companies (both for- and not-for-profit), such as Coursera, Udemy, and edX (a joint venture of Harvard and the Massachusetts Institute of Technology)—are targeting the hundreds of thousands of students now enrolled in hundreds of online courses available worldwide.

MOOCs herald an unbundling or decentralization of higher education. In this new context, students are studying and taking exams when they want and where they want. Time to learn is not necessarily dictated by the traditional model of set class time, lab time, and office hours, thus changing the rate at which students learn. Western Governors University, an entirely online degree program, reports the average time for a student to complete a bachelor's degree is under 2½ years. Opportunities for students promise to grow as universities begin to offer or accept online course credits from other universities, thereby providing a virtual smorgasbord of instructional options, potentially allowing students to craft an individualized program of the best of the best or a uniquely personal program rounded out by courses not commonly offered by mainstream campuses.

The programs mentioned in this section exemplify the variety and usefulness of new online programs. Undoubtedly, many more creative programs will emerge in the next several decades. The key question now—"Do they make a difference in learning?"—is what the next section addresses.

## Research Synthesis of Online Courses

American school achievement hasn't changed much in the last century, but the progress in technology in most realms has been astonishing, as can be seen in online instruction. A meta-analysis of 125 experimental and quasi-experimental studies revealed that students enrolled in online education courses through 2010 achieved better academically than students enrolled in traditional classroom instruction (Shachar & Neumann, 2010). Seventy percent of all 125 studies showed online education superior, and those after 2002 showed even more consistent results, with 84% superiority.

> *A U.S. Department of Education-funded meta-analysis and literature review of 51 studies comparing both online and blended learning environments to the face-to-face learning environment found that "on average, students in online learning conditions performed better than those receiving face-to-face instruction"*
> U.S. Department of Education, 2010

Undoubtedly because technology tends to improve, studies after 2002 showed not only consistent but a very large average effect of 0.403, corresponding roughly to what is learned in four tenths of a school year, which would put typical online education students at the 66th percentile, meaning they would exceed 66% of students conventionally taught. Moreover, most of the studies reviewed in the Shachar and Neumann (2010) meta-analysis concerned effects of a unit or at most a year of study, which could be multiplied over 12 years of schooling. The cumulative effect would suffice to rank American students first rather than as low as 32nd among countries in international achievement surveys.

Nearly all the studies were conducted before or shortly after the Internet became such a widespread means of communicating across the world. It can be imagined that the Internet will gain greater speeds and that online programs will continue to improve. More and more students will have access to and use online instruction. Today, for example, nearly all U.S. families have access to online computers, if only in neighborhood libraries and schools, allowing more and more opportunities to learn online.

Most of the comparative studies of online education concerned high school and college mathematics and science courses. No similarly extensive analysis has been made of younger students, but the What Works Clearinghouse (2009) found and reported on a rigorous reading study (a randomized field trial) of 4-year-olds. The study contrasted the computer-based Headsprout early reading program, discussed above, with more conventional programs. The computer-tutored children exceeded 81% of untutored, conventionally taught children. This gave them about the same sized achievement advantage over their same-age peers as much older step-tutored students had over their same-age peers.

A U.S. Department of Education-funded meta-analysis and literature review of 51 studies comparing both online and blended learning environments to the face-to-face learning environment found that "on average, students in online learning conditions performed modestly better than those receiving face-to-face instruction" (U.S. Department of Education, 2010, p. ix). Studies specifically focusing on blended environments found blended instruction to be more effective than face-to-face alone (U.S. Department of Education, 2010).

Online technology has the additional advantage of building mastery of Internet, digital devices, and other skills necessary for further learning in subsequent grades, in college, and on the job. A survey of 300 professionals, for example, showed they spend 40% of their time in online communities interacting with others, and twice that percentage participate in online groups to help others by sharing information, ideas, and experiences (Valsiner & van der Veer, 2000). In addition, as documented in this chapter, either by itself or "blended" with traditional classroom teaching, online technology continues to build an excellent record in raising student achievement more than traditional methods.

These studies demonstrate the effectiveness of online education and distance learning, particularly in instances where support for the online experience is provided. As noted by the International Association for K–12 Online Learning, "Larger-scale studies are needed to show the correlations between program models, instructional models, technologies, conditions, and practices for effective online learning" (Patrick & Powell, 2009, p. 9). In the meantime, available evidence supports some action principles that can be taken at the state, local, or school level to facilitate online and distance learning outcomes. These are described below.

## Action Principles

### State Education Agency

a. Compare the coverage of state curriculum requirements in candidate online and distance programs.
b. Survey current online and distance programs in terms of effectiveness and state applicability.
c. Compare the effectiveness and efficiency of available and state and locally grown online and distance programs.
d. Analyze and make known the cost (in money and resources) of creating an online course or program.

### Local Education Agency

a. Assist school authorities in understanding state online and distance requirements, research, and services.
b. Help school-level authorities choose, adapt, or develop the best online and distance programs uniquely suited for each school.

c. Offer explicit support for school administrators, teachers, and other school staff members in gaining knowledge of the effort required to develop, offer, conduct, and participate in an online or distance course.

**Schools**

a. Analyze state and local authorities' requirements and recommendations for online and distance education programs.
b. Choose the program best suited to the school for which they are responsible.
c. Cooperate with state and local authorities in mounting and enacting staff development and implementation activities.

## References

Achievement First. (2013). *Results across achievement first*. Brooklyn, NY, and New Haven CT: Author. Retrieved from http://www.achievementfirst.org/results/across-achievement-first/

Allen, I. E., & Seaman, J. (2011, November). *Going the distance: Online education in the United States*. Babson Park, MA: Babson Survey Research Group. Retrieved from http://sloanconsortium.org/publications/survey/going_distance_2011

Casey, A. M., & Lorenzen, M. (2010). Untapped potential: Seeking library donors among alumni of distance learning programs. *Journal of Library Administration, 50*(5), 515–529.

Cavanagh, S. (2012). States loosening entrenched "seat time" requirements. *Education Week, 31*(23), 12–15.

Clarfield, J., & Stoner, G. (2005). The effects of computerized reading instruction on the academic performance of students identified with ADHD. *School Psychology Review, 34*(2), 246–254.

Coleman, J. S. (1961). *The adolescent society: The social life of the teenager and its impact on education*. New York, NY: The Free Press.

Cossairt, A., Hall, R. V., & Hopkins, B. L. (1973). The effects of experimenter's instructions, feedback, and praise on teacher praise and student attending behavior. *Journal of Applied Behavior Analysis, 6*(1), 89.

DeSantis, N. (2012, January 23). Stanford professor gives up teaching position, hopes to reach 500,000 students at online start-up. *Chronicle of Higher Education*. Retrieved from http://chronicle.com/blogs/wiredcampus/stanford-professor-gives-up-teaching-position-hopes-to-reach-500000-students-at-online-start-up/35135

Dickey, M. D. (2005). Three-dimensional virtual worlds and distance learning. *British Journal of Educational Technology, 36*(3), 439–451.

Ely, D. P., & Plomp, T. (Eds.). (1996). *International encyclopedia of educational technology* (2$^{nd}$ ed.). London: Emerald Group Publishing.

Embry, D. D. (2002). The good behavior game: A best practice candidate as a universal behavioral vaccine. *Clinical Child and Family Psychology Review, 5*(4), 273–297.

Fuchs, L. S. (1986). Monitoring progress among mildly handicapped pupils: Review of current practice and research. *Remedial and Special Education, 7*(5), 5–12.

Gettinger, M., & Seibert, J. K. (2002). Best practices in increasing academic learning time. In A. Thomas (Ed.), *Best practices in school psychology IV* (4$^{th}$ ed., Vol. 1, pp. 773–787). Bethesda, MD: National Association of School Psychologists.

Goldiamond, I., & Dyrud, J. (1966). Reading as operant behavior. In J. Money (Ed.), *The disabled reader: Education of the dyslexic child* (pp. 93–120). Baltimore, MD: Johns Hopkins Press.

Hall, R. V., Delquadri, J., Greenwood, C. R., & Thurston, L. (1982). The importance of opportunity to respond in children's academic success. In E. Edgar, N. Haring, J. Jenkins, & C. Pious (Eds.), *Serving young handicapped children: Issues and research* (pp. 107–140). Baltimore, MD: University Park Press.

Huffstetter, M., King, J. R., Onwuegbuzie, A. J., Schneider, J. J., & Powell-Smith, K. A. (2010). Effects of a computer-based early reading program on the early reading and oral language skills of at-risk preschool children. *Journal of Education for Students Placed at Risk, 15*(4), 279–298.

Khan Academy. (2013). *A free world-class education for anyone anywhere.* Retrieved from http://www.khanacademy.org/about#faq

KIPP. (2013). *Results.* Retrieved from http://www.kipp.org/results

Kulik, C. L. C., Kulik, J. A., & Bangert-Drowns, R. L. (1990). Effectiveness of mastery learning programs: A meta-analysis. *Review of Educational Research, 60*(2), 265–299.

Layng, T. V. J., Stikeleather, G., & Twyman, J. (2006). Scientific formative evaluation: The role of individual learners in generating and predicting successful educational outcomes. In R. Subotnik & H. Walberg (Eds.), *The scientific basis of educational productivity* (pp. 29-43). Charlotte, NC: Information Age Publishing.

Mimio. (2013). *Reading instruction: Mimio offers research-based and proven supplementary reading instruction for a variety of elementary grade levels and learning needs.* Retrieved from http://www.mimio.com/en-NA/Products/Reading-Instruction.aspx

National Center for Education Statistics. (2011). *Digest of education statistics: 2011.* (Table 250. Selected statistics for degree-granting institutions enrolling more than 15,000 students in 2010: Selected years, 1990 through 2009–10.) Washington, DC: Author. Retrieved from http://nces.ed.gov/programs/digest/d11/tables/dt11_250.asp?referrer=list

National Institute of Child Health and Human Development. (2000). *Report of the National Reading Panel. Teaching children to read: An evidence-based assessment of the scientific research literature on reading and its implications for reading instruction: Reports of the subgroups* (NIH Publication No. 00-4754). Washington, DC: U.S. Government Printing Office.

Noer, M. (2012, November 19). One man, one computer, 10 million students: How Khan Academy is reinventing education. *Forbes.* Retrieved from http://www.forbes.com/sites/michaelnoer/2012/11/02/one-man-one-computer-10-million-students-how-khan-academy-is-reinventing-education/

Oblinger, D. G. (2000, March/April). The nature and purpose of distance education. *The Technology Source.* Retrieved from http://www.technologysource.org/article/348/

Patrick, S., & Powell, A. (2009). *A summary of research on the effectiveness of K–12 online learning. International Association for K–12 Online Learning* (iNACOL). Retrieved from http://www.inacol.org/cms/wp-content/uploads/2012/11/iNACOL_ResearchEffectiveness.pdf

Rasicot, J. (2011, August 5). Education review: Web site offering free math lessons catches on 'like wildfire'. *Washington Post.* Retrieved from http://www.washingtonpost.com/lifestyle/magazine/web-site-offering-free-online-math-lessons-catches-on-like-wildfire/2011/07/15/gIQAtL5KuI_story_1.html

Shachar, M., & Neumann, Y. (2010). Twenty years of research on the academic performance differences between traditional and distance learning: Summative meta-analysis and trend examination. *MERLOT Journal of Online Learning and Teaching, 6*, 318–334.

Siemens, G. (2012). What is the theory that underpins our MOOCs? *Elearnspace.* Retrieved from http://www.elearnspace.org/blog/2012/06/03/what-is-the-theory-that-underpins-our-moocs/

Stockard, J. (2009). *Promoting early literacy of preschool children: A study of the effectiveness of Funnix Beginning Reading*. Eugene, OR: Retrieved from http://www.nifdi.org/pdf/Technical%20Report-Funnix_2009-1.pdf

Touchette, P. E., & Howard, J. S. (1984). Errorless learning: Reinforcement contingencies and stimulus control transfer in delayed prompting. *Journal of Applied Behavior Analysis, 17*(2), 175.

Twyman, J. S. (in press). Technology to accelerate school turnaround. In S. Redding & L. M. Rhim (Eds.), *Handbook on state management of school turnaround*. San Francisco, CA: West Ed.

Twyman, J. S., Layng, T. V. J., Stikeleather, G., & Hobbins, K. A. (2004). A non-linear approach to curriculum design: The role of behavior analysis in building an effective reading program. In W. L. Heward et al. (Eds.), *Focus on behavior analysis in education* (Vol. 3, pp. 55–68). Upper Saddle River, NJ: Merrill/Prentice–Hall.

U.S. Department of Education. (2013). *Competency-based learning or personalized learning*. Washington, DC: United States Government. Retrieved from: http://www.ed.gov/oii-news/competency-based-learning-or-personalized-learning

U.S. Department of Education, Office of Planning, Evaluation, and Policy Development. (2010). *Evaluation of evidence-based practices in online learning: A meta-analysis and review of online learning studies*. Washington, DC: Author. Retrieved from http://www2.ed.gov/rschstat/eval/tech/evidence-based-practices/finalreport.pdf

Valsiner, J., & van der Veer, R. (2000). *The social mind: Construction of the idea*. New York, NY: Cambridge University Press.

What Works Clearinghouse, U.S. Department of Education. (2009, October). *Intervention: Headsprout Early Reading*. Washington, DC: Author. Retrieved from http://ies.ed.gov/ncee/wwc/interventionreport.aspx?sid=211

Young, J. (2010, June 6). College 2.0: A self-appointed teacher runs a one-man 'academy' on YouTube. *The Chronicle of Higher Education*. Retrieved from http://chronicle.com/article/College-20-A-Self-Appointed/65793/

# Learning, Schooling, and Data Analytics
*Ryan S. J. d. Baker*

Since the 1960s, methods for extracting useful information from large data sets, termed *analytics* or *data mining*, have played a key role in fields such as physics and biology. In the last few years, the same trend has emerged in educational research and practice, an area termed *learning analytics* (LA; Ferguson, 2012) or *educational data mining* (EDM; Baker & Yacef, 2009). In brief, these two research areas seek to find ways to make beneficial use of the increasing amounts of data available about learners in order to better understand the processes of learning and the social and motivational factors surrounding learning. The goal of these efforts is to produce more efficient, more effective, and deeper learning in the context of increasingly positive learning experiences.

The emergence of EDM/LA is a recent phenomenon. The first meetings of scientists in this area were the Educational Data Mining workshops, which started in 2005 and became an annual conference series in 2008. This conference series was joined by the Learning Analytics and Knowledge conference series in 2011. The two research areas of EDM and LA, emerging from different communities of scientists and practitioners, have somewhat different goals; discussing these differences is outside the scope of this report (see Siemens & Baker, 2012). In brief, the validity of models of learners and learning is perhaps the key focus of the EDM community, whereas the use of the results of analysis to drive changes in practice by instructors is perhaps the key focus of the LA community. The conferences in EDM and LA were followed by the establishment of journals devoted to the topics, with the *Journal of Educational Data Mining* commencing publication in 2009 and the *International Journal of the Society for Learning Analytics Research* expected to commence publication in 2013. As of this writing, the

International Educational Data Mining Society has approximately 150 members and over 600 subscribers on its mailing lists.

A range of methods has been developed by these two communities, drawing from areas such as data mining, computational science, statistics, psychometrics, and social network analysis. (A selection of these methods will be discussed below; a fuller review can be found in Baker & Siemens, in press).

## Research Synthesis

The methods of EDM have been applied to accomplish a range of objectives. This section reviews some of the applications which have had relatively large impacts or have relatively large potential, focusing on applications of particularly strong relevance to the readers of this *Handbook*.

One of the first applications of EDM was the development of models that could infer a student's knowledge as he or she worked through educational software. These inferences are in turn used to drive adaptation by the system. This application in fact preceded the existence of EDM or LA as research areas. Though student knowledge modeling began as a research area in the 1970s (Goldstein, 1979), the first model, which was both based on automated exploration of data and which achieved widespread dissemination in educational software, was Corbett and Anderson's (1995) Bayesian knowledge tracing (BKT) algorithm. One key difference between this algorithm and the types of student knowledge modeling used previously by the psychometrics community, for example in testing, was that BKT explicitly accounts for the fact that the student is learning at the same time he or she is being assessed; in other words, student knowledge is treated as a moving target. BKT was then incorporated into Cognitive Tutor software curricula for algebra and geometry (Koedinger & Corbett, 2006), sold by Carnegie Learning Inc., which was used by around 5% of U.S. high school students each year throughout the first decade of the 2000s. This software used BKT to decide when to advance the student on to new material, implementing an approach termed "mastery learning" (Bloom, 1968), in which the student does not advance until he or she demonstrates proficiency. By integrating BKT into mastery learning, Cognitive Tutor Algebra I was able to improve student test scores, with replication, in a range of settings (Koedinger & Corbett, 2006), although performance for geometry has been more mixed (Pane, McCaffrey, Slaughter, Steele, & Ikemoto, 2010). It is important to note that the automated algorithms and learning support in Cognitive Tutor replaced the workbook rather than the teacher; in Cognitive Tutor classrooms, the teacher spends more time interacting with students in one-on-one learning support sessions than in full-class teaching (Schofield, 1995), perhaps another reason for this approach's success.

Since the implementation of Cognitive Tutors, new online learning systems have added emphasis on providing actionable and formative information to teachers. For example, the ASSISTment system (it "assesses while it assists") has created a reporting system that teachers can use to determine both what material specific students are struggling with and what items the entire class is struggling with (Feng & Heffernan, 2006). Teachers using the system review student homework before class and are able to change the focus of classroom activities based on data on student understanding, leading to better classroom performance than is seen with traditional homework (Koedinger, McLaughlin, & Heffernan, 2010; Mendicino, Razzaq, & Heffernan, 2009).

The types of formative information that can be assessed by online learning systems have gone beyond just student knowledge in recent years. Algorithms for assessing disengaged behaviors have been developed for learning systems recently (Baker, 2007; Baker, Corbett, & Koedinger, 2004; Pardos, Baker, San Pedro, Gowda, & Gowda, 2013; San Pedro, Baker, & Rodrigo, 2011), making it possible to assess with reasonable accuracy whether students are careless, off-task, or intentionally misusing educational software, among other disengaged behaviors. These algorithms have been extended to also infer student emotion during learning, just from data readily available to computer systems (i.e., no physiological sensors; see Baker et al., 2012; Pardos et al., 2013; Sabourin, Rowe, Mott, & Lester, 2011). As these models are built into systems such as ASSISTments or Crystal Island, increasing amounts of information will be available to classroom teachers; the key challenge will be providing it to teachers in useful and timely fashions.

> *Teachers using the system review student homework before class and are able to change the focus of classroom activities based on student understanding...*

Another direction for integrating EDM and LA research into educational practice is to predict student dropout and course failure, a step towards providing early intervention. One particularly successful example is the Purdue Signals Project, reported to have significantly improved student outcomes at Purdue University (Arnold, 2010). This system uses prediction models to infer early in the semester which students are likely to fail or drop out of a course; a list of students at risk is generated and sent to an instructor, along with recommended template emails for these students which inform them about help resources available. This type of system is being implemented at an increasing number of universities, both in independent projects (Ming & Ming, 2012) and through a commercial vendor, Ellucian, which is distributing the Signals software to additional universities.

While dropout and failure prediction at the K–12 level have not yet reached the level of deployment and demonstrated success of the Purdue Signals Project, there are several examples of successful prediction of student dropout at the K–12 level. To give just a few examples, Tobin and Sugai (1999) predict high school dropout from middle school disciplinary records; Bowers (2010) uses changes in student achievement to predict high school dropout as early as third grade; San Pedro, Baker, Bowers, and Heffernan (in press) use data on middle school student emotion and learning within the aforementioned ASSISTment system to predict which students will attend college. Each of these approaches has the potential to be used at scale; the challenges to doing so are organizational rather than technical.

Beyond supporting specific changes in practice, EDM and LA research has played an increasingly important role in supporting basic discovery in education research. The opportunity to leverage very fine-grained data (often multiple data points per minute) across entire years of data for a specific student, in combination with automated methods for sifting through that data, has been an excellent opportunity for better understanding learners and learning.

> *The opportunity to leverage very fine-grained data...across entire years of data for a specific student...has been an excellent opportunity for better understanding learners and learning.*

Types of EDM methods, such as discovery with models and structure discovery algorithms, have enabled a variety of analyses, including discovery of which exploratory learning strategies are most effective (Amershi & Conati, 2009), which patterns of group work lead to more successful group projects (Perera, Kay, Koprinska, Yacef, & Zaiane, 2009), which meta-cognitive behaviors lead to deep learning (Baker et al., 2012), and how small-scale choices in the design of educational software can lead to substantial differences in student engagement (Baker et al., 2009).

## Action Principles

In this section, I propose a set of action principles for schools, local education agencies (LEAs), and state education agencies (SEAs), suggesting how the emerging fields of learning analytics and educational data mining can be used to improve their practice.

### Action Principles for Schools

**Provide formative data to teachers on student learning.** In recent years, the advent of learning systems such as ASSISTments (but also Cognitive Tutors, Reasoning Mind, Aleks, LearnBop, and many others) has presented an opportunity to provide teachers with considerably more information on their students' learning, generally in easy-to-interpret formats. Depending on a school's goals, some of these systems (such as Cognitive Tutors and Reasoning Mind) can be adopted as an entire curriculum; others, such as ASSISTments and LearnBop, simply replace existing homework or seatwork and can be used with a variety of curricula.

These systems provide teachers with information on which students are struggling and what they are struggling on. This enables teachers to identify what material these students need support with, so that the teacher can provide them with extra assistance (Schofield, 1995). Sometimes, a teacher can also see by using these systems that a specific topic is difficult for all students; this is also possible to determine when the teacher grades by hand, but the teacher is informed earlier by automated systems, thus supporting timely intervention.

**Predict which students are at risk for dropping out.** As discussed above, one of the key successes of learning analytics at the undergraduate level is predicting which students are at risk of failing or dropping out. At that level, success has been achieved not only in predicting who is at risk but also in embedding this information in effective interventions used to reduce dropout (Arnold, 2010).

Several research projects have demonstrated that the same type of prediction is possible for K–12 schools. The work by Bowers (2010) in predicting high school dropout from grades students receive in elementary school demonstrates that this type of prediction is possible just from the data already available in schools. Similarly, data on disciplinary referrals (e.g., fighting) during middle school can predict who will drop out in high school (Tobin & Sugai, 1999). However, both of these types of indicators may be identifying students at very high risk, students whose problems are outside those that are easily addressed by schools. Dropout prediction from interactions with educational software may provide a way to identify at-risk students whose challenges can be more easily addressed, and may provide more precise information on the factors causing those students to be at risk. For example, recent work has indicated that educational software can infer not just student knowledge but also multiple dimensions of student engagement. Long-term prediction from educational software is still emerging (San Pedro et al., in press) but is likely to be available in an increasing number of educational software packages used in schools in the years to come.

**Identify learning topics that are being learned less well within school.** Recent educational software is able to identify which skills and topics are being learned less well than others within a specific classroom or school. This type of information is available in reports from many modern learning software packages, including but not limited to ASSISTments, the Cognitive Tutor, LearnBop, and Reasoning Mind. This type of information does not require using a software package—it is possible to think of teachers across schools recording homework data, tagging it by topic, and looking together for topics where performance is poor—but it is much easier to do in schools and classrooms that use educational software since the bookkeeping and data integration is offloaded to a computer system.

Understanding the topics for which a school's current curriculum and pedagogical approaches are working less effectively creates opportunities to redesign teaching in those areas or to supplement current practice with other resources. If a school is generally performing poorly on division of fractions across teachers, for example, it is probably not a flaw in one person's teaching but instead a flaw in the curriculum being used, a flaw that can be addressed throughout the school.

**Capture and respond to changes in student engagement.** In 2013, the automated assessment of student engagement and emotion remains primarily within research classrooms, but it is emerging within a range of learning systems, making it likely that it will become generally available in classrooms in the coming years. As automated assessment of student engagement and emotion becomes increasingly feasible to integrate within online learning systems, such as ASSISTments, it is likely to become useful to teachers. When it is available, teachers and school psychologists will be able to use it to identify early students who have become disengaged across classes, potentially identifying a student in need of an intervention. If problem behaviors are below the threshold of office referrals, a student's general changes in behavior may not be noticed; with this type of technology, it may be possible to identify shifts in engagement quickly. Even within a single class, emotion- and engagement-sensing technology may prove quite useful. For example, if a teacher can identify that a student was frustrated during his or her online homework the night before, it may be possible to talk to the student to better understand why the material was particularly difficult.

## Action Principles for Local Education Agencies

**Identify specific areas of excellence and high success in teaching practice.** When educational software that assesses engagement and learning is used in schools, it can be beneficial not just to individual teachers and schools but to local education agencies (LEAs) as well. This type of assessment can provide information that can help LEAs to identify teachers that are successful in promoting engagement and learning in specific areas. The expertise these teachers have can then be leveraged by their LEA. For example, if a teacher is succeeding at teaching a topic that other teachers are known to struggle with—as manifested by better performance by his/her students on that topic—that teacher could give a brief workshop on his or her teaching strategies. Similarly, if one teacher's classes generally experience less boredom (while learning equally well), it may be worth having this teacher mentor other teachers in engaging their students. In this fashion, it may be possible to identify exact areas of excellence and share them across a school district.

Although these methods can be used to identify exemplary teachers, rewarding teachers who are particularly successful according to these types of internal measures may have undesired effects. If teacher pay were linked to evidence of frustration in a system like ASSISTments, some teachers might alter their classroom practice in undesirable ways, to try to "game the system," for example, by walking around the classroom, immediately giving answers to every struggling student. Even if this did not improve the assessment of engagement by the software, it might still be attempted, with unpredictable and likely undesirable results. Automated detectors will be more effective, and more useful, if there is not an attempt to subvert them (necessitating automated detectors of subversion, as seen in Baker et al., 2004). In sum, integrating automated assessment systems into reward structures has the potential to reduce their effectiveness for other goals.

**Identify students who could benefit from enrichment programs**. Another upcoming opportunity for LEAs is to identify specific students who could benefit from enrichment programs. Across the U.S., after-school, weekend, and summer programs are available to learners, funded by federal agencies—such as the National Science Foundation's Innovative Technology Experiences for Students and Teachers (ITEST) program—state agencies, foundations, and private funders. However, there remains insufficient capacity to provide enrichment programs to all students who want to enroll in them, and the students who do enroll are often drawn from wealthier groups (Gardner, Roth, & Brooks-Gunn, 2009). In addition, not all enrichment programs are the same; there is a question of fit when selecting students for an enrichment program.

When technology becomes readily available to assess engagement in class, it will be increasingly possible to identify students who are highly engaged in specific subjects. These students—especially if they are disadvantaged—should be particularly strong candidates for enrichment programs, and efforts should be made to place them in enrichment programs that fit their interests and will help them develop their interests in these specific areas.

**Develop internal expertise in learning analytics**. A third recommendation for local education agencies is to develop internal expertise in learning analytics. In recent years, there has been an explosion of data that can be used for a wide range of purposes, as indicated in the recommendations above (both those for schools and for local education agencies). Local education agencies can play an essential role in fulfilling both of these recommendations, conducting analyses at the district level and supporting schools in conducting school-level analyses (or even conducting analyses for schools).

The cost of hiring one or more learning analytics experts or of training an existing member of the LEA in learning analytics methods may in the future be seen as a relatively small expense in relation to the benefits that can be achieved. There are increasing opportunities to train LEA personnel, including the upcoming fall 2013 massive online open course (MOOC) within Coursera, Big Data in Education, and an annual MOOC on learning analytics provided by the Society for Learning Analytics Research. Also, an increasing number of graduate programs specialize in this area. As of this writing, programs in learning analytics or related areas are offered at Teachers College Columbia University, Carnegie Mellon University, and Worcester Polytechnic Institute, programs creating an increasing pool of trained individuals who can provide this type of expertise to schools.

**Develop data management and sharing plans to support partnerships with university researchers in line with legal obligations.** Beyond hiring their own staff in learning analytics, school districts may be able to leverage the expertise of universities. There is growing pool of university faculty, postdoctoral researchers, and graduate students who are deeply interested in learning analytics and EDM and want to use these methods to benefit American education, at a wide range of institutions, even beyond those officially offering training in these areas. These researchers are a resource that LEAs can leverage to conduct analyses beyond their own capacities. Such collaborations are likely to benefit all but the largest and wealthiest school districts; even for those districts, there may be expertise in learning analytics located in specific university research groups that is duplicated nowhere else.

However, these collaborations will not occur unless appropriate institutional, legal, and infrastructural arrangements are made. One key step is the creation of procedures for quickly de-identifying data sets (removing all potentially identifying information) so they can be shared with university researchers without violation of relevant federal privacy laws and guidelines, such as the Family Educational Rights and Privacy Act (FERPA), the federal law that protects the privacy of student education records. Creating procedures for sending de-identified data to researchers but being able to link findings from those researchers back to individual students within the LEA will be essential in order to benefit those students, using the information obtained in research. Policies for such de-identification would prevent identifiable information from being transmitted outside the school district and designate some individual within the LEA to hold a strictly guarded key, so that the findings can be tracked back to students within the LEA. In addition, LEAs should instruct their institutional review boards to follow relevant federal law and guidelines for fast-tracking research with minimal risk of harm to students, for research projects classified as exempt from review or fit for expedited review under the federal guidelines. Currently, many LEAs—particularly in larger cities—choose not to follow federal guidelines for review of research, instead creating onerous review processes that lead many research groups to avoid working with those LEAs. The result is that students in suburban school districts benefit more from the university researchers in major urban centers than students in those urban centers, reinforcing inequities. Even after approving research, many LEAs currently require extensive legal agreements, again well beyond federal or state requirements, delaying or preventing research collaborations. In general, streamlining procedures for learning analytics research (while following all federal laws and guidelines, and protecting student privacy) is likely to benefit students considerably and facilitate the task of LEAs in supporting their students.

## Action Principles for State Education Agencies

**Capture data about students according to broad-based range of indicators**. One important way that state education agencies (SEAs) can support learning analytics is by taking steps to collect a broad range of types of data. Many types of data are now available about learners and schools beyond what routinely make it to state education agencies—from log files, to automated assessments, to data from classroom observations. By having a range of types of data, SEAs will be able to conduct analyses of the factors leading to better performance on state standardized exams, higher college attendance, and so on. States should partner with resource centers to select which indicators to capture and encourage vendors to provide understandable and reasonably complete data to their SEA as a condition. Similarly, SEAs should incentivize schools and LEAs to also collect a broad range of data and provide it to SEAs. An SEA's data is unlikely to reach its full potential except in partnership with LEAs that are collecting a broad range of useful data.

While different schools may collect and use data that is not fully compatible, making sure that all of this data is available at the state level will be a useful step towards supporting state-level analyses. For example, even if one learning system tends to predict higher engagement than another learning system, having data from both learning systems will make it possible to see statewide trends.

**Form practices for aligning student data even in the face of mobility**. School mobility is a fact of 21st-century education; because American society is highly mobile, students are likely to change schools repeatedly during their education. While school mobility may not be problematic for students of high socioeconomic status (SES), it is associated with poorer outcomes among lower SES and minority students, especially if a student changes schools several times (Xu, Hannaway, & D'Souza, 2009). Mobility can also be a problem for tracking students and applying learning analytics to the data from these students; it is easier to obtain data for and therefore apply predictive models to students who do not change school districts, implying that prediction of at-risk status will be least effective for students who are already at risk due to their mobility.

State education agencies can play a key role in tracking these students by using state-level identifiers to track student progress even if the student moves. Equally importantly, SEAs should encourage LEAs and schools to store all data in terms of state-level identifiers and should support LEAs and schools in obtaining student data from other LEAs and schools (ideally through state-level databases that all LEAs provide data to and draw from). In that fashion, learning analytics analyses can leverage all of the data available for a specific student.

States can further support local districts by identifying effective practices for forming partnerships with university and corporate researchers focused on data use. As discussed above, several benefits may accrue to LEAs in forming partnerships with university researchers. SEAs have a key role to play in setting the tone for collaboration and nudging LEAs to develop and conduct these partnerships appropriately. SEAs should educate LEAs about—and encourage them to follow—federal and state guidelines so that LEAs avoid unnecessary and unproductive roadblocks which prevent interventions that would benefit students, while also avoiding violating federal or state laws or violating student privacy.

**Identify exemplary teachers and schools**. SEAs, even more than LEAs, have the potential to identify schools or teachers who are succeeding at promoting engagement and learning in specific areas. Across a state, there are likely to be exemplary practices, often in unexpected places, that can be identified through learning analytics. These practices can then be studied and communicated across the state in collaboration with resource centers. It is worth noting that, as with LEAs, the indicators that are useful for these types of analyses are better used in a formative fashion than to drive financial incentives (or firings); the incentives for gaming the system or even cheating are substantial if financial incentives are used and doing so would reduce the potential for disseminating exemplary practices statewide.

**Identify regional gaps in enrichment programs**. As discussed above, enrichment programs are not currently available to all students who want to enroll in them, and the students who do enroll are often drawn from wealthier groups (Gardner, Roth, & Brooks-Gunn, 2009), in part due to regional disparities. While some of the factors leading to these differences are difficult to address (e.g., parental choice and funding choices made by private foundations and individuals), better data on where the needs are may help to influence the allocation of government resources and potential private funding as well. By identifying the number of at-risk students and students likely to benefit from programs, and comparing these numbers to the availability of program slots in different regions, SEAs will be able to identify which regions have an insufficient quantity of enrichment programs and support program expansion and creation. Simply publishing data on where needs exist is likely to influence funding decisions, not just by private foundations and individuals but by programs funded by the federal government. For example, federal programs like National Science Foundation's ITEST might be more likely to fund programs in specific regions declared in need by SEAs than in regions shown to have a relative oversupply of enrichment programs.

Learning analytics may also have the potential to identify more quickly which enrichment programs are working. If an enrichment program is provided to elementary school students, any evidence of its effect on high school dropout rates or college attendance is a distant prospect. Obtaining data on learning and engagement from schools in the year following a student's participation in an enrichment program may provide more rapid signals as to which programs are succeeding in their goals.

## Acknowledgements

The author would like to thank Lisa Rossi, Janet Twyman, Marilyn Murphy, and Stephen Page for helpful comments and suggestions.

## References

Amershi, S., & Conati, C. (2009). Combining unsupervised and supervised machine learning to build user models for exploratory learning environments. *Journal of Educational Data Mining, 1*(1), 71–81.

Arnold, K. E. (2010). Signals: Applying academic analytics. *Educause Quarterly, 33*, 1–10.

Baker, R. S. J. d. (2007). *Modeling and understanding students' off-task behavior in intelligent tutoring systems.* In Proceedings of ACM CHI 2007: Computer-human interaction, 1059–1068.

Baker, R. S., Corbett, A. T., & Koedinger, K. R. (2004). *Detecting student misuse of intelligent tutoring systems.* Proceedings of the 7th International Conference on Intelligent Tutoring Systems, 531–540.

Baker, R. S. J. d., de Carvalho, A. M. J. A., Raspat, J., Aleven, V., Corbett, A. T., & Koedinger, K. R. (2009). *Educational software features that encourage and discourage "gaming the system."* Proceedings of the 14th International Conference on Artificial Intelligence in Education, 475–482.

Baker, R. S. J. d., Gowda, S. M., Wixon, M., Kalka, J., Wagner, A. Z., Salvi, A.,...Rossi, L. (2012). *Sensor-free automated detection of affect in a Cognitive Tutor for algebra.* Proceedings of the 5th International Conference on Educational Data Mining, 126–133.

Baker, R. S. J. d., & Siemens, G. (in press). Educational data mining and learning analytics. In K. Sawyer (Ed.), *Cambridge handbook of the learning sciences* (2nd ed.). Cambridge, MA: Cambridge University Press.

Baker, R. S. J. d., & Yacef, K. (2009). The state of educational data mining in 2009: A review and future visions. *Journal of Educational Data Mining, 1*(1), 3–17.

Bloom, B. S. (1968). Learning for mastery. *Evaluation Comment, 1*(2), 1–12.

Bowers, A. J. (2010). Analyzing the longitudinal K–12 grading histories of entire cohorts of students: Grades, data driven decision making, dropping out, and hierarchical cluster analysis. *Practical Assessment, Research & Evaluation (PARE), 15*(7), 1–18.

Corbett, A. T., & Anderson, J. R. (1995). Knowledge tracing: Modeling the acquisition of procedural knowledge. *User Modeling and User-Adapted Interaction, 4*, 253–278.

Feng, M., & Heffernan, N. T. (2006). Informing teachers live about student learning: Reporting in the ASSISTment system. *Technology, Instruction, Cognition, and Learning Journal, 3*(1–2), 1–8.

Ferguson, R. (2012). *The state of learning analytics in 2012: A review and future challenges* (Tech. Rep. No. KMI-12-01). Milton Keynes, UK: Open University, Knowledge Media Institute. Retrieved from http://kmi.open.ac.uk/publications/techreport/kmi-12-01

Gardner, M., Roth, J. L., & Brooks-Gunn, J. (2009, October). *Can after-school programs help level the playing field for disadvantaged youth?* (Equity Matters: Research Review, 4). New York, NY: Campaign for Educational Equity, Teachers College, Columbia University.

Goldstein, I. J. (1979). The genetic graph: a representation for the evolution of procedural knowledge. *International Journal of Man-Machine Studies, 11*(1), 51–77.

Koedinger, K. R., & Corbett, A. T. (2006). Cognitive tutors: Technology bringing learning science to the classroom. In K. Sawyer (Ed.), *The Cambridge handbook of the learning sciences* (pp. 61–78). New York: Cambridge University Press.

Koedinger, K. R., McLaughlin, E. A., & Heffernan, N. T. (2010). A quasi-experimental evaluation of an on-line formative assessment and tutoring system. *Journal of Educational Computing Research, 43*(4), 489–510.

Mendicino, M., Razzaq, L., & Heffernan, N. T. (2009). A comparison of traditional homework to computer-supported homework. *Journal of Research on Technology in Education, 41*, 331–358.

Ming, N. C., & Ming, V. L. (2012). *Predicting student outcomes from unstructured data.* Proceedings of the 2nd International Workshop on Personalization Approaches in Learning Environments, 11–16.

Pane, J. F., McCaffrey, D. F., Slaughter, M. E., Steele, J. L., & Ikemoto, G. S. (2010). An experiment to evaluate the efficacy of Cognitive Tutor Geometry. *Journal of Research on Educational Effectiveness, 3*(3), 254–281.

Pardos, Z. A., Baker, R. S. J. d., San Pedro, M. O. C. Z., Gowda, S. M., & Gowda, S. M. (2013). *Affective states and state tests: Investigating how affect throughout the school year predicts end of year learning outcomes.* To appear in Proceedings of the 3rd International Conference on Learning Analytics and Knowledge.

Perera, D., Kay, J., Koprinska, I., Yacef, K., & Zaiane, O. R. (2009). Clustering and sequential pattern mining of online collaborative learning data. *IEEE Transactions on Knowledge and Data Engineering, 21*(6), 759–772.

Sabourin, J., Rowe, J., Mott, B., & Lester, J. (2011). *When off-task in on-task: The affective role of off-task behavior in narrative-centered learning environments.* Proceedings of the 15th International Conference on Artificial Intelligence in Education, 534–536.

San Pedro, M. O. C., Baker, R., & Rodrigo, M. M. (2011). *Detecting carelessness through contextual estimation of slip probabilities among students using an intelligent tutor for mathematics.* Proceedings of 15th International Conference on Artificial Intelligence in Education, 304–311.

San Pedro, M. O. Z., Baker, R. S. J. d., Bowers, A. J., & Heffernan, N. T. (in press). *Predicting college enrollment from student interaction with an intelligent tutoring system in middle school.* To appear in Proceedings of the 6th International Conference on Educataional Data Mining.

Schofield, J. W. (1995). *Computers and classroom culture.* Cambridge, MA: Cambridge University Press.

Siemens, G., & Baker, R. S. J. d. (2012). Learning analytics and educational data mining: Towards communication and collaboration. *Proceedings of the 2nd International Conference on Learning Analytics and Knowledge,* 252–254.

Tobin, T. J., & Sugai, G. M. (1999). Using sixth-grade school records to predict violence, chronic discipline problems, and high school outcomes. *Journal of Emotional and Behavioral Disorders, 7*(1), 40–53.

Xu, Z., Hannaway, J., & D'Souza, S. (2009). *Student transience in North Carolina: The effect of school mobility on student outcomes using longitudinal data* (CALDER Working Paper 22). Washington, DC: The Urban Institute.

# Part 4
# Reports From the Field: Innovation in Practice

# Idaho Leads: Applying Learning In and Out of the Classroom to Systems Reform
*Lisa Kinnaman*

During the 2011 legislative session, Idaho passed an unprecedented education reform package, Students Come First, which included a mandate for increased technology in schools, limited collective bargaining, and increased accountability through pay-for-performance. The legislation was bold and fomented divisiveness between lawmakers and practitioners. It also created a sense of urgency and uncertainty among education stakeholders statewide as to how they would quickly implement the new requirements. Thus was born the grant-funded Idaho Leads project with a vision to help build leadership capacity in districts across the state—many of which are rural, remote, and lack the capacity to implement change, much less institute such sweeping reforms on their own. This effort would require something vastly different from the typical "drive-by" professional development. Consequently, the Idaho Leads project was designed to deeply engage a wide variety of education stakeholders over a significant period of time in regional networks and in-district support. Ultimately, the Students Come First legislation was overturned in a referendum vote in the fall of 2012. Despite this undoing of the mandate for change, systemwide reform had been sparked across the state, and Idaho Leads was there to help.

The Idaho Leads project was developed in partnership between the Boise State University Center for School Improvement & Policy Studies and the J. A. and Kathryn Albertson Foundation, which provided the center with a $3.85 million dollar grant to start the project in January 2012 and recently refunded it for $2.7 million to continue work through the 2013–2014 school year.

The goal of the Idaho Leads project is to provide essential technical assistance and professional development to Idaho administrators, teachers, and community members to build the needed leadership capacity to ensure the success of all Idaho students in the 21st century. This capacity building cannot be accomplished by working with one school at a time, but rather by addressing the entire "mega system," including the state, regional, and local communities, districts, and schools (Redding, 2006). This may sound like a flashy goal, but the design is strong, and early efforts have produced impressive forward movement throughout the state.

Applying the concept of "learning in and out of the classroom" to this systems reform effort, the Idaho Leads project pursues its goal by facilitating professional development in regional networks and by putting boots on the ground in districts across Idaho between professional development sessions. Just as students must learn in and out of the classroom, education stakeholders must have opportunities to learn in and out of the traditional professional development setting. Thus, a team was assembled to serve as the Idaho Leads project staff, including faculty from the Boise State University College of Education, teachers pulled fresh from the classroom to serve as instruction and technology specialists, communications specialists, recently retired superintendents and principals, and support staff. They develop and deliver content for regional networks—networks currently representing 43 of the state's 115 districts, plus six charter schools—cultivate district teams engaged in local work, and work intensively with identified "studio districts" (currently, seven districts).

**Figure 1: The Weave**

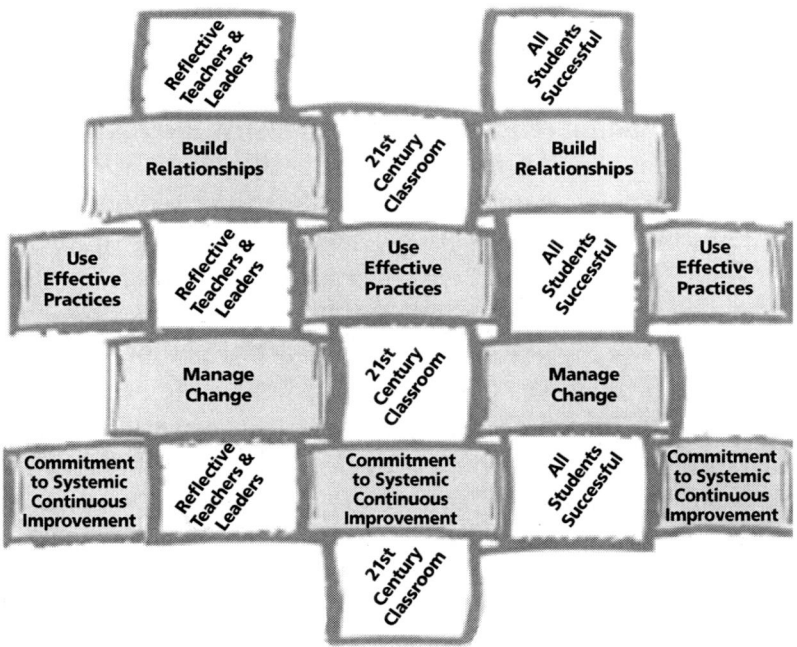

The backbone and guide for content development is based on what has been called "the Weave" (see Figure 1). The Weave is a framework for building high levels of leadership capacity and system improvement. The key strands of the Weave are represented horizontally: building relationships, using effective practices, managing change, and committing to continuous improvement. These horizontal strands form a foundation on which school leaders can address the ever-changing challenges of education. The vertical strands represent selected characteristics of high-functioning systems in which teachers and leaders continuously seek ways to improve. In Idaho, the first current vertical strand is "reflective teachers and leaders," which reflects Idaho Lead's efforts to implement Danielson's (2007) framework as a statewide instructional and evaluation model, and a response to pay-for-performance issues. The second vertical strand, "21st-century classrooms," includes efforts to combine both the Common Core State Standards and effective pedagogy with new technologies. The third strand, "all students successful," aims at high levels of learning for each individual as we seek to improve student achievement results that frequently rank Idaho near the bottom of the pack (Education Week, 2013). Table 1 presents the research base underlying each Weave component.

**Table 1: Idaho Leads Research Base**

| Weave Component | Research Base |
| --- | --- |
| **Building Relationships** | The Arbinger Institute, 2008; Fullan, 2010; Sanborn, 2004; Zander & Zander, 2000 |
| **Using Effective Practices** | Brookhart, 2010; Dean, Hubbell, Pitler, & Stone, 2012; Marzano, 2003, 2007; Parrett & Budge, 2012; Schmoker, 2006; Walberg, 2007 |
| **Managing Change** | Fullan, 2010; Heath & Heath, 2010; Hiatt & Creasey, 2003; Mauer, 2010; Pfeffer & Sutton, 2000 |
| **Commitment to System Continuous Improvement** | Fullan, 2011; Joyce & Showers, 2002; Supovitz, 2006; Walberg, 2007 |
| **Reflective Teachers and Leaders** | Danielson, 2007; Marzano, Waters, & McNulty, 2005; Spillane, 2009 |
| **21st Century Classrooms** | Fullan, 2013; Kendall, 2011; The National Research Council, 2000 |
| **All Students Successful** | Chenoweth, 2008, 2009; Hattie, 2009; Parrett & Budge, 2012 |

Although these are the current vertical strands in Idaho, they will change over time. In other educational systems with different areas of focus, different strands would be substituted. If leadership capacity is built across a system to operate within this framework, stakeholders will be ready to tackle each new opportunity and challenge. When the horizontal and vertical strands are woven together in practice, district leaders have a framework for implementing change within their systems.

The design for delivery of Idaho Leads professional development and technical assistance is modeled on the seven categories of standards for professional development defined by Learning Forward (formerly the National Staff Development Council): learning communities, leadership, resources, data, learning designs, implementation, and outcomes (Learning Forward, 2011). This approach provides a solid framework for creating and delivering meaningful support to Idaho education stakeholders.

## Support and Resources for All

The Idaho Leads project applies a differentiated approach to technical assistance and professional development. At the most basic level, a high-quality, user-friendly website has been established and is updated daily with implementation and support resources and stories of success, following a "drip irrigation philosophy," by which information is continually provided in manageable chunks.[1]

Additionally, the Idaho Leads project actively uses a variety of multimedia tools to disseminate information and communicate with educators statewide. Facebook, Twitter, blogging, Edmodo, and YouTube[2] are just a few of the dissemination methods used. Live podcasts and webcasts are also provided, including an interview with Sal Khan, recently featured on *60 Minutes* for his ground-breaking work with the Khan Academy.

Idaho Leads staff are continually developing resources and tools—including research, examples of best practice, and sample templates—to assist educators statewide in implementing sound educational reform practices. These resources and tools are posted on the Idaho Leads website, disseminated during Idaho Leads events, and at times delivered during an onsite visit to work directly with a particular district or group of districts. All resources are provided in print-friendly formats and are designed for easy modification and use at the local level. In alignment with the project goal of building leadership capacity at the local level, it is intended that these resources will jump-start districts engaged in continuous improvement, may be adapted by local personnel according to their needs, and freely replicated in the future.

Finally, to facilitate the sharing of accurate and timely information, an Idaho Leads team member ("real person, real help") is always available to answer frequently asked questions and help broker responses to more challenging information requests.

---

[1] See https://education.boisestate.edu/idaholeads/
[2] http://www.youtube.com/idaholeadsproject

## Regional Networks for the Willing

A key tenant of Idaho Leads is participation of district teams in regional networks. The goal of the regional network meetings is to provide participants with timely and useful resources to support the implementation of sound reform practices and also to offer a continuing forum for positive discussion and collaboration. With this goal in mind, there was much discussion regarding the best model for delivery. Idaho is a geographically diverse state, making it critical to bring the support to various regions of the state and to facilitate the development of regionally based learning communities. There has long been a perception that in order to get assistance or engage in professional learning, educators from around the state must always travel to Boise. Yet the context and needs of districts across the state often differ from those of the districts in the state's capitol city.

For the purposes of this project, three regional networks—north, southwest, and southeast—were established. Within each regional network, participating districts identified teams of 10 members to represent the district and participate in regional network meetings and activities. The members of each district team were required to represent, at a minimum, six roles: superintendent, principal, board member, teacher, parent, and student. The four remaining team positions could include additional teachers and students, community members, or district office staff, such as business managers or technology coordinators.

Participation in a regional network and accompanying supports were made available to all districts and charters in Idaho. Forty-nine districts and charter schools elected to participate in the project. One district team even included a mayor! The full Idaho Leads community is nearly 500 strong. A breakdown of participants by role is presented in Table 2.

**Table 2: Idaho Leads Participants**

| Participant's Local Role | North | Southeast | Southwest | Statewide |
|---|---|---|---|---|
| Board Member | 11 | 28 | 22 | **61** |
| Central Office Staff | 23 | 33 | 33 | **89** |
| Parent or Community Member | 5 | 11 | 10 | **26** |
| Principal | 26 | 32 | 27 | **85** |
| Student | 14 | 25 | 23 | **62** |
| Superintendent | 13 | 24 | 21 | **58** |
| Teacher | 19 | 57 | 31 | **107** |
| TOTAL | 111 | 210 | 167 | **488** |

In total, these districts' and charters' supporting teams represent approximately 138,000, or roughly 50%, of Idaho's students and over 20,300, or 47%, of its administrators and teachers. A critical mass embracing innovation and continuous improvement is on the rise in Idaho.

Regional network meetings were held in the three regions in February, April, and November of 2012, for a total of nine regional network meetings. Each regional network meeting was carefully designed and delivered by the Idaho Leads staff and external consultants selected for their expertise in areas of focus, including Michael Fullan, one of the world's leading experts in education reform; his associate Joanne Quinn; and Joe Morelock, innovative technology director from the Canby School District in Oregon. A combination of presented content using cutting-edge professional development techniques, work time for district teams, and breakout sessions for job-alike groups was provided at each network meeting. This has provided a well-balanced approach to scaling reform and providing much-needed opportunities for team building and networking both within and among districts.

In their job-alike groups, students, teachers, principals, district office staff, parents, and community members were able to meet with others representing their same role and dig deep into topics such as: teaching and learning, the common core, educational technology, and change management. All content was designed to meet the current needs of Idaho districts and to achieve the project goal of building leadership capacity in districts to manage change in a continuous improvement cycle through the building of relationships and use of effective practices. Another round of regional network meetings are slated for delivery through the end of the 2013–2014 school year.[3]

Each regional network meeting was followed by a variety of between-meeting supports and onsite work with participating districts. Some districts were provided with technology audits, a process developed in response to a request from the field. Others were provided with support in developing data profiles and guided deep analyses of student learning gaps. Onsite, between-meeting work was tailored to each district. In addition to the development of regional networks and ongoing technical assistance to all stakeholders, the Idaho Leads project is working to foster reciprocal, working partnerships with the legislature, associations, and organizations connected to education and the future workforce in Idaho.

## Onsite Adventures

The Idaho Leads team believes that the conversation about education in Idaho—too often focusing on deficiencies—needs to shift its focus to the "bright spots" (Heath & Heath, 2010). Idaho educators have a responsibility to advocate for their profession and to tell positive stories of educational reform and successes happening across the state. To help redirect the conversation, the

---

[3]A video overview of an Idaho Leads network meeting can be accessed at http://www.youtube.com/watch?v=sgh2HrmC_Yw&list=PL74653402632CD6CA&index=9

Idaho Leads team visited all 49 districts and charter schools participating in the project. A protocol was used during the onsite visits to gather evidence and data, resulting in numerous articles published in local newspapers, in education publications, and in "bright spot" stories posted on the Idaho Leads website.[4] In addition to gathering data about observed "bright spots," the Idaho Leads team offered technical assistance during these visits, deepening relationships with district leaders, which in turn frequently facilitated access to working directly with teachers in the classroom and enabled the team to ask questions and provide tailored support to individual districts.

Visiting communities across the state and directly observing reform efforts in schools has been a powerful component of Idaho Leads. The onsite visits and resulting documentation have not only raised public appreciation of the work of creative and innovative educators, but have also served to disseminate a knowledge of emerging best practices and efforts to scale up many of these innovations.

## Studio Districts

Of the 49 districts participating in the regional networks, seven districts were identified through a rigorous set of selection criteria to participate as "studio districts" that could function in a creative space somewhat like an artists' studio. In a time of numerous top-down mandates, districts were interested in entering a creative space focused on innovation from within. The intent behind the studio districts was to provide an opportunity for a smaller group of districts—representing all regions of the state, identified as ready to benefit, and prepared to engage in substantial innovation—to extend their learning from regional network meetings in this smaller learning community setting.

In addition to participating in the regional network meetings, the studio districts convened into a single learning community, each district represented by five members from its larger Idaho Leads team, including the superintendent, a board member, a principal, a teacher, and a fifth member selected at the group's discretion. These teams were provided with additional content and learning—including direct collaboration with Michael Fullan—to extend their implementation efforts beyond those planned in regional network meetings.

Studio districts have also experienced intensive support through the services of the Idaho Leads staff, who are equipped to provide onsite tailored support to help studio districts innovate, continuously improve, and meet their established goals for positively impacting the "instructional core" (City, Elmore, Fiarman, & Teitel, 2009). For example, Idaho Leads staff conducted a data analysis of 2012 Idaho Standards Achievement Test results for all seven studio districts' Grades 5, 8, and 10. The achievement of each measurable demographic group was

---

[4]https://education.boisestate.edu/idaholeads/

compared to the whole group to ascertain success of typically underperforming groups. This data was presented to the seven superintendents, each of whom shared this information with his or her leadership team and staff.

Ultimately, Idaho Leads envisions that studio districts will not only benefit from their own learning experience and support in the project, but that they will also then share lessons learned and best practices with other districts across the state. Just like good art is eventually put on display for others to see, so will the best practices of the studio districts be showcased.

## Showcasing Innovation

As planned in the original project design, the Idaho Leads community assembled at the conclusion of a year of working together to celebrate accomplishments and share best practices. The day-long convening of the 500-plus Idaho Leads community included general sessions, breakout sessions with district participants discussing their innovations and bright spots, and time devoted to district teams planning their next steps.

> *"The Idaho Leads project provides a unique and valuable opportunity for our district community to sharpen leadership skills and find the innovative ways to embrace change."*
> Charles Shackett, Bonneville School District Superintendent

In order to spread the word about innovative bright spots in Idaho education, an evening celebration in Boise also included several hundred legislators, community leaders, and other stakeholders from across the state. A significant component of this evening celebration highlighted and honored the studio districts and their extra work throughout the year. The Idaho Leads staff presented seven 3-minute videos of each studio district's accomplishments as assessed by interviewed stakeholders and observations during additional onsite visits. The videos were viewed one by one, after which each studio district team was recognized on stage.[5]

## Voices from the Field

The initial feedback on the Idaho Leads project from participants and other observers has been strongly positive. Charles Shackett, Bonneville School District superintendent, reported, "The Idaho Leads project provides a unique and valuable opportunity for our district community to sharpen leadership skills and find innovative ways to embrace change." Jennifer Branz, a parent of a child in the Wallace School District, said, "The Idaho Leads project is critical for schools in

---

[5] The evening celebration and studio district highlight videos can be viewed at http://www.youtube.com/idaholeadsproject

Idaho to make the technological advancements necessary for a 21st-century education." Kent Jackson, the technology director for the Minidoka School District, gave high marks to a regional network meeting, stating, "We went from 7 a.m. to 7 p.m. and not one minute was wasted and not one person was anxious to get it over with and go home. It was that good."

## Participating District Vignettes

While these quotations testify to positive participants' experiences, the following vignettes provide a brief snapshot into the improvement journey a few districts have had in the Idaho Leads community and actual changes in practice that have resulted from their learning and work.

### Boundary County School District

Boundary County School District is a small, rural district located in northern Idaho. The district serves over 1,600 students at five locations, including a high school, middle school, and three elementary schools. Fifty-six percent of Boundary County's students are eligible to receive free or reduced-price lunches.

When Boundary County School District administrators examined their technology capabilities as part of the Idaho Leads project, they came to an uncomfortable realization. As curriculum director Jan Bayer put it, "We needed HELP!" As a result, Boundary personnel requested a technology audit to help them better assess their district's capabilities.

> *"The focus shifted from devices to how technology will improve student achievement.*
> Jan Bayer, Curriculum Director

Bayer says, "We needed to know what was possible from an infrastructure, policy, and people perspective." Idaho Leads staff partnered with an external expert, created a technology audit protocol, conducted the requested audit, and provided the district with a report that included bright spots, challenges, and quick wins.

"We focused on the quick wins," Bayer says. "The focus shifted from devices to how technology will improve student achievement. We are still working and learning, but most importantly, we are shifting!"

Technology use in Boundary County now looks dramatically different. All of the schools will soon have robust wireless networks, and all have increased their bandwidth by 30%. Teachers have taken the lead in integrating technology into their practices by conducting professional development sessions on technology tools like Prezi, Wordle, Glogster, and Xtranormal. A high school biology teacher is piloting a one-to-one iPad program in her classes, and soon the district will be offering a class for teachers called "Technology as a Resource for Learning," which will focus on district policies, technology as a resource to increase student achievement, and 21st-century skills. Boundary County has made a significant shift in its thinking about educational technology and taken action so as to provide all students in the district success in the 21st century.

## Castleford School District

Located in southern rural Idaho, the Castleford School District serves about 300 students at three schools located in one building, 63% eligible to receive free or reduced-price lunch. After engaging in deep discussion about technology and a new era of teaching and learning in the Idaho Leads project, Castleford staff decided to take action towards better preparing students for life in the 21st century. The Castleford Idaho Leads team loaded up a big white school bus and took a field trip to Canby, Oregon, where they were provided with an in-district opportunity to observe technology integrated with effective pedagogy as guided by Joe Morelock, special consultant to the Idaho Leads project. Canby has been engaged in educational technology reform for a number of years, and its demonstration schools and classrooms provide an observable, live example of new tools and pedagogy in action. The Castleford team returned determined to implement such practices in their own district. Local donations from a community club started a flurry of fundraising; now every student in Grades 9 through 12 has an iPad, and elementary classrooms are using iPads, iPad minis, and iPods. The districtwide science textbook is electronic, and next year Castleford is looking to shift language arts to digital texts as well.

> *Students can now see the places they learn about.*

Superintendent Andy Wiseman reports that teachers are enthusiastic about the benefits of increased student engagement and collaborative learning that have accompanied the increased use of technology in the district. Teacher Darrell Edson finds the advent of technology nothing less than revolutionary for both students and faculty:

> Students can now see the places they learn about. They can zoom in on the Mediterranean and identify some of the city-states of the Fertile Crescent. They have visited Egypt to view the Great Pyramid of Giza and can trace the trade route of the ancient Minoan culture all the way to Norway. Lessons like these give the students a feel for where world events take place and how those places differ from their experience. These fantastic changes force me to evaluate my strategies constantly. Our classes are now concentrating on higher-level thinking skills as well as skills of creativity, collaboration, and adaptability. I attribute this to having and using iPads, applications, and web-based resources in our classes.

Castleford's data further validates the district's willingness to invest in innovative practices. The district has eliminated the achievement gap and now places a remarkable number of its students in postsecondary programs. Its leadership has provided students with opportunities never before available in rural Idaho.

## Garden Valley School District

Garden Valley School District is a rural district located in west central Idaho, serving approximately 240 students at four locations, 58% eligible to receive free or reduced-price lunches. Since 2008, Garden Valley has met its AYP targets and has consistently achieved a graduation rate of over 91%. While Garden Valley's students have historically performed well on achievement measures, the district has struggled with offering a robust set of course offerings due to its rural location and small student population.

To meet these challenges, the Garden Valley School District is breaking down the walls of a traditional educational offering—literally. Superintendent Randy Schrader created the Garden Valley Digital Learning Academy so students are no longer restricted to what their handful of rural teachers are certified to teach. Students are now able to take Mandarin Chinese, World Religions, and European History, courses that were not previously available. Not only have new course offerings been provided, students now experience a greater level of flexibility in when they take courses, rather than being trapped by a traditional schedule. About 15 students per period are learning flexibly online, including six middle school students who are taking high school classes and a 12-year-old enrolled in a freshman-level class that meets his academic needs while still participating in a class of peers matching his social needs.

Because of technology, the learning opportunities are now limitless. Plus, students can drive their own education. They can take any class they want from educators all over the world at the level of their skills. Students are tapping into lessons from the Khan Academy and enrolling in classes taught by highly qualified educators within the state of Idaho and without. While the Garden Valley Digital Learning Academy provides students with any class they want, it also keeps them enrolled in the district under the supervision and guidance of the Garden Valley teaching staff. Even though students are learning online, they still have access to direct instruction, rich discussion, and support from certified teachers with whom they have built a relationship within the context of the more traditional classroom. Schrader said, "We didn't have any other choice here but to become experts in technology; to know what's out there and anticipate what's next. We want to be a high-tech high school while keeping the standards tight." In other efforts to be a high-tech district, Garden Valley is nearly paperless with most districtwide communication transmitted by e-mail or e-text, and all secondary teachers are certified to instruct dual-credit classes.

## Twin Falls School District

Located in southeast Idaho, Twin Falls School District is the eighth largest district in the state, serving nearly 8,000 students at 13 locations, including seven elementary schools, two middle schools, two high schools, one alternative middle school, and one alternative high school. Sixty-two percent of the student population is eligible for free or reduced-price lunches.

In conjunction with their participation in the Idaho Leads project, teachers in Twin Falls School District are participating in a groundbreaking professional development pilot program facilitated by representatives from the educational social media site Edmodo. Edmodo is a free, web-based platform which allows teachers to interact with students in a safe, social media environment and to connect with educators all over the world. Some call it the education version of Facebook, with stellar safety features built into the system. As a result of this project, Twin Falls has seen significant growth in a number of areas: More staff are now delivering high-quality, technology-enriched learning experiences, and they have increased in- and out-of-school engagement for teachers and students.

Participating teacher Ron Withers assessed the use of this technology, "Edmodo is not designed to take the place of effective teaching, but rather is a valuable tool to enhance and supplement learning. It can be used both in and out of the classroom to help student learning." Edmodo additionally introduces teachers to a global community of educators and provides them with opportunities to share ideas for better student engagement and discuss new programs and materials.

## Looking Ahead

As the Idaho Leads project moves into the next phase, its focus will narrow to intensive work on the implementation of the Common Core State Standards and new student achievement measures, while remaining committed to the key tenants of building relationships, using effective practices, managing change, and committing to systemic continuous improvement. Participation will be offered both to the original group and to additional districts that may be interested in joining the learning network.

Throughout the duration of the project, the Idaho Leads team will continue to research best practices in educational reform and engage in substantial data collection and evaluative analysis. A variety of data points, both quantitative and qualitative, are being collected on a regular basis in order to provide formative and summative evaluation measures. This data will guide ongoing project design and implementation. Based on this research, the team will continually develop supports for educators across the state to build capacity to lead and deliver an education system that prepares all Idaho students for success in the 21st century.

Regional networks are established, and the culture is set for a positive and rigorous systems approach to professional development in and out of the school setting. Bright spots are abundant in the state of Idaho, and there is a buzz of energy and innovation as educators statewide engage in collaborative continuous improvement.

# References

The Arbinger Institute. (2008). *The anatomy of peace: Resolving the heart of conflict.* San Francisco, CA: Berrett-Koehler.

Brookhart, S. (2010). *How to assess higher-order thinking skills in your classroom.* Alexandria, VA: ASCD.

Chenoweth, K. (2008). *"It's being done": Academic success in unexpected schools.* Cambridge, MA: Harvard Education Press.

Chenoweth, K. (2009). *How it's being done: Urgent lessons from unexpected schools.* Cambridge, MA: Harvard Education Press.

City, E., Elmore, R., Fiarman, S., & Teitel, L. (2009). *Instructional rounds in education: A network approach to improving teaching and learning.* Cambridge, MA: Harvard Education Press.

Danielson, C. (2007). *Enhancing professional practice: A framework for teaching.* Alexandria, VA: ASCD.

Dean, C., Hubbell, E., Pitler, H., & Stone, B. (2012). *Classroom instruction that works: Research-based strategies for increasing student achievement* (2nd ed.). Alexandria, VA: ASCD.

Education Week. (2013). *Quality counts 2013.* Langhorne, PA: Editorial Projects in Education.

Fullan, M. (2010). *Motion leadership: The skinny on becoming change savvy.* Thousand Oaks, CA: Corwin.

Fullan, M. (2011). *The moral imperative realized.* Thousand Oaks, CA: Corwin.

Fullan, M. (2013). *Stratosphere: Integrating technology, pedagogy, and change knowledge.* Don Mills, Ontario, Canada: Pearson.

Hattie, J. (2009). *Visible learning: A synthesis of over 800 meta-analyses relating to achievement.* New York, NY: Routledge.

Heath, C., & Heath, D. (2010). *Switch: How to change things when change is hard.* New York, NY: Broadway Books.

Hiatt, J. M., & Creasey, T. J. (2003). *Change management: The people side of change.* Loveland, CO: Prosci Research.

Joyce, B., & Showers, B. (2002). *Student achievement through staff development.* Alexandria, VA: ASCD.

Kendall, J. (2011). *Understanding common core standards.* Alexandria, VA: ASCD.

Learning Forward. (2011). *Standards for professional learning.* Oxford, OH: Author.

Marzano, R. (2003). *What works in schools: Translating research into action.* Alexandria, VA: ASCD.

Marzano, R. (2007). *The art and science of teaching: A comprehensive framework for effective instruction.* Alexandria, VA: ASCD.

Marzano, R., Waters, T., & McNulty, B. (2005). *School leadership that works: From research to results.* Alexandria, VA: ASCD.

Mauer, R. (2010). *Beyond the wall of resistance: Why 70% of all changes still fail—and what you can do about it.* Austin, TX: Bard Press.

The National Research Council. (2000). *How people learn: Brain, mind, experience, and school.* Washington, DC: National Academy Press.

Parrett, W., & Budge, K. (2012). *Turning high-poverty schools into high-performing schools.* Alexandria, VA: ASCD.

Pfeffer, J., & Sutton, R. (2000). *The knowing–doing gap: How smart companies turn knowledge into action.* Boston, MA: Harvard Business School Press.

Redding, S. (2006). *The mega system—deciding, learning, connecting: A handbook for continuous improvement within a community of the school.* Lincoln, IL: The Academic Development Institute.

Sanborn, M. (2004). *The Fred factor.* New York, NY: Doubleday.

Schmoker, M. (2006). *Results now: How we can achieve unprecedented improvements in teaching and learning.* Alexandria, VA: ASCD.

Spillane, J. P. (2009). Engaging practice: School leadership and management from a distributed perspective. In A. Hargreaves & M. Fullan (Eds.), *Change wars* (pp. 201–220). Bloomington, IN: Solution Tree.

Supovitz, J. A. (2006). *The case for district-based reform: Leading, building, and sustaining school improvement.* Cambridge, MA: Harvard Education Press.

Walberg, H. (Ed.). (2007). *Handbook on restructuring and substantial school improvement.* Charlotte, NC: Information Age Publishing.

Zander, R., & Zander, B. (2000). *The art of possibility: Transforming professional and personal life.* New York, NY: Penguin Group.

# Using Response to Intervention Data to Advance Learning Outcomes
*Amanda M. VanDerHeyden*

Response to intervention (RtI) is a system of service delivery that uses student data to evaluate and repair core instruction and to provide increasingly intensive intervention supplements to students who need it to meet expected learning outcomes. Universal screening is conducted to identify students who are likely to experience academic failure and to indicate the general adequacy of instruction for the system. Screening data are used to indicate a need for core instruction enhancements that affect all students and to evaluate the extent to which such enhancements improve the effects of instruction for all students. Universal screening data are also used to identify students who require supplemental instruction to attain important learning objectives. RtI (now often called multi-tiered systems of support) is generally presented as a filtered system whereby student data are collected to identify risk. Based on that data, increasingly intensive interventions are provided to subgroups of students, with (a) most students successfully responding to core instruction alone, (b) a small subset of students requiring supplemental intervention support to experience success, and (c) a smaller subset requiring intensive individualized intervention to attain important learning outcomes.

When used effectively, RtI systems generate data that indicate the general effectiveness of instruction in a system; that is, the percentage of students requiring intervention should be below 20% and should decrease over time with core instructional enhancements (O'Connor, Fulmer, Harty, & Bell, 2005; Shapiro & Clemens, 2009). RtI systems also generate data that may be used to identify children for special education eligibility, particularly under the category of specific learning disability (Kovaleski, VanDerHeyden, & Shapiro, in press).

RtI came to the forefront in the 1990s as an innovative means of using data to determine when and for which students instruction was working and what types of adjustments were needed for students who were not learning successfully. The RtI framework has its roots in precision teaching, direct instruction, curriculum-based measurement, and school-based consultation. It has been widely studied with encouraging results (Burns, Appleton, & Stehouwer, 2005), endorsed and recommended by numerous policy groups as a method of system reform (Batsche et al., 2005; Bradley, Danielson, & Hallahan, 2002; Donovan & Cross, 2002), and permitted as a method of eligibility determination under Individuals with Disabilities Education Act and state regulations (IDEA, 2004). While promising, however, the effects attained depend upon the quality with which components are implemented, and quality of implementation varies greatly across sites. This chapter will demonstrate how to use student performance data to make decisions about core instruction adequacy, to guide instructional enhancements to core instruction, to identify small groups and individual students for intervention, to guide small-group and individual intervention, and to evaluate the effects of instructional changes so that implementation can be managed effectively and desired student learning improvements can occur.

## Key Action 1: Conduct Screening to Yield High-Quality Data

Universal screening is the starting point for any RtI implementation. Brief academic assessments are administered schoolwide, typically in reading and in mathematics, to characterize student performance by school, grade, and class. Universal screening data are a rich resource that is often underexploited by decision makers. Investing the time needed to ensure that the screening is conducted with sufficient quality to yield meaningful data is time well spent because screening data can be used to accomplish several objectives (which will be explained below). Adequate universal screening measures should (a) yield reliable scores, (b) forecast future learning success or outcomes, (c) be administered efficiently, and (d) reflect the mastery of key academic objectives (Kovaleski et al., in press). Screening measures can be selected to reflect a performance standard that children are already expected to have mastered because mastery of that skill or skills is an essential prerequisite to the instruction that students will experience. The screening must be administered correctly and scored accurately. For efficiency, curriculum-based measurement probes in reading and mathematics function well as screening devices, and it is possible for schoolwide screening to occur within a single day, requiring no more than 45 minutes in any class. Universal screening typically occurs three times per year. Screening scores should be organized by content area (e.g., reading, mathematics), school, grade, and class. Because screening yields data upon which important decisions will be based (e.g., who receives intervention), it is important to verify that high-quality screening has occurred. When training professionals to collect screening data,

*Using Response to Intervention Data*

the following indicators may be used as a guide to determine that a professional has been adequately prepared to conduct high-quality screening.

**Table 1. Key Action 1: Indicators That Trainee Is Proficient in Screening**

| |
|---|
| Faculty overview has been provided and screening materials selected. |
| Screening has been scheduled to occur on a single day, and screening schedule has been planned. |
| All materials for screening are available and have been organized by class, including a written protocol for screening. |
| Trainee has been observed to correctly administer and score screening materials. |

## Key Action 2: Interpret Screening Data Beginning With an Aerial View

Screening data can be examined to identify schoolwide, gradewide, and classwide problems. Decision makers should begin at the district or school level—the aerial view—and work their way down through the data to the grade, class, and, finally, individual students. A schoolwide learning problem is detected when more than half the grades within a school exhibit a gradewide problem. A gradewide problem is detected when more than half the classes in a grade exhibit a classwide problem. A classwide problem is defined as the median score for the class falling within the risk range associated with the screening tool.

In the example shown in Figure 1, a gradewide problem in mathematics was detected by a screening that was conducted in February of the third-grade year after multiplication facts 0–9 had been taught and students were expected to demonstrate proficient performance of that skill. Figure 1 shows that, in 8 of 12 classes, the majority of students performed in the risk range and therefore constituted a classwide problem. Because more than half of the classes at this grade level scored in the risk range during screening, a gradewide problem is indicated. There is no need to look further at individual classes or individual students because the gradewide problem should be addressed first.

**Figure 1. Instructional Effects, Grade 3. Assessment: Math, Multiplication, Multiplication Facts 0–9**

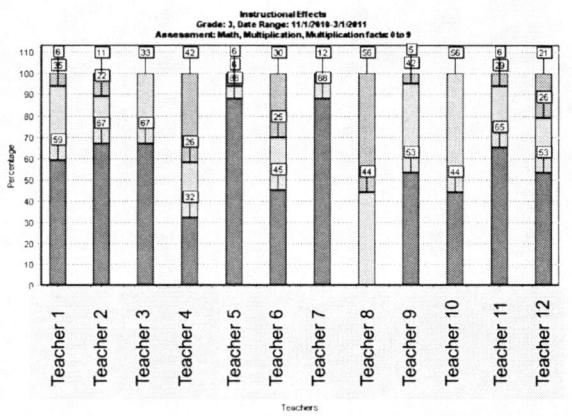

209

Handbook on Innovations in Learning

The data team should next examine other grade levels to determine if they show a similar gradewide learning problem in mathematics. Figure 2 shows the universal screening data for second-grade mathematics in the same school.

**Figure 2. Instructional Effects, Grade 2. Assessment: Math, Subtraction, 2-Digit Number from a 2-Digit Number, Regrouping**

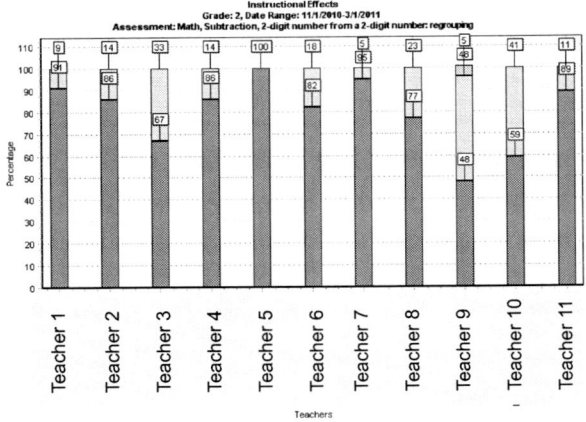

Second grade was also administered a 2-digit addition probe with regrouping, with the results shown in Figure 3.

**Figure 3. Instructional Effects, Grade 2. Assessment: Math, Addition, Two 2-Digit Numbers Regrouping**

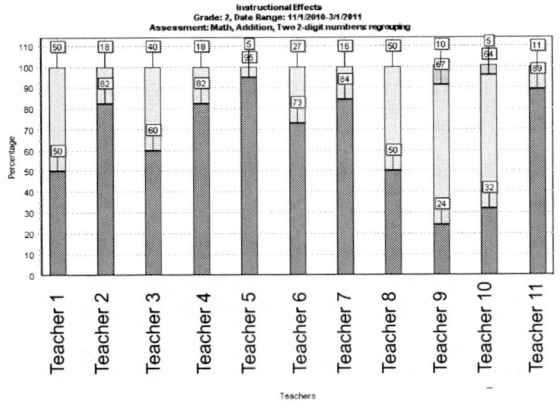

Thus, a schoolwide learning problem in mathematics was identified for this elementary school serving Grades 1 through 3.

Let's consider reading performance for the same grade level as indicated in Figure 4.

**Figure 4.** Instructional Effects, Grade 3. Assessment: DIBELS K–6, Oral Reading Fluency, Grade 3

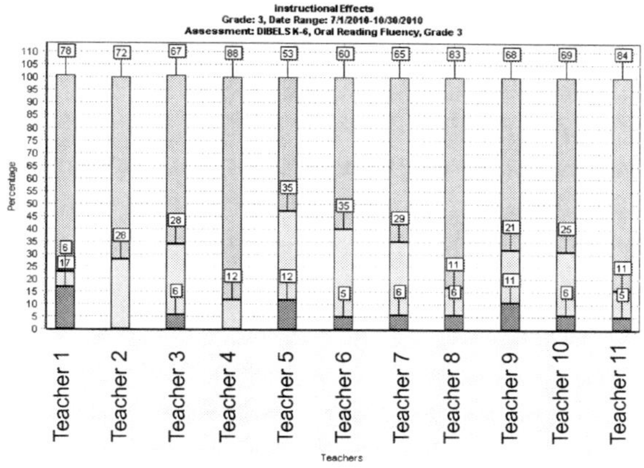

Here we reach a different conclusion. In this example, screening reveals no classwide problem—and therefore no gradewide problem—in reading. For the school, then, only the schoolwide problem in mathematics needs to be addressed through systemic solutions. In reading, individual children can be selected for further assessment and possibly intervention. Data teams will want to verify that the screening task was appropriately selected at each grade level (the difficulty of the screening task was well aligned with standard learning expectations at each grade level). Systemic performance problems should be treated with systemic solutions, which will be briefly discussed in the next section. When training professionals to interpret screening data, the indicators presented in Table 2 may be used to examine mastery of screening data interpretation.

**Table 2.** Key Action 2: Indicators That Trainee Is Proficient in Data Interpretation

| |
|---|
| Trainee has ruled out school-level, grade-level, and whole-class performance problems prior to selecting individual children for follow-up assessment and possibly intervention. |
| Data have been organized by grade and by class. |
| Data have been examined for identified vulnerable or high-risk groups of students to identify potential performance patterns (e.g., high numbers of new students scoring in the risk range, disproportionately high numbers of special education students scoring in the risk range). |

## Key Action 3: Treat Systemic Problems With Systemic Solutions

Systemic problems deserve systemic solutions. So when a schoolwide learning problem is detected, the first step to be taken by the data team should be to verify that research-supported curriculum materials are available to all teachers. The data team should also verify that the teachers understand what learning outcomes are expected of students and have a clear calendar of instruction

that specifies the time points by which certain learning outcomes will have been attained. Next, the data team should examine the quality of instruction in the classroom; team observations should answer questions such as the following:
- Is adequate instructional time allocated?
- Are students actively engaged during the instructional period?
- Does the teacher have a system for knowing which skills students have mastered and which skills require additional support to reach mastery?
- Does the teacher align instructional efforts with student needs (e.g., acquisition supports for skills that have not been established, fluency-building supports when student responses are accurate but slow, systematic practice applying learned skills to solve more complex problems or in different contexts)?

The data team should establish priorities for improvement and determine a timeline. So, if a schoolwide problem were detected at all grade levels, the data team may choose to begin a classwide intervention for all classes at one grade level, while simply monitoring performance weekly in the other grades and providing feedback to teachers. If systemic performance problems were detected in reading and mathematics, the data team may choose to target one content area initially and add the second only after improvements are attained for the first. Both of these approaches allow for a staggered or incremental solution implementation, which allows the data team to implement the intervention with quality, ensure that performance gains occur, troubleshoot any implementation challenges, and expand to new areas as capacity for implementation is increased.

In each class with a classwide problem (i.e., median score in the risk range), a classwide supplemental intervention should be conducted. Building fluency in prerequisite skills (i.e., skills that have been taught but which students have not mastered and which are required for successful goal-level performance) is an ideal target for a classwide intervention. Classwide intervention can occur daily within about 20 minutes and can produce large returns on proximal (targeted skills) and distal (more comprehensive or multicomponent skills, including content and skills not directly taught during the intervention) measures (Codding, Chan-Iannetta, Palmer, & Lukito, 2009; Fuchs, Fuchs, Mathes, & Simmons, 1997; VanDerHeyden, McLaughlin, Algina, & Snyder, 2012). When a classwide intervention has been initiated, progress monitoring should occur weekly. Weekly progress monitoring is used to determine when to advance task difficulty of the intervention and to signal the need for in-class coaching to support the fidelity of intervention implementation.

Data teams should examine and respond to implementation effects each month. The data demonstrating a systemic problem and the intervention data reflecting improvements gained through intervention should be shared with decision makers in the system's feeder pattern. Instructional leaders should consider and identify ways to prevent the same problem in the future and provide supports to ensure maintenance of intervention gains over time and across grade levels. One common need identified during multigrade and multischool troubleshooting sessions is an increased rigor of learning expectations and practice opportunities at earlier grade levels. Improved rigor will "reduce the load" experienced at subsequent grade levels and help prevent the emergence of gradewide performance problems. Progress monitoring data should reflect that at-risk performance by demographic categories becomes proportionate over time with intervention improvements. The percentage of students not at risk should increase following intervention. Systems can define and track their own long-term outcomes, such as the percentage of students enrolling in and passing algebra, advanced placement course enrollments and advanced placement test scores, and the percentage of students taking and meeting the ACT benchmarks for college readiness.

When an isolated classwide learning problem is detected (the majority of classes at a grade level are doing fine, but a minority of classes—one or more—have more than half of their students in the risk range at screening), classwide intervention can be started immediately. While training the teacher (or teachers) to implement a classwide intervention, the coach can assist the teacher to improve core instructional procedures (e.g., Does the teacher follow the master schedule? Does the lesson plan include time for establishing new skills, verifying understanding of new skills and information, providing guided practice with corrective feedback for new skills, providing fluency-building support for established skills, monitoring student performance for mastery, and providing structured support to generalize skills and connect newly learned information to existing knowledge?). The classwide intervention can be used to establish mastery-level performance of prerequisite skills and serve as a training vehicle to provide the teacher with an expanded skill set to enhance the quality of core instruction. The classwide intervention can be delivered following a standard, scripted intervention protocol (e.g., Vanderbilt Kennedy Center, n.d.; http://www.gosbr.net/).

Children who successfully respond to intervention should surpass the screening risk criterion at higher rates on subsequent screenings. Students receiving intervention should also pass the year-end accountability tests at higher rates following intervention. Unsuccessful responders should qualify for more intensive instruction at higher rates. Students successfully responding to intervention and students not successfully responding to intervention should be proportionate by demographics.

Only after systemic problems have been ruled out should individual children be considered for intervention support. The utility of a decision rule to determine academic risk status is affected by the prevalence of risk in the group within which the decision rule will be applied. Providing classwide intervention in classes where a classwide problem has been identified is more efficient than working with individual children, more effective in terms of showing learning gains for all students, and results in more accurate decision making in subsequent risk decisions because it reduces prevalence of risk within the group. Indicators that a professional has been adequately trained and equipped to deploy systemwide interventions are provided in Table 3.

**Table 3. Key Action 3: Indicators That Trainee Is Proficient in Treating Systemic Solutions**

| |
|---|
| Classwide interventions have been started in classes with classwide problems. |
| Data teams have examined core instructional procedures in classes and grades with systemic problems. |
| Vertical teaming has occurred across grades and schools within the feeder pattern to share screening data and systemic intervention data. |
| Lower percentages of students fall in the risk range across consecutive screenings within and across years. |
| Higher percentages of students meet the proficiency criterion on the year-end accountability measure over time. |
| Historically vulnerable students show learning gains and fall into the risk range at lower rates. Performance gaps between those at risk and not at risk are reduced with intervention. |
| All students, including those in the higher performing groups and the lower performing groups, show gains with intervention and over time. |
| Students found to be at risk become proportionate by demographics with interventions. |

## Key Action 4: Monitor Implemented Solution Effects and Manage Implementation Effectively

Once systemic problems have been detected and addressed through intervention, the data team can identify individual students for assessment and intervention. Individual children falling in the risk range should participate in brief follow-up assessments to verify risk-range performance, test the effect of rewards on performance, reduced task difficulty, and brief instructional trials on learning. This type of assessment is referred to as "functional assessment" or "brief experimental analysis" in the intervention literature (Daly, Witt, Martens, & Dool, 1997; Wagner, McComas, Bollman, & Holton, 2006) and explains the process of aligning instructional strategies with student skills for optimal intervention effects. The purpose of functional assessment is to identify an intervention that will work (i.e., has a functional relationship with student learning) when the intervention is properly used. If several children at a given grade level perform similarly (require instruction on the same content and subskill, require the same type of instruction), those students may be organized into a small group for supplemental instruction. Small-group intervention should occur daily with weekly progress monitoring and weekly adjustments as students' performances change. So called "standard protocol interventions" can be especially useful supplemental interventions (i.e., Tier 2) that generally involve teaching grade-level skills in a more explicit fashion with more opportunities to practice and receive corrective feedback. Children whose scores improve outside of the risk range on the lesson objectives and the screening criterion can be exited from the small-group intervention. Some children will require individualized intervention (i.e., Tier 3) to attain expected learning outcomes. These children should participate in an individual functional assessment to develop and test an intervention that will be conducted individually each day. During the individual assessment session, intervention targets should be specified, an effective intervention should be identified, and baseline performance should be quantified. Intervention progress should be examined weekly (five data points per week), and the intervention should be adjusted to accelerate growth when needed. Individual growth should be detectable within about 2 weeks. After ruling out poor fidelity when the intervention does not produce growth, data teams should troubleshoot and adjust the intervention (Fixsen & Blasé, 1993; Noell & Gansle, 2006).

In the implementation of an intervention, the lack of fidelity to its design is a persistent and ubiquitous threat. To prevent fidelity problems, coaches should provide adequate support for correct intervention implementation with ongoing monitoring of student outcomes. Where student outcomes lag, in-class coaching support, following a process known as "performance feedback" (Noell et al., 2005), should be provided.

Each week, the data team should examine growth in each classroom to verify that gains are being made. Where gains are not occurring, a trainer or coach should visit the classroom during intervention to verify correct intervention use or provide support and coaching for stronger intervention implementation (i.e., provide performance feedback). Figure 5 below presents the data from a class that is working on a particular skill target; growth each week is monitored and reflects steady, upward gains and the class's meeting the goal within a few weeks of the start of intervention.

**Figure 5. 2-Digit Addition With and Without Regrouping**

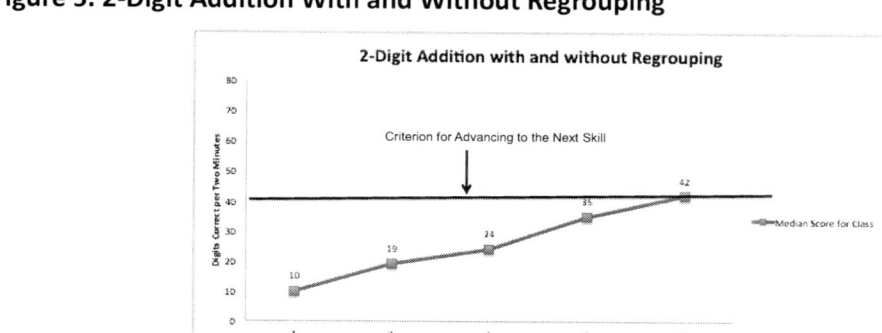

Where classwide intervention is occurring in many classes, data teams should identify those that "lag" relative to classes in the same grade at the same school in terms of the number of trials needed to reach the criterion (or duration of time required to meet the goal). That is, lagging classes can be identified by tracking the number of targeted skills mastered by class, as demonstrated in Figure 6. Maintaining these data is an efficient way to identify lagging classes each week so that a trainer or coach can visit those classes and provide support for greater intervention gains. In Figure 6, Classes 3 and 8 are lagging behind the other classes—all given the same classwide intervention—in terms of skill gains. Classes 1, 9, and 10 also require in-class coaching and support to maximize intervention gains.

**Figure 6. Number of Skills Mastered**

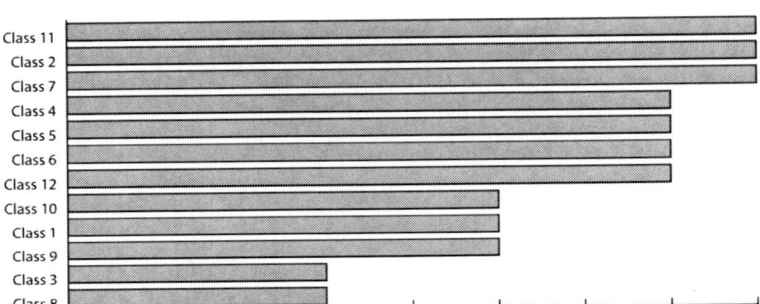

Figure 6. Number of Skills Mastered

Interventions that are not actively managed for fidelity and consistency will not be effective. One of the most important functions of the data team at a school is to actively manage intervention implementation, which includes monitoring intervention effects and providing support in classrooms where gains are not observed. In Table 4, indicators are provided for effective intervention implementation management that could be useful when training professionals to manage intervention or evaluating the quality with which interventions are being managed in a system.

**Table 4. Key Action 4: Indicators That Trainee Is Proficient in Monitoring Intervention Effects and Managing Implementation**

| |
|---|
| Interventions have written protocols available for teachers to use. |
| The teacher has been provided with all needed materials to conduct the intervention and has demonstrated correct and independent use of the intervention prior to being considered trained. |
| An in-class trainer or coach is available to model correct intervention use and provide in-vivo training for the teacher. |
| A tracking log is available showing at a glance who is experiencing intervention in the school. |

| A master schedule is followed to deliver classwide, small-group, and individual interventions. |
|---|
| Weekly progress monitoring data are collected for all children experiencing intervention. |
| Progress monitoring data are graphed, and interventions are adjusted weekly with in-class support where growth is not occurring as anticipated. |

## Key Action 5: Conduct Follow-up Screening to Verify Improvements

Intervention should produce appreciable effects for students in the school. Subsequent screenings should show that fewer children fall into the risk range, as shown in Figure 7. In Figure 7, the paired bars show the percentage of students at risk (black) during the fall and winter screening, respectively, for each teacher. So, for example, for Teacher 1, 81% of children in her class score in the risk range during the fall screening, and 59% of children score in the risk range during the winter. Comparing fall and winter screenings reveals that for all 12 teachers the percentage of students at risk is decreasing with intervention.

**Figure 7. Instructional Effects, Grade 3. Assessment: Math, Multiple Skills, Mixed Addition Problems With and Without Regrouping**

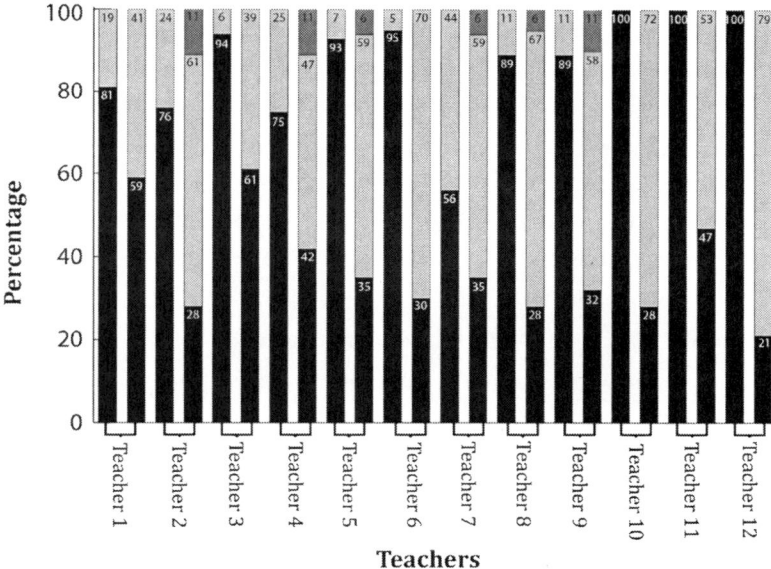

Similar data could be accumulated for all grades to show schoolwide progress. In any case, individual students who experience intervention should perform above the risk range on subsequent screenings and score at higher rates in the proficient range on the year-end accountability measure. Figure 8, a classwide screening graph, shows the baseline reading performance of students in a fourth-grade class (i.e., black bars). A follow-up assessment tested the effect of incentives on performance, and the gray bars next to the black bars show the students' scores upon being given an opportunity to earn a reward for beating the previous score. Based on the screening and follow-up assessment with incentives, three children were identified for individual reading intervention in this class.

**Figure 8. Assessment 9/9/2010—Reading, Maze, Grade 4**

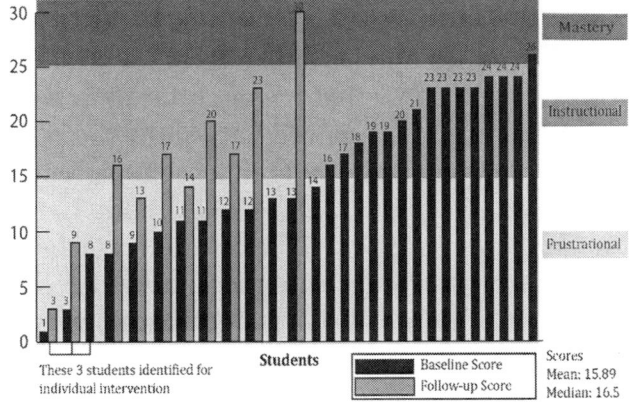

These three children participated in intervention that was actively managed. The subsequent classwide screening graph (for the winter screening) is shown in Figure 9. Here we see that two of the three children exposed to intervention now perform outside of the risk range for the class at the winter screening. Performance outside of the risk range during subsequent screenings is an indicator with great consequential and social validity and indicates that the interventions are having positive effects on important outcomes for the school. Key indicators of adequate use of follow-up screening data to verify intervention gains are provided in Table 5.

**Figure 9. Assessment 1/21/2011—Reading, Maze, Grade 4**

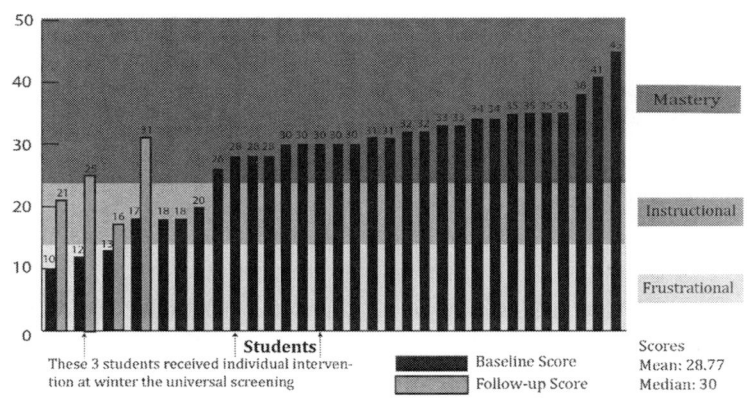

**Table 5. Key Action 5: Indicators that Trainee is Proficient in Organizing Follow-up Data to Verify Improvements**

| The data team organizes data across consecutive screenings to show a reduced risk status accompanying the intervention. |
|---|
| Intervention effects are monitored for vulnerable or at-risk students over time. |

When data are used to track instructional effects schoolwide and to make adjustments to instruction, learning outcomes can be accelerated. In the preceding case example, Figures 1–9, I have illustrated how universal screening data can be used to identify systemic problems, to monitor and manage intervention effects, and to evaluate intervention effects for the system. This case example ends with a caveat. Three of the most common errors in data-driven instructional decision making are (a) to collect too much of the wrong data, (b) to fail to expect intervention integrity errors, and (c) to fail to actively manage intervention to avoid fidelity errors. In this case example described above, the process for active management of intervention has been highlighted. The remaining space will used to explain how to avoid overassessment.

One of the most common implementation pitfalls in RtI is overassessment. Overassessment involves collecting data that provides redundant information or does not provide useful information. In many RtI systems, implementers conduct multiple screenings to determine which students are at risk. Overassessment is a costly waste of resources and comes with a direct cost to instructional time. Further, overassessment reduces the probability that the data will be used because implementers are overwhelmed by so much data and unsure how to translate the data into actions that make a difference.

To avoid the pitfall of overassessment, data teams should take an assessment inventory and verify that each assessment has a unique purpose. Further, data teams should verify that the intended purpose is served by each assessment in the least costly way possible. Where multiple assessments are being administered to inform the same decision, the data team should use local data to examine which measures provide the best utility for decision making. Data teams should examine local data to verify that publisher-suggested cutscores are serving the decisions well (accurate, sensitive, and efficient).

One metric for comparing the utility of each test measure is the AUC. The AUC stands for "area under the curve," and it is the probability that the results of a given test will rank a student who fails the criterion lower than it would rank a student who passes the criterion. It also is equivalent to the average sensitivity over all false positive rates. AUCs range from .5 (no value) to 1.0 (perfect value), and some groups (e.g., rti4success) recommend an AUC of at least .80 to consider a test potentially useful. The AUC is derived from a receiver operating characteristics (ROC) curve analysis. As shown in Figure 10 and Table 6, ROC analysis considers the full range of available screening scores and, for all possible decision thresholds (i.e., the number of unique test scores minus 1) on the test, plots the sensitivity of that score against the false positive rate for that score if it were used as the cutoff value in predicting the criterion (in this case, proficient performance on the year-end accountability measure). Thus, data teams can scan the associated AUC values and identify those with the greatest relative predictive value. In Figure 10, ROC curves have been plotted for each of the possible screening measures so that data teams can visually identify the relative merit of each screening. Generally speaking, as in Figure 10, trend lines closer to the upper left quadrant of the graph (as high vertically as possible indicating very strong sensitivity and as close to the y-axis as possible indicating very few false positive errors) are stronger and will have stronger AUC values; screening measures analyzed in Figure 10 show little difference among their ROCs and equally high relative predictive value.

**Figure 10. ROC Curve**

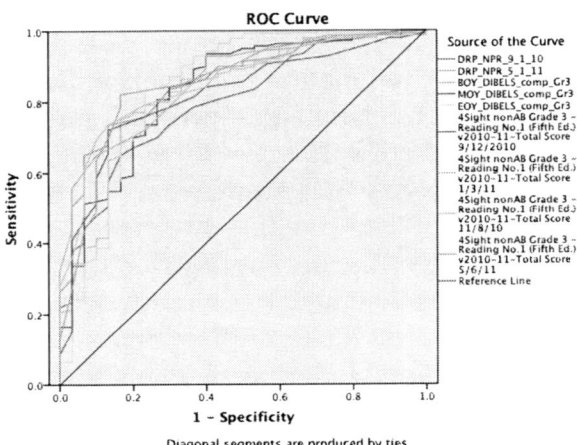

**Table 6. Receiver Operating Characteristics (ROC) Curve Analysis**

| Screening | Correlation With State Annual Proficiency Assessment in Reading | Percentage Nonproficient (Nonproficient on State Test = 23%) | AUC |
|---|---|---|---|
| DRP Fall | .74 | 32% | .797 |
| DRP Spring | .79 | 28% | .857 |
| DIBELS Fall | .66 | 19% | .827 |
| DIBELS Winter | .78 | 26% | .832 |
| DIBELS Spring | .77 | 25% | .841 |
| 4Sight Fall 1 | .72 | 34% | .816 |
| 4Sight Fall 2 | .79 | 24% | .856 |
| 4Sight Winter | .76 | 18% | .852 |
| 4Sight Spring | .78 | 10% | .855 |

The value of each screening measure can be further evaluated by considering the measure's sensitivity and specificity, as indicated in Table 7. To do this, we must tabulate all the cases in the sample and identify whether the screening measure was passed or failed and whether the criterion measure was passed or failed.

Table 7. Predictive Value of Screening Tools as Determined by Sensitivity, Specificity, and Likelihood Ratios

| Screening | Sensitivity[a] | Specificity[a] | Positive Likelihood Ratio[b] | Negative Likelihood Ratio[b] | Posttest Probability of Failing Year-End Test for those who FAILED Screener[b] | Posttest Probability of Failing Year-End Test for those who PASSED Screener[b] |
|---|---|---|---|---|---|---|
| DRP Fall | .70 | .80 | 3.5 | .38 | 51% | 10% |
| DRP Spring | .30 | .66 | .88 | 1.06 | 21% | 24% |
| DIBELS Fall | .58 | .89 | 5.27 | .47 | 61% | 12% |
| DIBELS Winter | .74 | .89 | 6.72 | .29 | 67% | 8% |
| DIBELS Spring | .75 | .91 | 8.33 | .27 | 71% | 8% |
| 4Sight Fall 1 | .77 | .79 | 3.67 | .29 | 52% | 8% |
| 4Sight Fall 2 | .68 | .89 | 6.18 | .36 | 65% | 10% |
| 4Sight Winter | .58 | .97 | 9.67 | .45 | 74% | 12% |
| 4Sight Spring | .37 | .99 | 37.00 | .64 | 92% | 16% |

[a]Sensitivity = number of correctly identified positives (i.e., correctly identified students with nonproficient year-end test scores) divided by the total number of positives (i.e., total number of students with nonproficient year-end test scores).

Specificity = number of correctly identified negatives (i.e., correctly identified students with proficient year-end test scores) divided by the total number of negatives (i.e., total number of students with proficient year-end test scores).

[b]Positive Likelihood Ratio = (sensitivity) / (1 − specificity)
Negative Likelihood Ratio = (1 − sensitivity) / (specificity)
Pretest Probability = .23 (23% of students failed the year-end test)
Pretest Odds = Pretest Probability / (1-Pretest Probability) or .23 / .77 = .30
Posttest Odds = Pretest Odds x Likelihood Ratio
Posttest Probability = Posttest Odds / (1 + Post test Odds)

Sensitivity is the power of the test to detect positives and is calculated as the number of correctly identified positives (test positive plus gold-standard positive cases) divided by the total number of gold-standard positives. Specificity is the power of the test to detect negatives and is calculated as the total number of correctly identified negatives (test negative plus gold standard negative cases) divided by the total number of gold-standard negatives. False-positive errors in this example are cases that were predicted to fail the year-end accountability measure based on the screening score but actually passed the year-end accountability measure. False-negative errors are cases that were predicted to pass the year-end accountability measure based on the screening score but actually failed the year-end accountability measure.

From sensitivity and specificity values, likelihood ratios can be calculated. The positive likelihood ratio (ratio of true positives to false positives) is computed as sensitivity divided by (1-specificity). The negative likelihood ratio (ratio of false negatives to true negatives) is computed as (1-sensitivity) divided by specificity. Sensitivity pertains only to those cases that are test-positive and/or criterion-positive while specificity pertains only to those cases that are test-negative and/or criterion-negative. Thus, sensitivity and specificity cannot be considered in isolation from one another; instead, sensitivity and specificity must be considered in tandem. Likelihood ratios provide a single value that incorporates sensitivity and specificity and allow for the calculation of posttest probability for test-positive and test-negative cases. Posttest probabilities are important because knowing that a test is capable of detecting 50% of actual positives (i.e., sensitivity = .50) or knowing how much more likely a positive result is for a person who truly has a condition (i.e., positive likelihood ratio) gives us good information when selecting a test for use in a particular context, but tells users nothing about how to interpret the test findings clinically for a given case or set of cases. The posttest probability values allow users to readily communicate to teachers what the calculated probability of failing the year-end test is for students who have failed the screening test and for students who have passed the screening test in a way that is superior to positive predictive value and negative predictive value (see VanDerHeyden, 2010a, 2010b, 2011 for a more complete analysis of the limitations of positive and negative predictive value). In the range of considered screening instruments in Table 7, the data team should discuss the cost associated with the time and materials needed to conduct each screening. The lowest-cost options can be identified for fall, winter, and spring. Next, the data team should discuss and ask teachers about what other useful data may be garnered from each screening score and determine whether teachers prefer one screening over another. Finally, the data team should identify the least costly measure that provides the most useful information at each screening occasion. Given the data in Table 7, the DIBELS and 4Sight screening measures could be supported as viable screening tools for use in the school (meaning one of those two should be selected for use, and the other, along with the DRP screening measure, could and should be discontinued).

## Conclusion

Student performance data offers an efficient and accurate guide for instructional actions. If one wants to know whether a program of instruction is effective, there is no better metric than the student's learning (Bushell & Baer, 1994; Deno & Mirkin, 1977). RtI is a framework for using student performance data to reach actionable conclusions for system improvement. There is no question that RtI systems work, but making them work requires that key components be implemented well. In this chapter we have highlighted key actions, including:

- conducting screening to yield high-quality data
- interpreting screening data beginning with an aerial view
- treating systemic problems with systemic solutions
- monitoring implemented solution effects and managing implementation effectively
- conducting follow-up screening to verify improvements

Key indicators of successful completion of each of these actions were provided in Tables 1–5 within the chapter and are summarized here for convenience.

## Action Principles

### Key Action 1: Conduct Screening to Yield High-Quality Data

a. Faculty overview has been provided and screening materials selected.
b. Screening has been scheduled to occur on a single day, and screening schedule has been planned.
c. All materials for screening are available and have been organized by class, including a written protocol for screening.
d. Trainee has been observed to correctly administer and score screening materials.

### Key Action 2: Interpret Screening Data Beginning With an Aerial View

a. Trainee has ruled out school-level, grade-level, and whole-class performance problems prior to selecting individual children for follow-up assessment and possibly intervention.
b. Data have been organized by grade and by class.
c. Data have been examined for identified vulnerable or high-risk groups of students to identify potential performance patterns (e.g., high numbers of new students scoring in the risk range, disproportionately high numbers of special education students scoring in the risk range).

### Key Action 3: Treat Systemic Problems With Systemic Solutions

a. Classwide interventions have been started in classes with classwide problems.

    b. Data teams have examined core instructional procedures in classes and grades with systemic problems.
    c. Vertical teaming has occurred across grades and schools within the feeder pattern to share screening data and systemic intervention data.
    d. Lower percentages of students fall in the risk range across consecutive screenings within and across years.
    e. Higher percentages of students meet the proficiency criterion on the year-end accountability measure over time.
    f. Historically vulnerable students show learning gains and fall into the risk range at lower rates. Performance gaps between those at risk and not at risk are reduced with intervention.
    g. All students, including those in the higher performing groups and the lower performing groups, show gains with intervention and over time.
    h. Students found to be at risk become proportionate by demographics with interventions.

## Key Action 4: Monitor Implemented Solution Effects and Manage Implementation Effectively

    a. Interventions have written protocols available for teachers to use.
    b. The teacher has been provided with all needed materials to conduct the intervention and has demonstrated correct and independent use of the intervention prior to being considered trained.
    c. An in-class trainer or coach is available to model correct intervention use and provide in-vivo training for the teacher.
    d. A tracking log is available showing at a glance who is experiencing intervention in the school.
    e. A master schedule is followed to deliver classwide, small-group, and individual interventions.
    f. Weekly progress monitoring data are collected for all children experiencing intervention.
    g. Progress monitoring data are graphed, and interventions are adjusted weekly with in-class support where growth is not occurring as anticipated.

## Key Action 5: Conduct Follow-up Screening to Verify Improvements

    a. The data team organizes data across consecutive screenings to show a reduced risk status accompanying the intervention.
    b. Intervention effects are monitored for vulnerable or at-risk students over time.

## References

Batsche, G., Elliott, J., Graden, J., Grimes, J., Kovaleski, J. F., Prasse, D.,...Tilly, W. D. (2005). *IDEA 2004 and response to intervention: Policy considerations and implementation*. Alexandria, VA: National Association of State Directors of Special Education.

Bradley, R., Danielson, L., & Hallahan, D. P. (Eds.). (2002). *Identification of learning disabilities: Research to practice*. Mahwah, NJ: Lawrence Erlbaum.

Burns, M. K., Appleton, J. J., & Stehouwer, J. D. (2005). Meta-analysis of response-to-intervention research: Examining field-based and research-implemented models. *Journal of Psychoeducational Assessment, 23*, 381–394.

Bushell, D., & Baer, D. M. (1994). Measurably superior instruction means close, continual contact with the relevant outcome data. Revolutionary! In R. Gardner, D. M. Sainato, J. O. Cooper, & T. E. Heron (Eds.), *Behavior analysis in education* (pp. 3–10). Belmont, CA: Wadsworth.

Codding, R. S., Chan-Iannetta, L., Palmer, M., & Lukito, G. (2009). Examining a classwide application of cover-copy-compare with and without goal setting to enhance mathematics fluency. *School Psychology Quarterly, 24*, 173–185. doi:10.1037/a0017192

Daly, E. J., III, Witt, J. C., Martens, B. K., & Dool, E. J. (1997). A model for conducting a functional analysis of academic performance problems. *School Psychology Review, 26*, 554–574.

Deno, S. L., & Mirkin, P. K. (1977). *Data-based program modification: A manual*. Reston, VA: Council for Exception Children.

Donovan, S., & Cross, C. (2002). *Minority students in special and gifted education*. Washington, DC: National Academy Press.

Fixsen, D. L., & Blasé, K. A. (1993). Creating new realities: Program development and dissemination. *Journal of Applied Behavior Analysis, 26*, 597–615.

Fuchs, D., Fuchs, L. S., Mathes, P. G., & Simmons, D. C. (1997). Peer-assisted learning strategies: Making classrooms more responsive to diversity. *American Educational Research Journal, 34*, 174–206.

Individuals with Disabilities Education Act of 2004, Pub. L. No. 108-466. (2004).

Kovaleski, J., VanDerHeyden, A. M., & Shapiro, E. (in press). *The RtI approach to evaluating learning disabilities*. New York, NY: Guilford.

Noell, G. H., & Gansle, K. A. (2006). Assuring the form has substance: Treatment plan implementation as the foundation of assessing response to intervention. *Assessment for Effective Intervention, 32*, 32–39.

Noell, G. H., Witt, J. C., Slider, N. J., Connell, J. E., Gatti, S. L., Williams, K. L.,...Duhon, G. J. (2005). Treatment implementation following behavioral consultation in schools: A comparison of three follow-up strategies. *School Psychology Review, 34*, 87–106.

O'Connor, R. E., Fulmer, D., Harty, K., & Bell, K. (2005). Layers of reading intervention in kindergarten through third grade: Changes in teaching and child outcomes. *Journal of Learning Disabilities, 38*, 440–455. doi: 10.1177/00222194050380050701

Shapiro, E. S., & Clemens, N. H. (2009). A conceptual model for evaluating system effects of response to intervention. *Assessment for Effective Intervention, 35*, 3–16. doi: 10.1177/1534508408330080

Vanderbilt Kennedy Center. (n.d.). *Peer-assisted learning strategies* (PALS) [Website]. Nashville, TN: Author. Retrieved from http://kc.vanderbilt.edu/pals

VanDerHeyden, A. M. (2010a). Determining early mathematical risk: Ideas for extending the research [Invited commentary]. *School Psychology Review, 39*, 196–202.

VanDerHeyden, A. M. (2010b). Use of classification agreement analyses to evaluate RTI implementation. *Theory into Practice, 49*, 281–288.

VanDerHeyden, A. M. (2011). Technical adequacy of RtI decisions. *Exceptional Children, 77*, 335–350.

VanDerHeyden, A. M., McLaughlin, T., Algina, J., & Snyder, P. (2012). Randomized evaluation of a supplemental grade-wide mathematics intervention. *American Educational Research Journal, 49*(6), 1251–1284.

Wagner, D., McComas, J. J., Bollman, K., & Holton, E. (2006). The use of functional reading analysis to identify effective reading interventions. *Assessment for Effective Intervention, 32*, 40–49.

# Innovation in Career and Technical Education Methodology
*Mark Williams*

Innovation in career and technical education (CTE) resides in the practical attempts by educators to break down the ancient divide that separates vocational training from academic learning. The ubiquitous presence of digital technology in the workplace has accelerated the need to redefine CTE, but the reshaping of the school curriculum to accommodate preparation for both college and career predates the Information Age. Over the past century, as proponents of vocational training and academic learning jockeyed for position in the school curriculum, they sought to divide the available instructional time between two worthy purposes.

This division was achieved by separating the students into different curricular tracks. More recently, as success in life has come to depend more and more on knowledge and skills drawn from both curricular strands, vocational and academic, stakeholders have acknowledged that all students benefit from schooling in both. CTE innovators strive to integrate the strands of CTE and traditional academics within the time constraints of the school days and years, without diluting the quality of either and overcoming differences in individual student capabilities.

A fresh way of thinking about CTE, emphasizing the importance of students acquiring an understanding of theories of work (general and specific to occupations) and the ethics of work, promises to shake up the world of CTE and introduce an innovative component to it. In reinventing itself, CTE is reintroducing excellence in work through an understanding of theories of work, occupational ethics, and the practical application of these mindsets. The exclusionary tendencies that traditionally exist between the workplace and school are shattered by more coherently integrating classroom learning with occupational experience.

This approach to integrating the mindsets of work and occupational ethics with the practical skills of a specific occupation is akin to the ancient practices of guilds and apprenticeships.

## Background

In 1917, the United States government sought to support and promote vocational training through the passage of the Smith-Hughes Act, legislation that focused primarily, but not exclusively, on strengthening the skills of agricultural workers (Vocational Education Act of 1917). Based on Charles Prosser's earlier 1914 report to Congress (Commission on National Aid to Vocational Education), this legislation was the beginning of the "comprehensive" high school, a local institution that brought together students who anticipated entering the workforce directly upon graduation with those who would be attending college. The students typically followed separate curriculum tracks. Federal support for vocational education has since evolved through a series of revisions over the last century, but has retained the original intent of the 1917 legislation: to make vocational education available as a means of educating America's youth and bolstering economic and workforce development.

In 2006, Congress's most recent reauthorization of the act bears a title that signals a new direction: *The Carl D. Perkins Career and Technical Education Improvement Act*. The reauthorized law replaces the term "vocational education" with "career and technical education" (terms introduced in the 1998 act) and incorporates new language, such as "career pathways" and "programs of study." With the addition of the word "improvement," the Perkins Act further establishes as a priority for career and technical education (CTE) its embracing of opportunities for innovation which reflect changing demands of the workforce. The word also highlights the role that CTE can play in reshaping the purpose and structure of the American high school and in affecting the curriculum of elementary and middle schools as well.

By uniting rigorous career preparation, occupational mindsets, and rigorous academic studies, CTE will become a key element in school improvement by supporting the goal of higher student academic achievement while providing those same students with clear direction for their future careers. Providing students with relevant and interesting study connected to their career aspirations will attack the root causes of dropout and student malaise.

What does this innovation look like? When CTE and academics are effectively integrated, with a focus on occupational mindsets and ethics as well as practical skills, the result is characterized by the following:

    a. academic content in CTE, and CTE content in non-CTE courses, strengthening both career and academic preparation

    b. increased comprehension and retention of academic learning by applying academics to real-world, hands-on, and engaging work

c. intentional connections between the student's educational pursuits and career aspirations
d. appreciation for the attitudinal perspectives of journeymen and professionals who understand the dignity and value of their work and the ethics of occupational practice

An understanding of this integration requires examining (a) the origins of the educational divide, (b) the methodology that bridges it, and (c) the promising potential for education standards and innovative practice.

## How Did the Divide Begin?

The Smith-Hughes Act of 1917 repeatedly stipulated that vocational education "shall be to fit for useful employment; that such education shall be of less than college grade" (p. 86). This division was reinforced by the typical physical separation of students and classes into separate spaces. Agricultural and industrial instruction was relegated to a separate building with differently credentialed teachers (Vocational Education Act of 1917). Students chose or were placed in one of two curricular tracks: Good vocational preparation could allow a student to enter directly into the workforce, or the successful completion of a good general education would equip a high school graduate to begin college. College-bound students were schooled in isolation from vocational course work, and vocational students were discouraged from choosing higher level, demanding academics. General education students (including the college bound) could take an occasional vocational class, such as home economics or shop class. The vocational students *per se* would have primarily purely vocational classes directed toward a specific occupation, chosen by the student from the menu of available options. Their instruction was typically isolated to the targeted technical skill itself, without linking the technical application to the general principles that supported it in the academic realm. For example, students in a blueprint reading class would not be required to have an understanding of the geometric principles behind the angles drawn, even though a fuller knowledge of geometry would have been a career asset. It was not the charge of shop class to establish "the learning of aesthetic, mathematical, and physical principles through the manipulation of material things" (Crawford, 2009, p. 31). Thus, the divide was institutionalized in the American high school and would powerfully influence future generations, not only of students but the entire American workforce: "Such a partition of thinking from doing has bequeathed us the dichotomy of white collar versus blue collar, corresponding to mental versus manual" (Crawford, 2009, p. 31), a separation of "hand and brain, mind and work" (Rose, 2008, p. 632). Coincidentally, this division reflected Henry Ford's assembly line, "the nascent two-track educational scheme mirrored the assembly line's severing of the cognitive aspects of manual work from its physical execution" (Crawford, 2009, p. 31).

This educational divide was not created by the Smith-Hughes Act: It is a longstanding schism in Western culture. It echoes an ancient distinction between *artes liberals* and *artes serviles*, wherein education in one arena would exclude its graduate from service within the other. Those trained in the servile arts would serve the common need; those educated in the liberal arts would serve the common good (Pieper, 1952). Obviously, low academic ability practically excludes students from those professions that demand high levels of that ability. The continued divide, however, reinforces the presumption that the technical or manual trades are only suitable to or desirable for those of lower raw intelligence. This presumption neglects the realities of the contemporary work world: Many manual arts are both intellectually demanding and engaging, while many "white collar" jobs are neither intellectually demanding nor personally engaging. To sustain such a dichotomy limits the possibilities for a good number of students who, in a "college-for-all" educational culture, are steered away from technical areas of study as well as from educational experiences that show practical, real-world application of academic content.

In his book *Shop Class as Soulcraft*, Matthew Crawford illustrates the effect of this dichotomy by citing the experience of one CTE instructor who had discovered that "in schools we create artificial learning environments for our children that they know to be contrived and undeserving of their full attention and engagement. Without the opportunity to learn through the hands, the world remains abstract and distant, and the passions for learning will not be engaged" (Crawford, 2009, p. 11). In continuing the traditional separation of academics and CTE in high school, educators risk reinforcing a prejudice between vocational education and lesser intellectual demand (Rose, 2008). Keeping CTE and rigorous academics disintegrated reinforces the presumption that manual work is stupid, or that the manual trades are neither intellectually demanding nor stimulating.

> **In continuing the traditional separation of academics and CTE in high school, educators risk reinforcing a prejudice between vocational education and lesser intellectual demand.**
>
> Rose, 2008

## Why Integration?

The desire to integrate what historically has been divided—namely academic (including theories of work and occupational ethics) and career and technical education—is not new. Unification of the two has been taking place in isolated schools or certain networks of schools for some time. The momentum toward integration of academics and CTE was first formalized in the 1990 federal vocational legislation and has gathered force in successive reauthorizations, culminating in the Perkins Act of 2006. The 2006 law requires professional development that promotes "the integration of coherent and rigorous academic content standards and career and technical education curricula, including through opportunities for the appropriate academic and career and technical education teachers to jointly develop and implement curricula and pedagogical standards" (S. 250–36). Practically speaking, the law requires a new pedagogy, one that demands collaboration among academic teachers and career and technical teachers be the norm. New pedagogy requires changes in teachers' preservice and inservice education.

This new norm is necessary for two reasons: It addresses low student achievement and widespread student disengagement. Regarding low student achievement, there is well-established concern that students are not being adequately prepared to meet the challenges of a rapidly changing economy. Indeed, school improvement has been the center of education efforts, expenditures, and policies since the publication of *A Nation at Risk* in 1983 and continues in federal initiatives to reform public education, initiatives such as the School Improvement Grant (SIG) program, waivers to requirements of the Elementary and Secondary Education Act, and the Race to the Top grant program. Career and technical education is not immune to the problem of low student achievement. For example, the Conference Board (Casner-Lotto, Barrington, & Wright, 2006) stated that employers report common applicant deficiencies in math, computer, and problem-solving skills. A wide variety of studies and indicators have demonstrated that our education system continues to fail to prepare many students for the emerging economy (Manufacturing Institute, 2011). Innovative integration of CTE with academics is key to meeting the increasing needs of industry while supporting the high academic standards necessary for success in a career and in college (Pearson et al., 2010; Institute for a Competitive Workforce, 2008).

In addition to concerns about student achievement, there is also widespread concern that high school students are increasingly disengaged from their studies and, because of this disengagement, are not finishing high school. A 2006 report, *The Silent Epidemic: Perspectives of High School Dropouts* (Bridgeland, DiIulio, & Morison, 2006), indicates that nearly half of dropouts reported that a reason for leaving was that classes were not interesting, and 7 in 10 respondents indicated that they were not motivated or inspired to work hard. Based on such student responses, the report advocates that high schools improve teaching and curricula to make education more relevant and engaging and enhance the connection between schools and work. In others words, practical application united with theories of work and occupational ethics can enliven the educational experience. The innovative, systemic merger of academics and CTE is the ideal delivery system for this kind of educational experience. Vocational education should no longer be seen as another set of subjects competing for students' time. It should be a set of activities that help students use, understand, and appreciate what they are learning in other courses (Houghlander, 1999). This kind of vocational education can increase students' long-term productivity as workers by encouraging them to understand the principles and ideas underlying the work they do (Stern, Hoachlander, Choy, & Benson, 1986).

Given the current low student achievement and high student disengagement, the standard practice of CTE classrooms is unlikely to assist the preparation of students in the higher academic skills necessary for the changing workplace. The National Assessment of Vocational Education (NAVE) reported that, on average, vocational courses as traditionally structured do not appear to contribute to an increase in students' academic achievement (Silverberg, 2002). Both low student achievement and high student disengagement are perpetuated by the continued disjunction of academic and career/technical tracks.

> **The highest rigor for students can occur in classrooms that demand high levels of knowing and doing.**

Integration of vocational and academic studies is supported by the Rigor/Relevance Framework tool developed by the International Center for Leadership in Education. The tool illustrates the important connection between thinking and doing and the close tie between the acquisition of knowledge and its application. According to the tool's developers, the greatest academic rigor is revealed in authentic application. The highest rigor for students can occur in classrooms that demand high levels of knowing and doing; the CTE classroom that embraces such rigor should be able to demonstrate correspondingly high levels of knowledge development, application, and transfer (International Center for Leadership in Education, 2013).

## How is Integration Accomplished?

The efforts to integrate career and technical education have focused on two separate but related strategies: (a) a systemic integration through "pathways" of interconnected academic and CTE coursework; and (b) the development of instructional approaches that, at the classroom level, make explicit connections between academic and technical content. These two strategies are exemplified by the work of many organizations, each approaching them for a different purpose and with its own efforts to innovate, including the following:

a. The movement to establish career-themed high school academies, "career academies" that incorporate small learning communities, deliver a college preparatory curriculum within specific career themes, and partner with business, postsecondary institutions, and the broader community to introduce students to the broader relevance of their career studies (College and Career Academy Support Network, http://casn.berkeley.edu/)

b. Linked Learning is a California initiative that seeks to integrate "rigorous academics with career-based learning and real world workplace experiences." Sixty-four California districts have joined an ongoing pilot that seeks to benefit students by creating meaningful and relevant learning experiences using career-oriented pathways that will help students connect their classroom learning to the attainment of their academic and career goals. Participating districts realign their curriculum, schedule, and professional development to intentionally innovate their present practice to serve the goal of rigorous career-focused instruction for all students; each district will implement 6–8 Linked Learning Pathways. Integral to the approach is collaboration with local business and industry, postsecondary institutions and other community stakeholders to shape the changes taking place in the school (ConnectEd, http://www.connectedcalifornia.org/linked_learning).

c. The National Association of State Directors of Career Technical Education Consortium (n.d.) promotes statewide efforts to implement "programs of study" required by the Perkins Act of 2006. NASDCTE has also supported the recent creation of the Common Career Technical Core that provides content structure to programs of study across 16 clusters that represent most contemporary career areas.

d. The Southern Regional Education Board's High Schools That Work initiative advocates high-quality implementation of integrated CTE and academics as a driver of increased student learning outcomes and school performance (Southern Regional Education Board, n.d.a) .

e. The International Center for Leadership in Education (n.d.) focuses its services on curriculum integration.

f. Edutopia's Problem- and Project-based Learning Initiatives introduce blended instructional designs and media-rich environments (Edutopia, n.d.).

**The Pathways Approach**

The first method of integration seeks to join coursework to a student's future career plans by presenting to the student a choice of career pathways that reflect both the student's career interest and the curriculum that the school and other partners can provide. By examining a variety of available career pathways in collaboration with a school counselor and parents, a student can develop an individual program of study. This strategy imagines a student who is carefully weighing different career possibilities, who is actively engaged in schoolwork, and who works to achieve at a high level because the coursework is relevant to his or her career goals. In recent years, this approach has led to the design of model high schools wherein career relevance drives student engagement and achievement. These designs have become more accepted; consequently, efforts to replicate the approach have become more widespread.

Efforts like these integrative projects have been given further impetus in the recent *Pathways to Prosperity* report from the Harvard Graduate School of Education (Symonds, Schwartz, & Ferguson, 2011). This report calls for a dramatic reenvisioning of the American high school experience with the purpose of allowing all students the choice of career pathways and the rigorous, relevant instruction necessary to make every pathway a road to a student's career success. From the standpoint of innovation, this is a new way of managing curriculum and personalizing learning.

One note of caution: While presently, in some parts of the nation, considerable efforts and resources are being directed toward the creation of career pathways in high schools, it is difficult to measure the value of this approach. The initiative has many interrelated objectives: high student academic achievement, mastery of appropriate technical and career skills, successful graduation from high school, and transition into postsecondary education or training or transition directly into the workplace. These many targets make evaluation difficult, and those educators championing pathway approaches are developing a methodology to measure the quality of these efforts, which include criteria for high-quality systems and programs, quality indicators linking core elements to participant outcomes, interim participant outcome metrics, and performance outcome metrics (Alliance for Quality Career Pathways, 2013).

**The Integrated Classroom Approach**

More directly related to individual course curricula and teacher pedagogy, substantial research investigating the use of integrated, enhanced coursework offers insight into how to replace, not simply improve, the current standards of curricular and instructional practice. Recent evidence supports the focused integration of rigorous academics with CTE instruction and demonstrates that integrated methodology effectively eliminates the educational disconnect that results from teaching only specific skills and only low-level, minimally relevant academics to CTE students. By consistently demonstrating the practical relationship between technical skill and strong academics, this integration strengthens student acquisition of both. In addition, students who are supported in making connections between academic and real-world learning through their use of higher level mathematics, reading, and writing in their assignments are able to link their skill and knowledge, which increases continued engagement and strengthens the link between student career aspirations and daily classroom experience (Bottoms, Young, & Han, 2009). This integration encompasses explicit "strategies that connect academic and vocational content [that] usually result[s] in content that is primarily academic with vocational elements woven throughout, or primarily vocational with academic elements woven throughout. In curriculum integration, the content can be neither purely academic not purely vocational" (Johnson, Charner, & White, 2003, p. 43). In short, the integration approach consistently demonstrates a "relationship between academic and occupational or career–technical subject matter that goes beyond what would normally occur in the delivery of either the academic or occupational/career–technical subject matter alone" (Johnson et al., 2003, p. v).

Not all approaches to integration are created equal. James Stone compares two distinct modes of implementation: the context-based approach and the contextualized approach (Pearson et al., 2010). "Context-based approaches," also known as "applied academics," introduces academic content artificially situated in an *imagined* application in an *imagined* workplace setting. For example, problems in an applied math workbook published in 2004 required students to use trigonometric functions and the Pythagorean theorem to determine requested measurements of a roof rafter or the slope of a wheelchair ramp. But the problems were not part of a particular CTE course—for example, building trades—and did not relate to each other. No construction projects from a CTE class were involved, and students could not apply the problem-solving exercises to any real, hands-on work within their daily school experience. The potential for true integration was missed in this example because the rigor of trigonometry was not supported by practical application (Phagan, 2004). While this approach delivers academic instruction with a nod to occupational references, relevance to the student is negligible because the CTE context itself is neither the origin nor the focus of the instruction. The expectations of academic learning in this artificial context are typically low (Pearson et al., 2010).

In contrast, contextualized integration reflects a different strategy for delivering academically rigorous content using authentic CTE situations as the vehicle for the delivery starting point in instruction. Both the genesis and the focus are rooted in the CTE content of the lesson. Within the lesson, the embedded academic content is highlighted; it is not artificially linked to the lesson but authentically placed within the CTE learning objective. The development of the CTE skill remains primary, setting the stage for comprehension of the underlying academic content. For example, a CTE lesson with the objective of teaching students how to build roof gables using the Pythagorean theorem employs integration by beginning with a relevant CTE question: How can we calculate, cut, and assemble gable frames for a house? Note that the origin of the lesson is rooted in CTE, not the academic/mathematical concepts that will eventually be used to solve the problem. After introducing the construction/manufacturing concept of calculating cross gable framing angles, the teacher assesses student math awareness by asking relevant questions about slope and right angle trigonometry. Construction materials and techniques demonstration adds further opportunity for linking occupational relevance and academic knowledge. The students are able to visualize the math concepts embedded in the construction of a roof gable because the teacher then provides an opportunity to do something authentic and meaningful with this knowledge. As in the Geometry in Construction program, the students learn these techniques by building a house. The house provides the real world relevance for the students to not only learn by simulation but also learn in an authentic way lending itself naturally to mastery learning. In its purest form, contextualization focuses the majority of a student's learning on performing tasks using academic knowledge that is so often lost in traditional academic settings where students learn just enough to pass tests. In a true contextualized environment, students are forced to use knowledge to produce something while gaining employable skills and confidence along the way. Once students have mastered the CTE content, they are introduced to what a traditional "naked math" problem would be, using the same skills. Once they make this link between the real world and the simulated (traditional math) world, they typically report a different level of learning and confidence. Formal assessment of students is demonstrated by this successful construction (Geometry in Construction, 2011). "The academic concepts resident in authentic applications of CTE support the understanding of both; rigor resides in combining CTE and academic skills as applied to real-world problems" (Pearson et al., 2010, p. 10). Making it real links academic skills to the CTE skills, strengthening them both.

The National Research Center for Career and Technical Education (NRCCTE) conducted the first study to develop, implement, and evaluate such a contextualized approach. In this national Math-in-CTE study (Stone, Alfeld, & Pearson, 2008), CTE teachers collaborating with mathematics teachers were trained to use curriculum mapping tools connecting CTE content to academic content. The collaboration yielded enhanced CTE lessons in which math concepts were embedded in the real-world CTE lessons. The researchers identified seven elements of curriculum integration within the Math-in-CTE pedagogic framework. These elements include:

1. introducing the CTE lesson
2. assessing the students' math awareness as it relates to the CTE lesson
3. working the math example embedded in the CTE lesson
4. working through related, contextual math-in-CTE examples
5. working through traditional math examples
6. requiring students to demonstrate their understanding
7. incorporating math questions into formal assessments at the end of the CTE unit/course

Compared with a control group of teachers and students who did not use the math-enhanced CTE lessons, students in the collaborative classroom performed significantly better on two of three standardized measures of math achievement. In addition, the students retained a higher level of indicated math skills after the semester coursework. The benefits of the contextualized approach were clear: improved math performance, authentic CTE skills development, and improved retention. The researchers attributed the benefits to both the unique pedagogic framework and the professional development of both math and CTE teachers that fostered collaboration (Stone, 2013).

In subsequent years, many of the participating teachers in the Math-in-CTE project sustained the framework as well as the communities of practice. Using mapping tools, CTE and math teacher teams worked together to:

a. identify the mathematics content embedded within the technical objective;
   b. create curriculum maps pinpointing the intersection of occupational content and math concepts; and
   c. use a curriculum mapped by its scope and sequence by CTE teachers to guide implementation (Pearson et al., 2010).

Encouraged by the Math-in-CTE research results, Stone's team then applied an integrated approach to discipline-based literacy instruction in CTE. Using a similar framework, lessons in the Literacy-in-CTE project were developed to determine if disciplinary literacy strategies would impact CTE students' reading comprehension, vocabulary development, and motivation to read. Once again, the starting point for lesson development was the CTE objectives and the literacy demanded by the CTE discipline. Strategies employed included competition (any strategy using game-like qualities), social learning (small group discussion), prereading activities (previewing text to give direction), organization (arranging and managing text for understanding), and classroom interaction. The combination of reading with CTE activity enabled students to connect their work to the reading they had mastered. The academic relevance is essential: CTE students are expected to read technical texts that may pose an obstacle to struggling readers. Implementation of literacy strategies makes texts more accessible to these students. As a result of the Literacy-in-CTE integration, students showed a significant improvement of reading comprehension and discipline-specific vocabulary mastery (although it did not improve the students' motivation to read). Analysis of data from student focus groups revealed four themes: (a) students desired a utility value in their reading strategy; (b) they understood the importance of reading to their career; (c) they engaged in reading if they could apply the information; and (d) they desired a social aspect to reading to foster their motivation (Pearson et al., 2010).

Ongoing analysis of the Math-in-CTE and Literacy-in-CTE contextualizing approach enabled NRCCTE researchers to develop five best practices to guide the design of integrated CTE lessons in math and discipline literacy:
   a. Develop and sustain a community of practice among the teachers.
   b. Begin with the CTE curriculum and not the academic curriculum.
   c. Understand that academic knowledge is essential workplace knowledge.
   d. Maximize the academics in the CTE curriculum.
   e. Recognize that CTE teachers are teachers of academics-in-CTE and not academic teachers (Stone, Alfeld, & Pearson, 2008, p. 789).

Successful implementation of these principles depends heavily upon CTE and academic teachers' collaboration in the curriculum mapping required to relate CTE content to the embedded academic content. This collaboration requires scheduled time for interdisciplinary teams to meet and develop instructional plans.

Currently, researchers are studying the effects of contextualizing science in CTE education. The Science-in-CTE study will adapt the Math-in-CTE model (Pearson et al., 2010) for the integration of science concepts with agricultural and health science curricula. While early results have not indicated an overall effect, there are promising benefits for non-White male and female students (Stone, 2013).

Since the initial Math-in-CTE studies, teachers have continued to develop enhanced CTE lessons by systematically integrating classroom coursework. An example is the Geometry in Construction program developed at Loveland (Colorado) High School. This program targets any student who has completed Algebra I and who wishes to complete a geometry curriculum via math instruction linked to the hands-on experience of constructing a house. Recorded in students' transcripts as two separate classes, the integrated coursework is team-taught by a certified math and a certified CTE construction trades teacher. Students routinely take part in team-building exercises and demonstrate mastery of geometry problems that solve a specific task associated with the building project. In the application of the contextualizing approach refined by the NRCCTE studies, participating students consistently outperform students enrolled in standard geometry classes in the school (Geometry in Construction, n.d.). Collaborating instructors identify four key factors necessary for successful implementation:

    a. careful sequencing of the content to maximize contextual learning;
    b. instructors teaching side-by-side to a fully integrated cohort of students;
    c. explicitly highlighting each student's relative strength in both the building project and the classroom; and
    d. professional interaction between participating teachers (Michigan Association of Secondary School Principals, 2008).

Ongoing research from the NRCCTE indicates integrated CTE classes can be scaled to develop entire systems of coursework that enable students to obtain higher levels of academic and technical achievement. In a 2010 summary, NRCCTE researchers suggest that the greatest impact of a contextualizing approach could move beyond CTE instruction by augmenting the overall high school education outcome when applied systemically. Such a system would be designed to accomplish the combined objectives of higher student achievement in academics and career skill readiness, higher student engagement and retention, greater student awareness of career options and command of the transition from high school into the world of work or transition to postsecondary education or training (Pearson et al., 2010).

Currently, this outcome is being manifested in the High Schools That Work (HSTW) network of schools, the largest comprehensive high school reform program in the United States, with over 1,000 schools in more than 30 states participating (Young, Cline, King, Jackson, & Timberlake, 2011). Established in 1987, the

HSTW operational framework builds on the fundamental expectation that most students can master complex academic and technical concepts if schools create an environment that encourages students to make the effort to succeed. The project's efforts to develop a secondary school environment unite high expectations and integrated academic/CTE experiences to effective implementation and student performance. The framework connects 10 identified key practices to student academic and technical skills (Southern Regional Education Board, n.d.b):

   a. motivating more students to meet high expectations by integrating those expectations into classroom practices and giving students frequent feedback;
   b. requiring each student to complete an upgraded academic core and a concentration;
   c. teaching more students the essential concepts of the college preparatory curriculum by encouraging them to apply academic content and skills to real-world problems and projects;
   d. providing more students access to intellectually challenging CTE studies in high-demand fields that emphasize higher level mathematics, science, literacy, and problem-solving skills;
   e. enabling students and their parents to choose from programs that integrate high school studies and work-based learning—programs that are planned by educators, employers, and students;
   f. providing multidisciplinary teams of teachers time to integrate reading, writing, and speaking instruction into all parts of the curriculum and to integrate mathematics into science and career/technical classrooms;
   g. engaging students in academic and career/technical classrooms in proficient-level assignments using research-based instructional strategies and technology;
   h. involving students and their parents in an advising system that ensures completion of an accelerated program of study with an academic or career/technical concentration;
   i. providing a structured system of assistance to students in completing accelerated programs of study with high-level academic and technical content; and
   j. using student assessment and program evaluation data to continuously improve school culture, organization, management, curriculum, and instruction to advance student learning.

HSTW technical assistance requires participating sites to conduct assessments every two years in order to determine the level of academic performance of the students and to correlate that performance with the degree of fidelity with which the 10 key practices have been implemented. Thus, member schools are able to substantiate the contextualizing approach with data which is timely and relevant.

Sites that have implemented the model with a high degree of fidelity, as evidenced by the locally self-reported indices of school practices and experiences, show the largest score gains on three NAEP-like assessments for reading, math, and science. The gains are significantly higher than the results in schools with low implementation of the model (Young et al., 2011). This correlation indicates, in a general way, that a systemic implementation of the contextualizing approach can increase student achievement.

As always, success requires both the adoption of the model and its faithful implementation. To achieve successful integration, schools must align a sequence of well-developed CTE courses with college- and career-readiness standards through relevant and intellectually challenging learning experiences, motivating students toward academic and technical mastery. The best CTE teachers equip students to connect academic and real-world learning by showing students that they are using high-level mathematics, reading, and writing in their assignments (Bottoms, Young, & Berto, 2012). Surveying its sites, HSTW observes that network schools implement the key practices in widely varying degrees; this variation impacts the CTE student's experience. A CTE student who has experienced a rigorous assignment will report having been given at least four of the following eight opportunities to

a. develop a logical argument for the solution to a problem;
b. make inferences from information provided to develop that solution;
c. use math to solve complex problems related to CTE area;
d. apply academic knowledge and skills to CTE area;
e. apply technical knowledge and skills to a new situation;
f. develop and test a hypothesis;
g. complete an extended project that requires planning and developing a solution or product and presenting the results orally or in writing; and/or
h. use computer skills to complete an assignment in CTE class at least weekly. (Southern Regional Education Board, n.d.a)

HSTW research has determined that students with CTE concentrations (at least four credits in CTE) who reported that they frequently completed intensive CTE assignments requiring them to read and write, interpret technical books and manuals, use computer skills, and apply mathematics were more likely than students not reporting these activities to meet college readiness goals in reading and mathematics (Bottoms, Young, & Han, 2009). The intensive CTE assignments encouraged by HSTW are also foundational to a related initiative of the Southern Regional Education Board for secondary CTE centers known as Tech Centers That Work (TCTW). In a recent study of TCTW student outcomes examining achievement and survey data from 2012, HSTW researchers established that, of those students who did not experience rigorous CTE assignments, only 40% met college and career readiness standards in reading, math, and science. Of those students who experienced rigorous CTE assignments, readiness was met by

60%. In addition, the report demonstrated a strong positive correlation between the percentage of students receiving rigorous CTE assignments and mean scores in reading, math, and science (Bottoms, 2013).

Whether in a tech center or a high school classroom, the contextualized approach requires enterprising educators who are prepared to articulate the systemic changes necessary for integration implementation. Committed stakeholders will help institute necessary instructional changes through professional development and other supports and provide opportunities for structured collaboration among teachers.

## Lifelong Learning and the Pursuit of Excellence

The world of learning and the world of work are usually seen as mutually exclusive, with one serving as antecedent to the other. However, learning is not a prerequisite to work, but rather a kind of work itself, one that provides the satisfaction of a young mind's curiosity and the development of focused interests through a directed exposure to the unknown. Once the unknown "starts to provide feedback to the person's skills, it usually tends to be intrinsically rewarding" (Csikszentmihalyi, 1991, p. 68). If the experiences of learning and work are simultaneous and engaging, a student begins to develop a positive, personal understanding of the relationship between the two. The effort and involvement required by the interplay of learning and work presages enjoyment and intellectual growth. This type of immersion is inherent to quality instruction, in both the academic and CTE spheres.

In CTE, this immersion creates a seamless classroom–workplace continuity and an entrance into a community of others who embody lifelong learning in order to become and remain excellent in a particular manual or technical field. As Crawford writes, "craftsmanship means dwelling on a task for a long time and going deeply into it, because you want to get it right" (Crawford, 2009, p. 20). Formal education begins a practice of learning that will define how a person continues to learn and develop skills in the workplace. This habit of workplace learning will then determine much of the satisfaction that individuals will derive from work and the level of excellence sought. To this end, CTE can initiate a student into a distinct community of those who possess a high degree of skills that have objective standards of performance, forming a crew of craftsmen. This community celebrates excellence in skill itself, the habits of learning inherent in continuing that excellence, the benefit that that skill provides to a larger community, and finally the camaraderie of those who share a passion for the craft. Crawford continues, "On a crew, skills become the basis for a circle of mutual respect among those who recognize each other as peers, even across disciplines…there is a sort of friendship or solidarity that becomes possible at work when people are open about differences of rank, and there are clear standards" (Crawford, 2009, p. 160). In a CTE classroom, as novices entering a community of learning, students can develop and refine a personal standard of excellence through which they also affirm the standards of the community of craftsmen. This standard requires a perpetual state of learning and the ongoing satisfaction of inquiry.

## Conclusion

The increased attention to CTE may have its origin in concern about employment or global competitiveness, but the value of CTE to students goes deeper than these expediencies; indeed, CTE brings value beyond the commodification of the individual in supplying the employment pipeline. It can foster a deeper, more satisfying approach to work and life. Because of the focus that high schools laudably place on higher education, the desire to promote learning is already present. Even if it can be demonstrated that CTE can lead to better economic outcomes, can keep kids in schools, or provide multiple pathways for a high school student to succeed, perhaps the best case for CTE is what it can offer to enlarge the lasting perspective of its students, by making connections between different domains, seeing the interrelations of the world around them, and embracing the task of lifelong learning.

## Action Principles

**For State Education Agencies**
   a. Establish incentives for high schools to participate in national student organizations that provide opportunities to learn, compete, and be acknowledged for attaining high levels of technical skill and leadership promise (such as SkillsUSA; FFA; Family, Career, and Community Leaders of America; DECA; Future Business Leaders of America; Health Occupations Student Association; National Technology Student Association).
   b. Identify and incentivize the implementation of effective practices in academic and CTE integration.
   c. Provide platforms for statewide collaboration between education and industry, adults, and students.
   d. Discuss the incorporation of interdisciplinary approaches to instruction with teacher preparation institutions.
   e. Include CTE as a full partner in school improvement efforts.
   f. Establish organizational ties with national organizations seeking to implement career pathways and programs of study.

**For Local Education Agencies**
   a. In curriculum planning, include the cultivation of employability skills, workplace ethics, and the habits of adult learning.
   b. Work with local industry to identify opportunities for work-based learning and real-world problems for classroom projects.

c. Prioritize time and resources for interdisciplinary curriculum mapping and planning.
  d. Establish collaboration with local postsecondary institutions regarding effective transition for career pathways.
  e. Provide students with tools for development of career portfolios.
  f. Discuss with local employers their practical needs for the incoming workforce and the talents and skills needed for those workers' advancement.

**For Schools**
  a. Find opportunities to celebrate the combination of academic inquiry and craftsmanship.
  b. Seek opportunities for interdisciplinary content planning and delivery.
  c. Work on career awareness, planning, and development for all students.
  d. Make time for teachers to collaborate within and across disciplines.
  e. Create challenging assignments that help students achieve at a high level in both academic and technical skills.
  f. Require students to read technical materials and write in the language of their career field.

## References

Alliance for Quality Career Pathways. (2013, February). *A framework for measuring career pathways innovation*. Washington, DC: Center for Postsecondary and Economic Success. Retrieved from http://www.clasp.org/admin/site/publications/files/CLASP-AQCP-Metrics-Feb-2013.pdf

Bottoms, G. (2013, January). *Signature features of CT program of study: How do we give students access to more of them?* Atlanta, GA: Southern Regional Education Board.

Bottoms, G., Young, M., & Berto, J. (2012). *Recognizing academic achievement in career and technical education: Conditions for awarding academic credit for career/technical courses*. Atlanta, GA: Southern Regional Education Board.

Bottoms, G., Young, M., & Han, L. (2009, November). *Ready for tomorrow: Six proven ideas to graduate and prepare more students for college and 21st century careers*. Atlanta, GA: Southern Regional Education Board.

Bridgeland, J. M., DiIulio, J. J., & Morison, K. B. (2006, March). *The silent epidemic: Perspectives of high school dropouts*. Washington, DC: Civic Enterprises.

Carl D. Perkins Career and Technical Education Improvement Act of 2006. Pub L. No. 109-270. 120 Stat. 683 (2006).

Casner-Lotto, J., Barrington, L., & Wright, M. (2006). *Are they really ready to work?* New York, NY: The Conference Board.

Commission on National Aid to Vocational Education. (1914). *Report of the Commission on National Aid to Vocational Education together with the hearings held on the subject*. Washington, DC: U.S. Government Printing Office. Retrieved from http://archive.org/stream/vocationaleduca00smitgoog#page/n5/mode/2up

Crawford, M. B. (2009). *Shop class as soulcraft: An inquiry into the value of work*. New York, NY: Penguin Press.

Csikszentmihalyi, M. (1991). *Flow: The psychology of optimal experience*. New York, NY: Harper Perennial.

Edutopia. (n.d.). What is project-based learning? [Webpage]. San Rafael, CA: The George Lucas Educational Foundation. Retrieved from http://www.edutopia.org/project-based-learning

Geometry in Construction. (2011). *Geometry in construction: Math problem of the month: Cross gable framing angles.* Loveland, CO: Author. Retrieved from http://www.geometryinconstruction.org/mathproblemofthemonth/index.php?id=6875616344938561749

Geometry in Construction. (n.d.). Geometry in construction: History [Webpage]. Loveland, CO: Author. Retrieved from http://www.geometryinconstruction.org/about/about/history.html

Houghlander, G. (1999). Integrating academic and vocational curriculum: Why is theory so hard to practice? *Centerpoint, 7,* 2–11. Retrieved from http://files.eric.ed.gov/fulltext/ED433454.pdf

Institute for a Competitive Workforce. (2008). *The skills imperative: How career and technical education can solve the U.S. talent shortage.* Washington, DC: U.S. Chamber of Commerce.

International Center for Leadership in Education. (n.d.). Integrating CTE and academic education [Webpage]. Retrieved from http://www.leadered.com/integratingCTE.html

International Center for Leadership in Education. (n.d.). Rigor/relevance framework [Webpage]. Retrieved from http://www.leadered.com/rrr.html

Johnson, A. B., Charner, I., & White, R. (2003). *Curriculum integration in context: An exploration of how structures and circumstances affect design and implementation.* St. Paul, MN: National Research Center for Career and Technical Education, University of Minnesota.

Manufacturing Institute. (2011). *Boiling point? The skills gap in U.S. manufacturing.* Washington, DC: Author.

Michigan Association of Secondary School Principals. (2008). The ultimate in career–academic integration: Geometry/construction program [Webpage]. Retrieved from http://mymassp.com/content/ultimate_careeracademic_integration_geometryconstruction_program

National Association of State Directors of Career Technical Education Consortium. (n.d.). Career clusters at a glance [Webpage]. Silver Spring, MD: Author. Retrieved from http://www.careertech.org/career-clusters/glance/

Pearson, D., Sawyer, J., Park, T., Santamaria, L., van der Mandele, E., Keene, B., & Taylor, M. (2010, March). *Capitalizing on context: Curriculum integration in career and technical education.* Louisville, KY: National Research Center for Career and Technical Education. Retrieved from http://www.nrccte.org/resources/publications/capitalizing-context-curriculum-integration-career-and-technical-education-0

Phagan, R. J. (2004). *Applied mathematics.* Tinley Park, IL: Goodheart-Wilcox.

Pieper, J. (1952). *Leisure as the basis of culture.* London, UK: Faber and Faber.

Rose, M. (2008). Intelligence, knowledge, and the hand/brain divide. *Phi Delta Kappan, 89*(9), 632–639.

Silverberg, M. W. (2002). *National assessment of vocational education.* Washington, DC: U.S. Department of Education.

Southern Regional Education Board. (n.d.a). High schools that work [Webpage]. Atlanta, GA: Author. Retrieved from http://www.sreb.org/page/1078/high_schools_that_work.html

Southern Regional Education Board. (n.d.b). Key practices [Webpage]. Atlanta, GA: Author. Retrieved from http://www.sreb.org/page/1139/key_practices.html

Stern, D. H., Hoachlander, E. G., Choy, S., & Benson, C. S. (1986). *One million hours a day: Vocational education in California's secondary schools* (Report to the California Policy Seminar). Berkeley, CA: University of California at Berkeley.

Stone, J. (2013, January). *Evidence based curriculum integration.* Presentation given at the National Technology Centers That Work Leaders Forum: Technology Centers of the Future, Greenville, SC. Retrieved from http://www.nrccte.org/sites/default/files/publication-files/nrccte_stone_2013_tctw_keynote_address.pdf

Stone, J. R., Alfeld, C., & Pearson, D. (2008). Rigor and relevance: Enhancing high school students' math skills through career and technical education. *American Educational Research Journal, 45*(3), 767–795.

Symonds, W. C., Schwartz, R., & Ferguson, R. F. (2011, February). *Pathways to prosperity: Meeting the challenge of preparing young Americans for the 21st century.* Cambridge, MA: Harvard University Graduate School of Education.

Vocational Education Act of 1917. P.L. 64-347; 39 Stat. 929 (1917).

Young, J. W., Cline, F., King, T. C., Jackson, A. D., & Timberlake, A. (2011). *High Schools That Work: Program description, literature review, and research findings.* Princeton, NJ: Educational Testing Service.

# GLOSSARY

*Robert Sullivan*

**1:1 technology**: every student has a laptop or tablet; to individualize learning, increase independence, and extend academics outside the classroom

**Achievement First**: a charter school operator in the U.S., currently a network that includes 22 schools in four cities serving 7,000 students in Grades K–12

**adaptive learning**: software (usually) that automatically adapts instructional level, content, and pacing to the current abilities of the user; related to individualized learning, personalized learning

**a la carte model (formerly self-blended learning)**: a form of blended learning where students take one or more courses entirely online with an online teacher of record, while continuing to have brick-and-mortar educational experiences

**A Nation at Risk: The Imperative for Educational Reform**: the 1983 report of American President Ronald Reagan's National Commission on Excellence in Education, which is considered a landmark event in modern American educational history, contributing to the ever-growing assertion that American schools were failing and touching off a wave of local, state, and federal reform efforts

**app**: short for application software; a term commonly used for software designed for specific purposes and generally used on mobile devices such as smart phones or tablet computers

**Applied Minds**: a company founded in 2000 by ex-Disney Imagineers Danny Hillis and Bran Ferren that provides technology, design, R&D, and consulting services to multiple firms, including General Motors, Intel, Northrop Grumman, Lockheed Martin, Herman Miller, Harris Corporation, Sony, and Sun MicroSystems

**ARPANet**: the Advanced Research Projects Agency Network, one of the world's first operational packet switching networks, the first network to implement TCP/IP (Transmission Control Protocol/Internet Protocol), and the progenitor of what was to become the global Internet

**ASCD**: formerly the Association for Supervision and Curriculum Development, a membership-based nonprofit organization with more than 175,000 members from over 100 countries, including superintendents, principals, teachers, professors of education, and other educators, initially founded with a focus on curriculum and supervision but now providing its members with professional development, educational leadership, and capacity building

**assistive technology (AT)**: an umbrella term that includes assistive, adaptive, and rehabilitative devices for people with disabilities and also includes the process used in selecting, locating, and using them

**asynchronous**: interaction between teachers and students occurs intermittently online with time between responses; users do not have to be logged on simultaneously; examples are self-paced courses taken via the Internet or CD-ROM, Q&A mentoring, online discussion groups, and email

**attention deficit hyperactivity disorder (ADHD)**: a psychiatric disorder of the neurodevelopmental disorder class in which there are significant problems of attention and/or hyperactivity and acting impulsively that are not appropriate for a person's age

**Audacity**: a free open source digital audio editor and recording computer software application, available for Windows, Mac OS X, Linux, and other operating systems

**augmented reality (AR)**: live, direct or indirect, view of a physical, real-world environment whose elements are augmented by computer-generated sensory input such as sound, video, graphics, or GPS data

**automatic system recovery (ASR)**: a device or process that detects a computer failure and attempts recovery

**avatar**: a graphical image that represents a person

**big data**: a collection of data sets so large and complex that it becomes difficult to process using on-hand database management tools or traditional data processing applications

**blended learning**: instructional context where students learn at school and also engage with content delivered online; models may be rotation, flex, self-blend, and enriched virtual; also called hybrid learning

**blog**: online journal, displaying most recent posting first

**Breakthrough Center**: an internal Maryland State Department of Education operation dedicated to coordinating, brokering, and delivering support to districts and schools across Maryland. It aims to maximize the state's comparative advantage by partnering with local school districts to determine needs and necessary supports; identify, target, and maximize resources in education, business, government, and research centers; and create cross-district and cross-sector access to people, programs, and resources

**broadcast**: simultaneously send the same message or online content to multiple recipients

**BYOD (bring your own device or BYOT–bring your own technology)**: movement where districts or schools encourage students and teachers to bring and utilize the technology they already have

**career academies**: career-themed high school academies that incorporate small learning communities; deliver a college preparatory curriculum within specific career themes; and partner with business, post-secondary institutions, and the broader community to introduce students to the broader relevance of their career studies

**Career and Technical Education (CTE)**: a program that prepares students for employment and/or postsecondary education in current or emerging professions; provides students with competency-based and applied learning opportunities that build academic knowledge, higher-order reasoning skills, problem-solving skills, work attitudes, general employability skills, technical skills, occupation-specific skills, and knowledge of all aspects of an industry

**Career and Technical Student Organization (CTSO)**: one of several vocational organizations primarily based in high schools and career technology centers; often, on the state level, they are integrated into departments of education or incorporated as nonprofit organizations

**Carl D. Perkins Career and Technical Education Improvement Act**: the reauthorization of a 1984 act, signed into law in 2006, that aims to increase the quality of technical education within the U.S. in order to help the economy. The reauthorization contained three major areas of revision—using the term "career and technical education" instead of "vocational education," maintaining the Tech Prep program as a separate federal funding stream within the legislation, and maintaining state administrative funding at 5% of a state's allocation—while also including new requirements for "programs of study" that link academic and technical content across secondary and postsecondary education and strengthening local accountability provisions that will ensure continuous program improvement

**change agent**: a person from inside or outside the organization who helps an organization transform itself by focusing on such matters as organizational effectiveness, improvement, and development

**change management**: an approach to transitioning individuals, teams, and organizations to a desired future state

**chat room**: an Internet site allowing users to communicate in real time via transmission of text messages from sender to receiver

**Children's Internet Protection Act (CIPA)**: a U.S. federal law requiring that K–12 schools and libraries in the U.S. use Internet filters and implement other measures to protect children from harmful online content as a condition for the receipt of certain federal funding

**Children's Online Privacy Protection Act of 1998 (COPPA)**: a U.S. federal law that applies to the online collection of personal information by persons or entities under U.S. jurisdiction from children under 13 years of age. It details what a website operator must include in a privacy policy, when and how to seek verifiable consent from a parent or guardian, and what responsibilities an operator has to protect children's privacy and safety online, including restrictions on the marketing to those under 13

**ClassDojo**: a free classroom tool, available on the Internet, designed to help teachers improve classroom behavior and to capture and generate data on behavior that teachers can share with parents and administrators

**classroom chronotope**: a shared conception of how a student moves through the spaces and times of a classroom

**client-based**: pertaining to an application that runs on a work station or personal computer in a network and is not available to others in the network (as opposed to cloud-based)

**cloud-based**: pertaining to an application where end users access the application through a web browser or a lightweight desktop or mobile app while the business software and user's data are stored on servers at a remote location

**cloud computing**: services and applications that host data, files, and information at remote servers around the country/globe to be accessed from any device; "in the cloud"

**cognitive science**: the interdisciplinary scientific study of the mind and its processes

**collaborative asynchronous**: characterizes work during which students provide input at various times, such as in discussion forums and social networking

**collaborative synchronous**: describes work where students engage in communications at the same time, such as in chat rooms, face-to-face meetings, or on the phone

**Common Core State Standards (CCSS)**: an education initiative sponsored by the National Governors Association (NGA) and the Council of Chief State School Officers (CCSSO) that seeks to bring diverse state curricula into alignment with each other by following the principles of standards-based education reform

**competency-based learning**: students advance upon mastery of explicit, measurable, transferable learning objectives that empower students. Assessment is meaningful and students receive timely, differentiated support based on their individual needs. Learning outcomes include competencies in application and creation of knowledge along with the development of skills

**computer game**: an electronic game that is usually more complex than a video game, with an interface that can be more elaborate, controls that are more detailed, and movements that are more precise; aka digital games

**computer simulation**: a computer program, run on a single computer or a network of computers, that attempts to simulate an abstract model of a particular system; aka computer model or computational model

**computer-supported collaborative learning (CSCL)**: a pedagogical approach wherein learning takes place via social interaction using a computer or through the Internet. This kind of learning is characterized by the sharing and construction of knowledge among participants using technology as their primary means of communication or as a common resource. It can be implemented in online and classroom learning environments and can take place synchronously or asynchronously

**content acquisition podcast (CAP)**: short, multimedia-based instructional vignettes that use still images and occasional on-screen text and contain carefully constructed narration to deliver instruction for one vocabulary term/concept, fact/event, or other singular piece of information

**context analysis**: a strategy readers use to infer or predict a word from the context in which it appears

**Council of Chief State School Officers (CCSSO)**: a nonpartisan, nonprofit organization of public officials who head departments of elementary and secondary education in the states, the District of Columbia, the Department of Defense Education Activity, and five U.S. territories

**course management system (CMS)**: software applications that help with online course administration (e.g., enroll students, document and track progress, and provide reporting); may also assemble, personalize, and deliver learning content; aka learning management system (LMS)

**Coursera**: an educational technology company offering massive open online courses (MOOCs) and working with universities to make some of their courses available online, offering courses in engineering, humanities, medicine, biology, social sciences, mathematics, business, computer science, and other areas

**Co-Writer**: a word prediction program designed to help individuals who struggle with writing

**crowdsourcing**: outsourcing tasks to an undefined, distributed group of people (the public) rather than specific individuals; process can occur online and offline

**cultural modeling**: a mental framework based on shared ideas, attitudes, and modes of behavior that span a society

**culture of innovation**: an environment that supports creative thinking and advances efforts to extract economic and social value from knowledge, and, in doing so, generates new or improved products, services, or processes

**curator/digital curator**: generally, the process of establishing and developing repositories of digital assets for current and future reference; curators collect and manage those resources

**dashboard/dashboard technologies**: a user interface that organizes and presents information in an easy-to-recognize/read interface; likely to be interactive; goal is to automatically show a user useful data, info, and other objects

**DECA**: previously known as Delta Epsilon Chi and Distributive Education Clubs of America, an international association of high school and college students and teachers of marketing, management, and entrepreneurship in business, finance, hospitality, and marketing sales and service

**dialogic book reading**: a form of shared reading; more specifically, an interaction between an adult and a child in which they take turns in a conversation about a book

**DIBELS (Dynamic Indicators of Basic Early Literacy Skills)**: a series of short tests that assess early childhood (K–6) literacy

**differentiated learning**: programs or tools that present learning materials that match each student's individual learning level; tools used depend on the student, however, learning goals are the same for everyone

**digital badges**: icons that represent academic achievements or skills; online record of knowledge or skill achievements

**digital immigrant**: someone who was born before the existence of digital technologies and adopted it to some extent later in life

**digital native**: generation of students that have grown up in the digital world using technology to communicate, educate, share, record, and learn about society; implies that students have an easier sense of how to use technology

# Glossary

**digital object identifier (DOI)**: a character string used to uniquely identify an object such as an electronic document

**digital tourist**: an inexperienced searcher in the digital environment

**discussion board**: an online discussion site where people can hold conversations in the form of posted messages, differing from chat rooms in that messages are at least temporarily archived; aka Internet forum or message board

**disruptive innovation**: an innovation that helps create a new market and value network and eventually goes on to disrupt an existing market and value network, displacing an earlier technology

**distance learning**: any type of learning that takes place with the student and instructor geographically distant from each other

**download**: to transfer (data or programs) from a server or host computer to one's own computer or device

**e-books**: completely digital books that are usually read on computers, tablets, or e-readers

**Edmodo**: a social learning platform for teachers, students, and parents, commonly thought of as the Facebook of schools

**educational data mining (EDM)**: a research field concerned with the application of data mining (the computational process of discovering patterns in large data sets) to information generated from educational settings (e.g., universities and intelligent tutoring systems)

**effectiveness**: improved student learning, including cognitive, social–emotional, and psychomotor skills and knowledge

**efficient**: evidence of a gain in student learning achieved by the innovation that is greater than that achieved by the standard practice over a similar or lesser amount of time

**e-learning**: the use of electronic media and information and communication technologies (ICT) in education, inclusive of and is broadly synonymous with multimedia learning, technology-enhanced learning (TEL), computer-based instruction (CBI), computer-based training (CBT), computer-assisted instruction or computer-aided instruction (CAI), Internet-based training (IBT), web-based training (WBT), online education, virtual education, and virtual learning environments (VLE)

**Elementary and Secondary Education Act (ESEA)**: an act passed as part of President Lyndon B. Johnson's "War on Poverty" and the most far-reaching federal legislation affecting education ever passed by Congress. The act is an extensive statute that funds primary and secondary education, while explicitly forbidding the establishment of a national curriculum; it emphasizes equal access to education and establishes high standards and accountability; and it aims to reduce the achievement gaps between students by providing each child with fair and equal opportunities to achieve an exceptional education

**emerging promising practice**: a practice that seems likely to replace the standard by being more effective but lacks sufficient evidence to be called an innovation

**enriched virtual model**: a form of blended learning providing a whole-school experience, where students divide their time between attending a brick-and-mortar campus and learning remotely using online delivery of content and instruction, differing from the flipped classroom in that students seldom attend the brick-and-mortar campus every weekday, and differing from the a la carte model in that it is a whole-school experience, not a course-by-course model

**Facebook**: an online social networking service whose name stems from the colloquial name for the book given to students at the start of the academic year by some university administrations in the U.S. to help students get to know each other

**Family, Career, and Community Leaders of America (FCCLA)**: formerly the Future Homemakers of America (FHA), a nonprofit U.S. career and technical student organization for young men and women in family and consumer science education in public and private schools through grade 12 across the U.S.

**Family Educational Rights and Privacy Act of 1974 (FERPA)**: a U.S. federal law that gives students access to their education records, an opportunity to seek to have the records amended, and some control over the disclosure of information from the records. With several exceptions, schools must have a student's consent prior to the disclosure of education records after that student is 18 years old. The law only applies to educational agencies and institutions that receive funding under a program administered by the U.S. Department of Education

**fan fiction**: stories about characters or settings written by fans of the original work, rather than by the original creator

**feature phone**: a mobile phone intended for customers who want a moderately priced and multipurpose phone without the expense of a high-end smartphone, having additional functions over and above a basic mobile phone which is only capable of voice calling and text messaging

**FFA (National FFA Organization)**: formerly the Future Farmers of America, an American youth organization, specifically a career and technical student organization based on middle and high school classes that promote and support agricultural education

**flex model**: a form of blended learning where face-to-face support is provided on a flexible and adaptive as-needed basis through activities such as small-group instruction, group projects, and individual tutoring, but where the backbone of student learning, even if it directs students to offline activities at times, is online learning

**flipped classroom**: term used to describe a reversed model where instruction is delivered at home through interactive, teacher-created videos or screencasts and teachers use class time for collaborative learning environments or more 1:1 time with students —as most notably exemplified by Khan Academy (see below)

**forum**: an online meeting or assembly for the open discussion

**Funnix**: an interactive computer CD program for parents and other educators to teach children reading or mathematics using Direct Instruction techniques

**Future Business Leaders of America (FBLA)**: an American career and technical student nonprofit organization of high school, middle school, and college students, as well as professional members who primarily help students transition to the business world

**game**: structured playing, usually undertaken for enjoyment and sometimes used as an educational tool

**game-based learning (GBL)**: a type of game play that has defined learning outcomes; generally, GBL is designed to balance subject matter with gameplay and to enhance the ability of the player to retain and apply said subject matter to the real world

**gamification**: using game design and mechanics to drive motivation and increase engagement in learning

**Glogster**: a social network that allows users to create free interactive posters, or Glogs, short for "graphics blogs," which are interactive multimedia images

**Goalbook**: a secure platform for schools to manage and collaborate around student individual learning plans (ILPs), designed to help educators collaborate more effectively, streamline communication, engage parents, and increase student agency through goal setting

**Google**: the most used search engine on the Internet (also used as a verb meaning to search on the Internet)

**Headsprout**: an online reading program that takes a nonreader to mid-2nd grade level in 80 lessons. The program, acquired by DYMO/Mimio ITT in 2011, is used in thousands of classrooms, learning labs, and homes in the U.S. and 87 other countries. The patented adaptive software adjusts to each learner's needs, facilitating success in phonemic awareness, phonics, fluency, vocabulary, and comprehension

**high-functioning autism (HFA)**: a term applied to people with autism who are deemed to be cognitively "higher functioning" (IQ>70) than other people with autism, exhibit deficits in areas of communication, emotion recognition and expression, and social interaction; aka Asperger syndrome

**High Schools That Work (HSTW)**: the nation's largest school improvement initiative for high school leaders and teachers, with more than 1,200 HSTW sites in 30 states and the District of Columbia currently using the framework of HSTW Goals and Key Practices to raise student achievement and graduation rates

**hip hop**: a music genre consisting of a stylized rhythmic music that commonly accompanies rapping, a rhythmic and rhyming speech that is chanted

**HOSA-Future Health Professionals**: formerly known as Health Occupations Students of America, a national student organization endorsed by the U.S. Department of Education and the Health Science Education Division of the Association for Career & Technical Education, with the two-fold mission of promoting career opportunities in the health care industry and enhancing the delivery of quality health care to all people

**hybrid course**: a blend of face-to-face interaction such as in-class discussions, active group work, and live lectures, with typically web-based educational technologies such as online information and assignments, discussion boards, and other web-assisted learning tools

**hyperlink**: a reference to data that the computer user can directly follow or that is followed automatically

**HyperStudio**: a multimedia authoring tool software program distributed by Software MacKiev, that provides relatively simple methods for combining varied media

**hypertext**: text displayed on a computer display or other electronic device with references (hyperlinks) to other text which the computer user can immediately access, or text that can be revealed progressively at multiple levels of detail

**HyperText Markup Language (HTML)**: the main markup language for creating webpages and other information that can be displayed in a web browser

**HyperText Transfer Protocol (HTTP)**: an application protocol for distributed, collaborative, hypermedia information systems

**HyperText Transfer Protocol Secure (HTTPS)**: a communications protocol for secure communication over a computer network, with especially wide deployment on the Internet. Technically, it is not a protocol in and of itself, but rather the result of simply layering the Hypertext Transfer Protocol (HTTP) on top of the SSL/TLS protocol, thus adding the security capabilities of SSL/TLS to standard HTTP communications

**implementation science**: the study of the process of implementing evidence-based programs and practices

**indicator of effective practice**: a concrete, behavioral expression of a professional practice that research demonstrates contributes to student learning

**Indistar®**: a web-based system implemented by a state education agency, district, or charter school organization for use with district and/or school improvement teams to inform, coach, sustain, track, and report improvement activities

**individual rotation model**: a form of rotation model in which, within a given course or subject, students rotate on an individually customized, fixed schedule among learning modalities, at least one of which is online learning

**Individuals with Disabilities Education Act (IDEA)**: a U.S. federal law that governs how states and public agencies provide early intervention, special education, and related services to children with disabilities

**Information Age**: a period in human history characterized by the shift from traditional industry that the Industrial Revolution brought through industrialization to an economy based on information computerization

**information and communication technology (ICT)**: extended synonym for information technology (IT); emphasizes the role of unified communications, integration of telecommunications, computers, software, storage, and audiovisual systems; enables users to access, store, transmit, and manipulate information

**innovation**: may be a change in methods, change in technology, or both; it replaces the standard (best) practice with a more effective or efficient one, thus creating a new standard

**innovation fatigue**: what happens when a group of people is subjected to vague innovation talk and badly explicated innovation projects to the point where the very reference to "innovation" triggers feelings of boredom and meaninglessness

**Institute of Education Sciences (IES)**: the primary research arm of the U.S. Department of Education, created as part of the Education Sciences Reform Act of 2002

**instructional core**: the teacher and the student in the presence of content—the relationship between the teacher, the student, and the content, and not the qualities of any one of them by themselves, determining the nature of instructional practice

**instructional productivity**: indicated by the ratio of effectiveness to resource allocation

**interactive media**: digital and analog materials, including software programs, applications (apps), broadcast and streaming media, some children's television programming, e-books, the Internet, and other forms of content designed to facilitate active and creative use by young children and to encourage social engagement with other children and adults

**interactive multimedia**: technology that allows users to work with any combination of video, audio, animation, text, and graphics

**interactive whiteboard**: a large interactive display that connects to a computer, with a projector projecting the computer's desktop onto the board's surface, where users control the computer using a pen, finger, stylus, or other device

**Internet**: a global system of interconnected computer networks that use the standard Internet protocol suite (TCP/IP) to serve several billion users worldwide. It is a network of networks that consists of millions of private, public, academic, business, and government networks, of local to global scope, that are linked by a broad array of electronic, wireless, and optical networking technologies. The Internet carries an extensive range of information resources and services, such as the interlinked hypertext documents of the World Wide Web (WWW) and the infrastructure to support e-mail

**Internet protocol suite**: the networking model and a set of communications protocols used for the Internet and similar networks. Commonly known as TCP/IP, because its most important protocols, the Transmission Control Protocol (TCP) and the Internet Protocol (IP), were the first networking protocols defined in this standard

**intranet**: a computer network that uses Internet Protocol technology to share information, operational systems, or computing services within an organization

**Investing in Innovation (I3)**: the flagship innovation grant program from the U.S. Department of Education. The program, managed by the Office of Innovation and Improvement, is available to Local Educational Agencies (school districts) in partnership with nonprofit organizations. There are three funding categories for I3 grants: Development, Validation, and Scale-up

**iOS**: a mobile operating system developed and distributed by Apple, Inc. that supports Apple's iPhone, iPod Touch, iPad, and second-generation Apple TV; previously iPhone OS

**iPad**: a line of tablet computers designed and marketed by Apple, Inc., which runs Apple's iOS

**iPod**: a line of portable media players designed and marketed by Apple, Inc.

**just-in-time learning**: the acquisition of knowledge or skills at the time they are needed rather than in advance. Rather than sitting through hours of traditional classroom training, users can tap into Web-based tutorials, interactive CD-ROMs, and other tools to zero in on just the information they need to solve problems, perform specific tasks, or update their skills

**K12, Inc.**: a for-profit education company that sells online schooling and curriculum to state and local governments

**keyword mnemonic instruction**: the linking of new information to keywords that are already encoded to memory

**Khan Academy**: a nonprofit educational website created in 2006 by educator Salman Khan that supplies a free online collection of more than 4,300 micro lectures via video tutorials stored on YouTube, teaching mathematics, history, healthcare, medicine, finance, physics, chemistry, biology, astronomy, economics, cosmology, organic chemistry, American civics, art history, macroeconomics, microeconomics, and computer science

**Kid Pix**: a bitmap drawing program aimed at children, first released for the Macintosh in 1989 and subsequently published in 1991 by Brøderbund

**Knowledge Is Power Program (KIPP)**: a nationwide network of free, open-enrollment, college-preparatory schools in under-resourced communities throughout the United States. KIPP schools are usually established under state charter school laws, KIPP being America's largest network of charter schools

**Kurzweil 3000**: an assistive technology which provides a reading, writing, and study platform aimed at people with learning disabilities or other disabilities that make reading or writing difficult

**lab-rotation model**: a form of rotation model in which, within a given course or subject, students rotate on a fixed schedule or at the teacher's discretion among locations on the brick-and-mortar campus, at least one of which is a learning lab for predominantly online learning, differing from the station location in that they are not confined to a single classroom

**learning analytics (LA)**: the measurement, collection, analysis, and reporting of data about learners and their contexts for purposes of understanding and optimizing learning and the environments in which it occurs

**Learning Forward**: formerly the National Staff Development Council, an association devoted exclusively to advancing professional learning for student success

**learning management system (LMS)**: software applications that help with online course administration (e.g., enroll students, document and track progress, and provide reporting); may also assemble, personalize, and deliver learning content; aka course management system (CMS)

**lexical abilities**: abilities relating to words or the vocabulary of a language as distinguished from its grammar and construction

**Linked Learning**: an improvement approach for California high schools that connects strong academics with real-world experience in a wide range of fields, such as engineering, arts and media, and biomedical and health sciences, helping students gain an advantage in high school, college, and career

**low evidence**: based on expert opinion derived from strong findings or theories in related areas and/or expert opinion buttressed by direct evidence that does not rise to moderate or strong level

**massively multiplayer online role-playing game (MMORPG)**: a genre of role-playing video games or web-browser-based games in which a very large number of players interact with one another within a virtual game world

**metacognitive skills**: "cognition about cognition," or "knowing about knowing"; the individual's own awareness and consideration of thinking/learning processes and strategies

**microblogging**: a type of short message blogging, often made via mobile device (e.g., using Twitter)

**microformats**: a web-based approach to semantic markup which seeks to reuse existing HTML/XHTML tags to convey metadata and other attributes in webpages and other contexts that support (X)HTML

**MimioReading**: a state-of-the-art instructional program that provides broad and effective lessons for schools that want to improve their reading comprehension performance in Grades 3–8

**MimioSprout**: a program for Grades preK–2 that incorporates hundreds of instructional routines that automatically adapt to the specific needs and learning pace of each student

**Minecraft**: a computer game that allows players to build constructions out of textured cubes in a 3D procedurally generated world and to participate in exploration, gathering resources, crafting, and combat

**m-learning (mobile learning)**: any sort of learning that happens when the learner is not at a fixed, predetermined location, or learning that happens when the learner takes advantage of the learning opportunities offered by mobile technologies

**mobile operating system**: the operating system that operates a smartphone, tablet, PDA, or other digital mobile device; aka mobile OS

**moderate evidence**: requires (1) studies that support strong causal conclusions but where generalization is uncertain, or (2) studies that support the generality of a relationship but where the causality is uncertain

**MOOC (massive open online course)**: a recent development in distance education, a MOOC is an online course aimed at large-scale interactive participation and open access via the World Wide Web. In addition to traditional course materials such as videos, readings, and problem sets, MOOCs provide interactive user forums that help build a community for the students, professors, and teaching assistants. Also SMOOC, for smaller, or synchronized, massive open online course

**morpheme**: the smallest grammatical unit in a language

**morphemic analysis**: a strategy in which the meanings of words can be determined or inferred by examining their meaningful parts (i.e., prefixes, suffixes, roots, etc.)

**National Early Literacy Panel (NELP)**: panel convened in 2002 to conduct a synthesis of the scientific research on the development of early literacy skills in children ages zero to five

**National Reading Panel**: a U.S. government body formed in 1997 at the request of Congress with the stated aim of assessing the effectiveness of different approaches used to teach children to read

**National Technology Student Association**: a nonprofit national student organization devoted to teaching technology education to young people

**netiquette**: social etiquette rules when communicating over computer networks

# Glossary

**networked book**: an open book (such as Wikipedia) designed to be written, edited, and read in a networked environment; also a platform for social exchange, potentially linked to other books and other discussions

**networked learning**: a process of developing and maintaining connections with people and information and communicating in such a way so as to support one another's learning

**new and emerging technologies**: reflects current advances and innovation in various fields and disciplines

**No Child Left Behind Act of 2001 (NCLB)**: a United States Act of Congress that is a reauthorization of the Elementary and Secondary Education Act; supports standards-based education reform based on the premise that setting high standards and establishing measurable goals can improve individual outcomes in education

**Number Munchers**: one of the two original games in the Munchers series of edutainment computer games produced by the Minnesota Educational Computing Consortium (MECC) for several operating systems, which were popular among American schoolchildren in the 1980s and 1990s, the other being Word Munchers

**online assessment**: the process used to measure certain aspects of information for a set purpose where the assessment, usually some type of educational test, is delivered via a computer connected to a network. Different types of online assessments contain elements of one or more of the following components, depending on the assessment's purpose: formative, diagnostic, or summative. Instant and detailed feedback, as well as flexibility of location and time, are two benefits associated with online assessments, and there are many resources available that provide online assessments, some free of charge and others that charge fees or require a membership

**open educational resource (OER)**: digital information/materials available for reuse and repurposing in teaching, researching, and learning; open licenses allow use through means not normally permitted under copyright

**Oregon Trail**: a computer game originally produced by the Minnesota Educational Computing Consortium (MECC) in 1974, designed to teach school children about the realities of 19th century pioneer life on the Oregon Trail

**personal digital assistant (PDA)**: a mobile device that functions as a personal information manager; aka palmtop computer or personal data assistant

**personalization of learning**: the tailoring for each student of the pace, content, and goals of learning, with the learner exercising significant choice and direction in the learning process; personalization ensues from the relationships among teachers and learners and the teacher's orchestration of multiple means for enhancing every aspect of each student's learning and development

**phonemic awareness**: the ability to notice, think about, and work with the individual sounds in words

**phonological sensitivity**: an individual's sensitivity to the phonological structure, or sound structure, of spoken words

**PLATO (Programmed Logic for Automatic Teaching Operations)**: the first generalized computer-assisted instruction system that, by the late 1970s, comprised several thousand terminals worldwide on nearly a dozen different networked mainframe computers

**podcast**: a type of digital media consisting of an episodic series of audio radio, video, PDF, or ePub files subscribed to and downloaded through web syndication or streamed online to a computer or mobile device, the word being a neologism derived from "broadcast" and "pod" from the success of the iPod, as audio podcasts are often listened to on portable media players

**Prezi**: a U.S. software company, producing a cloud-based presentation software and storytelling tool for presenting ideas on a virtual canvas

**private social network (PSN)**: a closed network of online users, such as EveryMe or Yammer, designed in part to increase privacy and confidentiality

**productive innovation**: an innovation that achieves the same learning outcomes as the standard practice but at less cost (time, money, and other resources) or better learning outcomes than the standard practice at the same or lesser cost

**pull technology**: when people use software such as a web browser to locate and "pull down" (get) information for themselves

**push technology**: when information is sent directly to a user's computer without them having to go get it

**Quest Atlantis**: a 3D, multiuser, computer graphics learning environment that utilizes a narrative programming toolkit to immerse children ages 9–15 in meaningful inquiry tasks

**Race to the Top**: a U.S. Department of Education contest created to spur innovation and reforms in state and local district K–12 education

**Reader Rabbit**: an edutainment software franchise created in 1986 by The Learning Company with games for infancy through second grade featuring Reader Rabbit

**Reading First Program**: a federal education program mandated under the No Child Left Behind Act and administered by the U.S. Department of Education requiring that schools funded by Reading First use "scientifically based" reading instruction

**real-time communication**: when information is received (nearly) at the instant it's sent; characteristic of instant messaging; synchronous learning

**relational suasion**: the teacher's ability to influence a student's learning, motivation to learn, metacognitive competencies, and social and emotional competencies by virtue of the teacher's personal knowledge of and interaction with the student and the student's family

**Response to Intervention (RtI)**: a system of service delivery that uses student data to evaluate and repair core instruction and to provide increasingly intensive intervention supplements to students who need it to meet expected learning outcomes

**rotation model**: a form of blended learning where students rotate between in-class and homework activities (such as small-group or full-class instruction, group projects, individual tutoring, and pencil-and-paper assignments) and online learning

**RSS (really simple syndication)**: a method by which web content can be easily and quickly distributed when it is changed or newly entered into a web site or blog; most blogs automatically include an RSS feed. This feed automatically sends out formatted releases of new posts that are received by those who use RSS news readers and subscribe to that particular feed

**rti4success.org (National Center on Response to Intervention)**: a center housed at the American Institutes for Research, working in conjunction with researchers from Vanderbilt University and the University of Kansas and funded by the U.S. Department of Education's Office of Special Education Programs (OSEP), with the mission of providing technical assistance to states and districts and building the capacity of states to assist districts in implementing proven models for Response to Intervention (RTI)

**scalability**: the degree to which a program, process, tool, or application can increase in number of users served, locations, etc., and continue to function properly (little or no degradation in function).

**schema theory**: the theory that people make sense of new experiences and the world by activating the mental representations or schemata stored in their memory. New experiences and information are interpreted according to how they fit into their schemata. Information that does not fit may be misunderstood or not comprehended

**School Improvement Grant (SIG)**: a grant awarded by the U.S. Department of Education to state education agencies (SEAs) under Section 1003(g) of the Elementary and Secondary Education Act of 1965 (aka ESEA, reauthorized by the No Child Left Behind Act [NCLB] in 2002). The SEAs, in turn, award subgrants to local educational agencies (LEAs, also known as school districts) for the purpose of supporting focused school improvement efforts

**School Improvement Plan (SIP)**: strategies and steps that a school will utilize to raise student achievement which may involve new programs, more assistance for students, new curricula, and/or teacher training

**Schoolwide Positive Behavior Support (SWPBS)**: a proactive approach based on a three-tiered model of prevention and intervention aimed at creating safe and effective schools

**screen capturing**: a computer user's taking of an image to record the visible items displayed on the monitor, television, or another visual output device; aka screen shot or screen grab

**screencast**: digital recording (movie) of interactions of a computer screen (often with audio), to be viewed by others remotely or at a later date (also known as video screen capture)

**search engine**: a software system that is designed to search for information on the Internet

**self-paced asynchronous**: refers to learning where the student is allowed the autonomy and freedom to complete work at his/her own speed, through such means as online self-tutorials and archived podcasts

**serious game**: a game designed for a primary purpose other than pure entertainment; aka applied game

**student information management system (SIMS)**: software to securely manage individual student data, including demographics and learning information, usually at the state, district, or school level

**SimCity**: an open-ended city-building computer and console video game series

**simulation**: interactive applications in which learners role play in or model a scenario; allows practice in a risk-free environment

**simulation game**: an electronic game that represents or simulates an environment accurately, representing the interactions between the playable characters and the environment realistically

**simulation software**: a program that allows the user to observe an operation through simulation without actually performing that operation

**SkillsUSA**: a U.S. career and technical student organization serving more than 320,000 high school and college students and professional members enrolled in training programs in technical, skilled, and service occupations, including health occupations

**smartpen**: a high-tech writing tool that records spoken words and synchronizes them with notes users write on special paper

**smartphone**: a mobile phone built on a mobile operating system with more advanced computing capability and connectivity than a feature phone

**Smith-Hughes National Vocational Education Act of 1917**: an act of the U.S. Congress that promoted vocational agriculture to train people "who have entered upon or who are preparing to enter upon the work of the farm" and provided federal funds for this purpose

**Software & Information Industry Association (SIIA)**: a software trade association that lobbies U.S. policymakers as well as conducting surveys and research and many conferences and webcasts

**SSL/TSL**: Secure Sockets Layer (SSL) and its successor, Transport Layer Security (TLS), are cryptographic protocols that provide communication security over the Internet

**station-rotation model**: a form of rotation model in which, within a given course or subject, students rotate on a fixed schedule or at the teacher's discretion among classroom-based learning modalities, including at least one station for online learning

**student response system (SRS)**: using a web-based software (or PowerPoint), teachers ask questions and students use a device (clicker or, increasingly, smartphones and tablets) to respond to that question, providing real-time results for the teacher

**standard practice**: the best known practice prior to the replacement by an innovation

**strong evidence**: requires (1) studies whose designs can support causal conclusions (internal validity), and (2) studies that in total include enough of the range of participants and settings on which the recommendation is focused to support the conclusion that the results can be generalized to those participants and settings (external validity)

**subnotebook**: a class of laptop computers that are smaller and lighter than a typical notebook; aka ultraportable or mini notebook

**synchronous**: interactions that occur at the same time (in real time)

**synchronous communication**: communications in which the message occurs in real time, so when you speak or write, someone could immediately respond to your message

**tablet computer**: a one-piece mobile computer, typically having a touchscreen, with finger or stylus gestures replacing the conventional computer mouse

**TeachMeet**: an unconference; an informal gathering of educators that encourages sharing of ideas and lessons used in their classrooms

**technology**: the use and knowledge of tools, techniques, systems, or methods in order to solve a problem or serve some purpose; can significantly affect the ability to control and adapt to the environment

**TED lectures**: a series of video talks freely available online, originally concerning the fields of technology, entertainment, and design (TED), but later expanded to include science, philosophy, music, philanthropy, and many other fields

**Trends in International Mathematics and Science Study (TIMSS)**: an international assessment of the mathematics and science knowledge of 4th and 8th graders around the world, developed by the International Association for the Evaluation of Educational Achievement (IEA) to allow participating nations to compare students' educational achievement across borders

**turnaround**: a dramatic and comprehensive intervention in a low-performing school designed to produce significant gains in achievement and to ready the school for the longer process of transformation into a high-performance organization

**Twitter**: an online social networking service and microblogging service that enables its users to send and read text-based messages of up to 140 characters, known as "tweets"

**Ultrabook**: a specification and brand developed by Intel for a class of high-end subnotebooks which are designed to feature reduced bulk without compromising performance and battery life

**Universal Design for Learning (UDL)**: framework for the design of online learning and environments ensuring accessibility for all users; framework for designing flexible curriculum and learning environments for all students

**upload**: to transfer (data or programs), usually from a peripheral computer or device to a central, often remote computer

*Glossary*

**URI (uniform resource identifier)**: a string of characters used to identify a name or a web resource

**URL (uniform resource locator)**: address of a specific web page, technically a type of URI

**UI/UX**: user interface/user experience; user interface being the system by which people (users) interact with a machine, and user experience involving a person's emotions about using a particular product, system, or service

**video capturing**: converting an analog video signal, such as that produced by a video camera or DVD player, to digital video

**video game**: an electronic game that involves human interaction with a user interface to generate visual feedback on a video device, the term usually referring to the earliest simpler video games such as Atari and Pong

**video game console**: an interactive computer that produces a video display signal which can be used with a display device (a television, monitor, etc.) to display a video game; the term is used to distinguish a machine designed for people to buy and use primarily for playing video games on a television, monitor, etc., in contrast to arcade machines, handheld game consoles, or home computers

**virtual desktop**: a user's desktop environment (icons, folders, toolbars, wallpaper, windows, etc.) is stored remotely on a server, not on the local device (desktop virtualization software separates the desktop operating systems, applications, and data from the hardware client, storing this virtual desktop on a remote server)

**virtual learning**: any learning that occurs where either the instructor or student is present for an educational event in a digital (virtual) rather than physical form

**virtual private network (VPN)**: the extension of a private network across a public network, such as the Internet, enabling a computer to send and receive data across shared or public networks as if it were directly connected to the private network, while benefitting from the functionality, security, and management policies of the private network. This is done by establishing a virtual point-to-point connection through the use of dedicated connections, encryption, or a combination of the two

**virtual reality (VR)**: artificial, computer-generated environment experienced via sensory input; special equipment allows users to interact with the environment

**virtual university**: a university that provides higher education programs through electronic media, typically the Internet, some being brick-and-mortar institutions that provide online learning as part of their extended university courses, while others solely offer online courses

**Walt Disney Imagineering**: the design and development arm of The Walt Disney Company, responsible for the creation and construction of Disney theme parks worldwide; aka WDI or Imagineering

**Web 2.0**: World Wide Web current age; used for interacting with web apps, collaboration, and sharing with others

**Web 3.0**: World Wide Web future age; a term coined by John Markoff of *The New York Times* to refer to a supposed third generation of Internet-based services that collectively comprise what might be called "the intelligent Web"—such as those using semantic web, microformats, natural language search, data-mining, machine learning, recommendation agents, and artificial intelligence technologies—which emphasize machine-facilitated understanding of information in order to provide a more productive and intuitive user experience

**web accessibility**: the inclusive practice of making websites usable by people of all abilities and disabilities

**Web Accessibility Evaluation Tool**: an online tool to evaluate web accessibility, made available as a free community service by WebAIM, a nonprofit organization within the Center for Persons with Disabilities at Utah State University

**Web Accessibility Initiative (WAI)**: the World Wide Web Consortium (W3C)'s effort to improve the accessibility of the World Wide Web for people with disabilities

**web browser**: a software application (such as Google and Internet Explorer) for retrieving, presenting, and traversing information resources (each identified by its Uniform Resource Identifier, usually a URL) on the World Wide Web

**webcast**: a media presentation distributed over the Internet using streaming media technology to distribute a single content source to many simultaneous listeners/viewers

**Web Content Accessibility Guidelines 2.0 (WCAG 2.0)**: the current version of the Web Content Accessibility Guidelines (part of a series of Web accessibility guidelines published by the W3C's Web Accessibility Initiative) consisting of a set of guidelines for making content accessible, primarily for disabled users

**webpage**: a web document that is suitable for the World Wide Web and the web browser

**What Works Clearinghouse (WWC)**: an initiative of the Institute for Education Sciences (IES) at the U.S. Department of Education, administered by the National Center for Education Evaluation within IES, with the goal of being a resource for informed education decision making

**Wi-Fi**: a popular technology that allows an electronic device to exchange data or connect to the Internet wirelessly using radio waves

**Wii**: a home video game console released by Nintendo

**wiki**: web application developed collaboratively that allows anyone visiting a website to edit content on it

**Wikipedia**: a collaboratively edited, multilingual, free Internet encyclopedia supported by the nonprofit Wikimedia Foundation

**wireless network**: any type of computer network that utilizes some form of wireless network connection

**WordAssist**: a word prediction program designed to help individuals who struggle with writing

**Wordle**: a toy for generating "word clouds" from text provided by the user, giving greater prominence to words that appear more frequently in the source text

**WordQ**: assistive technology software developed by Quillsoft Ltd. and Holland Bloorview Kids Rehabilitation Hospital, designed to help individuals who struggle with writing

**World of Warcraft (WoW)**: a massively multiplayer online role-playing game (MMORPG) by Blizzard Entertainment

**World Wide Web**: a system of interlinked hypertext documents accessed via the Internet. With a web browser, one can view webpages that may contain text, images, videos, and other multimedia, and navigate between them via hyperlinks

**World Wide Web Consortium (W3C)**: the main international standards organization for the World Wide Web

**Xbox 360**: the second video game console developed by and produced for Microsoft, and the successor to the Xbox

**Xtranormal**: a digital entertainment company that produces do-it-yourself animation software for the World Wide Web and desktop; turns words from a script into an animated movie using text-to-speech and animation technologies

**YouTube**: a video-sharing website created by three former PayPal employees in February 2005 and owned by Google since late 2006, on which users can upload, view, and share videos

# Authors' Biographies

**Ryan Shaun Joazeiro de Baker, Ph.D.,** is the Julius and Rosa Sachs Distinguished Lecturer at Teachers College, Columbia University. He earned his Ph.D. in Human–Computer Interaction from Carnegie Mellon University. Dr. Baker was previously Assistant Professor of Psychology and the Learning Sciences at Worcester Polytechnic Institute, and he served as the first Technical Director of the Pittsburgh Science of Learning Center DataShop, the largest public repository for data on the interaction between learners and educational software. He is currently serving as the founding President of the International Educational Data Mining Society and as Associate Editor of the *Journal of Educational Data Mining*. His research combines educational data mining and quantitative field observation methods in order to better understand how students respond to educational software and how these responses impact their learning. He studies these issues within intelligent tutors, simulations, multiuser virtual environments, and educational games.

**Joseph R. Boyle, Ph.D.,** is currently an associate professor of special education in the College of Education at Temple University in Philadelphia, PA. He received his Ph.D. from the University of Kansas in special education in 1993. His current research interests include examining the effectiveness of teaching techniques/interventions for students with mild disabilities in general education and inclusive classrooms. As a result, he has developed a number of classroom interventions for students with mild disabilities in the areas of reading, writing, and note-taking. Dr. Boyle has over 40 publications that include books, research articles, and research-to-practice articles. He is currently P.I. of a $906,000 Institute of Education Sciences (IES) grant titled *Improving the Science Performance of Students with Disabilities through Strategic Note-taking*, which is examining the effects of strategic note-taking on the science learning of middle school students with learning disabilities. Dr. Boyle has taught or currently teaches courses to university students in undergraduate, graduate, and doctoral programs, including Critical Issues in Special Education and Technology in Special Education.

**Ronnie Detrich, Ph.D.,** is currently a Senior Fellow at the Wing Institute, a relatively new nonprofit organization in Oakland, CA with the mission of promoting evidence-based practices in education. Prior to coming to the Wing Institute, Dr. Detrich spent over 30 years delivering evidence-based interventions in educational settings. Most recently, he served as Clinical Director of a large nonprofit, private special education school for children with serious educational and behavioral challenges and codirected a large public school consultation project. He has also served as director for a residential/educational program for children with autism and director of a program for adolescent status offenders. Dr. Detrich's current interest in evidence-based education is in the large-scale implementation of effective interventions in typical service settings. He is also interested in issues of effective staff training and practical methods for assessing and assuring high levels of treatment integrity. He has authored several papers on issues related to evidence-based practice in school settings in the last few years.

**Michael L. Kamil, Ph.D.,** has been a professor of education at Stanford University and has recently been named professor emeritus. Dr. Kamil served as a consultant to several laboratories in the regional educational laboratory system and the research panel of the New York State English Language Arts Standards revision. Dr. Kamil's work involves the effects of technology on literacy and literacy acquisition and assistive technologies. His work examines the appropriate application of new technologies and suggests a thoughtful approach to adapting untried technological strategies. His current research involves an examination of recreational reading in ELL students, software for literacy development, effects of technology on literacy, and cognitive processes in reading electronic text. He was a member of the National Reading Panel, for which he chaired the subgroup on technology; the RAND Reading Study Group; the National Literacy Panel; and the Carnegie Corporation Advisory Council on Advancing Adolescent Literacy.

**Lisa Kinnaman, Ed.D.,** is currently codirecting the Idaho Leads Project, funded by the Albertson Foundation, a project designed to build leadership capacity at all stakeholder levels (superintendents, board members, principals, teachers, students, central office staff, and community members) while shifting to systemwide 21st-century learning and meeting the needs of every individual learner. Formerly, she served as the director of statewide school improvement programs for the Idaho State Department of Education, where she designed and implemented the Idaho Building Capacity Project. Dr. Kinnaman led the adoption and statewide rollout of the Indistar school improvement planning tool and process (developed by the Center on Innovation & Improvement) in Idaho and has provided consultation services to a number of other states regarding issues of school improvement. Additionally, Dr. Kinnaman was an education professor at Northwest Nazarene University and a high school social studies and sheltered instruction teacher, and she has participated in various projects, trainings, and consultations at the state, district, and local levels on topics including state standards, standardized assessments, sheltered instruction, coaching, school improvement planning and implementation, and instructional strategies that promote individualized learning and achievement for all students.

**T. V. Joe Layng, Ph.D.,** has over 35 years of experience in the learning sciences and holds a Ph.D. in behavioral science (biopsychology) from the University of Chicago. While at the university, he performed basic research and developed some of the key elements of what has become known as generative instruction. As an undergraduate student at Western Illinois University, he founded the Centre for Innovative Design and Programmed Instruction. With a staff of 23, he designed and implemented learner-verified instructional programs for 19 university courses, developed tutoring methods for the Office of Academic Services for underprepared students, and established a universitywide self-paced learning center. Dr. Layng cofounded Headsprout located in Seattle, WA, and from 1999 to 2011 served as the company's senior scientist, where he led the scientific team that developed Headsprout's patented Generative Learning Technology. This technology forms the basis of the company's online MimioSprout early reading program and MimioReading reading comprehension programs, for which Dr. Layng was the chief architect. Dr. Layng serves as director of learning sciences at Newell-Rubbermaid Corporation; Headsprout has merged with that company's interactive teaching technologies division. He serves on the board of trustees for TCS Education System, The Chicago School for Professional Psychology, Pacific Oaks College, and The Cambridge Center for Behavioral Studies, where he also serves as a member of its board of directors.

**Maureen M. Mirabito, M.A.,** has assisted states, districts, and schools in examining and aligning their organizational, operational, and behavioral practices in pursuit of improved efficiency and increased student learning. Ms. Mirabito is the architect of the

Maryland State Department of Education's Breakthrough Center, the driver of Maryland's school reform efforts and Race to the Top initiatives. The discontinuation of ineffective practices in favor of identifying and scaling proven learning innovations throughout the state is central to the work of The Breakthrough Center, particularly related to the success of students receiving special education and English language learners. Ms. Mirabito has aided in the conceptualization, development, and production of Indicators in Action, an online, video-based professional development course that brings research-based instructional, operational, and leadership practices to life with actual classroom footage and interviews. She previously served as the special assistant to the superintendent of the Howard County Public School System in Maryland, spearheading policy development and the district's strategic planning efforts, which relied on creative and effective strategies to build school and teacher capacity to improve every student's learning.

**Marilyn Murphy, Ed.D.**, is the Director of the Center on Innovations in Learning (CIL). She also serves as the Interim Executive Director of the Institute for Schools and Society (ISS), the research branch of the Temple University College of Education, and team leader of the $E = mc^2$ program (Educating Middle School Teachers for Challenging Contexts). $E = mc^2$ is a Transition to Teaching program funded by the U.S. Department of Education; it trains candidates transitioning from math and science careers as middle school teachers in math and science for underserved schools. Previously, Dr. Murphy was the codirector of the Laboratory for Student Success (LSS), the mid-Atlantic Regional Educational Laboratory at Temple University, and LSS's director of outreach and dissemination. She received her doctorate in education from Temple University in curriculum, instruction, and technology in education. Her research interests include communication processes, engagement theory, learning theory, and the use of metaphor by children and adults. She has made frequent contributions to numerous educational publications, including a chapter in the CII volume *Handbook on Strengthening the Statewide System of Support*, the *Handbook on Effective Implementation of School Improvement Grants*, and is coeditor and contributor to the *Handbook on Family and Community Engagement*.

**Sam Redding, Ed.D.**, is the Senior Learning Specialist of the Center on Innovations in Learning (CIL). Since 1984, Dr. Redding has served as the Executive Director of the Academic Development Institute (ADI), and from 2005 to 2011 as Director of the Center on Innovation & Improvement. He codeveloped Indistar, a web-based school improvement technology, and Indicators in Action, web-based tutorials for online professional development for educators. Dr. Redding is a former high school teacher and college dean and vice president. He received the "Those Who Excel" Award from the Illinois State Board of Education in 1990, the Ben Hubbard Leadership Award from Illinois State University in 1994, and the Ernie Wing Award for Excellence in Evidence-Based Education from the California-based Wing Institute in 2012. He has been executive editor of the *School Community Journal* since 1991 and was a senior research associate of the Laboratory for Student Success (LSS) at Temple University from 1995 to 2005, where he led the Lab's work on comprehensive school reform. He has edited four books on family–school relationships, authored a book on school improvement and personalized learning, edited books on statewide systems of support, and written articles and chapters in the areas of school management, school improvement, and factors affecting school learning. He has consulted with more than 30 SEAs on their systems for school improvement.

**Catherine Schifter, Ph.D.**, is an associate professor in the Departments of Curriculum, Instruction, and Technology in Education (CITE) and of Psychological Studies in Education at Temple University and is a Carnegie Scholar (2000–2001). In her time at Temple, she has been director of the Online Learning Program (1997–2000), the founding director of the Temple Teaching and Learning Center (2002–2004), and chair of the CITE Department in the College of Education (2007–2009). Her research has focused on distance education and technology integration in education, with recent interest in using game-based design to assess understanding of science inquiry. In addition to publishing numerous articles, she coedited *The Distance Education Evolution: Issues and Case Studies* (2004), solely authored *Infusing Technology into the Classroom: Continuous Practice Improvement* (2008), and coedited *New Media in Education: Beyond Constructivism* (2010). Dr. Schifter's work has focused on the impact of new media or technologies in supporting teaching and learning at the individual level.

**Michael W. Smith, Ph.D.**, a professor in Temple University's College of Education, joined the ranks of college instructors after 11 years of teaching high school English. His research focuses on how experienced readers read and talk about texts as well as what motivates adolescents' reading and writing both in and out of school. He uses that research as a lens to examine the curricular and instructional innovations most likely to foster adolescents' achievement and engagement. He has been chair of the Literature Special Interest Group of the American Educational Research Association, cochair of the National Council of Teachers of English Assembly for Research, and coeditor of *Research in the Teaching of English*. He is a Fellow of the National Conference on Research in Language and Literacy. He has written, cowritten, or edited 13 books and monographs, including *Reading Don't Fix No Chevys: Literacy in the Lives of Young Men*, for which he and his coauthor Jeff Wilhelm received the 2003 David H. Russell Award for Distinguished Research in the Teaching of English. His writing has appeared in such journals as *Communication Education, English Journal, Journal of Adolescent and Adult Literacy, Journal of Educational Research, Journal of Literacy Research*, and *Research in the Teaching of English*.

**Janet S. Twyman, Ph.D., BCBA**, is the Director of Innovative Technologies for the Center on Innovations in Learning (CIL). Dr. Twyman is a career educator and has been a preschool and elementary school teacher, a principal and administrator, and a university professor. She has worked directly on improving the personalization of learning and engineering self-paced learning with typically developing students, preschoolers with intellectual disabilities, adolescents with emotional and behavioral problems, and learners with autism spectrum disorders. For over a decade, she has worked at the forefront of merging evidence-based educational methods with new and emerging technologies, including selecting technologies that support personalized learning and adaptive instructional systems. As a vice president at Headsprout, she led the design, development, and dissemination of the company's Internet-based reading programs and oversaw their implementation in over 1,500 public and private schools. These programs featured built-in, data-based decision-making and real-time, individualized use of data to inform instruction. In 2007–2008, she served as president of the Association for Behavior Analysis International. Currently an associate professor of pediatrics at the

University of Massachusetts Medical School, Dr. Twyman's research interests involve understanding basic learning processes so that we may build meaningful instructional technology programs for use with all learners.

**Amanda M. VanDerHeyden, Ph.D.**, is a private consultant and researcher who has worked as a researcher, consultant, and trainer in a number of school districts and has published more than 60 scholarly articles and chapters related to Response to Intervention (RtI). She has directed numerous RtI implementation efforts, and her work has been featured by the U.S. Department of Education on "Education News Parents Can Use" on PBS and The Learning Channel. Dr. VanDerHeyden serves as advisor to the RtI Action Network at the National Center for Learning Disabilities, the Education Programs Committee for the National Center for Learning Disabilities, and iSTEEP (a web-based data management system). She has consulted for Renaissance Learning, Vanderbilt's National Comprehensive Center for Teacher Quality, and several state departments of education to offer guidance on RtI implementation and evaluate implementation effects. Dr. VanDerHeyden is associate editor for *School Psychology Review* and serves on the editorial boards for *School Psychology Quarterly*, *Journal of School Psychology*, *Topics in Early Childhood Special Education*, and *Journal of Learning Disabilities*. Dr. VanDerHeyden is a standing panel member for the Institute for Education Sciences at the U.S. Department of Education.

**Herbert J. Walberg, Ph.D.**, is a Distinguished Visiting Fellow at the Hoover Institution, Stanford University. He formerly taught at Harvard University and is Emeritus University Scholar and professor of education and psychology at the University of Illinois at Chicago. He has written more than 70 books and written about 300 articles on such topics as educational effectiveness and exceptional human accomplishments. Dr. Walberg served as a founding member of the National Assessment Governing Board, referred to as "the national school board," given its mission to set education standards for U.S. students and measure progress in achieving them. In 2005, he was also confirmed by the Senate as a presidential appointment to the National Board for Educational Sciences, which provides policy guidance and oversight for about $600 million in federal education research, including the What Works Clearinghouse. He has frequently testified before U.S. Congressional committees, state legislators, and federal courts. In his research, Dr. Walberg employs analyses of large national and international data sets to discover the factors in homes, schools, and communities that promote learning and other human accomplishments. He also employs research synthesis to summarize effects of various educational conditions and methods on learning and other outcomes, the results of which have important bearings on education policy and practice. For the past two decades, he has concentrated on educational productivity—that is, increased learning at lower costs.

**Mark Williams, M.A., S.T.L.**, is the Vice President for Institutional Advancement at the Academic Development Institute (ADI), where he is responsible for working with state and district partners to provide research, training, and tools for leadership and supervision of rapid district and school improvement. A former high school teacher, from 2005 to 2012 he served as the Illinois State Director for Career and Technical Education, during which time he received several awards for his contribution to Career and Technical Education (CTE) as well as exercised national leadership in organizations dedicated to CTE and the promotion of college and career readiness. In this position, he oversaw the policy and programs relating to secondary CTE, as well as alignment of K–12 career awareness, exploration, and development. He has worked extensively with Illinois's Department of Commerce and Economic Opportunity and the Illinois Business Roundtable , including the Illinois Innovation Talent Initiative that linked high school students with industry scientists, engineers, and experts in real world projects. He was also one of the three original designers of the Illinois Pathways Initiative, which partners business and industry with the world of public education to enhance the educational experiences of young Illinoisans. Mark holds a bachelor's degree in behavioral science from the University of Chicago, a master's degree from the Pontifical University of St. Thomas in Rome, Italy.

CPSIA information can be obtained at www.ICGtesting.com
Printed in the USA
BVOW07s0855130314

347468BV00003B/4/P